Dynamic Economic Analysis

Focusing on deterministic models in discrete time, this concise yet rigorous textbook provides a clear and systematic introduction to the theory and application of dynamic economic models. It guides students through the most popular model structures and solution concepts, from the simplest dynamic economic models through to complex problems of optimal policy design in dynamic general equilibrium frameworks. Chapters feature theorems and practical hints, and seventy-five worked examples highlight the various methods and results that can be applied in dynamic economic analysis. Notation and formulation is uniform throughout, so students can easily discern the similarities and differences between various model classes. Chapters include more than sixty exercises for students to self-test their analytical skills, and password-protected solutions are available for instructors on the companion website. Assuming no prior knowledge of dynamic economic analysis or dynamic optimization, this textbook is ideal for advanced students in economics.

Gerhard Sorger is Professor of Economics at the University of Vienna, Austria where he teaches primarily in the areas of macroeconomics, mathematical economics, and dynamic economic analysis.

'This book offers a comprehensive vision of economic dynamics suitable for graduate students and professionals alike. Gerhard Sorger is a leading researcher with a flair for presenting mathematically challenging theories carefully and rigorously. His text emphasizes the interplay between formal theory and applications, with detailed developments of a catalogue of economic models and examples drawn from macroeconomics, growth theory and game theory.

The book's structure builds on deterministic discrete time dynamical systems following a thorough development of basic graphical and analytical solution methods for difference equations. Highlights include the detailed presentation of basic stability theories for linear and non-linear difference equations followed by a treatment of bifurcation theory. In all cases there are numerous detailed economically motivated examples constructed to teach readers techniques and appreciate many subtle elements in the constructions. There is no other single book readily accessible in the economics literature covering the same wide range of deterministic dynamics and optimization theories with detailed illustrations of those theories in action. For example, chapters on dynamic games and time consistency illustrate basic applications with careful attention to details such as the difference between Markov perfect strategies and closed-loop ones. Recursive and Lagrangean optimization methods are compared and contrasted in the context of dynamic equilibrium models, including an application to the Ramsey problem of optimal taxation.

Sorger's book is accessible to students engaged in a self-study programme for students engaging with dynamical systems for the first time. Better yet, it offers the topics and treatments for a course in dynamics. Indeed, that is a course I would love to teach our graduate students.'

Robert A. Becker, Professor of Economics, Indiana University (Bloomington)

'This is a beautifully written book, providing a completely self-contained introduction to dynamic economic methods and models for graduate students in economics. The masterly exposition strikes a perfect balance between a user-friendly approach and a completely rigorous presentation of the subject matter. The style of writing is marked by exceptional clarity, very much in keeping with the high standards set by the author in his research contributions. The book is neatly divided into two parts, the first providing a comprehensive account of the theory of dynamical systems, and the second the theory and applications of dynamic optimization in settings with single and multiple decision makers. The chapters on autonomous difference equations and optimization techniques are real gems, and should form the core material in any course on dynamic economic analysis.'

Tapan Mitra, Goldwin Smith Professor of Economics, Cornell University

'Up to now, there are very few books available at the graduate level that introduce the necessary mathematical techniques to study macroeconomics from the viewpoint of non-linear dynamics. Gerhard Sorger is one of the few theorists who have made profound contributions to the subject. His book beautifully introduces the basic results and synthesizes the latest developments in the discrete time non-linear growth models. This book is ideally suited as a textbook for graduate courses in macroeconomics and mathematical economics. Gerhard Sorger should be congratulated on his efforts to educate young researchers. I highly recommend this book.'

Kazuo Nishimura, RIEB, Kobe University

Dynamic Economic Analysis
Deterministic Models in Discrete Time

GERHARD SORGER

CAMBRIDGE
UNIVERSITY PRESS

CAMBRIDGE
UNIVERSITY PRESS

University Printing House, Cambridge CB2 8BS, United Kingdom

Cambridge University Press is part of the University of Cambridge.

It furthers the University's mission by disseminating knowledge in the pursuit of education, learning and research at the highest international levels of excellence.

www.cambridge.org
Information on this title: www.cambridge.org/9781107443792

© Gerhard Sorger 2015

First published 2015

A catalogue record for this publication is available from the British Library

ISBN 978-1-107-44379-2 Paperback

To Renate and Helene

Contents

List of figures

Preface

The present textbook grew out of lecture notes for courses on the methods and applications of dynamic economic analysis that I have been teaching to graduate students over the years. The book is not meant to cover the whole state of the art in this area but to provide a compact presentation of the most essential concepts and results and to illustrate them by selected applications from various fields of economic research. The target readership consists of students and researchers who have little or no experience with solution techniques for dynamic economic models but who have a decent background knowledge in economics, calculus, and linear algebra. I hope that the book helps its readers to get acquainted with the basic issues and the most popular modelling frameworks of dynamic economic analysis and that it raises the appetite of its audience for a more complete and detailed study of this area.

Dynamic economic analysis is a vast area and the relevant literature is extensive. In order to achieve my goal of a compact presentation, I deliberately make two important restrictions that are also reflected in the title of the book. First, I only consider models, that are formulated in discrete time and, second, I do not deal with stochastic dynamics. The main justification of the first restriction is that I want to provide an overview of the most important concepts and methods of dynamic economic analysis without getting lost in technicalities. For some dynamic economic models, the choice between a discrete-time formulation and a continuous-time formulation is simply a matter of taste, whereas for others this choice is driven by the quest for analytical tractability. Moreover, there exist dynamic economic models that generate quite different predictions depending on which of the two formulations of time is applied. In my opinion, however, the basic issues arising in dynamic economic analysis can be illustrated with less technical effort in a discrete-time setting than in a continuous-time setting, which is why I restrict the presentation to the former case. By no means do I consider the discrete-time formulation as more relevant or more realistic than its continuous-time counterpart.

The restriction to deterministic models is a much more substantial one. Many economic situations include stochastic elements in a natural and essential way. Examples include dynamic economies that are buffeted by sequences of aggregate or idiosyncratic shocks, intertemporal decision making in the presence of uncertainty or risk, or randomization devices and mixed strategies in dynamic games. By not discussing models with these features, I do not intend to indicate that I regard them as unimportant. Rather, I have chosen not to deal with them because my own expertise is mostly in deterministic modelling and because I do not see how the methods of dynamic economic analysis for both deterministic and stochastic models can be treated in a single, reasonably sized textbook. As a consequence, there are only two instances in this book where I refer to stochastic concepts such as random variables or expected values. The first one is section 3.5 where I talk about the existence of sunspot equilibria in deterministic models with extrinsic uncertainty and the second one is section 6.3 where I discuss optimization in a deterministic environment but under partial commitment. Both of these sections can be skipped on a first reading without losing the thread.

In addition to restricting the presentation to deterministic models in discrete time, I also make many other deliberate choices on the selection of topics and the depth of their discussion. These choices are mostly based on my assessment of the relative importance of various modelling frameworks and solution techniques but also on my personal taste.

Having talked about the most important restrictions of my approach, let me also emphasize two of its focal points. The first one is that the book is targeted towards students and researchers who are primarily interested in the analytical solution or the qualitative analysis of small-scale dynamic economic models. Consequently, I refrain from discussing issues regarding the numerical implementation of the solution methods for dynamic economic models and I present many examples for which solutions can be characterized (at least qualitatively) by analytical means. And even when I discuss methods that are used in computational approaches, I focus on those aspects of these methods that are also helpful for studying dynamic models using paper and pencil. In section 5.5, for example, when introducing the value iteration method of dynamic programming – a standard method to obtain numerical solutions to dynamic optimization problems – I show how this algorithm can be used to obtain closed-form solutions of the Bellman equation as well as qualitative properties of the optimal value function.

The second point that I would like to emphasize is that I believe that the concepts and methods of dynamic economic analysis can only be properly understood by the reader if he or she has successfully applied them to specific problems. This belief results in my way of presenting the material: a blend of formal theorems (some with, others without proofs), hints about practical applications of these results, and worked out examples in the main text as well as end-of-chapter exercises. For example, even if it is tedious to derive the trajectories of a system of three or four linear difference equations, the solution to a Bellman equation in a dynamic optimization problem, or the various equilibria of dynamic games or dynamic competitive economies, I take the reader through these calculations because I consider this as essential for a thorough understanding of the proposed solution concepts in a more general setting. Sometimes

I even introduce concepts by means of examples before I define them formally; on other occasions, the examples are used to illustrate the application of the various methods in economic contexts. As a result of this approach, the text contains more than 70 worked-out examples and more than 60 end-of-chapter exercises that form an integral part of the book.

Let me now briefly outline the structure and the contents of the book. The material is organized according to the different modelling frameworks and the corresponding solution methods. Part I deals with those models that do not involve dynamic optimization. It is entitled 'Difference equations' and consists of four chapters. In chapter 1, I introduce the basic terminology for the study of difference equations and I explain what is understood by a solution to such an equation. I start with the simple case of one-dimensional maps and show how the solutions of these equations can conveniently be studied by graphical means. I then turn to more general explicit difference equations, distinguishing between first-order equations and higher-order equations, between autonomous ones and non-autonomous ones, and between pre-determined variables and jump variables. Some basic results about the existence of solutions as well as about their dependence on initial conditions are also presented. Finally, I point out that implicit difference equations may have no solutions at all or that they may have multiple solutions. Chapter 1 also introduces many examples of dynamic economic models, including the Solow–Swan growth model, the replicator dynamics from evolutionary game theory, the cobweb model (or hog cycle model), the basic New-Keynesian model for monetary policy analysis, and a simple version of an overlapping generations model with money.

Chapter 2 is devoted to the study of linear difference equations. After introducing some terminology for this type of equation, I show that the set of all trajectories of a linear difference equation forms a linear manifold of the same dimension as the system domain and I explain how this result suggests a general procedure for determining the trajectories of homogeneous and non-homogeneous linear difference equations starting in a given initial state. I then consider the special case of homogeneous linear difference equations with constant coefficients, and derive the form of all basis solutions by separately treating the four possible combinations of single or multiple and real or complex eigenvalues of the system matrix. Quite deliberately, I present this material not in an abstract way using the Jordan normal form of the system matrix but in a way that is hopefully more accessible to beginners. I continue with a detailed discussion of systems of two linear difference equations with constant coefficients and the extremely useful tool of the (T, D)-diagram. The application of this device is illustrated by the analysis of Samuelson's multiplier-accelerator model and the basic New-Keynesian model. Finally, I show how particular solutions of non-homogeneous linear difference equations can be found by the variation-of-constants formula or by a guess-and-verify approach.

In chapter 3, I turn to non-linear but autonomous difference equations. After introducing the important concepts of invariant sets, fixed points, and periodic points and stating a few fundamental results about these concepts, I explain the Hartman–Grobman theorem which provides the basis for all local linearization techniques. After that, various definitions of stability or instability of fixed points and periodic points are presented and the corresponding stability conditions are derived. In addition to those that can be obtained by local linearization techniques, we also encounter Lyapunov's direct method which requires neither smoothness nor hyperbolicity. Section 3.4 introduces the definition of saddle point stability by means of a simple overlapping generations model with capital, and argues that this concept of stability is the appropriate one for economic models including jump variables. The connections between the numbers of pre-determined variables and jump variables, on the one hand, and the occurrence of saddle point stability and indeterminacy, on the other hand, are clearly spelt out. Several examples illustrate these phenomena. The chapter concludes with a discussion of sunspot equilibria and their relation to the indeterminacy of fixed points.

Chapter 4, the last one in the first part of the book, discusses a number of more advanced results on one-dimensional maps. In particular, I treat monotonicity properties of trajectories, local bifurcations, and deterministic chaos. The occurrence of all these phenomena in economic models is illustrated by examples. This chapter is primarily meant to serve as an appetizer for students who want to obtain a deeper understanding of the intricacy and beauty of dynamical systems theory and its applications in economics. The presentation is deliberately restricted to one-dimensional maps, although many of the concepts and results are relevant for and can be generalized to higher-dimensional systems of difference equations.

Part II of the book is entitled 'Dynamic optimization' and also consists of four chapters. It deals with economic models in which some agents make intertemporal choices. Chapter 5 sets the stage by formulating a class of standard infinite-horizon dynamic optimization problems, and by explaining the most popular solution methods for this class of problems. I deal in turn with the Euler equation, the transversality condition, the Lagrangian approach, and the recursive approach (dynamic programming). For each of these approaches, I derive necessary and sufficient optimality conditions and apply them to the tradeoff between consumption and saving that is ubiquitous in optimal growth models and in many other economic situations as well. Special attention is devoted to the class of stationary discounted problems, which occur frequently in economic applications. For this class of problems, there exist additional results on the local dynamics around optimal steady states (turnpike theorems) as well as very strong results related to the recursive approach. In particular, I present sufficient conditions for the convergence of the value iteration algorithm and I use this algorithm to derive monotonicity, concavity, and smoothness properties of the optimal value function.

In all the models and examples from chapter 5, the principle of optimality applies, which means that it is irrelevant whether the decision maker solves the model once and for all at the start of the planning horizon or whether he or she solves the model sequentially in each period of time. Chapter 6, on the other hand, deals with dynamic optimization models in which changes in the constraints or the preferences of the optimization problem occur over the course of time, which implies that the optimal solution from a certain point in time onwards may differ from what the decision maker considered optimal at an earlier time. In such a situation, it makes a difference whether the decision maker optimizes once and for all and commits to that solution or whether he or she optimizes sequentially. In the literature, this difference is discussed under the heading of 'commitment versus discretion'. I start by describing various mechanisms that lead to the dynamic inconsistency of optimal solutions, that is, to situations in which the decision maker wants to deviate from previously made plans. Optimal solutions in these situations can only be implemented if commitment is possible. I continue by explaining solution concepts for models in which the decision maker lacks any commitment power. Finally, I consider an intermediate case and discuss a model in which it is assumed that the decision maker has limited or partial commitment power.

The last two chapters of the book deal with two classes of models that are frequently used in economic research: dynamic games and dynamic competitive equilibrium models. In both of these frameworks, there exist multiple interacting decision makers. Whereas the decision makers in a dynamic game are aware of these interactions and exploit them strategically, the interactions in a competitive model are indirect ones and the decision makers are not aware of them. Various solution concepts for these types of models are presented and discussed. In chapter 7 on dynamic games, I emphasize the generic multiplicity of Nash equilibria, a phenomenon that is rooted in the different possible presentations of optimal solutions (informational non-uniqueness). I also show how the equilibrium refinement of Markov perfection can be applied to obtain unique predictions. Finally, I point out a number of technical and conceptual difficulties that arise in dynamic games with a hierarchical decision making process (for example, dynamic Stackelberg games).

Chapter 8 presents two different definitions of a dynamic competitive equilibrium: the sequence formulation and the recursive formulation. I illustrate by examples from industrial organization and macroeconomics how these definitions can be applied. After doing that, I turn to policy problems in which, in addition to the competitively acting agents, there also exists a policy maker. The policy maker is able to affect the preferences and constraints of all competitive agents by his or her choice of the policy variables and acts like a Stackelberg leader in a game. The structure of equilibria in these models is already quite complex and only very limited results can be obtained by analytical means. I present two such applications from the area of fiscal and monetary policy. The situation becomes especially complicated if we assume that the policy maker lacks commitment power and seeks a dynamically consistent solution. The discussion in this chapter clearly illustrates the limits of a pencil-and-paper approach to the study of realistic dynamic economic models with multiple interacting agents, and it underlines the need for computational methods. The presentation of such methods, however, should be left to those who have sufficient expertise in developing and applying them and is therefore beyond the scope of the present book.

I have taught various selections of the material covered in this book to students of economics both at Master level and at Ph.D. level. I do not think that the book is suitable for Bachelor students of economics. In the Master program in economics, I usually teach selected material from chapters 1, 2, 3, and 5, leaving out some details and proofs but illustrating all concepts and results by economic examples. Sometimes I add material from chapter 4 at the end in order to encourage the students to delve deeper into dynamical systems theory. In the Ph.D. program in economics, I usually start with chapter 5 (going through all the proofs) and continue by presenting material from chapters 6–8 along with original journal articles. In all my courses on dynamic economic analysis, I require the students to solve problem sets on a regular basis. You can find many of these problems in the exercises collected at the end of each chapter.

I would like to thank the institutions at which I was encouraged to teach courses on dynamic economic analysis, and the students who challenged me to convey my knowledge in a comprehensible way. In addition, I would like to acknowledge the encouragement, support, and guidance that I have received from the following three colleagues: Gustav Feichtinger introduced me to dynamic optimization and its applications in economics more than 30 years ago. He thereby sowed the seeds for my interest in dynamic economic analysis and prepared the stage for my academic career. Ngo Van Long supported me at various phases throughout my career in a number of ways: as a host, a co-author, and a friend. Last but not least, Tapan Mitra's sharp insights into dynamic models and his incredible clear way of thinking and writing have been constant sources of inspiration for me. Of course, none of these persons is responsible for any shortcomings or mistakes in the present textbook. Finally, I would like to thank my family for letting me spend hours and hours in front of my laptop preparing the manuscript. I hope that they do not resent me for having focused so much on this project.

Difference equations

1 Basic concepts

Difference equations are formal models of dynamical systems in which time is assumed to evolve in discrete periods. Models of this kind are used in many areas of economic research, including macroeconomics, monetary economics, resource economics, game theory, etc. In this chapter, we introduce some basic concepts and illustrate them by a number of selected examples. Throughout the book, we restrict the presentation to deterministic systems, that is, we do not consider any models involving uncertainty.

One of the simplest types of difference equations arises through repeated iterations of one-dimensional maps. Because of their conceptual simplicity, we start our discussion of difference equations with these models, proceeding rather informally and without proving any theorems. Later in chapter 4, we shall see that even these simple difference equations can generate surprisingly rich dynamics. In section 1.2, we continue by introducing a general class of explicit difference equations and by extending the basic concepts to this framework. We also increase the level of rigor and formally prove several properties of the solutions of explicit difference equations including their existence and their uniqueness for a complete set of initial or boundary conditions. Finally, in section 1.3, we argue that economic models often take the form of implicit difference equations. Unfortunately, neither the existence nor the uniqueness of solutions to such equations can be ensured, a fact that we illustrate by means of a detailed economic example.

1.1 One-dimensional maps

Suppose that the economic system under consideration can be described by a single variable $x \in X$, where $X \subseteq \mathbb{R}$ is a non-empty interval on the real line. Depending on the context, the variable x can measure the productive capital available in the economy, the price of a commodity, the stock of a resource, the fraction of the population with a certain characteristic, etc. We shall refer to x as the *system variable* and to X as the *system domain*. The system domain contains all possible values of the system variable. Suppose furthermore that the economic system is a dynamic one, that is, that

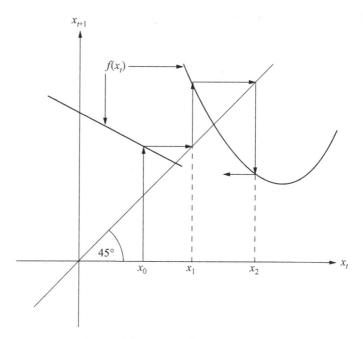

Figure 1.1 Construction of a trajectory

the value of x may change over the course of time. We assume that time is measured in discrete periods $t \in \mathbb{N}_0 = \{0, 1, 2, \ldots\}$ and that the variable x can change its value at most once in every period. The set $\mathbb{N}_0$ of all periods is called the *time domain* or *time horizon*. The interpretation of time periods is also dependent on the context. For example, the variable t may refer to calendar time (days, quarters, years, etc.) or to notional time (decision periods, applications of an operator, generations, etc.). Throughout this book, we indicate the time period by a subscript. In particular, x_t is the value of the system variable in period t. The dynamic evolution of the system is described by a function $f : X \mapsto X$, which is often called the *law of motion* or the *system dynamics*. More specifically, if the system variable has the value x_t in period $t \in \mathbb{N}_0$, then it has the value

$$x_{t+1} = f(x_t) \tag{1.1}$$

in period $t + 1$.

Equation (1.1) is an example of a *difference equation*, because it relates the values of the system variable in different time periods to each other. A solution to this equation is a sequence $(x_t)_{t=0}^{+\infty}$ such that $x_t \in X$ and (1.1) hold for all $t \in \mathbb{N}_0$. Such a sequence is referred to as a *trajectory* of (1.1).

There exists an extremely simple but powerful method for analyzing the dynamics generated by equation (1.1). To apply this method, we must draw the graph of the function f as well as the $45°$ line into a (x_t, x_{t+1})-diagram as shown in figure 1.1.

Suppose that the system has initially the value x_0. We start by locating the point $(x_0, 0)$ on the horizontal axis and by drawing a vertical line from this point to the graph of f. Because of (1.1), it follows that the intersection of this vertical line with the graph of f occurs at the point (x_0, x_1). Starting at that point, we then draw a horizontal line to the 45° line to get to the point (x_1, x_1). We can repeat the same construction over and over again, that is, starting from the most recently determined system value we first draw a vertical line to the graph of the function f and then a horizontal line to the 45° line. In this way, we can construct as many elements of a trajectory of the difference equation (1.1) as we wish. It should be emphasized that this technique does not require any continuity properties of the system dynamics f.

In the following example, the graphical method is applied to a famous model of economic growth.

Example 1.1   The Solow–Swan model is an aggregative model of economic growth. Suppose that the aggregate capital stock available in the economy at the beginning of period t is K_t and that the size of the labour force in period t is L_t. The labour force is assumed to grow at the exogenously given rate $n > -1$ such that

$$L_{t+1} = (1 + n)L_t$$

holds for all $t \in \mathbb{N}_0$. Using its factor endowments with capital and labour, K_t and L_t, respectively, the economy is able to produce the amount $F(K_t, L_t)$ of output in period t, where $F : \mathbb{R}_+^2 \mapsto \mathbb{R}_+$ is the aggregate production function. This output can be used for consumption or it can be invested to form new capital. One of the central assumptions of the Solow–Swan model is that in every period the same fraction of output is invested. Denoting this fraction by $s \in [0, 1]$, it follows that aggregate investment in period t is equal to $sF(K_t, L_t)$, whereas aggregate consumption in period t is $(1 - s)F(K_t, L_t)$. By the elementary rules of bookkeeping, it follows that the aggregate capital stock at the beginning of period $t + 1$ is equal to the aggregate capital stock that was available at the beginning of period t, plus investment during period t and minus depreciated capital. Assuming finally that a constant fraction $\delta \in [0, 1]$ of existing capital depreciates in every period, it follows that

$$K_{t+1} = K_t + sF(K_t, L_t) - \delta K_t.$$

This equation is not of the form (1.1) as it contains both the capital stock and the labour force. However, if we assume that the production technology exhibits constant returns to scale, that is, that the function F is homogeneous of degree 1, then we can rewrite the above equation in the form of (1.1). The function F is homogeneous of degree 1 if and only if $F(\lambda K, \lambda L) = \lambda F(K, L)$ holds for all triples of non-negative numbers (K, L, λ). Dividing the displayed equation from above by $(1 + n)L_t$ and using

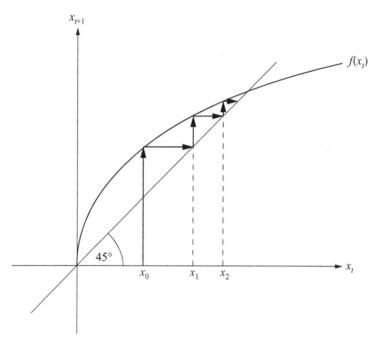

Figure 1.2 Construction of a trajectory of the Solow–Swan model

homogeneity of degree 1 of F plus the fact that $(1 + n)L_t = L_{t+1}$ holds, it follows that

$$\frac{K_{t+1}}{L_{t+1}} = \frac{K_t/L_t + sF(K_t/L_t, 1) - \delta K_t/L_t}{1 + n}.$$

Finally, by introducing the system variable $x_t = K_t/L_t$, which denotes the capital stock per worker, we obtain equation (1.1) with

$$f(x) = \frac{(1 - \delta)x + sF(x, 1)}{1 + n}.$$

As for the system domain, we may choose $X = \mathbb{R}_+$.

Figure 1.2 shows the graph of the function f in the case where the production function F is given by $F(K, L) = \sqrt{KL}$. The figure also shows the 45° line and illustrates how a trajectory of the Solow–Swan model can be constructed along the lines explained above.

The graphical method also helps to identify the so-called *fixed points* of equation (1.1), that is, those values of the system variable which remain fixed under the law of motion f. These fixed points are simply the intersections of the graph of f and the 45° line. In the example depicted in figure 1.2, we can see two such fixed points. One of them is $x = 0$, whereas the other one is in the interior of the system domain $X = \mathbb{R}_+$. It is straightforward to see from the figure that all trajectories of the Solow–Swan model, except for the one emanating from the initial value $x = 0$, converge monotonically to the interior fixed point.

Before we discuss more general types of difference equations, let us consider two more examples of one-dimensional maps, one from evolutionary game theory and another one without any economic background.

Example 1.2 Consider the doubly symmetric two-player normal form game with payoff matrix

$$\begin{pmatrix} a & 0 \\ 0 & b \end{pmatrix},$$

where a and b are positive numbers. We denote the strategy corresponding to the first row or column by A and the strategy corresponding to the second row or column by B. The payoff matrix says that the players receive a if both of them choose A, they receive b if both of them play B, and they receive 0 otherwise. Since a and b are positive, it follows that the players are better off if they choose the same strategies than if they choose different ones. The game is therefore called a coordination game.

The above game has two pure strategy Nash equilibria, (A, A) and (B, B), and one mixed strategy Nash equilibrium in which A is chosen with probability $\bar{x} = b/(a + b)$. There is no obvious reason why one of these equilibria should be preferred over the others. The replicator dynamics have been suggested as a selection device. To explain this device, suppose that there exists a continuum of measure 1 of players who are randomly matched in every period to play the game. Denote the fraction of players who choose A in period t by x_t. The expected payoff of an A-player is therefore ax_t and the expected payoff of a B-player is $b(1 - x_t)$. The average payoff in the entire population is given by $ax_t^2 + b(1 - x_t)^2$.

According to the discrete-time replicator dynamics the growth factor of the measure of players who play a certain strategy is given by the ratio of the expected payoff of players choosing that strategy and the average payoff in the entire population, that is

$$\frac{x_{t+1}}{x_t} = \frac{ax_t}{ax_t^2 + b(1 - x_t)^2}.$$

Multiplication by x_t shows that this equation has the form of (1.1) with

$$f(x) = \frac{ax^2}{ax^2 + b(1 - x)^2}.$$

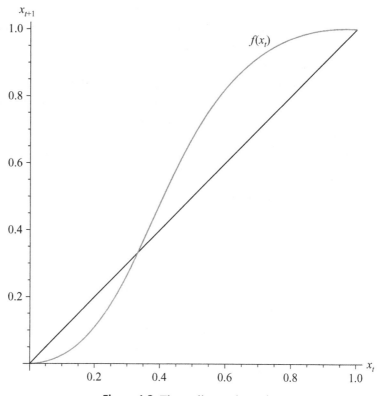

Figure 1.3 The replicator dynamics

If there are no A-players in period t, that is, if $x_t = 0$, then there will be no A-players in the next period either. This is the case because $f(0) = 0$. Analogously, if $x_t = 1$, then there will be no B players in period $t + 1$, because $f(1) = 1$. Thus, the entire population playing the same pure strategy corresponds to a fixed point of the replicator dynamics. There exists, however, a third fixed point, that is, a third solution to the equation $f(x) = x$. This solution is given by $x = \bar{x} = b/(a + b)$. Whenever the population consists of exactly $\bar{x}$ agents who play strategy A and exactly $1 - \bar{x}$ players who choose strategy B, then it follows that this situation will persist forever. Note that the fraction of A-players in this fixed point coincides exactly with the probability of playing A in the mixed strategy Nash equilibrium.

The set of all possible values of the system variable x in this example is the unit interval $X = [0, 1]$. Figure 1.3 displays the graph of the function f along with the 45° line for the case where $a = 2$ and $b = 1$. We can clearly see the three fixed points corresponding to the three Nash equilibria. Graphical analysis along the lines suggested above shows that all trajectories of the replicator dynamics converge to one of these fixed points. More specifically, whenever $x_0 \in (\bar{x}, 1]$, then it follows that the trajectory emanating from x_0 converges to 1, and whenever $x_0 \in [0, \bar{x})$, then it converges to 0. If $a > b$ (as is the case in the example depicted in figure 1.3), then it holds that $1 - \bar{x} > \bar{x}$ such that the set of initial distributions of strategies from which the fixed point corresponding to the Nash equilibrium (A, A) is reached is larger than the set from which the fixed point corresponding to (B, B) is reached. The mixed strategy Nash equilibrium seems to be particularly fragile in the replicator dynamics as it is not reached from any initial distribution that differs from $\bar{x}$. Using the size of the set from which a given fixed point (that corresponds to a Nash equilibrium) is reached as an equilibrium selection criterion therefore leads to the selection of the pure strategy Nash equilibrium (A, A).

The last example in this section, although not originating from any economic application, has strong similarities to the previous example. It shows how an appropriately defined dynamic model can be used to single out one of multiple solutions of a purely static problem. Once again, the graphical method for the analysis of one-dimensional maps turns out to be very useful.

Example 1.3 Let $a > 0$ be given and consider the expression

$$x = a^{a^{a^{\cdot^{\cdot^{\cdot}}}}}, \tag{1.2}$$

that is, the infinitely continued exponentiation of the positive real number a. To compute the value of x for a given value of a, we could exploit the fact that whenever x is given by (1.2) then it must obviously satisfy the equation

$$x = a^x. \tag{1.3}$$

We could therefore try to solve (1.3) instead of (1.2). Unfortunately, this does not necessarily yield a unique answer. For example, if $a = \sqrt{2}$, then both $x = 2$ and $x = 4$ are solutions of (1.3) such that the static model given by equation (1.3) yields an ambiguous answer. Let us therefore try to make the interpretation of (1.2) more precise by using a recursive (dynamic) approach. One possibility to do this is to define x as the limit of the sequence

$$a, a^a, a^{a^a}, \ldots .$$

A more practical way of expressing this is $x = \lim_{t \to +\infty} x_t$, where $x_0 = a$ and $x_{t+1} = f(x_t)$ for all $t \in \mathbb{N}_0$ and where the function $f : \mathbb{R}_+ \mapsto \mathbb{R}_+$ is defined by $f(x) = a^x$. Note that every solution to (1.3) qualifies as a fixed point of the above one-dimensional map. Plotting the graph of the function f for the parameter value $a = \sqrt{2}$ (see figure 1.4) and applying the graphical method introduced earlier in the present section, it is easy to verify that no trajectory emanating from an initial

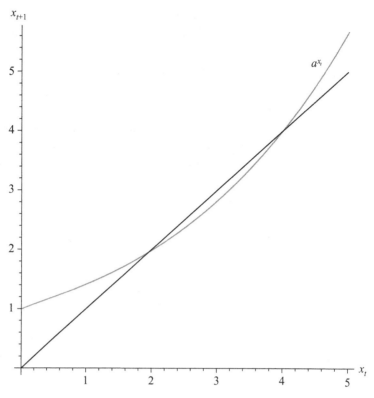

Figure 1.4 The graph of the function a^x for $a = \sqrt{2}$

value $x_0 \neq 4$ can ever approach the fixed point $x = 4$. In particular, the trajectory starting at $x_0 = a = \sqrt{2}$ does not converge to the limit 4 but to the limit 2. This shows that when $a = \sqrt{2}$ the only solution to equation (1.2) that is consistent with the recursive definition of the infinitely continued exponentiation is $x = 2$.

1.2 ## Explicit difference equations

We now generalize the class of difference equations discussed in the previous section in three different ways. First, we consider systems that are described by a finite-dimensional vector rather than by a single real number; second, we allow the system dynamics f to change in the course of time; and, third, we drop the assumption that the value of the system variable x in a given period depends only on the corresponding value in the immediately preceding period.

Let the *system domain* X be an arbitrary non-empty subset of the n-dimensional Euclidean space $\mathbb{R}^n$, where n is a fixed positive integer. We continue to denote the *time domain* by $\mathbb{N}_0 = \{0, 1, 2, \ldots\}$. Thus, in any given period $t \in \mathbb{N}_0$, the system under consideration can be described by a n-dimensional vector

$$x_t = \begin{pmatrix} x_{t,1} \\ x_{t,2} \\ \vdots \\ x_{t,n} \end{pmatrix}.$$

As before, we refer to the variables collected in the vector x_t as the *system variables*.

An *explicit* difference equation is an equation of the form

$$x_{t+1} = f(x_t, x_{t-1}, \ldots, x_{t-k+1}, t), \tag{1.4}$$

where k is a positive integer called the *order* of the difference equation and where $f : X^k \times \mathbb{N}_0 \mapsto X$ is the *system dynamics*. Here $X^k = X \times X \times \cdots \times X$ is the k-fold Cartesian product of the system domain X. The difference equation (1.4) is said to be 'explicit' because it is explicitly solved for the system variable with the highest time-index, x_{t+1}. In economic applications, difference equations do not necessarily occur in this explicit form. We shall therefore also discuss 'implicit' difference equations in section 1.3 below. To simplify the presentation, however, we will omit the label 'explicit' from now on and refer to (1.4) simply as a 'difference equation'.

Note that the function f takes values in $X \subseteq \mathbb{R}^n$, that is, it is a vector-valued function with n components. Thus, we could write (1.4) equivalently in the form of the n equations

$$x_{t+1,\ell} = f_\ell(x_{t,1}, x_{t,2}, \ldots, x_{t,n}, x_{t-1,1}, x_{t-1,2}, \ldots, x_{t-1,n}, \ldots,$$
$$x_{t-k+1,1}, x_{t-k+1,2}, \ldots, x_{t-k+1,n}, t),$$

where, for all $\ell \in \{1, 2, \ldots, n\}$, the function f_ℓ is real-valued and defined on the domain $X^k \times \mathbb{N}_0$.

A sequence $(x_t)_{t=0}^{+\infty}$ for which $x_t \in X$ and (1.4) hold for all $t \in \mathbb{N}_0$ is a *trajectory* of the difference equation (1.4). The following result ensures that explicit difference equations admit trajectories and that for any given k-tuple of *initial values* $(x_0, x_1, \ldots, x_{k-1}) \in X^k$ there exists a unique trajectory of (1.4).

Theorem 1.1 Let k and n be positive integers, let $X \subseteq \mathbb{R}^n$ be a non-empty set, and let $f : X^k \times \mathbb{N}_0 \mapsto X$ be a function. For every k-tuple $(x_0, x_1, \ldots, x_{k-1}) \in X^k$, there exists a unique trajectory of (1.4) with these initial values.

PROOF: The statement follows immediately from an inductive argument. Given the initial values $(x_0, x_1, \ldots, x_{k-1}) \in X^k$, we can set $t = k - 1$ in (1.4) to compute the unique value of x_k. Then, given $(x_1, x_1, \ldots, x_k)$, equation (1.4) with $t = k$ determines a unique value x_{k+1}. Proceeding in this fashion, we can construct the entire trajectory $(x_t)_{t=0}^{+\infty}$, and this construction produces obviously a unique result.

To illustrate the above theorem, consider the following example.

Example 1.4   Assume that $X = \mathbb{R}$, $f(x, t) = x(x - t/3)$, and $x_0 = 1$. Then it follows that $x_1 = 1$, $x_2 = 2/3$, and $x_t = 0$ for all $t \geq 3$. The unique trajectory starting from $x_0 = 1$ is therefore $(1, 1, 2/3, 0, 0, \ldots)$.

Note that theorem 1.1 establishes the uniqueness of a trajectory of the kth-order difference equation (1.4) only under the assumption that k initial values $x_0, x_1, \ldots,$ x_{k-1} are given. If more than k initial values are given, there usually does not exist any trajectory of (1.4) that satisfies all of these initial conditions simultaneously. On the other hand, if only $\ell < k$ initial values are known, say $x_0, x_1, \ldots, x_{\ell-1}$, then we can construct infinitely many trajectories of (1.4) that satisfy these initial conditions by choosing arbitrary values for the system variables in those $k - \ell$ periods $\ell, \ell + 1, \ldots,$ $k - 1$ for which no initial values are given. Whether a difference equation like (1.4) has a solution or not and whether such a solution is unique depends always on the number of initial (or boundary) conditions that are given.

A special case of (1.4) is the *first-order* difference equation

$$x_{t+1} = f(x_t, t), \tag{1.5}$$

which involves only a single time-lag. By a suitable redefinition of the system variables, we can convert every kth-order difference equation into a first-order difference equation. To see how this works, define $\hat{X} = X^k$ and

$$\hat{x}_t = \begin{pmatrix} \hat{x}_{t,1} \\ \hat{x}_{t,2} \\ \vdots \\ \hat{x}_{t,k} \end{pmatrix} := \begin{pmatrix} x_t \\ x_{t-1} \\ \vdots \\ x_{t-k+1} \end{pmatrix}.$$

Using this notation and (1.4), it follows that

$$\hat{x}_{t+1} = \begin{pmatrix} f(\hat{x}_{t,1}, \hat{x}_{t,2}, \ldots, \hat{x}_{t,k}, t) \\ \hat{x}_{t,1} \\ \vdots \\ \hat{x}_{t,k-1} \end{pmatrix}.$$

Obviously, this equation is of the form $\hat{x}_{t+1} = g(\hat{x}_t, t)$, that is, it is a first-order difference equation on the system domain $\hat{X}$. Because of this observation, it causes no loss of generality to restrict attention to first-order difference equations. We will often do so in the rest of this book. Whenever we write 'difference equation' without further qualification, we will implicitly assume that it is of order $k = 1$.

The difference equations (1.4) and (1.5) are called *autonomous* if the function f does not explicitly depend on t. Otherwise, they are called *non-autonomous*. Except for the next chapter on linear difference equations, we shall restrict ourselves to the analysis of autonomous difference equations. This has two reasons: on the one hand, many applications in economics involve autonomous equations and, on the other hand, every non-autonomous difference equation can be converted into an autonomous one which is defined on an augmented system domain. Indeed, equation (1.5) on the system domain $X \subseteq \mathbb{R}^n$ can be converted into the autonomous equation

$$\tilde{x}_{t+1} = g(\tilde{x}_t)$$

on the state space $\tilde{X} = X \times \mathbb{N}_0$, where the function $g : \tilde{X} \mapsto \tilde{X}$ is defined by

$$g(\tilde{x}) = g((x, t)) = \begin{pmatrix} f(x, t) \\ t + 1 \end{pmatrix}.$$

The reader should be warned, however, that the conversion of a non-autonomous difference equation into an autonomous one is not necessarily helpful because the analysis of the converted difference equation is rarely simpler than the analysis of the original equation.

Applying theorem 1.1 to the case of the first-order equation (1.5), we see that for every initial value $x_0 \in X \subseteq \mathbb{R}^n$ there exists a unique trajectory emanating from this initial value. It may happen, however, that not for all components $x_{t,\ell}$ of the system variable an initial value $x_{0,\ell}$ is given.[1] We call those components for which an initial value is given the *pre-determined variables*, because the values of these variables are determined by historical events prior to the initial period of the model. The components $x_{t,\ell}$ for which no initial values are given are called *jump variables*, because these variables are free to take on any feasible value at time 0. Whether a system variable is a pre-determined one or a jump variable is not a mathematical property of the difference equation but depends entirely on the economic interpretation of the model. Jump variables typically occur in economic models in which expectations about the future evolution of the system are formed in a rational, forward-looking way. We illustrate this by means of the examples in the rest of this section. Jump variables also occur naturally in dynamic optimization models, as will be seen in part II of this book.

---

[1] Recall that the system variable x_t is an n-dimensional vector with components $x_{t,1}, x_{t,2}, \ldots, x_{t,n}$.

Example 1.5 The model discussed in this example is known as the cobweb model or hog cycle model. It is a partial equilibrium model describing the dynamics of prices and quantities for a homogeneous good traded on a single market. Denote the demand for the good under consideration in period t by $D(p_t)$, where the demand function $D : \mathbb{R}_+ \mapsto \mathbb{R}_+$ is assumed to be strictly decreasing and invertible, and where p_t is the market price for the good in period t. This means that the demand for the good depends only on its current price. As for supply, we assume that it depends on the one-period-ahead forecast of the price. This assumption reflects the presence of a production lag. For example, pig farmers must decide how many pigs to breed one period before they can actually sell them on the market. As a consequence, the decision of how many pigs to supply to the market in period t must be made on the basis of a price forecast, here denoted by p_t^e, for the market price in period t. Formally, let us assume that the supply of the good is given by $S(p_t^e)$, where $S : \mathbb{R}_+ \mapsto \mathbb{R}_+$ is the supply function. Under our assumption that the demand function is invertible, we can write the market clearing condition $D(p_t) = S(p_t^e)$ in the form

$$p_t = f\left(p_t^e\right), \tag{1.6}$$

where $f(p) = D^{-1}(S(p))$.

We still have to specify how the price forecasts are formed. One popular assumption is that of adaptive expectations, which means that

$$p_t^e = (1 - \gamma)p_{t-1}^e + \gamma p_{t-1}, \tag{1.7}$$

where $\gamma \in [0, 1]$ is a weight parameter. This equation says that the forecast for the period-t price is a weighted average of the forecast for the previous price and the actual price from the previous period. We can write equation (1.7) also in the form

$$p_t^e = p_{t-1}^e - \gamma\left(p_{t-1}^e - p_{t-1}\right),$$

which shows that the price forecast for period t is equal to the price forecast for the previous period, p_{t-1}^e, minus γ times the forecast error from the previous period, $p_{t-1}^e - p_{t-1}$. In words, the agents form their forecast by adjusting the previous forecast in the direction opposite to the latest forecast error. It should be clear from this discussion that the price forecast p_t^e is entirely determined by events prior to period t and it follows that p_t^e is a pre-determined variable. If we assume the model to start in period 0, we must therefore specify an initial value for p_0^e.

Combining the definition of adaptive expectations (1.7) with equation (1.6) from above and advancing the result by one period, we obtain

$$p_{t+1}^e = (1 - \gamma)p_t^e + \gamma f\left(p_t^e\right).$$

This is a one-dimensional map that can be readily analyzed by the graphical method introduced in section 1.1. From theorem 1.1, we know that there exists a unique trajectory from every given initial value p_0^e.

A special case of the adaptive expectations assumption arises if $\gamma = 1$. In this case, we have $p_t^e = p_{t-1}$, which means that the producers simply assume that next period's price will be the same as this period's price. This form of expectation formation is called naive expectations. Note that under this assumption we can rewrite equation (1.6) also in the form[2]

$$D(p_{t+1}) = S(p_t). \tag{1.8}$$

In the literature, the dynamics of this difference equation are often analyzed by a graphical method that is a bit different but essentially equivalent to the one we have discussed in section 1.1. According to that method, we draw the graphs of the demand and supply curves into a (p_t, p_{t+1})-diagram as illustrated in figure 1.5. Starting from a given initial value $p_0 = p_1^e$ on the horizontal axis, we can use the supply curve to find the corresponding value $S(p_0)$. Note that this value is the supply of the good in period 1. Hence, for market clearing to occur in period 1, the price p_1 must be such that $S(p_0) = D(p_1)$, which means that the value of the demand function at p_1 must coincide with $S(p_0)$. We can therefore find the unique market clearing price p_1 by moving from the point $(p_0, S(p_0))$ on the supply curve horizontally to the graph of the demand curve, which yields the point $(p_1, D(p_1))$. The price p_1 can then be marked on the horizontal axis and we can repeat the procedure from that point onwards as long as we wish: vertically to the graph of the supply curve, horizontally to the graph of the demand curve. Under certain assumptions on the shapes of the demand and supply functions, this results in a picture like the one in figure 1.5 which resembles a cobweb. Note that the price sequence in that example displays damped period-two oscillations between high and low values. In the interpretation of the model mentioned above (pig market), this pattern is known as the hog cycle.

Finally, let us point out how we could apply the rational expectations hypothesis to the hog cycle model. In the fully deterministic context of the present example, this hypothesis boils down to the assumption of perfect foresight. This means that the agents (here, the pig farmers) correctly anticipate the future price, that is, $p_t^e = p_t$ for all $t \in \mathbb{N}_0$. Contrary to the situation of adaptive expectations formation, the perfect foresight assumption turns the system variable $p_t^e = p_t$ into a jump variable. This is the case because the forecast p_t^e is formed at the beginning of period t

---

[2] As before, we advance the equation by one period to get the form that we used in our earlier discussion of one-dimensional maps.

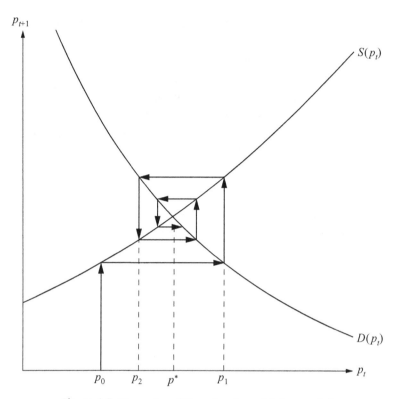

Figure 1.5 Dynamics of the cobweb model (hog cycle)

independently of past events. In particular, no initial value p_0 needs to be specified. Substituting $p_t^e = p_t$ into equation (1.6), we obtain $p_t = f(p_t)$, which is no longer a difference equation. Rather, this equation can be solved separately for each time period, which, in the situation depicted in figure 1.5, would yield $p_t = p^*$ for all $t \in \mathbb{N}_0$.

Example 1.6 Consider the standard New Keynesian model consisting of a (rational expectations-augmented) Phillips curve, a forward looking IS-curve, and an interest rate rule. The equation of the Phillips curve is given by

$$\pi_t = \beta \pi_{t+1} + \alpha y_t, \tag{1.9}$$

where π_t is the rate of inflation in period t (defined as the logarithm of P_t/P_{t-1}, with P_t denoting the price level in period t) and y_t is the output gap in period t (also measured in logarithmic terms). The parameters α and β are assumed to be positive with $\beta \leq 1$. The occurrence of π_{t+1} on the right-hand side of (1.9) reflects the dependence of current inflation on expected future inflation, where we apply the rational expectation hypothesis (perfect foresight).

The equation of the IS-curve takes the form

$$y_t = y_{t+1} - \gamma(i_t - \pi_{t+1}),$$

where i_t is the nominal interest rate in period t and where γ is another positive parameter. Again, rational expectations together with the fact that aggregate demand depends among other things on expected future output implies that y_{t+1} shows up on the right-hand side of the IS-curve. To summarize, both the Phillips curve and the IS-curve can be derived from underlying dynamic optimization problems, in which it is assumed that the economic agents of the model (households and firms) have rational expectations. This assumption is responsible for the occurrence of the forward-looking terms π_{t+1} and y_{t+1} on the right-hand sides of the Phillips curve and the IS-curve, respectively. Both π_t and y_t are therefore jump variables of the model.

Finally, let the interest rate rule be given by

$$i_t = a + b\pi_t + cy_t,$$

where $a \in \mathbb{R}$ and where the non-negative feedback coefficients b and c measure how strongly the central bank responds to changes in the rate of inflation and the output gap, respectively. It seems that there are three system variables: π_t, y_t, and i_t. However, we can use the interest rate rule to eliminate the interest rate from the IS-curve. Doing that and solving the resulting equation and the Phillips curve (1.9) for π_{t+1} and y_{t+1}, we obtain

$$\pi_{t+1} = \frac{1}{\beta}\pi_t - \frac{\alpha}{\beta}y_t,$$

$$y_{t+1} = \gamma\left(b - \frac{1}{\beta}\right)\pi_t + \left(1 + c\gamma + \frac{\alpha\gamma}{\beta}\right)y_t + a\gamma,$$

which is a first-order difference equation in the two system variables π_t and y_t. As has been pointed out before, both of these variables are jump variables for which no initial values are given.

Note that so far we have not imposed any particular structure on the system domain X, except that it is a non-empty subset of $\mathbb{R}^n$. The alert reader will have noticed that even the assumption of X being a subset of $\mathbb{R}^n$ was unnecessary for the analysis up to this point. The next theorem, however, discusses continuity properties of trajectories and therefore requires the system domain to have a topological structure. This is especially simple in the case where $X \subseteq \mathbb{R}^n$, because we can use the familiar topological properties of Euclidean spaces.

Let us introduce the following notation: by $q(x_0; t)$ we denote the tth element of the trajectory of (1.5) starting in x_0. Formally, this means that the function $q : X \times \mathbb{N}_0 \mapsto X$ is recursively defined by the equations

$$q(x; 0) = x$$

and

$$q(x; t + 1) = f(q(x; t), t)$$

for all $x \in X$ and all $t \in \mathbb{N}_0$.

Theorem 1.2   Let X be a non-empty subset of $\mathbb{R}^n$ and let $f : X \times \mathbb{N}_0 \mapsto X$ be a function such that for every $t \in \mathbb{N}_0$, $f(x, t)$ is continuous with respect to x. Then it follows that for every $t \in \mathbb{N}_0$, $q(x_0; t)$ is a continuous function of x_0.

PROOF: The proof is by induction. For $t = 0$, the statement holds because $q(x; 0)$ is the identity map which is continuous. For $t > 0$, the statement follows from $q(x; t + 1) = f(q(x; t), t)$ and the fact that the concatenation of finitely many continuous functions (here f and q) is itself continuous.

1.3   Implicit difference equations

In example 1.6, we discussed a model consisting of a Phillips curve and an IS-curve. When we specified these equations in the first place, we did not write them in such a way that the system variables π_{t+1} and y_{t+1} were expressed in terms of period-t variables. However, we were able to solve the two equations for π_{t+1} and y_{t+1}, thereby converting the model into a system of two explicit difference equations. The same approach also worked in some of the other examples discussed so far. In the present section, we want to show that this is not always possible. Indeed, there exist prominent examples of dynamic economic models which cannot be written as explicit difference equations, albeit they can be written as implicit difference equations. This gives rise to a number of technical difficulties for the analysis of such models.

An *implicit* difference equation (of order 1) on the state space $X \subseteq \mathbb{R}^n$ is an equation of the form

$$F(x_{t+1}, x_t, t) = 0, \tag{1.10}$$

where $F : X^2 \times \mathbb{N}_0 \mapsto \mathbb{R}^n$ is a given function. Suppose that for some $t \in \mathbb{N}_0$ the value x_t is known. Then there are three cases that can arise. If there exists a unique value

x_{t+1} satisfying (1.10), then we can write this value in the form $x_{t+1} = f(x_t, t)$. Thus, we are back in the case of the explicit difference equation (1.5). It could also be the case that there does not exist any value x_{t+1} satisfying (1.10) for the given values t and x_t. This means that there does not exist a trajectory of (1.10) that passes through the point x_t in period t. Finally, there could exist multiple values x_{t+1} satisfying (1.10). In this case, there exist several possibilities to continue the initial segment $(x_0, x_1, \ldots, x_t)$ of the trajectory beyond period t. The following example illustrates the emergence of all three of these cases by means of a simple overlapping generations model.

Example 1.7 Suppose that there exists an infinite sequence of generations, each one consisting of a continuum of unit mass of identical, two-period lived agents. The generation born in period $t \in \mathbb{N}_0$ will be referred to as generation t. Agents in their first period of life are called 'young', whereas those in their second period of life are called 'old'. In addition, there exists a generation of old agents of generation -1 who live in period 0 and whose life lasts for a single period only.

A young agent of generation t spends effort y_t to produce y_t units of a non-storable consumption good and sells this output at price p_t to the old agents from generation $t - 1$. In return, the young agent receives $m_t = p_t y_t$ units of money from the old agents. In the next period $t + 1$, when the agent has grown old, he or she spends the m_t units of money on consumption goods produced by young agents of generation $t + 1$. In other words, the old agents of generation t consume c_{t+1} units of the period-$(t + 1)$ consumption good, where $p_{t+1} c_{t+1} \leq m_t$. The old agents of generation -1 are endowed with M units of money which they spend on consumption goods produced in period 0.

Consumption of c units of output generates utility $u(c)$, and producing y units of output causes disutility $v(y)$. The representative agent of generation $t \in \mathbb{N}_0$ takes the prices p_t and p_{t+1} as given and seeks to maximize the lifetime utility function

$$-v(y_t) + u(c_{t+1})$$

subject to the budget constraints

$$p_{t+1} c_{t+1} \leq m_t = p_t y_t.$$

Note that the agent has to solve this problem at the start of period t. By assuming that the agent takes the future price p_{t+1} as given, we have implicitly imposed perfect foresight. We assume furthermore that the function $v : \mathbb{R}_+ \mapsto \mathbb{R}$ is smooth, strictly increasing, and convex with $v(0) = v'(0) = 0$, and $\lim_{y \to +\infty} v'(y) = +\infty$, and that the function $u : \mathbb{R}_+ \mapsto \mathbb{R} \cup \{-\infty\}$ is strictly increasing and concave and that it is smooth on the interior of its domain. Monotonicity of u implies that the first budget constraint must always be binding, that is, $p_{t+1}c_{t+1} = m_t$. We can therefore solve the two budget constraints for y_t and c_{t+1}, which allows us to rewrite the representative agent's objective function as

$$-v(m_t/p_t) + u(m_t/p_{t+1}).$$

Maximization with respect to m_t yields the necessary and sufficient first-order optimality condition

$$v'(m_t/p_t)/p_t = u'(m_t/p_{t+1})/p_{t+1}.$$

The total amount of money available in the economy in any period must coincide with the initial endowment M such that $m_t = M$ holds for all $t \in \mathbb{N}_0$. Goods market clearing in period t requires that $c_t = y_t$ holds for all t. Multiplying the first-order condition from above by M, it can therefore be rewritten as

$$V(y_t) = U(y_{t+1}), \tag{1.11}$$

where $V(y) = yv'(y)$ and $U(y) = yu'(y)$. Relation (1.11) summarizes all equilibrium conditions in a single implicit difference equation. The only system variable is y_t, which is the amount of the consumption good produced in period t. The price of the consumption good in period t is given by $p_t = M/y_t$. Note that neither y_t nor p_t are pre-determined variables, because their values are determined by the market clearing conditions in period t and not by any historical events that took place prior to period t. Consequently, no initial value for the difference equation (1.11) is given and every sequence of non-negative numbers $(y_t)_{t=0}^{+\infty}$ that satisfies this equation for all $t \in \mathbb{N}_0$ qualifies as an equilibrium of the overlapping generations economy.

To study the structure of equilibria, first note that the assumptions that we have imposed on the function v imply that V is a strictly increasing one-to-one mapping from $\mathbb{R}_+$ to itself. Hence, this function has an inverse and we can write (1.11) as

$$y_t = V^{-1}(U(y_{t+1})).$$

This equation expresses the period-t system variable y_t as a function of the period-$(t + 1)$ system variable y_{t+1}. We call such an equation a description of the *backward dynamics* of the model. We can use a graphical method analogous to that described in section 1.1 to determine for all t_0 and y_{t_0} the unique trajectory $(y_t)_{t=-\infty}^{t_0}$ ending at time t_0 in the system value y_{t_0}. To obtain a description of the usual forward dynamics for the overlapping generations model, however, we would have to solve (1.11) for y_{t+1}. We shall illustrate the various possibilities that can arise by assuming specific functional forms.

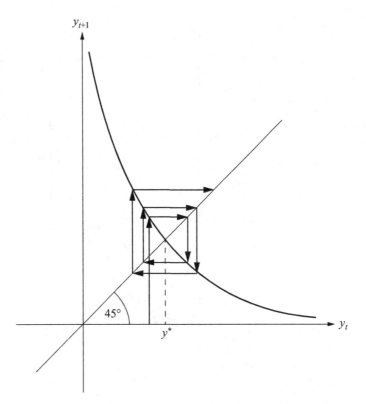

Figure 1.6 Dynamics for $v(y) = y^2/2$ and $u(c) = -1/c$

Suppose first that $u(c) = \ln c$, which implies that $U(y) = 1$ holds for all $y \in \mathbb{R}_+$. In this case, equation (1.11) is not a difference equation, because y_{t+1} drops out of the equation. For a logarithmic utility function, it follows therefore that every equilibrium must satisfy $V(y_t) = 1$ for all $t \in \mathbb{N}_0$. This implies that there exists a unique equilibrium path $(y_t)_{t=0}^{+\infty}$ given by $y_t = V^{-1}(1)$ for all $t \in \mathbb{N}_0$. In this equilibrium, all agents produce the same amount and the price level $p_t = M/V^{-1}(1)$ is also constant throughout the entire time horizon.

Next suppose that $u(c) = c^{1-\sigma}/(1-\sigma)$, with $\sigma > 0$ and $\sigma \neq 1$. In this case, it holds that $U(y) = y^{1-\sigma}$, which can be inverted. The implicit difference equation (1.11) can therefore be written in the explicit form $y_{t+1} = f(y_t)$, where

$$f(y) = U^{-1}(V(y)).$$

If $\sigma > 1$, then it follows that U and, hence, also f are strictly decreasing functions. For example, if $v(y) = y^2/2$ and $u(c) = c^{1-\sigma}/(1-\sigma)$ with $\sigma = 2$, we get $f(y) = 1/y^2$, which is displayed in figure 1.6. It can be seen that there exists a unique fixed point at

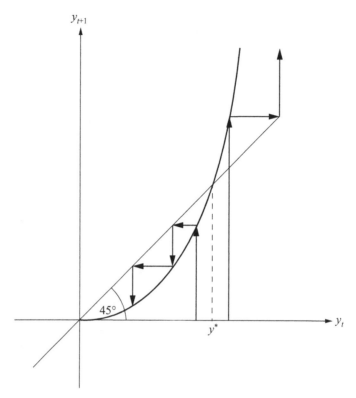

Figure 1.7 Dynamics for $v(y) = y^2/2$ and $u(c) = 2\sqrt{c}$

$y^* = 1$, characterized by the condition $U(y^*) = V(y^*)$, and that all solutions of (1.11), except for the fixed point itself, display explosive period-two oscillations. Whereas the equilibrium $(y_t)_{t=0}^{+\infty}$ with $y_t = y^*$ for all $t \in \mathbb{N}_0$ looks similar to the unique equilibrium in the case of the logarithmic utility function, the oscillating sequences represent a new type of equilibrium. Both the quantities produced and their prices are non-constant with an infimum of 0 and a supremum of $+\infty$. Thus, along this equilibrium, periods with high inflation (y_{t+1} is much smaller than y_t and, hence, p_{t+1} is much higher than p_t) alternate with periods of high deflation (y_{t+1} is much higher than y_t and, hence, p_{t+1} is much smaller than p_t). We would like to emphasize once more that y_t is a jump variable in this model such that we can choose any positive initial value y_0. It follows that in addition to the constant equilibrium $(y^*, y^*, \ldots)$ there exists a continuum of equilibria displaying explosive oscillations of inflations and deflations.

If we assume instead that $\sigma < 1$, the function U and its inverse U^{-1} are strictly increasing functions such that f is also strictly increasing. Figure 1.7 shows the graph of f for the case where $v(y) = y^2/2$ as before and where $u(c) = c^{1-\sigma}/(1-\sigma)$ with

$\sigma = 1/2$. We obtain $f(y) = y^4$ and see from the diagram that there exist two fixed points at $y = 0$ and $y = y^* = 1$. The fixed point $y = y^*$ corresponds to the one we saw before in the case of a logarithmic utility function and the case where $\sigma > 1$. The other fixed point at $y = 0$ represents a very peculiar equilibrium. Note that $y_t = 0$ implies that $p_t = M/y_t = +\infty$. In this equilibrium, agents expect that in their second period of life the price of consumption will be prohibitively high such that no matter how much money they earn during their youth they will not be able to buy any consumption goods. As a consequence, they find it optimal to spend no effort at all in their first period of life. If all agents of all generations behave like that, the situation indeed qualifies as an equilibrium. An alternative interpretation of this equilibrium is that it is one in which money has no value: it is a non-monetary equilibrium. However, since consumption goods are non-storable by assumption, money is the only asset in the economy. If this asset has no value, there will be no trade, no production, and no consumption. Finally, we see from figure 1.7 that all trajectories starting to the left of the positive fixed point y^* converge to the fixed point $y = 0$, that is, to the non-monetary equilibrium. Along such a trajectory, y_t decreases and the price level $p_t = M/y_t$ increases. Hence, the non-monetary equilibrium is approached via an inflation of infinite duration. On the other hand, all trajectories starting to the right of y^* diverge to $+\infty$. Along these trajectories the price level monotonically decreases to 0 (deflation) and output approaches $+\infty$.

Finally, we analyze the model under the assumption that $u(c) = -e^{-\alpha c}$ with $\alpha > 0$. In this case, we have $U(y) = \alpha y e^{-\alpha y}$, which is a non-monotonic function that cannot be inverted. As for the function v, we continue to assume that $v(y) = y^2/2$, which implies $V(y) = y^2$. The backward dynamics are described by

$$y_t = e^{-(\alpha/2)y_{t+1}} \sqrt{\alpha y_{t+1}}, \tag{1.12}$$

which is depicted in figure 1.8. Note that there exist again two fixed points, one at 0 and the other one – again denoted by y^* – in the interior of the system domain. However, if $y_0 = y^*$, this does not necessarily mean that $y_t = y^*$ holds for all t. Indeed, as indicated in the diagram, y_1 could also be much smaller than y^*. Alternatively, consider an initial value such as $y_0 = \tilde{y}$ in the figure. Again, there are two possible values y_1 that satisfy the difference equation (1.11). In choosing the larger one, it turns out that there does not exist any feasible value y_2. More generally, whenever $y_t > \bar{y}$ there does not exist any value y_{t+1} such that (1.11) holds. To summarize, as in the previous case there exist a non-monetary equilibrium corresponding to the fixed point $y = 0$, a constant monetary equilibrium corresponding to the fixed point $y = y^*$, and infinitely many other equilibria that can display quite complicated sequences of inflationary and deflationary periods. In contrast to the previous cases, output along every equilibrium must remain bounded from above by $\bar{y}$. Most importantly,

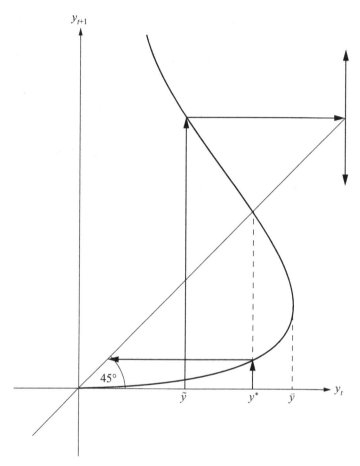

Figure 1.8 Dynamics for $v(y) = y^2/2$ and $u(c) = -e^{-\alpha c}$

however, we note that equation (1.12) cannot be converted into an explicit difference equation.

1.4   EXERCISES

EXERCISE 1.1   At time 0, you borrow an amount x_0 to buy an apartment. Starting from the next period 1, you repay the fixed amount y per period. The interest rate (per period) on your mortgage is $r > 0$.

(a) Derive a difference equation that describes the evolution of your debt from period 0 onwards.

(b) Assume that the parameters are given by $x_0 = 1000$, $r = 5\%$, and $y = 150$. Compute the debt level for as many periods as it is positive.

(c) Is the debt level a pre-determined variable or a jump variable?

EXERCISE 1.2 Consider a tree farm with area equal to 1. The trees live for at most two periods. Trees of age 1 are called 'young' trees and trees of age 2 are 'old' trees. The area that is covered by old trees at the beginning of period t is denoted by x_t. The remaining area $1 - x_t$ is covered by young trees. In each period t, the following events happen. First, all old trees are cut down because they are going to die anyway. Second, the farmer cuts down the fraction $z \in [0, 1]$ of all young trees. Finally, the farmer plants new trees without wasting any space, that is, the entire area that is available after tree-cutting is replanted with trees of age 0. These newly planted trees will be of age 1 at the beginning of the next period $t + 1$.

(a) Derive a difference equation (a one-dimensional map) that determines the sequence $(x_t)_{t=0}^{+\infty}$.

(b) Is x_t a pre-determined variable or a jump variable?

(c) Draw a diagram to study the dynamics of the difference equation and determine (graphically and analytically) all of the fixed points of the equation. Illustrate the evolution of the system variable if the initial value satisfies $x_0 = 1$ and the parameter z is either $z = 0$, $z = 1/2$, or $z = 1$.

EXERCISE 1.3 Consider the following simple macroeconomic model of a closed economy. Real GDP in period t is denoted by Y_t, aggregate demand for consumption goods in period t by C_t, and aggregate demand for investment goods by I_t. Market clearing requires that

$$Y_t = C_t + I_t.$$

Now assume that consumption demand is given by a linear Keynesian consumption function with a time-lag of one period. More specifically, assume that

$$C_t = b + cY_{t-1},$$

where b is autonomous consumption demand and c is the marginal propensity to consume. It is assumed that $0 < c < 1$ holds. As for investment demand, assume the following version of the accelerator principle to hold

$$I_t = \bar{I} + a(Y_t - Y_{t-1}).$$

The number $\bar{I}$ denotes autonomous investment demand and the parameter $a > 0$ describes how strongly investment demand reacts to changes in economic activity (as measured by real GDP). The justification for this equation is that investment decisions by firms are at least in part dependent upon expectations of future increases in demand, which may in turn be extrapolated from past increases in aggregate demand or output. Finally, assume that $a \neq 1$.

(a) Combine the above three equations to obtain an explicit difference equation of the form

$$Y_t = f(Y_{t-1}).$$

(b) Is Y_t a pre-determined variable or a jump variable?

(c) For each of the following four cases, draw the graph of f and indicate the nature of the solutions to the difference equation: $0 < a < c, c < a < (1+c)/2$, $(1+c)/2 < a < 1$, and $1 < a$.

EXERCISE 1.4 Let $a > 0$ be a given real number and consider the continued fraction

$$x = \cfrac{1}{a + \cfrac{1}{a + \cdots}}.$$

Convince yourself that a reasonable (and more precise) definition of x is $x = \lim_{t \to +\infty} x_t$, where $x_0 = 1/a$ and $x_{t+1} = 1/(a + x_t)$. Use this definition and the graphical method introduced in section 1.1 to derive a closed-form expression for x.

EXERCISE 1.5 Consider the New-Keynesian Phillips curve (1.9) from example 1.6 and assume in addition that the quantity equation

$$y_t = m_t - p_t$$

holds, where m_t is the logarithm of the nominal money supply in period t and where $p_t = \ln P_t$ is the logarithm of the price level. We assume that the nominal money supply grows at the constant rate μ such that $m_{t+1} - m_t = \mu$ holds for all $t \in \mathbb{N}_0$.

(a) Shift the quantity equation forward in time by one period and subtract the original (period-t) quantity equation. Show that this leads to

$$y_{t+1} - y_t = \mu - \pi_{t+1},$$

where $\pi_{t+1} = p_{t+1} - p_t$ denotes the rate of inflation.

(b) Rewrite the Phillips curve equation (1.9) and the equation derived in part (a) in the form of an explicit first-order difference equation in the two system variables π_t and y_t. Are these two variables pre-determined or are they jump variables?

(c) Show that the difference equations derived in part (b) are equivalent to those from example 1.6 for the special case where $\gamma = 1$ and where the interest rate rule does not respond to the state of the economy (that is, $b = c = 0$).

EXERCISE 1.6   Rewrite each of the following difference equations as an explicit first-order difference equation and compute the first five elements x_0, x_1, x_2, x_3, and x_4 of the trajectory starting at $x_0 = x_1 = 1$:

(a) $x_{t+1} = 3^t x_t - 4x_{t-1} + 1$.

(b) $x_{t+1} = -(x_{t-1} + t)^2$.

(c) $x_{t+1} = (x_{t-1} - t)^2$.

(d) $(1 + x_t^2)e^{x_{t+1} - x_{t-1}} = 1$.

EXERCISE 1.7   For each of the following implicit difference equations, check whether there exists one or several trajectories emanating from the given initial condition. If possible, compute the first five elements x_0, x_1, x_2, x_3, and x_4 of these trajectories.

(a) $(2x_t + x_{t+1})^{1/2} = 1 + x_t, x_0 = 2$.

(b) $(2x_t + x_{t+1})^{1/2} = 1 + x_t, x_0 = -2$.

(c) $(x_t + 2x_{t+1})^{1/2} = 1 + x_{t+1}, x_0 = 5$.

(d) $(x_t + 10x_{t+1} - 16)^{1/2} = 1 + x_{t+1}, x_0 = 5$.

EXERCISE 1.8   Consider the overlapping generations model discussed in example 1.7, but assume that young agents of generation t cannot perfectly anticipate next period's price p_{t+1}. Assume instead that they form a price forecast p_{t+1}^e by means of the adaptive expectations formula (1.7) with $\gamma \in (0, 1]$. Express the equilibrium conditions in the form of an implicit difference equation in the single system variable p_t^e. Is this variable pre-determined or a jump variable?

1.5   COMMENTS AND REFERENCES

Difference equations are frequently used in economics and, consequently, there exist several textbooks dealing with the most popular methods and applications in economics. A few examples, each with a different focus, are Ferguson and Lim [31], Galor [35], Gandolfo [36], Shone [84], or Sydsæter *et al.* [90]. Of course, there exist also good textbooks on difference equations that are not especially written for economists. One such example is Elaydi [29]. Finally, some books on economics (in particular on macroeconomics) such as Azariadis [5] contain material on difference equations.

   The Solow–Swan model presented in example 1.1 is the simplest neo-classical growth model. It originates from Solow [85] and Swan [89] and is discussed in all standard textbooks on economic growth (e.g. Acemoglu [1]) or macroeconomics (e.g. Blanchard [13]). The replicator dynamics introduced in example 1.2 belongs to the tool box of evolutionary biology and evolutionary game theory. Standard references in these areas include Hofbauer and Sigmund [40] or Weibull [94]. Example 1.3

is taken from Humenberger [42]. The cobweb model from example 1.5 was developed in the 1930s and received its name from Kaldor [44]. The hypothesis of rational expectations was introduced by Muth [71] and is nowadays a standard (but not undisputed) assumption in economics. For an in-depth discussion of the dynamics generated by the cobweb model, we refer the reader to Hommes [41] and the references therein. New-Keynesian models like the one presented in example 1.6 and exercise 1.5 form nowadays the most popular frameworks for monetary policy analysis. For a thorough derivation of these models, we refer to Galí [34] or Woodford [96]. The overlapping generations model is a general framework for dynamic macroeconomic analysis; see, for example, Champ and Freeman [20], De la Croix and Michel [25], or McCandless and Wallace [65]. The version of this model that is presented in example 1.7 is a special case of the one studied in Grandmont [37]. Exercise 1.3 is a simplified version of the multiplier-accelerator model from Samuelson [79]. The original version will be discussed as example 2.4 in chapter 2.

2 | Linear difference equations

Linear difference equations form a very special but important class of dynamical systems. The theory of linear difference equations is well developed and provides a complete characterization of the solutions of these equations. In the present chapter, we discuss some elements of this theory that are of high relevance for economists. The importance of linear difference equations stems, on the one hand, from numerous applications in many areas and, on the other hand, from the fact that under certain conditions the solutions to non-linear difference equations can be approximated by those of suitably linearized equations. Before we turn to non-linear equations in chapter 3, we must therefore deal with the linear case.

We start in section 2.1 by discussing the difference between homogeneous and non-homogeneous linear difference equations and by showing that the set of trajectories of a homogeneous linear difference equation forms a finite-dimensional vector space. This allows us to represent every trajectory of such an equation as a linear combination of finitely many basis solutions. In section 2.2, we derive explicit formulas for the basis solutions of homogeneous linear difference equations with constant coefficients, and in section 2.3 we deal with the important special case of a two-dimensional system domain. Finally, in section 2.4 we present two different approaches for solving non-homogeneous linear difference equations.

2.1 Terminology and general results

Throughout this chapter, we assume that the system domain X is the entire n-dimensional Euclidean space $\mathbb{R}^n$. A difference equation with system domain X is said to be *linear* if it is of the form

$$x_{t+1} = A(t)x_t + b(t), \tag{2.1}$$

where $A : \mathbb{N}_0 \mapsto \mathbb{R}^{n \times n}$ and $b : \mathbb{N}_0 \mapsto \mathbb{R}^n$ are a matrix-valued function and a vector-valued function, respectively. In words, the difference equation $x_{t+1} = f(x_t, t)$ is linear if the law of motion f is an (affine) linear function of the system variables.

By repeated application of equation (2.1), we obtain

$$x_t = A(t-1)x_{t-1} + b(t-1)$$
$$= A(t-1)[A(t-2)x_{t-2} + b(t-2)] + b(t-1)$$
$$= A(t-1)A(t-2)x_{t-2} + A(t-1)b(t-2) + b(t-1)$$
$$\vdots$$
$$= \left[\prod_{s=1}^{t} A(t-s)\right] x_0 + \sum_{s=1}^{t} \left[\prod_{\tau=1}^{s-1} A(t-\tau)\right] b(t-s). \qquad (2.2)$$

Hence, we can always express the value x_t along a trajectory of (2.1) as an (affine) linear function of the initial value x_0. However, this representation of the solution to (2.1) is hardly useful unless we can effectively compute the sums and products appearing in (2.2). Unfortunately, this is often not the case. In the remainder of this section, we therefore outline a different and more practical approach.

If $b(t) = 0$ holds for all $t \in \mathbb{N}_0$, then we call (2.1) a *homogeneous* linear difference equation, otherwise we call it a *non-homogeneous* linear difference equation. Moreover, we refer to the equation

$$x_{t+1} = A(t)x_t \qquad (2.3)$$

as the homogeneous equation corresponding to (2.1).

Lemma 2.1   Let $(\bar{x}_t)_{t=0}^{+\infty}$ be any trajectory of (2.1) and let $(x_t)_{t=0}^{+\infty}$ be any sequence satisfying $x_t \in \mathbb{R}^n$ for all $t \in \mathbb{N}_0$. The sequence $(x_t)_{t=0}^{+\infty}$ is a trajectory of the non-homogeneous equation (2.1) if and only if the sequence $(y_t)_{t=0}^{+\infty}$ defined by $y_t = x_t - \bar{x}_t$ for all $t \in \mathbb{N}_0$ is a trajectory of the corresponding homogeneous equation (2.3).

PROOF: Since $(\bar{x}_t)_{t=0}^{+\infty}$ is a trajectory of (2.1), it follows for all $t \in \mathbb{N}_0$ that

$$\bar{x}_{t+1} = A(t)\bar{x}_t + b(t). \qquad (2.4)$$

Using the fact that $x_t = y_t + \bar{x}_t$ holds by the definition of y_t, it follows that the sequence $(x_t)_{t=0}^{+\infty}$ satisfies (2.1) if and only if

$$y_{t+1} + \bar{x}_{t+1} = A(t)(y_t + \bar{x}_t) + b(t)$$

holds for all $t \in \mathbb{N}_0$. Because of (2.4), it is obvious that this condition is equivalent to $y_{t+1} = A(t)y_t$. This completes the proof of the lemma.

The above lemma suggests the following procedure for solving a non-homogeneous linear difference equation. First we determine the set S_{hom} of all solutions of the corresponding homogeneous equation as well as one particular solution $(\bar{x}_t)_{t=0}^{+\infty}$ of the non-homogeneous equation. The set of all solutions of the non-homogeneous equation is then given by

$$S_{non\text{-}hom} = \left\{ (x_t)_{t=0}^{+\infty} \mid x_t = y_t + \bar{x}_t \text{ for all } t \in \mathbb{N}_0, \ (y_t)_{t=0}^{+\infty} \in S_{hom} \right\}.$$

Regarding the set S_{hom}, we have the following result.

Lemma 2.2 Let $(x_t)_{t=0}^{+\infty}$ and $(x_t')_{t=0}^{+\infty}$ be two elements of S_{hom}, that is, let these two sequences be trajectories of the homogeneous linear difference equation (2.3). If α and β are arbitrary real numbers, then it follows that $(z_t)_{t=0}^{+\infty}$ defined by $z_t = \alpha x_t + \beta x_t'$ for all $t \in \mathbb{N}_0$ is also an element of S_{hom}.

PROOF: By assumption, we have $x_{t+1} = A(t)x_t$ and $x_{t+1}' = A(t)x_t'$ for all $t \in \mathbb{N}_0$. It follows therefore that

$$z_{t+1} = \alpha x_{t+1} + \beta x_{t+1}' = \alpha A(t)x_t + \beta A(t)x_t' = A(t)(\alpha x_t + \beta x_t') = A(t)z_t.$$

This completes the proof of the lemma.

Lemma 2.2 says that the set S_{hom} of all trajectories of the homogeneous linear difference equation (2.3) is a real vector space. The next theorem, which will be stated without proof, strengthens this result by showing that the vector space S_{hom} has the dimension n.

Theorem 2.1 There exist n different trajectories of the homogeneous linear difference equation (2.3), denoted by $(z(j)_t)_{t=0}^{+\infty}$, $j \in \{1, 2, \ldots, n\}$, such that the following statements are true:

(a) If there exist n real numbers $\alpha(j)$, $j \in \{1, 2, \ldots, n\}$, such that

$$\sum_{j=1}^{n} \alpha(j)z(j)_0 = 0$$

holds, then it follows for all $j \in \{1, 2, \ldots, n\}$ that $\alpha(j) = 0$.

(b) Every trajectory $(x_t)_{t=0}^{+\infty}$ of equation (2.3) has a unique representation of the form

$$x_t = \sum_{j=1}^{n} \alpha(j)z(j)_t \tag{2.5}$$

for all $t \in \mathbb{N}_0$, where $\alpha(j)$, $j \in \{1, 2, \ldots, n\}$, are real numbers.

Property (a) of theorem 2.1 implies that the trajectories $(z(j)_t)_{t=0}^{+\infty}, j \in \{1, 2, \ldots, n\}$, are linearly independent.[1] Property (b), on the other hand, implies that these trajectories form a basis of the vector space S_{hom}. Since the basis consists of n elements, the dimension of S_{hom} must be equal to n.

The representation of the trajectories of (2.3) that is stated in equation (2.5) is called the *general solution* to the homogeneous linear difference equation. The general solution expresses all trajectories of equation (2.3) as linear combinations of n *basis solutions* $(z(j)_t)_{t=0}^{+\infty}, j \in \{1, 2, \ldots, n\}$. The numbers $\alpha(j), j \in \{1, 2, \ldots, n\}$, appearing in (2.5) are free parameters. If we assign specific values to these parameters, we obtain a *particular solution* to the homogeneous linear difference equation. For example, by choosing $\alpha(j) = 0$ for all j, we obtain the *trivial solution* given by $x_t = 0$ for all $t \in \mathbb{N}_0$. Every homogeneous linear difference equation admits this trivial solution.

Combining theorem 2.1 with lemma 2.1, it follows that the general solution to the non-homogeneous linear difference equation (2.1) can be represented in the form

$$x_t = \bar{x}_t + \sum_{j=1}^{n} \alpha(j) z(j)_t, \qquad (2.6)$$

where $(\bar{x}_t)_{t=0}^{+\infty}$ is an arbitrary particular solution to equation (2.1). If we seek the (unique) trajectory of (2.1) that starts in a given initial value x_0, then we just need to determine the unknown coefficients $\alpha(j), j \in \{1, 2, \ldots, n\}$, in such a way that

$$\sum_{j=1}^{n} \alpha(j) z(j)_0 = x_0 - \bar{x}_0. \qquad (2.7)$$

Because theorem 2.1(a) ensures that the n vectors $z(j)_0, j \in \{1, 2, \ldots, n\}$, are linearly independent, it follows that there exists a unique n-tuple of parameters $\alpha(j)$ such that (2.7) holds.

To summarize, the standard method for solving the linear difference equation (2.1) consists of the following steps. First, we determine n linearly independent trajectories $(z(j)_t)_{t=0}^{+\infty}$ of the corresponding homogeneous difference equation (2.3). Second, we try to find one particular solution $(\bar{x}_t)_{t=0}^{+\infty}$ of the original (non-homogeneous) equation (2.1) (if the original equation itself is homogeneous, we simply set $\bar{x}_t = 0$ for all $t \in \mathbb{N}_0$). Third, the general solution to equation (2.1) is given by (2.6) and the unique trajectory emanating from a given initial point x_0 can be obtained by solving (2.7) for the n coefficients $\alpha(j), j \in \{1, 2, \ldots, n\}$.

So far, we have been silent about how to determine the basis solutions $(z(j)_t)_{t=0}^{+\infty}$, $j \in \{1, 2, \ldots, n\}$, and the particular solution $(\bar{x}_t)_{t=0}^{+\infty}$. We shall deal with these problems

---

[1] Using the fact that for all $j \in \{1, 2, \ldots, n\}$ the sequence $(z(j)_t)_{t=0}^{+\infty}$ is a trajectory of the difference equation (2.3), it is straightforward to see that the assumption $\sum_{j=1}^{n} \alpha(j) z(j)_0 = 0$ stated in part (a) of theorem 2.1 implies that $\sum_{j=1}^{n} \alpha(j) z(j)_t = 0$ holds for all $t \in \mathbb{N}_0$.

in sections 2.2 and 2.4 for the special case in which equation (2.1) has constant coefficients. This property, which means that the matrix $A(t)$ does not depend on t, is satisfied in many applications in economics.

2.2 Homogeneous equations

Consider a homogeneous linear difference equation with *constant coefficients*, that is, an equation of the form

$$x_{t+1} = Ax_t. \tag{2.8}$$

Here $x_t \in X = \mathbb{R}^n$ is the system variable and A is a real-valued $n \times n$ matrix with entries $A = (a_{ij})_{i,j=1}^n$. We shall refer to this matrix as the *system matrix* of equation (2.8). A more elaborate form of writing this equation is given by

$$\begin{pmatrix} x_{t+1,1} \\ x_{t+1,2} \\ \vdots \\ x_{t+1,n} \end{pmatrix} = \begin{pmatrix} a_{11} & a_{12} & \cdots & a_{1n} \\ a_{21} & a_{22} & \cdots & a_{2n} \\ \vdots & \vdots & \ddots & \vdots \\ a_{n1} & a_{n2} & \cdots & a_{nn} \end{pmatrix} \begin{pmatrix} x_{t,1} \\ x_{t,2} \\ \vdots \\ x_{t,n} \end{pmatrix}.$$

In the rest of this section, we present results that allow us to find n linearly independent trajectories of (2.8). As we shall see, this requires knowledge about the eigenvalues and eigenvectors of the matrix A. A real or complex number λ is an eigenvalue of A if there exists a non-zero (real or complex) n-dimensional vector w such that $Aw = \lambda w$. The vector w is called an eigenvector corresponding to the eigenvalue λ. The eigenvalues of the real matrix A are the roots of the characteristic polynomial $p(\lambda) = \text{Det}(A - \lambda I_n)$, where I_n denotes the $n \times n$ unit matrix.

We write complex numbers in the form $z = a + ib$, where $a \in \mathbb{R}$ and $b \in \mathbb{R}$ are referred to as the real part and the imaginary part, respectively, of z, and where $i = \sqrt{-1}$ is the imaginary unit. The absolute value (or modulus) of the complex number $z = a + ib$ is given by $r = \sqrt{a^2 + b^2}$. The phase (or argument) of z is given by $\theta = \arctan(b/a)$. Using this notation, we can write z also in the form $z = r[\cos(\theta) + i\sin(\theta)]$. The complex conjugate of the complex number $z = a + ib$ is given by $a - ib$. We are now ready to state the first result of this section.

Theorem 2.2 Consider the homogeneous linear difference equation (2.8).

(a) If λ is a real eigenvalue of the matrix A with corresponding eigenvector w, then it follows that the sequence $(z_t)_{t=0}^{+\infty}$ defined by

$$z_t = \lambda^t w$$

for all $t \in \mathbb{N}_0$ is a trajectory of (2.8).

(b) Let $r[\cos(\theta) + i\sin(\theta)]$ be a complex eigenvalue of the matrix A with corresponding eigenvector $w = u + iv$. Without loss of generality, we may assume that $r > 0$ and that $\sin(\theta) \neq 0$. The sequences $(z_t)_{t=0}^{+\infty}$ and $(\hat{z}_t)_{t=0}^{+\infty}$ defined by

$$z_t = r^t[\cos(\theta t)u - \sin(\theta t)v]$$
$$\hat{z}_t = r^t[\sin(\theta t)u + \cos(\theta t)v]$$

for all $t \in \mathbb{N}_0$ are linearly independent trajectories of (2.8).

PROOF: (a) It holds that $z_{t+1} = \lambda^{t+1}w = \lambda^t(\lambda w) = \lambda^t(Aw) = A(\lambda^t w) = Az_t$, where we have used the fact that w is an eigenvector of A corresponding to the eigenvalue λ.

(b) We start by explaining why it is no loss of generality to assume $r > 0$. Because r is the absolute value of a complex eigenvalue, it must be non-negative. If it were equal to 0, then the eigenvalue would be equal to 0, that is, a real number, and we have dealt with that case already in part (a). There is no loss of generality to assume that $\sin(\theta) \neq 0$, because the case where $\sin(\theta) = 0$ corresponds also to a real eigenvalue.

Since $u + iv$ is an eigenvector with eigenvalue $r[\cos(\theta) + i\sin(\theta)]$, it holds that $A(u + iv) = r[\cos(\theta) + i\sin(\theta)](u + iv)$, which is equivalent to $Au = r[\cos(\theta)u - \sin(\theta)v]$ and $Av = r[\sin(\theta)u + \cos(\theta)v]$. Consequently, we have

$$
\begin{aligned}
Az_t &= r^t[\cos(\theta t)Au - \sin(\theta t)Av] \\
&= r^{t+1}[\cos(\theta t)\cos(\theta)u - \cos(\theta t)\sin(\theta)v - \sin(\theta t)\sin(\theta)u - \sin(\theta t)\cos(\theta)v] \\
&= r^{t+1}\{\cos[\theta(t+1)]u - \sin[\theta(t+1)]v\} \\
&= z_{t+1},
\end{aligned}
$$

where we have used the addition formulas for trigonometric functions. In a completely analogous way, we can prove that $A\hat{z}_t = \hat{z}_{t+1}$.

It remains to be shown that the trajectories $(z_t)_{t=0}^{+\infty}$ and $(\hat{z}_t)_{t=0}^{+\infty}$ are linearly independent. Suppose that they are not. In this case, there must exist real numbers α and β, not both equal to 0, such that $\alpha z_t + \beta \hat{z}_t = 0$ holds for all $t \in \mathbb{N}_0$. For $t = 0$, this implies that

$$\alpha u + \beta v = 0. \tag{2.9}$$

For $t = 1$, we get $\alpha r[\cos(\theta)u - \sin(\theta)v] + \beta r[\sin(\theta)u + \cos(\theta)v] = 0$. Because of (2.9), $r > 0$, and $\sin(\theta) \neq 0$ this implies

$$-\alpha v + \beta u = 0. \tag{2.10}$$

Suppose now that $\alpha = 0$. Because we know that not both α and β are equal to 0, it must be the case that $\beta \neq 0$ and it follows therefore from (2.9) and (2.10) that $u = v = 0$. But this implies $w = u + iv = 0$, which contradicts the fact that w is an eigenvector of A. Hence, it holds that $\alpha \neq 0$ and we obtain from (2.10) that $v = (\beta/\alpha)u$. Substituting this into (2.9), it follows that $(\alpha^2 + \beta^2)u = 0$, which again implies that $u = v = 0$. Since this is impossible, the proof of the theorem is complete.

The following example illustrates the application of the above theorem in the case of a one-dimensional system domain $X = \mathbb{R}$.

Example 2.1 Consider the one-dimensional homogeneous linear difference equation

$$x_{t+1} = \lambda x_t, \tag{2.11}$$

where λ is a real number and $x_t \in X = \mathbb{R}$. In this situation, the system matrix $A = (\lambda)$ is just a real number, its only eigenvalue is obviously equal to λ, and a corresponding eigenvector is equal to $w = (1)$. Since λ is a real number, we can apply part (a) of theorem 2.2. Doing that we see that $z_t = \lambda^t$ is a trajectory of (2.11). Because of $n = 1$, we know from theorem 2.1 that there are no further linearly independent trajectories, and it follows that the general solution to (2.11) takes the form $x_t = \alpha\lambda^t$, where α is a real parameter. If an initial value x_0 is given, then it must hold that $\alpha = x_0$.

We can now determine how the qualitative behaviour of the trajectories of equation (2.11) depends on the parameter value λ. If $x_0 = 0$, then it holds obviously for all $t \in \mathbb{N}_0$ that $x_t = 0$, and we obtain the trivial solution. For the remainder of this example, let us therefore assume that $x_0 \neq 0$. If $\lambda = 0$, then $x_t = 0$ holds for all $t \geq 1$ and there is no movement after period 0. If $\lambda \in (0, 1)$, then it follows that $x_t = x_0\lambda^t$ converges from the given initial value x_0 monotonically to 0. If $\lambda \in (-1, 0)$, on the other hand, the trajectory $(x_0\lambda^t)_{t=0}^{+\infty}$ converges to 0, but in an oscillatory way. If $\lambda = 1$, then the equation reads $x_{t+1} = x_t$ so that $x_t = x_0$ holds for all t. In this case, there are no dynamics whatsoever. The system remains in its initial value forever. If $\lambda = -1$, then we have $x_t = x_0(-1)^t$, which shows that the system displays periodic oscillations of period 2. Next consider the case $\lambda > 1$. In this situation, it follows that the trajectory $(x_0\lambda^t)_{t=0}^{+\infty}$ diverges monotonically to plus or minus infinity. Finally, if $\lambda < -1$, then we get divergence to infinity again, but this time in an oscillatory way.

The above example illustrates all possible scenarios that can arise in the case of a one-dimensional system domain. Let us now turn to higher-dimensional systems of difference equations. If $r[\cos(\theta) + i\sin(\theta)]$ is a complex eigenvalue of the real matrix

A and $w = u + iv$ is the corresponding eigenvector, then $r[\cos(\theta) - i\sin(\theta)]$ must be an eigenvalue of A corresponding to the conjugate eigenvector $\bar{w} = u - iv$. Applying the construction from theorem 2.2(b) to this second eigenvalue, we get the trajectories $(z_t)_{t=0}^{+\infty}$ and $(-\hat{z}_t)_{t=0}^{+\infty}$. Hence, for every pair of complex conjugate eigenvalues of A, theorem 2.2 allows us to construct exactly one pair of linearly independent trajectories of (2.8).

The following lemma, which is stated without proof, shows that all the trajectories constructed according to theorem 2.2 are linearly independent, provided that the corresponding eigenvalues differ from each other.

Lemma 2.3 Consider the homogeneous linear difference equation (2.8). Let $\ell \leq n/2$ and $m \leq n - 2\ell$ be non-negative integers and suppose that for all $j \in \{1, 2, \ldots, \ell\}$ the matrix $A \in \mathbb{R}^{n \times n}$ has the pair of conjugate complex eigenvalues $\{r(j)[\cos(\theta(j)) + i\sin(\theta(j))], r(j)[\cos(\theta(j)) - i\sin(\theta(j))]\}$ and that for all $j \in \{2\ell + 1, 2\ell + 2, \ldots, 2\ell + m\}$ the matrix A has the real eigenvalue $\lambda(j)$. Suppose furthermore that all these eigenvalues are mutually different from each other. Then it follows that the corresponding $2\ell + m$ trajectories of (2.8) that are constructed according to theorem 2.2 are linearly independent.

If the system matrix A has n distinct (real or complex) eigenvalues (that is, if $2\ell + m = n$), then it follows from the above lemma that we can use the method described in theorem 2.2 to construct n linearly independent trajectories of equation (2.8), that is, a basis of the vector space S_{hom}. According to theorem 2.1, this implies that we can express the general solution to equation (2.8) in the form (2.5).

If A has less than n distinct eigenvalues, however, then theorem 2.2 may not be sufficient to determine a basis of the vector space S_{hom}. In order to deal with this case, we have to refer to a few results from linear algebra. First, recall that the characteristic polynomial of a real matrix A can be factored as

$$p(\lambda) = (-1)^n \prod_{j=1}^{J} [\lambda - \lambda(j)]^{m^a(j)},$$

where $\{\lambda(1), \lambda(2), \ldots, \lambda(J)\}$ are the distinct eigenvalues of the matrix A and where for every $j \in \{1, 2, \ldots, J\}$ the positive integer $m^a(j)$ is the algebraic multiplicity of the eigenvalue $\lambda(j)$. Of course, it must hold that $m^a(j) \geq 1$ for all j and $m^a(1) + m^a(2) + \ldots + m^a(J) = n$. If an eigenvalue λ has algebraic multiplicity m^a, then there exist at most m^a linearly independent eigenvectors corresponding to λ. The maximal number of linearly independent eigenvectors corresponding to λ is called its geometric multiplicity, and will be denoted by m^g. If the geometric multiplicity m^g of an eigenvalue λ is strictly smaller than its algebraic multiplicity m^a, then it is always possible to determine $m^a - m^g$ generalized eigenvectors corresponding to λ according to the following procedure.

Let $\{w(0, k) \mid k \in \{1, 2, \ldots, m^g\}\}$ be a set of linearly independent eigenvectors of A corresponding to the eigenvalue λ. For every $k \in \{1, 2, \ldots, m^g\}$, we determine a set of vectors $W_\lambda(k) = \{w(0, k), w(1, k), \ldots, w(\ell_k, k)\}$, where $\ell_k \geq 0$ is the largest integer such that the set $W_\lambda(k)$ consist of linearly independent vectors which satisfy the recursive formula

$$Aw(\ell, k) = \lambda w(\ell, k) + w(\ell - 1, k) \tag{2.12}$$

for all $\ell \in \{1, 2, \ldots, \ell_k\}$. Note that it can happen that $\ell_k = 0$, that is, that there exists no vector $w(1, k)$ which is linearly independent of the eigenvector $w(0, k)$ and which satisfies equation (2.12). The union of all these sets, that is

$$W_\lambda = \bigcup_{k=1}^{m^g} W_\lambda(k) \tag{2.13}$$

consists of m^g eigenvectors $\{w(0, k) \mid 1 \leq k \leq m^g\}$ plus $m^a - m^g$ generalized eigenvectors $\{w(\ell, k) \mid 1 \leq k \leq m^g, \ 1 \leq \ell \leq \ell_k\}$. It can be shown that the set

$$W = \bigcup_{j=1}^{J} W_{\lambda(j)}$$

consists of n linearly independent eigenvectors and generalized eigenvectors of A.

The following two theorems present the results and formulas that allow us to construct a basis of S_{hom} in the case where A has less than n distinct eigenvalues. We first deal with the case of multiple real eigenvalues (theorem 2.3) and then with the case of multiple complex eigenvalues (theorem 2.4).[2]

Theorem 2.3 Consider the homogeneous linear difference equation (2.8) and let λ be a real eigenvalue of the system matrix A. Assume that λ has algebraic multiplicity m^a and geometric multiplicity m^g and let $\{w(0, 1), w(0, 2), \ldots, w(0, m^g)\}$ be a set of linearly independent eigenvectors corresponding to λ. For every $k \in \{1, 2, \ldots, m^g\}$, let $W_\lambda(k) = \{w(\ell, k) \mid \ell \in \{0, 1, \ldots, \ell_k\}\}$ be a maximal set of linearly independent vectors satisfying the recursion (2.12), and let W_λ, as given by (2.13), be the full set of eigenvectors and generalized eigenvectors corresponding to λ. Then it follows that

---

[2] Since complex eigenvalues always arise as pairs of complex conjugate numbers, the case of multiple complex eigenvalues can only occur in difference equations defined on a system domain of dimension $n \geq 4$.

the trajectories $\{(z(\ell, k)_t)_{t=0}^{+\infty} \mid k \in \{1, 2, \ldots, m^g\}, \ell \in \{0, 1, \ldots, \ell_k\}\}$ defined by[3]

$$z(\ell, k)_t = \sum_{j=0}^{\ell} \binom{t}{j} \lambda^{t-j} w(\ell - j, k)$$

form a set of m^a linearly independent solutions of equation (2.8).

PROOF: It holds that

$$Az(\ell, k)_t = \sum_{j=0}^{\ell} \binom{t}{j} \lambda^{t-j} A w(\ell - j, k)$$

$$= \sum_{j=0}^{\ell-1} \binom{t}{j} \lambda^{t-j} [\lambda w(\ell - j, k) + w(\ell - j - 1, k)] + \binom{t}{\ell} \lambda^{t-\ell} \lambda w(0, k)$$

$$= \sum_{j=0}^{\ell} \binom{t}{j} \lambda^{t-j+1} w(\ell - j, k) + \sum_{j=1}^{\ell} \binom{t}{j-1} \lambda^{t-j+1} w(\ell - j, k)$$

$$= \lambda^{t+1} w(\ell, k) + \sum_{j=1}^{\ell} \left[\binom{t}{j} + \binom{t}{j-1} \right] \lambda^{t-j+1} w(\ell - j, k)$$

$$= \sum_{j=0}^{\ell} \binom{t+1}{j} \lambda^{t-j+1} w(\ell - j, k)$$

$$= z(\ell, k)_{t+1}.$$

The first line of this chain of equations uses the definition of the trajectory $(z(\ell, k)_t)_{t=0}^{+\infty}$; the second line uses equation (2.12) as well as the fact that $w(0, k)$ is an eigenvector corresponding to λ. Lines three and four involve only simple rearrangements of terms, whereas the fifth line uses a well-known formula for the binomial coefficients. The last step uses the definition of $(z(\ell, k)_t)_{t=0}^{+\infty}$ once more.

The above arguments prove that the m^a sequences $(z(\ell, k)_t)_{t=0}^{+\infty}, k \in \{1, 2, \ldots, m^g\}$, $\ell \in \{0, 1, \ldots, \ell_k\}$, qualify as trajectories of equation (2.8). It remains to be shown that these trajectories are linearly independent. Because $z(\ell, k)_0 = w(\ell, k)$ holds for all k and all ℓ, the linear independence of the trajectories follows immediately from the linear independence of the vectors in W_λ.

---

[3] The symbol $\binom{t}{j}$ denotes the binomial coefficient, which is defined by

$$\binom{t}{j} = \frac{t \times (t - 1) \times \ldots \times (t - j + 1)}{1 \times 2 \times \ldots \times j}.$$

Note that theorem 2.3 generalizes statement (a) of theorem 2.2. As a matter of fact, if $m^a = m^g = 1$, then it follows that $\ell_1 = 0$ and the formula in theorem 2.3 reduces to $z(0, 1)_t = \lambda^t w(0, 1)$, which is exactly the statement of theorem 2.2(a). The following example illustrates the application of the results derived so far.

Example 2.2 Consider the homogeneous system of four linear difference equations

$$x_{t+1,1} = -x_{t,3} + x_{t,4},$$

$$x_{t+1,2} = 2x_{t,2},$$

$$x_{t+1,3} = 2x_{t,3},$$

$$x_{t+1,4} = -x_{t,1} + 2x_{t,3}.$$

The matrix A is therefore given by

$$A = \begin{pmatrix} 0 & 0 & -1 & 1 \\ 0 & 2 & 0 & 0 \\ 0 & 0 & 2 & 0 \\ -1 & 0 & 2 & 0 \end{pmatrix}.$$

The characteristic polynomial of A is $P(\lambda) = (\lambda - 2)^2(1 + \lambda^2)$ and has the roots 2, i, and $-i$. Since 2 is a real eigenvalue with algebraic multiplicity $m^a = 2$, we have to apply theorem 2.3. Using the notation from that theorem, it is easy to see that both $w(0, 1) = (0, 1, 0, 0)^\top$ and $w(0, 2) = (0, 0, 1, 1)^\top$ are eigenvectors corresponding to the eigenvalue 2 and that these eigenvectors are linearly independent.[4] Hence, the algebraic multiplicity of the eigenvalue coincides with its geometric multiplicity: $m^a = m^g = 2$. Furthermore, an eigenvector corresponding to the complex eigenvalue $i = i \sin(\pi/2)$ is given by $w = (-i, 0, 0, 1)^\top$. From theorems 2.1–2.3, it follows therefore that the general solution to the above system of difference equations is given by

$$\begin{pmatrix} x_{t,1} \\ x_{t,2} \\ x_{t,3} \\ x_{t,4} \end{pmatrix} = \alpha(1)2^t \begin{pmatrix} 0 \\ 1 \\ 0 \\ 0 \end{pmatrix} + \alpha(2)2^t \begin{pmatrix} 0 \\ 0 \\ 1 \\ 1 \end{pmatrix} + \alpha(3) \begin{pmatrix} \sin(\pi t/2) \\ 0 \\ 0 \\ \cos(\pi t/2) \end{pmatrix} + \alpha(4) \begin{pmatrix} -\cos(\pi t/2) \\ 0 \\ 0 \\ \sin(\pi t/2) \end{pmatrix}$$

$$= \begin{pmatrix} \alpha(3) \sin(\pi t/2) - \alpha(4) \cos(\pi t/2) \\ \alpha(1)2^t \\ \alpha(2)2^t \\ \alpha(2)2^t + \alpha(3) \cos(\pi t/2) + \alpha(4) \sin(\pi t/2) \end{pmatrix}.$$

---

[4] The superscript $^\top$ denotes transposition of a vector or a matrix.

Difference equations

In the first line of this equation, we can see the four basis solutions multiplied by the undetermined coefficients $\alpha(j)$, $j \in \{1, 2, 3, 4\}$, and summed over all j. In the second line, the general solution is simply rewritten in a more compact form.

Now let us slightly modify the example. Suppose that the second difference equation is changed to $x_{t+1,2} = 2x_{t,2} - x_{t,3}$. Thus, the system matrix A is now given by

$$A = \begin{pmatrix} 0 & 0 & -1 & 1 \\ 0 & 2 & -1 & 0 \\ 0 & 0 & 2 & 0 \\ -1 & 0 & 2 & 0 \end{pmatrix}.$$

The characteristic polynomial of this matrix is exactly the same as that of the matrix in the previous example, and, hence, the eigenvalues are again given by 2, i, and $-i$. An eigenvector corresponding to the double eigenvalue 2 is given by $w(0, 1) = (0, 1, 0, 0)^\top$. In this case, however, there does not exist a second eigenvector that is linearly independent of $w(0, 1)$. Thus, we have to use theorem 2.3 again, but this time it holds that $m^g = 1 < m^a = 2$, and we need to calculate a generalized eigenvector corresponding to the eigenvalue 2. Indeed, it holds that $Aw(1, 1) = 2w(1, 1) + w(0, 1)$ provided that $w(1, 1) = (0, 0, -1, -1)^\top$. As in the previous example, an eigenvector corresponding to the complex eigenvalue i is given by $w = (-i, 0, 0, 1)^\top$. The general solution to the present system of difference equations is therefore

$$\begin{pmatrix} x_{t,1} \\ x_{t,2} \\ x_{t,3} \\ x_{t,4} \end{pmatrix} = \alpha(1)2^t \begin{pmatrix} 0 \\ 1 \\ 0 \\ 0 \end{pmatrix} + \alpha(2) \left[2^t \begin{pmatrix} 0 \\ 0 \\ -1 \\ -1 \end{pmatrix} + 2^{t-1}t \begin{pmatrix} 0 \\ 1 \\ 0 \\ 0 \end{pmatrix} \right]$$

$$+ \alpha(3) \begin{pmatrix} \sin(\pi t/2) \\ 0 \\ 0 \\ \cos(\pi t/2) \end{pmatrix} + \alpha(4) \begin{pmatrix} -\cos(\pi t/2) \\ 0 \\ 0 \\ \sin(\pi t/2) \end{pmatrix}$$

$$= \begin{pmatrix} \alpha(3)\sin(\pi t/2) - \alpha(4)\cos(\pi t/2) \\ [2\alpha(1) + \alpha(2)t]2^{t-1} \\ -\alpha(2)2^t \\ -\alpha(2)2^t + \alpha(3)\cos(\pi t/2) + \alpha(4)\sin(\pi t/2) \end{pmatrix}.$$

Finally, we discuss the case of multiple complex eigenvalues. Since the relevant formulas can be proved in an analogous way as are those for the case of multiple real eigenvalues, we state the theorem without proof.

Theorem 2.4 Consider the homogeneous linear difference equation (2.8), and let $\lambda = r[\cos(\theta) + i\sin(\theta)]$ be a complex eigenvalue of the system matrix A. Without loss of generality, we may assume $r > 0$ and $\sin(\theta) \neq 0$. Suppose that λ has algebraic multiplicity m^a and geometric multiplicity m^g, and let $\{w(0,1), w(0,2), \ldots, w(0,m^g)\}$ be a set of linearly independent eigenvectors corresponding to λ. For every $k \in \{1, 2, \ldots, m^g\}$, let $W_\lambda(k) = \{w(\ell, k) \mid \ell \in \{0, 1, \ldots, \ell_k\}\}$ be a maximal set of linearly independent vectors satisfying the recursion (2.12) and let W_λ, as given by (2.13), be the full set of eigenvectors and generalized eigenvectors corresponding to λ. We write $w(\ell, k) = u(\ell, k) + iv(\ell, k)$ for all $k \in \{1, 2, \ldots, m^g\}$ and all $\ell \in \{0, 1, \ldots, \ell_k\}$. Then it follows that the trajectories $(z(\ell, k)_t)_{t=0}^{+\infty}$ and $(\hat{z}(\ell, k)_t)_{t=0}^{+\infty}$ defined for all k and ℓ by

$$z(\ell, k)_t = \sum_{j=0}^{\ell} \binom{t}{j} r^{t-j} \left[\cos(\theta(t-j))u(\ell-j, k) - \sin(\theta(t-j))v(\ell-j, k) \right],$$

$$\hat{z}(\ell, k)_t = \sum_{j=0}^{\ell} \binom{t}{j} r^{t-j} \left[\sin(\theta(t-j))u(\ell-j, k) + \cos(\theta(t-j))v(\ell-j, k) \right]$$

form a set of $2m^a$ linearly independent solutions of equation (2.8).

For $m^a = m^g = 1$ and $\ell_1 = 0$, the above theorem reduces to statement (b) of theorem 2.2. The following example illustrates the application of theorem 2.4.

Example 2.3 Consider the homogeneous system of four linear difference equations

$$x_{t+1,1} = -x_{t,2},$$

$$x_{t+1,2} = x_{t,1},$$

$$x_{t+1,3} = x_{t,1} - x_{t,4},$$

$$x_{t+1,4} = -x_{t,2} + x_{t,3}.$$

The matrix A is therefore given by

$$A = \begin{pmatrix} 0 & -1 & 0 & 0 \\ 1 & 0 & 0 & 0 \\ 1 & 0 & 0 & -1 \\ 0 & -1 & 1 & 0 \end{pmatrix}.$$

The characteristic polynomial of A is $P(\lambda) = (\lambda^2 + 1)^2$ and has the roots i and $-i$, both with algebraic multiplicity $m^a = 2$. It is easy to see that both $w(0, 1) = (0, 0, 1, -i)^\top$

and $w(0, 2) = (1, -i, 0, 1)^\top$ are eigenvectors corresponding to the eigenvalue i and that these two eigenvectors are linearly independent. Hence, it holds that $m^g = m^a = 2$, and we can apply theorem 2.4 with $r = 1$, $\theta = \pi/2$, $u(0, 1) = (0, 0, 1, 0)^\top$, $v(0, 1) = (0, 0, 0, -1)^\top$, $u(0, 2) = (1, 0, 0, 1)^\top$, and $v(0, 2) = (0, -1, 0, 0)^\top$. According to theorems 2.1 and 2.4, the general solution to the above system of difference equations is given by

$$
\begin{pmatrix} x_{t,1} \\ x_{t,2} \\ x_{t,3} \\ x_{t,4} \end{pmatrix} = \alpha(1) \begin{pmatrix} 0 \\ 0 \\ \cos(\pi t/2) \\ \sin(\pi t/2) \end{pmatrix} + \alpha(2) \begin{pmatrix} 0 \\ 0 \\ \sin(\pi t/2) \\ -\cos(\pi t/2) \end{pmatrix} + \alpha(3) \begin{pmatrix} \cos(\pi t/2) \\ \sin(\pi t/2) \\ 0 \\ \cos(\pi t/2) \end{pmatrix}
$$

$$
+ \alpha(4) \begin{pmatrix} \sin(\pi t/2) \\ -\cos(\pi t/2) \\ 0 \\ \sin(\pi t/2) \end{pmatrix}
$$

$$
= \begin{pmatrix} \alpha(3)\cos(\pi t/2) + \alpha(4)\sin(\pi t/2) \\ \alpha(3)\sin(\pi t/2) - \alpha(4)\cos(\pi t/2) \\ \alpha(1)\cos(\pi t/2) + \alpha(2)\sin(\pi t/2) \\ [\alpha(1) + \alpha(4)]\sin(\pi t/2) + [\alpha(3) - \alpha(2)]\cos(\pi t/2) \end{pmatrix}.
$$

Now let us slightly modify the example. Suppose that the fourth difference equation is changed to $x_{t+1,4} = x_{t,3}$. Thus, the system matrix A is now given by

$$
A = \begin{pmatrix} 0 & -1 & 0 & 0 \\ 1 & 0 & 0 & 0 \\ 1 & 0 & 0 & -1 \\ 0 & 0 & 1 & 0 \end{pmatrix}.
$$

The characteristic polynomial of this matrix is the same as before and, hence, the eigenvalues are again given by i and $-i$, both with algebraic multiplicity $m^a = 2$. One eigenvector corresponding to the double eigenvalue i is given by $w(0, 1) = (0, 0, 1, -i)^\top$, and it is straightforward to verify that there does not exist a second eigenvector corresponding to this eigenvalue that is linearly independent of $w(0, 1)$. We thus have $m^g = 1 < m^a = 2$, and we need to compute a generalized eigenvector. Indeed, it holds that $Aw(1, 1) = iw(1, 1) + w(0, 1)$ provided that $w(1, 1) = (2, -2i, 0, 1)^\top$. Using theorems 2.1 and 2.4, the general solution to the present system of difference equations is therefore

$$
\begin{pmatrix} x_{t,1} \\ x_{t,2} \\ x_{t,3} \\ x_{t,4} \end{pmatrix} = \alpha(1) \begin{pmatrix} 0 \\ 0 \\ \cos(\pi t/2) \\ \sin(\pi t/2) \end{pmatrix} + \alpha(2) \left[\begin{pmatrix} 2\cos(\pi t/2) \\ 2\sin(\pi t/2) \\ 0 \\ \cos(\pi t/2) \end{pmatrix} + t \begin{pmatrix} 0 \\ 0 \\ \cos(\pi(t-1)/2) \\ \sin(\pi(t-1)/2) \end{pmatrix} \right]
$$

$$
+ \alpha(3) \begin{pmatrix} 0 \\ 0 \\ \sin(\pi t/2) \\ -\cos(\pi t/2) \end{pmatrix} + \alpha(4) \left[\begin{pmatrix} 2\sin(\pi t/2) \\ -2\cos(\pi t/2) \\ 0 \\ \sin(\pi t/2) \end{pmatrix} + t \begin{pmatrix} 0 \\ 0 \\ \sin(\pi(t-1)/2) \\ -\cos(\pi(t-1)/2) \end{pmatrix} \right]
$$

$$
= \begin{pmatrix} 2[\alpha(2)\cos(\pi t/2) + \alpha(4)\sin(\pi t/2)] \\ 2[\alpha(2)\sin(\pi t/2) - \alpha(4)\cos(\pi t/2)] \\ Q(t) \\ R(t) \end{pmatrix},
$$

where

$$
Q(t) = \alpha(1)\cos(\pi t/2) + \alpha(2)t\cos(\pi(t-1)/2) + \alpha(3)\sin(\pi t/2)
$$
$$
+ \alpha(4)t\sin(\pi(t-1)/2)
$$

and

$$
R(t) = [\alpha(1) + \alpha(4)]\sin(\pi t/2) + [\alpha(2) - \alpha(3)]\cos(\pi t/2) + \alpha(2)t\sin(\pi(t-1)/2)
$$
$$
- \alpha(4)t\cos(\pi(t-1)/2).
$$

Theorem 2.3 provides the formulas to construct, for every real eigenvalue with algebraic multiplicity m^a, exactly m^a linearly independent trajectories of the homogeneous linear difference equation (2.8). Analogously, theorem 2.4 tells us how to construct for every pair of complex conjugate eigenvalues with algebraic multiplicities m^a exactly $2m^a$ linearly independent trajectories. Because the sum of the algebraic multiplicities of all eigenvalues of an $n \times n$ matrix A is equal to n, these two theorems together are sufficient to construct n trajectories of (2.8). The following lemma, which is stated without proof, shows that this set consists of linearly independent trajectories such that it forms a basis of S_{hom}. This result therefore generalizes lemma 2.3 to the case of multiple eigenvalues.

Lemma 2.4 The n trajectories that we can construct using the formulas from theorems 2.3 and 2.4 form a basis of S_{hom}.

The results collected in the present section allow the derivation of closed-form expressions for the general solution to a homogeneous linear difference equation with constant coefficients. These closed-form expressions are not only useful for the actual computation of the trajectories, but they also facilitate the geometric visualization of the form of the trajectories. Since the trajectories are expressed as linear combinations of n basis solutions, the form of a trajectory can be understood as a superposition of these n basis solutions. Consider, for example, a basis solution of the form

$$z_t = \lambda^t w,$$

as it is described in theorem 2.2(a). If $\lambda > 1$, this basis solution moves in the direction of the eigenvector w in geometrically increasing steps away from the origin. If $\lambda \in (0, 1)$, on the other hand, the basis solution converges geometrically along the direction of $-w$ towards the origin. Negative values of λ correspond to period-two oscillations along the line determined by the eigenvector w, these being exploding or damped depending on whether $|\lambda|$ is larger or smaller than 1.

Basis solutions corresponding to complex eigenvalues as described in theorem 2.2(b) can be visualized in a similar way. They form expanding or damped spirals in the two-dimensional plane spanned by the vectors u and v. The phase θ determines the direction and speed of rotation and the modulus r determines how quickly the spirals expand from $(r > 1)$ or converge to $(r < 1)$, the origin.

2.3 Two-dimensional systems of homogeneous equations

In the present section, we consider the same class of difference equations as in the previous section, namely homogeneous linear difference equations with constant coefficients, but we restrict the system domain X to be equal to $\mathbb{R}^2$. The equations therefore take the form

$$\begin{pmatrix} x_{t+1,1} \\ x_{t+1,2} \end{pmatrix} = \begin{pmatrix} a_{11} & a_{12} \\ a_{21} & a_{22} \end{pmatrix} \begin{pmatrix} x_{t,1} \\ x_{t,2} \end{pmatrix}. \tag{2.14}$$

We denote the trace and the determinant of the system matrix

$$A = \begin{pmatrix} a_{11} & a_{12} \\ a_{21} & a_{22} \end{pmatrix}$$

by T and D, respectively, that is $T = a_{11} + a_{22}$ and $D = a_{11}a_{22} - a_{12}a_{21}$. Using these definitions, the eigenvalues of the system matrix can be written as

$$\lambda(1) = (T/2) + \sqrt{(T^2/4) - D} \quad \text{and} \quad \lambda(2) = (T/2) - \sqrt{(T^2/4) - D}. \tag{2.15}$$

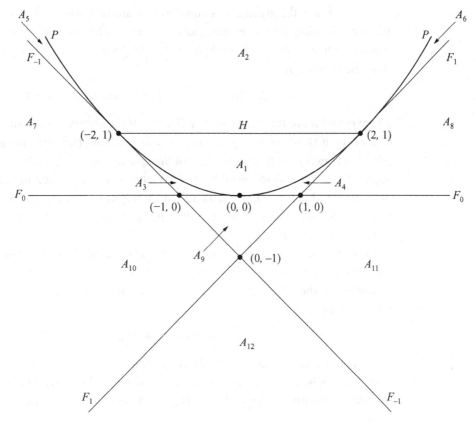

Figure 2.1 The (T, D)-diagram

The qualitative behaviour of the trajectories can most easily be characterized by drawing a (T, D)-diagram as in figure 2.1. This figure shows the parabola P defined by the equation $D = T^2/4$, the line segment $\{(T, D) \mid -2 < T < 2, D = 1\}$ labelled H, and the lines defined by $D = 0$, $D = T - 1$, and $D = -T - 1$ labelled F_0, F_1, and F_{-1}, respectively. These five curves partition the entire (T, D)-parameter region into the twelve areas $A_1, A_2, \ldots, A_{12}$. Every possible system matrix A corresponds to a unique point in the (T, D)-diagram.[5]

It follows from (2.15) that the two eigenvalues of A are complex conjugate numbers if $D > T^2/4$, and that they are real numbers otherwise. Hence, the parabola P separates the area of system matrices with complex eigenvalues from the area of matrices with real eigenvalues.

Let us start with the case of complex eigenvalues, that is, with matrices A that correspond to points above P. The absolute value of such an eigenvalue is equal

---

[5] Note, however, that the mapping between system matrices and points in the diagram is not one-to-one. All matrices that share the same trace and determinant are mapped to the same point in the diagram.

to $r = \sqrt{D}$, and the argument is equal to $\theta = \arctan(\sqrt{4D - T^2}/T)$. Let us denote the corresponding pair of eigenvectors by $u \pm iv$, where u and v are vectors in $\mathbb{R}^2$. According to theorem 2.2(b) or theorem 2.4, the general solution to equation (2.14) in this case is given by

$$x_t = D^{t/2}[\cos(\theta t)(\alpha u + \beta v) + \sin(\theta t)(\beta u - \alpha v)],$$

where α and β are undetermined coefficients. If the matrix A corresponds to a point in area A_1, it holds obviously that $D < 1$, and it follows therefore that all trajectories of (2.14) converge to the origin $(0, 0)$ of the system domain $X = \mathbb{R}^2$ in spirals, whose angle of rotation is determined by θ. For matrices in area A_2, on the other hand, the determinant D is larger than 1 and all trajectories of (2.14), except for the trivial one that starts in the origin of X take the form of expanding spirals and become unbounded as t approaches infinity.

Now suppose that $D < T^2/4$. In this case, the eigenvalues of A are real and different from each other. Let the corresponding eigenvectors be denoted by $w(1)$ and $w(2)$. According to the results from the previous section, the general solution to (2.14) can be written as

$$x_t = \alpha\lambda(1)^t w(1) + \beta\lambda(2)^t w(2), \tag{2.16}$$

where α and β are again undetermined coefficients. We claim that for all matrices in area A_3 it holds that both eigenvalues are in the interval $(-1, 0)$. This is equivalent to the two inequalities $-1 < \lambda(2)$ and $\lambda(1) < 0$. Using (2.15), the first inequality can be written as

$$\sqrt{(T^2/4) - D} < 1 + (T/2).$$

Since $T > -2$ holds in A_3, both sides of this inequality are non-negative and we can take the square on both sides. This yields, after simplifications, $D > -T - 1$, which is one of the defining properties of area A_3. Hence, $-1 < \lambda(2)$ has been proved. In an analogous way, we can verify the second inequality $\lambda(1) < 0$. Because both eigenvalues are contained in the interval $(-1, 0)$, it follows from (2.16) that all trajectories of (2.14) converge to the origin of X. Except for the trivial one starting in the origin, all these trajectories display damped oscillations of period 2 because the eigenvalues are negative.

The characterization of the qualitative behaviour of solutions of (2.14), when the system matrix A is in one of the remaining areas, can be obtained in a completely analogous way, which is why we restrict ourselves to presenting the results without detailed proofs. If the matrix A corresponds to a point in area A_4, both eigenvalues are located in the interval $(0, 1)$ and it follows that all trajectories converge eventually monotonically to the origin of X. For matrices in area A_5, it holds that both eigenvalues of A are real numbers smaller than -1. All trajectories of (2.14), except for the trivial one, diverge in an oscillatory way. For matrices in area A_6, the eigenvalues are real numbers greater than 1, and it follows that all trajectories, except for the trivial one, are eventually monotonic and become unbounded.

Next consider a matrix A that is located in area A_7. It holds that $\lambda(2) < -1 < \lambda(1) < 0$, that is, both eigenvalues are negative: one with absolute value smaller than 1, the other one with absolute value larger than 1. We observe so-called *saddle point dynamics*. As a matter of fact, it can be seen from (2.16) that every trajectory for which $\beta = 0$ holds converges to the origin $(0, 0)$, whereas every trajectory with $\beta \neq 0$ becomes unbounded. In other words, if the initial value x_0 for (2.14) is located in the subspace of $\mathbb{R}^2$ spanned by the eigenvector $w(1)$, then the trajectory converges to $(0, 0)$, otherwise it becomes unbounded. Since the eigenvalues are negative, the dynamics display oscillations of period 2. For matrices in area A_8, the situation is very similar, except that the eigenvalues are now positive. More specifically, we have $0 < \lambda(2) < 1 < \lambda(1)$. In this case, the trajectories emanating from the subspace spanned by $w(2)$ converge to $(0, 0)$, whereas all other trajectories become unbounded. The difference to the case described by A_7 is that the dynamics are now eventually monotonic because the eigenvalues are positive.

If the system matrix is located in area A_9, the eigenvalues satisfy $-1 < \lambda(2) < 0 < \lambda(1) < 1$. Because both eigenvalues are smaller than 1 in absolute value, it follows that all trajectories of (2.14) converge to $(0, 0)$. Whether this convergence occurs monotonically or in the form of oscillations depends on whether the coefficient β is equal to 0 or not. If it is, then the dynamics are monotonic, otherwise they exhibit fluctuations. Areas A_{10} and A_{11} are again parameter regions in which we observe saddle point dynamics. For matrices in area A_{10}, the eigenvalues satisfy $\lambda(2) < -1$ and $0 < \lambda(1) < 1$. Every trajectory with $\beta = 0$ converges monotonically to the origin. If β is different from 0, however, trajectories are non-monotonic and become unbounded. For matrices in A_{11}, it holds that the eigenvalues satisfy $-1 < \lambda(2) < 0$ and $\lambda(1) > 1$. In this situation, there is non-monotonic convergence to $(0, 0)$ if $\alpha = 0$ and unboundedness if $\alpha \neq 0$.

Finally, let us consider matrices corresponding to points in area A_{12} where we have $\lambda(2) < -1$ and $\lambda(1) > 1$. Every trajectory, except for the trivial one, becomes unbounded. If $\beta = 0$, these trajectories are monotonic, otherwise they are not.

Having characterized the behaviour of the trajectories of (2.14) for system matrices A located in all 12 areas $A_1, A_2, \ldots, A_{12}$, let us briefly discuss the boundaries of these areas. The parabola P separates the area of complex eigenvalues from the area of real eigenvalues. Along this curve, the discriminant of the characteristic equation of the system matrix A is equal to 0. This implies that the system matrix has a single real eigenvalue with multiplicity 2, that is, the trajectories will have the form described in theorem 2.3. The other boundaries H, F_0, F_1, and F_{-1} are of a different nature. Along F_0, one eigenvalue is equal to 0. This means that one of the terms on the right-hand side of (2.16) is equal to 0 for all $t \geq 1$. Along each of the boundaries H, F_1, and

F_{-1}, on the other hand, there exists at least one eigenvalue with absolute value equal to 1. Along H, the matrix A has a pair of complex conjugate eigenvalues on the unit circle of the complex plane, along F_1 it has the real eigenvalue 1, and along F_{-1} it has the real eigenvalue -1. To summarize, for system matrices located on any of the separating curves P, H, F_0, F_1, and F_{-1}, the behaviour of the trajectories of (2.14) is in a certain way degenerate. Note also that if some parameter of a difference equation changes in such a way that the system matrix crosses one of these separating curves, the behaviour of the trajectories changes in a qualitative sense, which is referred to as a *bifurcation*.[6]

The usefulness of the (T, D)-diagram for the analysis of dynamic economic models cannot be overemphasized. This is the case because many economic models give rise to difference equations on a two-dimensional system domain and because the (T, D)-diagram can be analyzed without explicitly computing the eigenvalues. Let us therefore conclude the present section by two examples illustrating this approach.

Example 2.4 Consider a variant of the multiplier-accelerator model discussed in exercise 1.3. More specifically, suppose that the accelerator principle is changed to $I_t = \bar{I} + a(C_t - C_{t-1})$ instead of $I_t = \bar{I} + a(Y_t - Y_{t-1})$, and that $b = \bar{I} = 0$. The former modification has the effect that the model is described by a second-order difference equation rather than by a first-order equation. The latter modification eliminates the non-homogeneity of the equation and turns it into a homogeneous difference equation. We can write the modified model in the form

$$\begin{pmatrix} Y_t \\ C_t \end{pmatrix} = \begin{pmatrix} (1+a)c & -a \\ c & 0 \end{pmatrix} \begin{pmatrix} Y_{t-1} \\ C_{t-1} \end{pmatrix}. \tag{2.17}$$

As in our presentation of the multiplier-accelerator model in exercise 1.3, we assume that $a > 0$ and $0 < c < 1$. Using the notation from above, we have $T = c + ac$ and $D = ac$. Consider any fixed value $c \in (0, 1)$ and treat T and D as functions of the accelerator $a \in (0, +\infty)$. Since both of these functions are linear and have the same slope c, it follows that the locus of all feasible pairs (T, D) forms a ray in the (T, D)-diagram that emanates from the point $(T, D) = (c, 0)$ (corresponding to $a = 0$) and points exactly in the north-east direction (to be more precise, the ray has slope 1). The situation is depicted in figure 2.2 in which the ray is labelled as R.

Obviously, the ray R starts in area A_4, then passes through A_1 and A_2, and finally ends up in area A_6. For small values of a, we therefore have $(T, D) \in A_4$, and it follows that all trajectories of (2.17) converge to the origin and do not display any fluctuations. As a increases, the point (T, D) crosses the parabola P into area A_1, which means

---

[6] See section 4.2 for a more detailed discussion of bifurcations in the special case of one-dimensional maps.

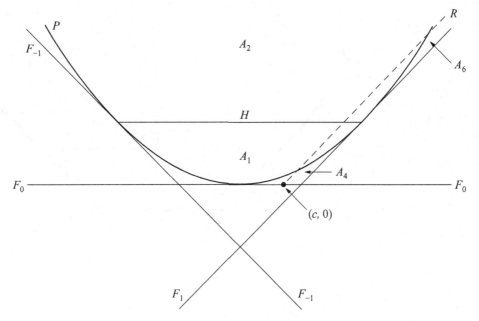

Figure 2.2 The (T, D)-diagram for the multiplier-accelerator model (2.17)

that the trajectories exhibit damped oscillations. For even higher values of a, the point (T, D) moves into areas A_2 and A_6, where the trajectories fail to converge to the origin. As in exercise 1.3, we conclude that the strength of the accelerator a is crucial for the qualitative behaviour of the trajectories.

Example 2.5 Reconsider the New Keynesian model from example 1.6 and assume that $a = 0$ such that the difference equation becomes homogeneous. For simplicity, assume furthermore that $c = 0$, which means that the nominal interest rate does not respond to the output gap. The system matrix in this case is given by

$$
A = \begin{pmatrix} \dfrac{1}{\beta} & -\dfrac{\alpha}{\beta} \\ \gamma\left(b - \dfrac{1}{\beta}\right) & 1 + \dfrac{\alpha\gamma}{\beta} \end{pmatrix}.
$$

We want to study how the behaviour of the solutions to the model depends on the reaction coefficient b that describes the sensitivity of the nominal interest rate with respect to inflation. The trace of A is given by

$$
T = 1 + \frac{1}{\beta} + \frac{\alpha\gamma}{\beta},
$$

Difference equations

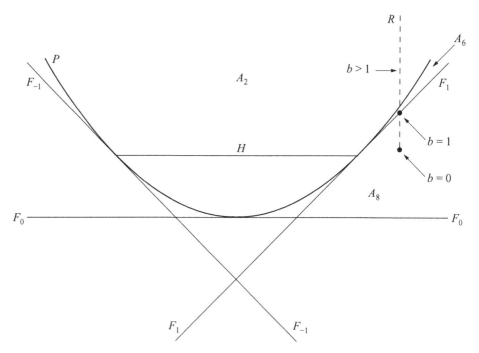

Figure 2.3 The (T, D)-diagram for the New Keynesian model of example 2.5

which is independent of b. The determinant, on the other hand, is given by

$$D = \frac{1 + \alpha \gamma b}{\beta},$$

which is a linear and increasing function of b. These properties as well as the assumed positivity of α, β, and γ imply that the locus of all points (T, D) as b varies in the feasible interval $[0, +\infty)$ is a ray in the (T, D)-diagram that starts at the point $(1 + 1/\beta + \alpha\gamma/\beta, 1/\beta)$ corresponding to the value $b = 0$ and extends vertically upwards. This ray is labelled as R in figure 2.3. Because of $\beta \leq 1$, it follows furthermore that $T > 2$ and $D > 1$ hold for all $b \geq 0$. Finally, it is easy to see that $D \leq T - 1$ holds if and only if $b \leq 1$. We can therefore conclude that whenever $b \leq 1$ the eigenvalues of the system matrix A are real and one of them is larger than 1, whereas the other one is smaller than 1 (area A_8). On the other hand, if $b > 1$, then the matrix A corresponds to a point either in A_6 or in A_2, where both eigenvalues of A are larger than 1 in absolute value. The relevance of this observation for the design of interest rate rules will be explained at a later stage in section 3.4. For the moment, we just mention that the condition $b > 1$ is crucial for stabilization policy and is referred to as the Taylor principle.

Non-homogeneous equations

Let us now consider non-homogeneous difference equations with constant coefficients, that is, difference equations of the form

$$x_{t+1} = Ax_t + b(t). \tag{2.18}$$

As in sections 2.1–2.2, the system domain is $X = \mathbb{R}^n$. We continue to refer to the matrix $A \in \mathbb{R}^{n \times n}$ as the system matrix and we call the vector-valued function $b : \mathbb{N}_0 \mapsto \mathbb{R}^n$ the *non-homogeneity*.

From lemma 2.1, we know that it is sufficient to find one particular solution to the non-homogeneous equation. A useful method for doing this is the *variation-of-constants* formula. To derive this formula, we consider the general solution to the homogeneous equation as stated in (2.5), but we allow the undetermined coefficients $\alpha(1), \alpha(2), \ldots, \alpha(n)$ to be time-dependent functions. That is, we consider the sequence $(\bar{x}_t)_{t=0}^{+\infty}$ defined by

$$\bar{x}_t = \sum_{k=1}^{n} \alpha(k)_t z(k)_t, \tag{2.19}$$

where $(z(k)_t)_{t=0}^{+\infty}$, $k \in \{1, 2, \ldots, n\}$, are n linearly independent trajectories of the homogeneous equation (2.8) and where $(\alpha(k)_t)_{t=0}^{+\infty}$ are real-valued sequences for all $k \in \{1, 2, \ldots, n\}$. Let $Z_t \in \mathbb{R}^{n \times n}$ be the matrix consisting of the columns $z(1)_t, z(2)_t, \ldots, z(n)_t$ and let $\alpha_t \in \mathbb{R}^n$ be the vector

$$\alpha_t = \begin{pmatrix} \alpha(1)_t \\ \alpha(2)_t \\ \vdots \\ \alpha(n)_t \end{pmatrix}.$$

These definitions imply that (2.19) can be written more compactly as

$$\bar{x}_t = Z_t \alpha_t \tag{2.20}$$

for all $t \in \mathbb{N}_0$. It follows that $(\bar{x}_t)_{t=0}^{+\infty}$ is a trajectory of (2.18) if and only if the equation

$$Z_{t+1}\alpha_{t+1} = AZ_t\alpha_t + b(t)$$

holds for all $t \in \mathbb{N}_0$. Moreover, since the vectors $z(k)_{t+1} \in \mathbb{R}^n$, $k \in \{1, 2, \ldots, n\}$, are linearly independent, it follows that the matrix Z_{t+1} is invertible, and we can rewrite the above condition as

$$\alpha_{t+1} = Z_{t+1}^{-1}AZ_t\alpha_t + Z_{t+1}^{-1}b(t).$$

Difference equations

Now recall that the columns of Z_t are trajectories of the homogeneous equation (2.8). This implies that $Z_{t+1} = AZ_t$, and it follows that the above equation reduces to

$$\alpha_{t+1} = \alpha_t + Z_{t+1}^{-1}b(t).$$

This is a non-homogeneous linear difference equation with constant coefficients for the variables $(\alpha_t)_{t=0}^{+\infty}$. It is easy to see that the solution to this equation is given by

$$\alpha_t = \alpha_0 + \sum_{s=1}^{t} Z_s^{-1}b(s-1).$$

Combining this with (2.20), we arrive at

$$\bar{x}_t = Z_t \left[\alpha_0 + \sum_{s=1}^{t} Z_s^{-1}b(s-1) \right]. \tag{2.21}$$

We summarize this finding in the following theorem:

Theorem 2.5 Consider the non-homogeneous linear difference equation (2.18). Let $(Z_t)_{t=0}^{+\infty}$ be a sequence of matrices whose columns form n linearly independent trajectories of the corresponding homogeneous equation (2.8), and let $\alpha_0 \in \mathbb{R}^n$ be an arbitrary vector. A particular solution to (2.18) is given by $(\bar{x}_t)_{t=0}^{+\infty}$, where $\bar{x}_t$ is defined by the variation-of-constants formula (2.21).

To illustrate the application of the variation-of-constants formula, let us consider the one-dimensional non-homogeneous linear difference equation

$$x_{t+1} = \lambda x_t + b(t), \tag{2.22}$$

where $x_t \in X = \mathbb{R}$, $b : \mathbb{N}_0 \mapsto \mathbb{R}$, and $\lambda \in \mathbb{R}$. A basis solution to the corresponding homogeneous equation $x_{t+1} = \lambda x_t$ is $(\lambda^t)_{t=0}^{+\infty}$. Using the terminology introduced above, we have $Z_t = (\lambda^t)$. It follows therefore from theorem 2.5 that a particular solution to the non-homogeneous equation is given by

$$\bar{x}_t = \lambda^t \left[\alpha_0 + \sum_{s=1}^{t} \lambda^{-s}b(s-1) \right]. \tag{2.23}$$

It depends on the form of the function b whether or not the term in brackets can be expressed in closed form. We illustrate some possibilities in the following example.

Example 2.6 Consider equation (2.22) with non-homogeneity $b(t) = \beta \mu^t$, where β and μ are real numbers with $\mu \neq \lambda$. In this case, we obtain from equation (2.23) that

$$\bar{x}_t = \lambda^t \left\{ \alpha_0 + \frac{\beta[1 - (\mu/\lambda)^t]}{\lambda - \mu} \right\} = \left(\alpha_0 + \frac{\beta}{\lambda - \mu} \right) \lambda^t - \frac{\beta \mu^t}{\lambda - \mu}.$$

Since α_0 can be freely chosen, we may as well choose $\alpha_0 = \beta/(\mu - \lambda)$, which yields the particular solution

$$\bar{x}_t = \frac{\beta \mu^t}{\mu - \lambda}.$$

Note that the assumption $\mu \neq \lambda$ was crucial for the feasibility of the above calculations. If $\mu = \lambda$, then we obtain from (2.23)

$$\bar{x}_t = \lambda^t \left(\alpha_0 + \frac{\beta t}{\lambda} \right) = \alpha_0 \lambda^t + \beta t \lambda^{t-1}.$$

Again, we may set α_0 to an arbitrary value, say $\alpha_0 = 0$. This yields the particular solution $\bar{x}_t = \beta t \lambda^{t-1}$. The case where the non-homogeneity is of the same form as a basis solution to the homogeneous equation (here, an exponential function of the form const. $\times \lambda^t$) is called *resonance*.

The next example deals essentially with the same non-homogeneous difference equation as the previous example, but this time we cast the equation in an economic context.

Example 2.7 Consider the multiplier-accelerator model from exercise 1.3, but assume that the consumption demand includes a seasonal component. More specifically, assume that

$$C_t = B(t) + c Y_{t-1},$$

where

$$B(t) = \begin{cases} B_1 & \text{if } t = 4k + 1, \\ B_2 & \text{if } t = 4k + 2, \\ B_3 & \text{if } t = 4k + 3, \\ B_4 & \text{if } t = 4k + 4. \end{cases}$$

The interpretation is that the period length is a quarter and that B_1, B_2, B_3, and B_4 are autonomous consumption demands in spring, summer, fall, and winter, respectively. Furthermore, we assume that the accelerator a is different from 1.

Combining this consumption demand with the accelerator principle and the goods market clearing condition (both stated in exercise 1.3), we obtain $Y_{t+1} = \lambda Y_t + b(t)$

with $\lambda = (c - a)/(1 - a)$ and $b(t) = [B(t + 1) + \bar{I}]/(1 - a)$. This is a difference equation of the same form as equation (2.22).[7]

According to theorem 2.5, a particular solution is given by

$$\bar{x}_t = \lambda^t \left[\alpha_0 + \sum_{s=1}^{t} \frac{B(s) + \bar{I}}{(1 - a)\lambda^s} \right] = -\frac{\bar{I}}{(1 - a)(\lambda - 1)} + \frac{\lambda^{t-1}}{1 - a} \sum_{s=0}^{t-1} \frac{B(s + 1)}{\lambda^s},$$

where we have chosen

$$\alpha_0 = -\frac{\bar{I}}{(1 - a)(\lambda - 1)}.$$

Evaluating this expression for the given periodic sequence of autonomous consumption demands, we get

$$\bar{x}_t = \begin{cases} \alpha_0 + \dfrac{(1 - \lambda^t)M}{1 - a} & \text{if } t = 4k, \\[2ex] \alpha_0 + \dfrac{\lambda(1 - \lambda^{t-1})M + B_1}{1 - a} & \text{if } t = 4k + 1, \\[2ex] \alpha_0 + \dfrac{\lambda^2(1 - \lambda^{t-2})M + \lambda B_1 + B_2}{1 - a} & \text{if } t = 4k + 2, \\[2ex] \alpha_0 + \dfrac{\lambda^3(1 - \lambda^{t-3})M + \lambda^2 B_1 + \lambda B_2 + B_3}{1 - a} & \text{if } t = 4k + 3, \end{cases}$$

where $M = (\lambda^3 B_1 + \lambda^2 B_2 + \lambda B_3 + B_4)/(1 - \lambda^4)$.

Even if the variation-of-constants formula (2.21) holds for all non-homogeneous linear difference equations of the form (2.18), it is often easier to find a particular solution by a guess-and-verify approach. This means that we postulate a functional form for the particular solution that contains a number of undetermined coefficients and then verify that this expression actually qualifies as a solution if the coefficients take appropriate values. In many cases, it is conducive to postulate a functional form for the particular solution that matches the form of the non-homogeneity $b(t)$. For example, if $b(t)$ is a polynomial of order m, then we try to seek a particular solution that is also a polynomial of order m. Or if $b(t)$ is an exponential function, then we postulate also an exponential function for the particular solution. This approach is illustrated in the following example.

---

[7] Note that a is different from 1, such that the expressions for λ and $b(t)$ make sense. Note also that $\lambda \neq 1$ because of $c \in (0, 1)$.

Example 2.8   Consider the one-dimensional linear difference equation

$$x_{t+1} = \lambda x_t + vt^2 + \mu^t,$$

where $x_t \in X = \mathbb{R}$, $(\lambda, \mu, v) \in \mathbb{R}^3$, and $\lambda \notin \{1, \mu\}$. The non-homogeneity is the sum of a quadratic polynomial and an exponential term. Therefore, we postulate a particular solution of the form $\bar{x}_t = At^2 + Bt + C + D\mu^t$ and try to determine the coefficients $\{A, B, C, D\}$ in such a way that $(\bar{x}_t)_{t=0}^{+\infty}$ is a trajectory of the given difference equation. By substituting the guess on both sides of the equation and collecting terms, we get

$$(A - \lambda A - v)t^2 + (2A + B - \lambda B)t + (A + B + C - \lambda C) + (\mu D - \lambda D - 1)\mu^t = 0.$$

This demonstrates that our guess is correct provided that

$$A = \frac{v}{1 - \lambda}, \quad B = \frac{-2v}{(1 - \lambda)^2}, \quad C = \frac{v(1 + \lambda)}{(1 - \lambda)^3}, \quad D = \frac{1}{\mu - \lambda}.$$

We can clearly see that the guess-and-verify approach works because we have ruled out resonance by the assumption $\lambda \notin \{1, \mu\}$. The resonance cases have to be dealt with separately and can usually be handled by adding a term that consists of the originally postulated form multiplied by t. To illustrate this, suppose that $\lambda = 1 \neq \mu$. In this case, there is resonance between the homogeneous equation $x_{t+1} = x_t$ and the polynomial term of the non-homogeneity. We therefore choose a particular solution of the form $\bar{x}_t = At^3 + Bt^2 + Ct + D\mu^t$. Proceeding in the same way as before, we can easily verify that this guess is correct provided that

$$A = \frac{v}{3}, \quad B = -\frac{v}{2}, \quad C = \frac{v}{6}, \quad D = \frac{1}{\mu - 1}.$$

There are two more resonance cases that can occur in the present example. The reader is asked to solve the equation for these cases in exercise 2.6 below.

2.5   EXERCISES

EXERCISE 2.1   Let $\lambda(1)$ and $\lambda(2)$ be two different real eigenvalues of the system matrix $A \in \mathbb{R}^{n \times n}$. Prove that the two corresponding trajectories that we can construct according to theorem 2.2(a) are linearly independent.

EXERCISE 2.2   Consider the second-order linear difference equation

$$x_{t+1} = 4(x_t - x_{t-1}).$$

(a) Rewrite the equation as a first-order equation on a two-dimensional state space.

(b) Determine the general solution to the equation.

(c) Determine the particular solution satisfying the initial conditions $x_0 = 1$ and $x_1 = 0$.

EXERCISE 2.3   The expectations-augmented Phillips curve has the form

$$\pi_t = \pi_t^e + \alpha y_t,$$

where π_t is the rate of inflation in period t, π_t^e is expected inflation in period t, and y_t is the output gap in period t. A simple form of a backward-looking IS-curve is

$$y_t = \beta y_{t-1} - \gamma(i_t - \pi_t^e),$$

where i_t is the nominal interest rate in period t. The parameters α, β, and γ are positive.

(a) Assume that expectations are formed naively (that is, $\pi_t^e = \pi_{t-1}$) and that the central bank sets a zero nominal interest rate (that is, $i_t = 0$ for all $t \in \mathbb{N}_0$). Write the model as a homogeneous linear difference equation in the variables π_t and y_t.

(b) In addition to the assumptions of part (a), suppose that $\alpha = 1$, $\beta = 4/9$, and $\gamma = 2/9$. Determine the general solution to the macroeconomic model.

(c) Under the same assumptions as in part (b), find the particular solution for the initial values $\pi_0 = 0$ and $y_0 = 1$.

(d) Repeat parts (a)–(c) with the assumption of a constant nominal interest rate ($i_t = 0$) replaced by the assumption that the nominal interest rate is set according to the rule $i_t = b\pi_{t-1}$, where b is a positive parameter. Set $\alpha = 1$, $\beta = 4/9$, $\gamma = 2/9$, and $b = 15/2$ when you calculate the general and the particular solution.

EXERCISE 2.4   Consider the same model as in exercise 2.3(d), that is, the Phillips curve

$$\pi_t = \pi_{t-1} + \alpha y_t,$$

the IS-curve

$$y_t = \beta y_{t-1} - \gamma(i_t - \pi_{t-1}),$$

and the interest rate rule

$$i_t = b\pi_{t-1}.$$

The parameters α, β, γ, and b are positive and it holds that $\beta < 1$. Consider α, β, and γ as fixed and analyze by means of the (T, D)-diagram how the qualitative behaviour of the solutions changes as b increases from 0 to $+\infty$.

EXERCISE 2.5   Consider the linear non-homogeneous difference equation

$$x_{t+1} = \lambda x_t + \alpha t,$$

where α and λ are real constants and $x_t \in X = \mathbb{R}$.
(a) Assume that $\lambda \neq 1$ and try to find a particular solution to the above difference equation. What is the general solution to the difference equation?
(b) Repeat the exercise for the case in which $\lambda = 1$.

EXERCISE 2.6   Solve the difference equation from example 2.8 in the two resonance cases $\lambda = \mu \neq 1$ and $\lambda = \mu = 1$.

EXERCISE 2.7   Consider the non-homogeneous linear difference equation

$$\begin{pmatrix} x_{t+1} \\ y_{t+1} \\ z_{t+1} \end{pmatrix} = \begin{pmatrix} -3/2 & 8 & 9/2 \\ -9/4 & 3 & 1/4 \\ 1/2 & 8 & 5/2 \end{pmatrix} \begin{pmatrix} x_t \\ y_t \\ z_t \end{pmatrix} + \begin{pmatrix} 0 \\ 10 \\ 0 \end{pmatrix}.$$

(a) Determine the general solution to the corresponding homogeneous equation.
(b) Determine the particular solution to the non-homogeneous equation satisfying the initial conditions $x_0 = y_0 = z_0 = 0$.

EXERCISE 2.8   Before the birth of her baby, a mother opens a saving account with a fixed annual interest rate r. On each birthday of the child, the mother deposits 100 times as many Euros as the current age of the child. Between every two consecutive birthdays, the bank pays interest into the account.

Derive a difference equation that describes the evolution of the balance of the saving account. What is the correct initial value for this difference equation? Determine a closed form expression for the balance of the saving account with t denoting the age of the child.

2.6   COMMENTS AND REFERENCES

Linear difference equations, especially those with constant coefficients, are treated in probably all textbooks that deal with discrete-time dynamic economic models. This includes in particular those books that we have already mentioned at the end of chapter 1, that is, Ferguson and Lim [31], Galor [35], Gandolfo [36], Shone [84], and Sydsæter *et al.* [90]. The style of presentation and the level of detail and rigor vary greatly among different books.

The theory of linear difference equations makes heavy use of linear algebra and matrix analysis. There are many good textbooks about this subject, for example, Lang [55] or Meyer [67].

The (T, D)-diagram has been used by many authors and is described in detail in, for example, Azariadis [5] or Grandmont *et al.* [38].

Example 2.4 is the famous multiplier-accelerator model from Samuelson [79]. We have encountered a simplified version of that model already in exercise 1.3. The same simplified version forms the basis for example 2.7. Example 2.5 is a deterministic version of the New Keynesian model that is nowadays frequently used for monetary policy analysis; see Galí [34] or Woodford [96].

3 Autonomous difference equations

In this chapter, we turn to the analysis of non-linear difference equations. Since most applications in economics assume a stationary environment, that is, an environment that does not change over time, the focus of our study will be on autonomous equations. Such equations typically admit constant solutions – so-called fixed points – or periodic solutions, and the first step of the analysis of an autonomous difference equation is often the identification of these simple types of solutions. Therefore, we collect in section 3.1 a number of results about fixed points and periodic points.

As a next step, we turn to the investigation of the dynamics locally around the fixed points and the periodic points, respectively. This is greatly facilitated by local linearization techniques and the Hartman–Grobman theorem, which we present in section 3.2. In section 3.3, we introduce the important notion of the stability of a fixed point or a periodic point and we derive stability criteria. Some of these criteria are based on local linearization techniques, whereas others involve Lyapunov functions.

As we shall see in section 3.4, the appropriate definition of stability for an economic problem depends on how many of the system variables are pre-determined and how many are jump variables. This will lead us to the concept of saddle point stability. Finally, in section 3.5 we demonstrate that in the case of 'too much stability', a notion that we will formally define, purely deterministic economic models can admit stochastic solutions if we properly take into account the influence that expectations have on the behaviour of economic agents.

3.1 Invariant sets, fixed points, and periodic points

In this section, we consider autonomous difference equations of the form

$$x_{t+1} = f(x_t), \tag{3.1}$$

where the law of motion $f : X \mapsto X$ is a given function and the system domain $X \subseteq \mathbb{R}^n$ is a non-empty set. Recall from chapter 1 that a solution to the difference equation is a sequence $(x_t)_{t=0}^{+\infty}$ satisfying (3.1) and $x_t \in X$ for all $t \in \mathbb{N}_0$, and that such a solution is called a trajectory. Recall furthermore that we have denoted the tth element of the trajectory that starts in the initial value x by $q(x;t)$. In the case of autonomous difference equations, it will be convenient to express $q(x;t)$ in terms of the value of the tth iterate $f^{(t)}$ of the function f. The iterates of f are recursively defined as follows: $f^{(0)} : X \mapsto X$ is the identity map on X and $f^{(t+1)} : X \mapsto X$ is defined by $f^{(t+1)}(x) = f(f^{(t)}(x)) = f^{(t)}(f(x))$ for all $x \in X$ and all $t \in \mathbb{N}_0$. Note that this definition implies that

$$f^{(t+s)}(x) = f^{(t)}(f^{(s)}(x)) = f^{(s)}(f^{(t)}(x))$$

holds for all $x \in X$, all $s \in \mathbb{N}_0$, and all $t \in \mathbb{N}_0$.

Using the above notation, we can therefore write $q(x;t) = f^{(t)}(x)$. The *orbit* of $x \in X$ is defined as the set

$$\mathcal{O}(x) = \{f^{(t)}(x) \,|\, t \in \mathbb{N}_0\}.$$

Note the difference between the orbit $\mathcal{O}(x)$, which is a set that contains each of its elements only once, and the trajectory $(f^{(t)}(x))_{t=0}^{+\infty}$, which is a sequence and, hence, can have the same element at different positions. The following example illustrates this distinction.

Example 3.1 Consider the autonomous difference equation $x_{t+1} = 1 - x_t$ on the system domain $X = \mathbb{R}$. The trajectory starting at $x_0 = 0$ is given by $(0, 1, 0, 1, 0, \ldots)$. The orbit corresponding to $x_0 = 0$ is $\mathcal{O}(0) = \{0, 1\}$. The trajectory starting at $x_0 = 1/2$ is given by $(1/2, 1/2, \ldots)$ and the orbit corresponding to $x_0 = 1/2$ is the singleton $\mathcal{O}(1/2) = \{1/2\}$.

A set $A \subseteq X$ is said to be *invariant* under f if $f(x) \in A$ holds for all $x \in A$. This implies of course that every trajectory of (3.1) that enters the set A in some period $t \in \mathbb{N}_0$ remains in A forever after. In other words, once the economic system enters an invariant set A, it is trapped in A. If A is an invariant set, then it follows also that the restriction of f to the set A maps A to A. This shows that (3.1), which has been defined as a difference equation on the original system domain X, can also be considered as a difference equation on any invariant subset A of X. This can be helpful if the invariant set A has properties which the system domain X lacks; see the discussion in example 3.2 below.

Every difference equation admits invariant sets. This is a consequence of the following simple lemma.

Lemma 3.1   Every orbit of the difference equation (3.1) is invariant under f.

PROOF: Let $x \in X$ be given and consider an arbitrary element y of the orbit $\mathcal{O}(x) = \{f^{(t)}(x) \mid t \in \mathbb{N}_0\}$. Then there must exist $t \in \mathbb{N}_0$ such that $y = f^{(t)}(x)$ holds and it follows that $f(y) = f(f^{(t)}(x)) = f^{(t+1)}(x) \in \mathcal{O}(x)$. This completes the proof of the lemma.

Let $p \in \{1, 2, \ldots\}$ be a positive integer. An element $x^* \in X$ satisfying $f^{(p)}(x^*) = x^*$ and $f^{(t)}(x^*) \neq x^*$ for all $t \in \{1, 2, \ldots, p-1\}$ is called a *periodic point* of the difference equation (3.1) with *period p*. A periodic point of period 1 is called a *fixed point*. Fixed points are therefore characterized by the equation $f(x^*) = x^*$. Fixed points and periodic points of an autonomous difference equation are of particular interest because they describe states of the system that recur regularly. The following theorem states two different sufficient conditions for the existence of fixed points.

Theorem 3.1   Consider the difference equation (3.1) on the system domain $X \subseteq \mathbb{R}^n$ and let $A \subseteq X$ be invariant under f.

(a) If A is compact and convex and if f is continuous on A, then it follows that there exists $x^* \in A$ such that x^* is a fixed point of (3.1).

(b) If A is closed and there exists $\kappa \in [0, 1)$ such that $\|f(x) - f(y)\| \leq \kappa \|x - y\|$ holds for all $(x, y) \in A^2$, then it follows that there exists a unique $x^* \in A$ such that x^* is a fixed point of (3.1).

PROOF: If condition (a) is fulfilled, then the result follows from Brouwer's fixed point theorem; if condition (b) holds, it follows from Banach's fixed point theorem (contraction mapping theorem).

Note that theorem 3.1(a) establishes only the existence of a fixed point (under the stated assumptions), whereas theorem 3.1(b) ensures also its uniqueness. As an application of part (a) of the theorem, let us consider the following example.

Example 3.2 The Solow–Swan model, which was introduced in example 1.1, gives rise to the autonomous difference equation $x_{t+1} = f(x_t)$ on the system domain $X = [0, +\infty)$, where

$$f(x) = \frac{(1 - \delta)x + sF(x, 1)}{1 + n}.$$

Suppose that $\delta + n > 0$, that the production function $F(x, 1)$ is non-negative and monotonically increasing with respect to x, and that it satisfies the Inada condition $\lim_{x \to +\infty} F_1(x, 1) = 0.$[1] Then it follows that $f'(x) < 1$ holds for all sufficiently large x. It is easy to see that these properties imply that there exists $M \in \mathbb{R}_+$ such that

$$f(x) \begin{cases} \in [0, M] & \text{if } x \in [0, M], \\ \in (M, x) & \text{if } x > M. \end{cases}$$

This, in turn, shows that every compact interval $A = [0, x]$, where $x \geq M$, is invariant under f. We can therefore conclude from theorem 3.1(a) that there must exist a fixed point $x^* \in [0, M]$. As we have seen in example 1.1, this fixed point is typically not unique. As a matter of fact, under standard assumptions, including the concavity of F, the second Inada condition $\lim_{x \to 0} F_1(x, 1) = +\infty$, and the requirement that capital is essential for the production (that is, $F(0, 1) = 0$), there exist exactly two fixed points in the Solow–Swan model: one of them is equal to 0, whereas the other one is located in the interior of the system domain X.

Let us now turn to periodic points. The following lemma collects a number of results that facilitate the identification of periodic points.

Lemma 3.2 Consider the autonomous difference equation (3.1) and let $p \geq 1$ be a positive integer.

(a) If $x^* \in X$ is a periodic point of (3.1) with period p, then it follows that x^* is a fixed point of the difference equation $x_{t+1} = f^{(p)}(x_t)$.

(b) If $x^* \in X$ satisfies $x^* = f^{(p)}(x^*)$, then it follows that there exists a positive integer q such that p is divisible by q without remainder and such that x^* is a periodic point of (3.1) with period q.

---

[1] Here and in the rest of the book, we indicate partial derivatives of functions of more than one variable by subscripts. For example, $F_1(x_t, 1)$ is the partial derivative of $F(K, L)$ with respect to its first argument evaluated at the point $(K, L) = (x_t, 1)$. To avoid ambiguity, we shall sometimes use the slightly longer notation $\partial F(x_t, 1)/\partial K$ to denote the very same object.

(c) If $x^* \in X$ is a periodic point with period p, then it follows that every element of the orbit $\mathcal{O}(x^*)$ is also a periodic point of period p.

PROOF: The proof of part (a) is obvious. To prove part (b), we proceed as follows. If there does not exist any $q \in \{1, 2, \ldots, p - 1\}$ such that $f^{(q)}(x^*) = x^*$, then it follows that x^* is a periodic point of (3.1) with period p and we are done. Suppose therefore that there exists a number q in the set $\{1, 2, \ldots, p - 1\}$ such that $f^{(q)}(x^*) = x^*$. Without loss of generality, we may assume that q is the smallest such number. All we need to show is that p is divisible by q without remainder. If this is not the case, then there must exist positive integers u and v such that $p = uq + v$ and $1 \le v < q$. From $f^{(p)}(x^*) = f^{(q)}(x^*) = x^*$, it follows therefore that $x^* = f^{(p)}(x^*) = f^{(uq+v)}(x^*) = f^{(v)}(f^{(uq)}(x^*)) = f^{(v)}(x^*)$. Because of $v < q$, this contradicts our assumption that q is the smallest integer in the set $\{1, 2, \ldots, p - 1\}$, which satisfies $f^{(q)}(x^*) = x^*$. This completes the proof of part (b).

To prove part (c), first note that the fact that x^* is periodic of period p implies that $\mathcal{O}(x^*) = \{f^{(q)}(x^*) \mid q \in \{0, 1, \ldots, p - 1\}\}$. We must therefore prove that

$$f^{(p)}(f^{(q)}(x^*)) = f^{(q)}(x^*)$$

holds for all $q \in \{0, 1, \ldots, p - 1\}$ and that

$$f^{(t)}(f^{(q)}(x^*)) \ne f^{(q)}(x^*)$$

holds for all $q \in \{0, 1, \ldots, p - 1\}$ and all $t \in \{1, 2, \ldots, p - 1\}$. The first statement follows easily from $f^{(p)}(f^{(q)}(x^*)) = f^{(q)}(f^{(p)}(x^*))$ and $f^{(p)}(x^*) = x^*$. In order to prove the second statement, let us assume that there exist $q \in \{0, 1, \ldots, p - 1\}$ and $t \in \{1, 2, \ldots, p - 1\}$ such that $f^{(t)}(f^{(q)}(x^*)) = f^{(q)}(x^*)$. Define $x = f^{(q)}(x^*) \in X$ and $s = 2p - (t + q) \ge 2$. From $f^{(t)}(x) = x$, it follows that $f^{(t+s)}(x) = f^{(s)}(x)$. But $f^{(t+s)}(x) = f^{(t+s+q)}(x^*) = f^{(2p)}(x^*) = f^{(p)}(x^*) = x^*$ and $f^{(s)}(x) = f^{(s+q)}(x^*) = f^{(2p-t)}(x^*) = f^{(p-t)}(x^*)$. Therefore, it must hold that $f^{(p-t)}(x^*) = x^*$, which contradicts the assumption that x^* is of period p. This concludes the proof.

We illustrate the identification of fixed points and periodic orbits in the following example.

Example 3.3 Consider the cobweb model with naive expectations that we have already discussed in example 1.5. Suppose that the demand and supply functions are given by

$$D(x) = \frac{A}{Ax^\alpha + 1} \quad \text{and} \quad S(x) = \frac{Bx^\beta}{x^\beta + 1},$$

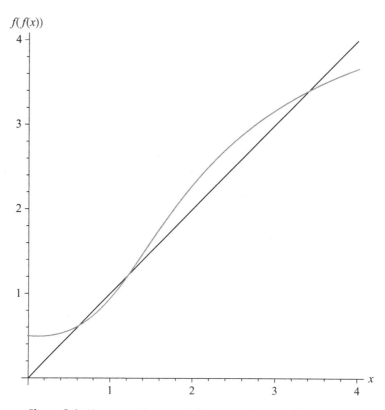

Figure 3.1 The second iterate of f for $A = \beta = 2$ and $B = \alpha = 1$

respectively, where x denotes the price and A, B, α, and β are positive parameters with $A \geq B$.[2] Note that both of these functions are continuous on $(0, +\infty)$, that D is strictly decreasing, and that S is strictly increasing. The range of the demand function is the interval $(0, A)$ such that the inverse demand function D^{-1} maps $(0, A)$ to $(0, +\infty)$. Since $A \geq B$ is assumed, it follows that the range of the supply function S, which is given by $(0, B)$, is contained in the domain of the inverse demand function. This shows that the cobweb model (1.8), that is, the implicit difference equation $D(x_{t+1}) = S(x_t)$, can equivalently be written in the following explicit form

$$x_{t+1} = D^{-1}(S(x_t)) = f(x_t) := \left(\frac{1}{Bx_t^{\beta}} + \frac{A-B}{AB} \right)^{1/\alpha}.$$

The fixed point equation $f(x) = x$ can be written as

$$x^{\alpha} = \frac{1}{Bx^{\beta}} + \frac{A-B}{AB}. \tag{3.2}$$

---

[2] When we introduced the cobweb model in section 1.2, we denoted the system variable by the letter p in order to indicate that it is a price. In the present section, the letter p is already used to denote the period of a periodic point, so that we use the letter x for the system variable.

Since the left-hand side of (3.2) is strictly increasing from 0 to $+\infty$ as x varies between 0 and $+\infty$, whereas the right-hand side is strictly decreasing from $+\infty$ to $(A - B)/(AB)$, it follows that there exists a unique fixed point x^*. In the special case $A = B$, this fixed point is given by $x^* = B^{-1/(\alpha+\beta)}$.

Now let us try to locate periodic points of period 2. If such points exist, they must be different from x^* and they must satisfy the equation $f^{(2)}(x) = x$. Let us start with the special case $A = B$ in which it holds that $f(x) = (Bx^\beta)^{-1/\alpha}$ and $f^{(2)}(x) = B^{(\beta-\alpha)/\alpha^2} x^{\beta^2/\alpha^2}$. If, in addition to $A = B$, it also holds that $\alpha = \beta$, then we have $f^{(2)}(x) = x$, and it follows therefore that every $x \in (0, +\infty)$, except for the fixed point x^*, qualifies as a periodic point of period 2. If $A = B$ but $\alpha \neq \beta$, however, the equation $f^{(2)}(x) = x$ has the unique solution $x = x^*$, and we can conclude that no periodic point with period 2 exists.

If $A \neq B$, the analysis is more complicated and we restrict ourselves to presenting a numerical example. More specifically, we choose the parameter values $A = 2$, $B = 1$, $\alpha = 1$, and $\beta = 2$. Substituting these values into (3.2), we obtain the cubic equation $2x^3 - x^2 - 2 = 0$, which has the unique real solution $x^* \approx 1.197$. The graph of $f^{(2)}$ is shown in figure 3.1. It is clearly seen from this graph that there are three solutions to the equation $f^{(2)}(x) = x$. The one in the middle corresponds to the fixed point x^*, whereas the other two are periodic points of period 2.

3.2 Local linearization

When studying an autonomous difference equation of the form (3.1), we often start with the determination of the fixed points. Having found a fixed point, it is useful to proceed with an analysis of the dynamics locally around that fixed point. If the right-hand side of (3.1) is a continuously differentiable function of x_t, then this is often easy to accomplish by a local linearization. Let us therefore assume that $X \subseteq \mathbb{R}^n$, that $x^* \in \text{int}(X)$ is a fixed point of (3.1), and that $f : X \mapsto X$ is continuously differentiable in an open neighbourhood of x^*. The local linearization of equation (3.1) around x^* is then given by

$$y_{t+1} = Jy_t, \qquad (3.3)$$

where $y_t = x_t - x^*$ are the local system variables and where

$$J = \begin{pmatrix} \partial f_1(x^*)/\partial x_1 & \partial f_1(x^*)/\partial x_2 & \cdots & \partial f_1(x^*)/\partial x_n \\ \partial f_2(x^*)/\partial x_1 & \partial f_2(x^*)/\partial x_2 & \cdots & \partial f_2(x^*)/\partial x_n \\ \vdots & \vdots & \ddots & \vdots \\ \partial f_n(x^*)/\partial x_1 & \partial f_n(x^*)/\partial x_2 & \cdots & \partial f_n(x^*)/\partial x_n \end{pmatrix}$$

is the *Jacobian matrix* of (3.1) evaluated at x^*. The entry $\partial f_k(x^*)/\partial x_\ell$ of the Jacobian matrix is the partial derivative of the kth component of the vector-valued function $f = (f_1, f_2, \ldots, f_n)$ with respect to the ℓth component of the system variable $x = (x_1, x_2, \ldots, x_n)$, evaluated at the fixed point x^*. Note that the linearized system (3.3) is a homogeneous linear difference equation such as those discussed in section 2.2.

In order to proceed, we need to introduce the concept of a homeomorphism and that of topological conjugacy. Consider two subsets U and V of the Euclidean space $\mathbb{R}^n$. A function $h : U \mapsto V$ is called a homeomorphism if it is continuous and invertible and if its inverse $h^{-1} : V \mapsto U$ is also continuous. If there exists a homeomorphism $h : U \mapsto V$, then the sets U and V are called homeomorphic. A homeomorphism can be considered as a continuous transformation of coordinates. Due to the assumptions imposed on h, both h and h^{-1} preserve all topological properties such as openness of sets or convergence of sequences. Now let two autonomous difference equations be given with system dynamics $f : X \mapsto X$ and $g : Y \mapsto Y$, respectively, where $X \subseteq \mathbb{R}^n$ and $Y \subseteq \mathbb{R}^n$. If there exist sets $U \subseteq X$ and $V \subseteq Y$ as well as a homeomorphism $h : U \mapsto V$ such that

$$h(f(x)) = g(h(x)) \tag{3.4}$$

holds for all $x \in U$, then we call the two difference equations topologically conjugate on U and V, respectively. To understand the meaning of topological conjugacy, consider any trajectory $(x_t)_{t=0}^{+\infty}$ of the difference equation $x_{t+1} = f(x_t)$. We can define a corresponding sequence $(y_t)_{t=0}^{+\infty}$ by $y_t = h(x_t)$ for all $t \in \mathbb{N}_0$. Because of (3.4), it holds that $y_{t+1} = h(x_{t+1}) = h(f(x_t)) = g(h(x_t)) = g(y_t)$ and it follows that $(y_t)_{t=0}^{+\infty}$ is a trajectory of the difference equation $y_{t+1} = g(y_t)$. Since h is invertible, we can also reverse this argument. We can therefore conclude that there exists a one-to-one relation between the trajectories of the first difference equation and those of the topologically conjugate equation. Furthermore, because h and its inverse are continuous, the trajectories of the two difference equations have the same qualitative properties. For example, if one trajectory of the equation $x_{t+1} = f(x_t)$ approaches another one of the same equation, then the corresponding trajectories of the equation $y_{t+1} = g(y_t)$ approach each other as well. In other words, the dynamics generated by topologically conjugate difference equations can be considered as qualitatively equivalent.

Consider a fixed point x^* of the autonomous difference equation (3.1). This fixed point is *hyperbolic* if the Jacobian matrix J has no (real or complex) eigenvalue with absolute value equal to 1. Otherwise, the fixed point is said to be *non-hyperbolic*. The following Hartman–Grobman theorem shows that locally around a hyperbolic fixed point x^* the original (non-linear) system (3.1) is topologically conjugate to the linearized system (3.3). Hence, in order to study the dynamics of the non-linear

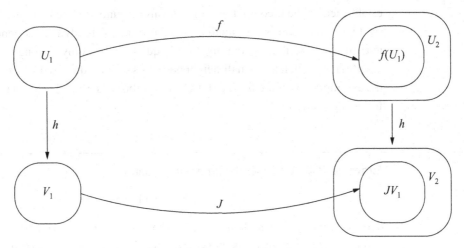

Figure 3.2 Illustration of theorem 3.2

difference equation (3.1) locally around a hyperbolic fixed point, it is sufficient to analyze the linear difference equation (3.3).

Theorem 3.2   Let x^* be a fixed point of (3.1) with $x^* \in \text{int}(X)$ and let f be continuously differentiable in an open neighbourhood of x^*. Let J be the Jacobian matrix of (3.1) at x^*, and suppose that x^* is hyperbolic. There exist open sets U_1, U_2, V_1, and V_2 and a homeomorphism $h : U_1 \cup U_2 \mapsto V_1 \cup V_2$ such that the following properties hold: $x^* \in U_1 \subseteq X$, $0 \in V_1 \subseteq \mathbb{R}^n$, $f(U_1) \subseteq U_2 \subseteq X$, $JV_1 \subseteq V_2 \subseteq \mathbb{R}^n$, and $h(f(x)) = Jh(x)$ for all $x \in U_1$.

We do not present a proof of theorem 3.2. However, a graphical illustration of the result is provided in figure 3.2. We shall use this powerful theorem primarily for the analysis of the stability properties of fixed points. For example, if the trajectory $(x_t)_{t=0}^{+\infty}$ converges to the fixed point x^*, that is, if $\lim_{t \to +\infty} x_t = x^*$ holds, then it follows from the continuity of h that $\lim_{t \to +\infty} y_t = \lim_{t \to +\infty} h(x_t) = h(x^*) = 0$.[3] Thus, every trajectory of (3.1) that converges to the fixed point x^* corresponds to a trajectory of the linearized system (3.3) that converges to its fixed point 0.

Let us emphasize that the Hartman–Grobman theorem 3.2 is a local result. The topological conjugacy between a non-linear difference (3.1) and its linearization

---

[3] The last equality can be proved as follows. The properties of h imply that $h(x^*) = h(f(x^*)) = Jh(x^*)$ or, equivalently, $(J - I_n)h(x^*) = 0$, where I_n is the unit matrix in $\mathbb{R}^n$. Because J does not have the eigenvalue 1, this is only possible if $h(x^*) = 0$.

established by the theorem holds only locally around the fixed points x^* and 0, respectively. In other words, the qualitative behaviour of the dynamics generated by (3.1) is correctly described by the linearized equation (3.3) only as long as we restrict our attention to sufficiently small neighbourhoods around the fixed points. Note also that the assumption that the fixed point x^* is hyperbolic is crucial. This is illustrated by the following example.

Example 3.4   Consider the difference equation

$$x_{t+1} = x_t(1 + x_t)$$

defined on the system domain $X = \mathbb{R}$. It is obvious that $x^* = 0$ is a non-hyperbolic fixed point. Graphical analysis as shown in figure 3.3 demonstrates that trajectories which start at $x_0 \in (-1, 0]$ converge to x^*, whereas all trajectories starting at $x_0 \in (0, +\infty)$ diverge to $+\infty$. The linearization around $x^* = 0$, however, is given by $y_{t+1} = y_t$, which shows that all trajectories of the linearized equation are constant. We can therefore see that the topological properties of the trajectories of the original difference equation are very different from those of the linearized equation, that is, the Hartman–Grobman theorem does not apply.

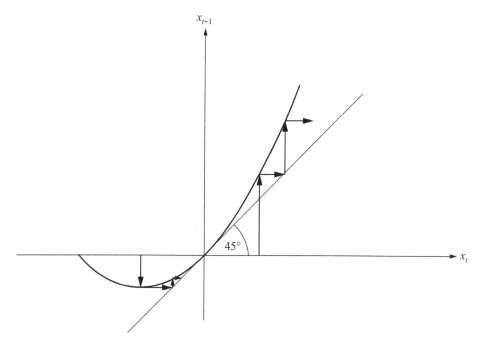

Figure 3.3 Dynamics of example 3.4

3.3 Stability

Throughout this section, let $x^* \in X \subseteq \mathbb{R}^n$ be a fixed point of the autonomous difference equation (3.1). For any two vectors $x = (x_1, x_2, \ldots, x_n)$ and $y = (y_1, y_2, \ldots, y_n)$ in $\mathbb{R}^n$, let us denote their Euclidean distance by[4]

$$\|x - y\| = \left[\sum_{k=1}^{n} (x_k - y_k)^2 \right]^{1/2}.$$

The open ε-ball around x^* is the set $B_\varepsilon(x^*)$ of all $x \in \mathbb{R}^n$ such that the distance between x and x^* is smaller than ε. Formally, we have $B_\varepsilon(x^*) = \{x \in \mathbb{R}^n \mid \|x - x^*\| < \varepsilon\}$. The closure of $B_\varepsilon(x^*)$ will be denoted by $\bar{B}_\varepsilon(x^*)$.

The fixed point x^* is called *stable* if for every $\varepsilon > 0$ there exists $\delta > 0$ such that the following condition holds for all $x \in B_\delta(x^*)$

$$f^{(t)}(x) \in B_\varepsilon(x^*) \qquad \text{for all } t \in \mathbb{N}_0.$$

If the fixed point x^* fails to satisfy this condition, then it is called *unstable*. If a fixed point is stable and if, in addition, there exists $\delta > 0$ such that, for all $x \in B_\delta(x^*)$, it holds that

$$\lim_{t \to +\infty} f^{(t)}(x) = x^*,$$

then we call x^* a *locally asymptotically stable* fixed point. In this case, we call the set

$$A(x^*) = \{x \in X \mid \lim_{t \to +\infty} f^{(t)}(x) = x^*\}$$

the *basin of attraction* of the fixed point x^*. If $A(x^*) = X$, then we call x^* a *globally asymptotically stable* fixed point.

Fixed points are of particular importance in many economic (and other) applications, as the system under consideration is at rest. Suppose that the system is at the fixed point x^* when some exogenous shock perturbs it. After the perturbation, the evolution of the system is described by the given difference equation, starting from the perturbed state $x_0 \neq x^*$. If the fixed point is stable, then it follows that a small perturbation cannot have a strong effect: whenever the system is perturbed by less than δ, it still remains within the distance ε from the fixed point. If the fixed point is also locally asymptotically stable, then it follows that the system returns asymptotically to the fixed point after the perturbation. Stability and local asymptotic stability therefore describe the robustness of the system under consideration with respect to small perturbations.

---

[4] Note that in this formula k is not a time-subscript but indicates the components of the n-dimensional vectors x and y.

For the analysis of dynamic models in economics, the notions of local and global asymptotic stability are more relevant than the concept of stability. Nevertheless, in the rest of this section we present conditions for all three stability notions. We also alert the reader that the distinction between pre-determined variables and jump variables has a bearing on the appropriate definition of stability. We will return to this important point in section 3.4 below, where we introduce saddle points and saddle point stability. For the moment, it is best to think of systems that contain only pre-determined variables but no jump variables.

Finally, let us mention that all of the above stability definitions can easily be applied to periodic points of (3.1) as well. Indeed, since we know from lemma 3.2(a) that every periodic point x^* of period p is a fixed point of the difference equation $x_{t+1} = f^{(p)}(x_t)$, we can say that x^* is stable (unstable, locally asymptotically stable, globally asymptotically stable) as a periodic point of (3.1) if it has the corresponding property as a fixed point of the equation $x_{t+1} = f^{(p)}(x_t)$. In what follows, we may therefore restrict ourselves to the stability analysis of fixed points.

How do we check the stability of a fixed point? The easiest way to proceed is via a local linearization. As a matter of fact, since we know from theorem 3.2 that the local dynamics around a hyperbolic fixed point can be inferred from the local linearization of the difference equation, we can simply compute the Jacobian matrix J and study the solutions of the linearized equation (3.3) by the methods discussed in section 2.2. The assumed hyperbolicity of the fixed point ensures that J has no eigenvalue with absolute value equal to 1. That is, all eigenvalues λ either have an absolute value greater than 1 or they have an absolute value smaller than 1. We refer to those with $|\lambda| > 1$ as unstable eigenvalues and to those with $|\lambda| < 1$ as stable eigenvalues. This makes sense because eigenvalues with absolute values greater than 1 give rise to basis solutions of the linearized system (3.3) that become unbounded, whereas those with absolute values smaller than 1 generate basis solutions converging to 0. We summarize these observations in the following theorem.

Theorem 3.3   Let the assumptions of theorem 3.2 be satisfied.

(a) If x^* is stable, then it follows that all eigenvalues of the Jacobian matrix J have absolute values smaller than 1.

(b) If all eigenvalues of the Jacobian matrix J have absolute values smaller than 1, then it follows that x^* is locally asymptotically stable.

Note that local or global asymptotic stability implies stability such that part (a) of the theorem not only provides a necessary condition for stability, but also for the stronger notions of local and global asymptotic stability. Note furthermore that under the assumptions of theorems 3.2 and 3.3, which include the requirement that x^* is a hyperbolic fixed point, stability and local asymptotic stability are equivalent properties. We now illustrate the application of theorem 3.3 by a simple example.

Example 3.5 Let us return to the cobweb model with naive expectations introduced in example 1.5. The model is described by the difference equation

$$p_{t+1} = D^{-1}(S(p_t)),$$

where D is the demand function and S the supply function. Assume that p^* is a fixed point of this equation, that is, $D(p^*) = S(p^*)$. Assume furthermore that both functions D and S are continuously differentiable and that $D'(p^*) \neq 0$. To check the stability of the fixed point p^*, we compute the Jacobian matrix, which in our case is just a single number $J = S'(p^*)/D'(p^*)$. Because we have assumed that D is decreasing while S is increasing, we must have $J \leq 0$. According to theorem 3.3, the fixed point x^* is locally asymptotically stable if $-1 < J$ and it is unstable if $J < -1$. The former condition translates into $S'(p^*) < -D'(p^*)$ or $S'(p^*) < |D'(p^*)|$. Thus, if the slope of the demand function at the fixed point exceeds (in absolute value) the slope of the supply function, then it follows that the fixed point is locally asymptotically stable. If, on the other hand, the supply function is steeper, then the fixed point is unstable.

Theorem 3.3 is of fundamental importance for the stability analysis of fixed points of autonomous difference equations. It is easy to apply since all that is required is the calculation of the Jacobian matrix along with its eigenvalues. Although these calculations may be cumbersome (especially in high-dimensional systems), they do not pose any conceptual problem. However, there are also several limitations of theorem 3.3. First, it requires continuous differentiability of the system dynamics at the fixed point. Non-smooth equations cannot be dealt with. Second, the theorem is silent about the stability of non-hyperbolic fixed points. Finally, the theorem cannot be used for checking global asymptotic stability. This is the case because it is entirely based on the local information that is contained in the Jacobian matrix.

An alternative way to study the stability of fixed points is the *direct method of Lyapunov*. It is not as straightforward to apply as theorem 3.3, but it neither requires assumptions on the differentiability of the system dynamics f nor on the hyperbolicity of the fixed point x^*.

Difference equations

Theorem 3.4 Consider the autonomous difference equation (3.1) with state space $X \subseteq \mathbb{R}^n$. Assume that f is a continuous function and that x^* is a fixed point of (3.1).

(a) Suppose that there exists a neighbourhood U of x^* and a continuous function $V : U \mapsto \mathbb{R}$ such that $V(x^*) = 0$, $V(x) > 0$ for all $x \in U \setminus \{x^*\}$, and

$$V(f(x)) \leq V(x) \text{ for all } x \in U. \tag{3.5}$$

Then it follows that x^* is stable.

(b) If, in addition to the properties mentioned in part (a), inequality (3.5) holds strictly for all $x \in U \setminus \{x^*\}$, then it follows that x^* is locally asymptotically stable.

PROOF: (a) Let $\varepsilon_1 > 0$ be given such that $\bar{B}_{\varepsilon_1}(x^*) \subseteq U$. Since f is continuous and $f(x^*) = x^*$, there exists $\varepsilon_2 \in (0, \varepsilon_1]$ such that $f(x) \in \bar{B}_{\varepsilon_1}(x^*)$ holds for all $x \in \bar{B}_{\varepsilon_2}(x^*)$. Now consider the set $C = \{x \in X \mid \varepsilon_2 \leq \|x - x^*\| \leq \varepsilon_1\}$. Since C is non-empty and compact and since the function V is continuous, it must hold that V attains a minimum on C. Because $V(x) > 0$ holds for all $x \in U \setminus \{x^*\}$, this minimum must be strictly positive. Let us denote it by m. Continuity of V together with $V(x^*) = 0$ implies that there exists $\delta \in (0, \varepsilon_2)$ such that $V(x) < m$ holds for all $x \in B_\delta(x^*)$.

We now show that $f^{(t)}(y) \in \bar{B}_{\varepsilon_1}(x^*)$ must hold for all $y \in B_\delta(x^*)$ and all $t \in \mathbb{N}_0$. Suppose that this is not the case. Because $\delta < \varepsilon_2 \leq \varepsilon_1$, there exists $t \in \mathbb{N}_0$ such that $f^{(t)}(y) \in B_{\varepsilon_2}(x^*)$ and $f^{(t+1)}(y) \notin B_{\varepsilon_2}(x^*)$. Without loss of generality, let t be the smallest such number. Because $f(x) \in \bar{B}_{\varepsilon_1}(x^*)$ holds for all $x \in B_{\varepsilon_2}(x^*)$, it follows that $f^{(t+1)}(y) \in C$ and, hence, $V(f^{(t+1)}(y)) \geq m$. On the other hand, we have $y \in B_\delta(x^*)$ and therefore $V(y) < m$. Obviously, these properties are inconsistent with (3.5), since (3.5) implies that $V(f^{(t)}(y))$ must be non-increasing with respect to t as long as $f^{(t)}(y) \in U$. This contradiction proves part (a).

(b) Let $y \in B_\delta(x^*)$ be given. From part (a), we know that $x_t := f^{(t)}(y) \in \bar{B}_{\varepsilon_1}(x^*)$ holds for all $t \in \mathbb{N}_0$. Defining $z_t = V(x_t)$, it follows from (3.5) that the real-valued sequence $(z_t)_{t=0}^{+\infty}$ is non-increasing and non-negative. Consequently, it has a limit v^*. Since $\bar{B}_{\varepsilon_1}(x^*)$ is compact, there exists a convergent subsequence of $(x_t)_{t=0}^{+\infty}$. Denoting this subsequence by $(x_{t_k})_{k=0}^{+\infty}$ and its limit by $\bar{x}$, and using the continuity of f and V, we get

$$v^* = \lim_{k \to +\infty} z_{t_k} = \lim_{k \to +\infty} V(x_{t_k}) = V(\bar{x})$$

and

$$v^* = \lim_{k \to +\infty} z_{t_k+1} = \lim_{k \to +\infty} V(x_{t_k+1}) = \lim_{k \to +\infty} V(f(x_{t_k})) = V(f(\bar{x})).$$

Together, these two equations imply that $V(\bar{x}) = V(f(\bar{x}))$. Because (3.5) holds with strict inequality whenever $x \in U \setminus \{x^*\}$, we must therefore have $\bar{x} = x^*$. To summarize, we have shown that every convergent subsequence of $(x_t)_{t=0}^{+\infty}$ has the limit x^*. Because of the compactness of $\bar{B}_{\varepsilon_1}(x^*)$ and the fact that $x_t \in \bar{B}_{\varepsilon_1}(x^*)$ holds for all $t \in \mathbb{N}_0$, this completes the proof of part (b) of the theorem.

There exists also a global version of this result, which can be proved in essentially the same way as part (b) of theorem 3.4.

Theorem 3.5 Consider the autonomous difference equation (3.1) with state space $X \subseteq \mathbb{R}^n$. Assume that X is compact, that f is continuous, and that x^* is a fixed point of (3.1). If there exists a continuous function $V : X \mapsto \mathbb{R}$ such that $V(x^*) = 0$, $V(x) > 0$, and $V(f(x)) < V(x)$ for all $x \in X \setminus \{x^*\}$, then it follows that x^* is globally asymptotically stable.

The function V appearing in theorems 3.4 and 3.5 is called a Lyapunov function. The crucial step in the application of these theorems is finding an appropriate Lyapunov function.

Example 3.6 Consider once more the cobweb model from example 3.5. Let us assume that both the demand function D and the supply function S are continuous and that the demand function is strictly decreasing. This implies that the dynamics can be written in the form

$$p_{t+1} = f(p_t),$$

where $f(p) = D^{-1}(S(p))$ is a continuous function. Let p^* be a fixed point of this difference equation. We define a Lyapunov function by $V(p) = [D(p) - q^*]^2$, where $q^* = D(p^*) = S(p^*)$. This function is obviously continuous and non-negative. Because D is strictly decreasing, it follows furthermore that $V(p) = 0$ holds if and only if $p = p^*$. It remains to verify condition (3.5). Because of $V(f(p)) = V(D^{-1}(S(p))) = [S(p) - q^*]^2$, this condition can be written as $[S(p) - q^*]^2 \leq [D(p) - q^*]^2$. Note that this inequality is equivalent to

$$\left| \frac{S(p) - q^*}{p - p^*} \right| \leq \left| \frac{D(p) - q^*}{p - p^*} \right|,$$

which implies once again that the fixed point p^* is stable if the supply function is less steep than the demand function. If this inequality holds strictly for all $p \neq p^*$, then we obtain from theorem 3.5 that p^* is globally asymptotically stable; if it holds only locally around p^*, then theorem 3.4 applies. Note that the above condition can be checked even if the functions D and S are not differentiable.

3.4 Saddle points

In this section, we continue to discuss the stability of a fixed point, but we now take into account that some system variables are jump variables. Recall that we have argued that stable or locally asymptotically stable fixed points are robust against small perturbations, where we meant by a small perturbation an exogenous change of the system variable from the fixed point x^* to some nearby value $x_0 \neq x^*$. Now suppose, for example, that the kth component of the system variable is a jump variable, which means that this component can adjust to any feasible value at the start of any given period. If a shock perturbs the fixed point x^* to some value x_0 with $x_{0,k} \neq x_k^*$, then this is of no relevance because, being a jump variable, component k can return immediately to its fixed point value x_k^* anyway. In other words, speaking of a perturbation of a jump variable does not really make sense and perturbations have an influence on the system only if they affect pre-determined variables.

The consequences of this observation for the very definition of the stability of a fixed point are obvious. We do not need to require that the system remains close to, or returns to the fixed point after all small perturbations of all components of the system variable, but only after those perturbations that affect the pre-determined variables. This suggests that a weaker notion of stability is relevant. In the present section, as well as in the next one, we make this idea precise and we discuss the implications of having too little or too much stability in the system. Let us begin by studying an example, namely a simple economic growth model with an overlapping generations structure.

Example 3.7 Consider the overlapping generations model from example 1.7, but assume that instead of money the only asset in the economy is physical capital, which is also used as a production input (in addition to labour). A household of generation $t \in \mathbb{N}_0$ chooses $\ell_t \geq 0$, the amount of labour (or effort) supplied to the firms during period t. Denoting by w_t the real wage in period t, the labour income of a young household in period t is $w_t \ell_t$. As in example 1.7, we assume that the household does not consume anything in its first period of life but that the entire income is saved. Physical capital is the only asset in the economy and we assume that it depreciates completely during production within one period. This implies that the capital stock of period $t + 1$ coincides with the labour income of period t, that is

$$k_{t+1} = w_t \ell_t.$$

In period $t + 1$, the household does not work but consumes its entire wealth. Denoting by c_{t+1} consumption by a household of generation t in period $t + 1$ and by r_{t+1} the rental rate of capital held from period t to period $t + 1$, we therefore obtain[5]

$$c_{t+1} = r_{t+1}k_{t+1}.$$

The household seeks to maximize its lifetime utility given by $-v(\ell_t) + u(c_{t+1})$ subject to non-negativity constraints on ℓ_t and c_{t+1} and subject to the two budget constraints displayed above. Throughout the present example, we assume that $v(\ell) = B\ell^{1+\eta}/(1 + \eta)$ and $u(c) = (c^{1-\sigma} - 1)/(1 - \sigma)$, where B, σ, and η are positive parameters.[6] Substituting the two budget constraints into the objective functional and maximizing the resulting expression with respect to k_{t+1}, we obtain the first-order condition

$$B\ell_t^{1+\eta} = c_{t+1}^{1-\sigma}.$$

Due to the smoothness and curvature properties of the functions v and u, this first-order condition is both necessary and sufficient for the optimal behaviour of the household. Households of generation -1 are endowed with k_0 units of capital at the start of period 0. They live for one period only, during which they consume the amount $c_0 = r_0 k_0$. We assume that the initial capital endowment k_0 is strictly positive.

There exists a continuum of measure 1 of identical competitive firms with access to a technology described by the Cobb–Douglas production function $F(k_t, \ell_t) = Ak_t^\alpha \ell_t^{1-\alpha}$, where $A > 0$ and $\alpha \in (0, 1)$ are fixed technology parameters. The rental rate of capital is given by

$$r_t = F_1(k_t, \ell_t) = \alpha A k_t^{\alpha-1} \ell_t^{1-\alpha},$$

whereas the real wage equals

$$w_t = F_2(k_t, \ell_t) = (1 - \alpha)Ak_t^\alpha \ell_t^{-\alpha}.$$

Finally, we have to discuss the market clearing conditions. Labour market clearing and capital market clearing have already been taken care of by identifying the factor supplies of the households with the factor demands by the firms. Output market clearing requires that $Ak_t^\alpha \ell_t^{1-\alpha} = c_t + k_{t+1}$. Due to Walras' law, however, this market clearing condition is redundant and can be neglected in the following analysis. An equilibrium for a given initial value k_0 is therefore a sequence of variables that satisfies the five conditions displayed above for all $t \in \mathbb{N}_0$.

Combining the first budget constraint of the households with the wage equation, we obtain

$$k_{t+1} = (1 - \alpha)Ak_t^\alpha \ell_t^{1-\alpha}. \tag{3.6}$$

---

[5] Since we assume capital to depreciate completely within one period, the rental income of the agent is all the income the household can use for consumption in period $t + 1$.

[6] If $\sigma = 1$, then the utility of consumption is given by $u(c) = \ln c$.

If $\sigma = 1$, then the first-order condition of the households' optimization problem yields $\ell_t = B^{-1/(1+\eta)}$ for all $t \in \mathbb{N}_0$. Substituting this into (3.6), we obtain a single difference equation for $(k_t)_{t=0}^{+\infty}$ describing the equilibrium dynamics. This equation is very similar to the one we encountered in the Solow–Swan model from example 1.1 and can be analyzed very much in the same way as outlined in section 1.1. Together with the initial value k_0, the equation determines a unique equilibrium path.

Let us now turn to the more interesting case $\sigma \neq 1$. Combining the second budget constraint with the equation for the rental rate of capital and (3.6), it follows that

$$c_{t+1} = \alpha A k_{t+1}^{\alpha} \ell_{t+1}^{1-\alpha} = \alpha(1-\alpha)^{\alpha} A^{1+\alpha} k_t^{\alpha^2} \ell_t^{\alpha(1-\alpha)} \ell_{t+1}^{1-\alpha}.$$

Substituting this relation into the first-order optimality condition for the households' problem and solving for ℓ_{t+1}, we obtain

$$\ell_{t+1} = C k_t^{-\alpha^2/(1-\alpha)} \ell_t^{(1+\eta)/[(1-\alpha)(1-\sigma)]-\alpha}, \tag{3.7}$$

where

$$C = \left[\frac{B^{1/(1-\sigma)}}{\alpha(1-\alpha)^{\alpha} A^{1+\alpha}} \right]^{1/(1-\alpha)}$$

is a positive constant. Thus, the equilibrium dynamics in the case $\sigma \neq 1$ are described by the system of first-order difference equations (3.6)–(3.7) in the two variables k_t and ℓ_t. The variable k_t is obviously a pre-determined variable, because its value at the beginning of period t is the result of the effort decisions made in period $t-1$. Accordingly, an initial value k_0 is given. The variable ℓ_t, on the other hand, is a jump variable because its value in period t does not depend on decisions or events prior to period t but is determined by the choice of the young households in period t. Thus, there are two system variables: one is pre-determined, whereas the other one is a jump variable.

It is straightforward to verify that there exists a unique fixed point $(k^*, \ell^*)^\top$ of (3.6)–(3.7) for which both k^* and ℓ^* are positive. In the remainder of this example, we discuss the stability of that fixed point. To this end, we could compute the Jacobian matrix at the fixed point. In the present case, however, there is a simpler approach due to the fact that the two equations (3.6)–(3.7) are linear in the logarithms of the two system variables. Indeed, if we define the local coordinates $x_t = \ln k_t - \ln k^*$ and $y_t = \ln \ell_t - \ln \ell^*$, then we can rewrite the system (3.6)–(3.7) as the following homogeneous linear difference equation

$$\begin{pmatrix} x_{t+1} \\ y_{t+1} \end{pmatrix} = \begin{pmatrix} \alpha & 1-\alpha \\ \dfrac{-\alpha^2}{1-\alpha} & \dfrac{1+\eta}{(1-\alpha)(1-\sigma)} - \alpha \end{pmatrix} \begin{pmatrix} x_t \\ y_t \end{pmatrix}. \tag{3.8}$$

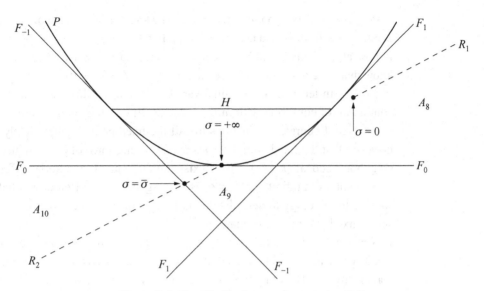

Figure 3.4 The (T, D)-diagram for equation (3.8)

Thus, the homeomorphism h from the Hartman–Grobman theorem 3.2 is given by the map $h(k, \ell) = (\ln k - \ln k^*, \ln \ell - \ln \ell^*)^\top$.

Since the linearized system (3.8) has a two-dimensional system domain, we can apply the techniques from section 2.3. The system matrix has the trace $T = (1 + \eta)/[(1 - \alpha)(1 - \sigma)]$ and determinant $D = \alpha(1 + \eta)/[(1 - \alpha)(1 - \sigma)]$. The (T, D)-diagram is shown in figure 3.4. As σ varies from 0 to $+\infty$, the point (T, D) moves along the two rays R_1 and R_2, both of which are part of the line $D = \alpha T$. For $\sigma = 0$, we have $T = (1 + \eta)/(1 - \alpha)$ and $D = \alpha(1 + \eta)/(1 - \alpha)$, which corresponds to the left endpoint of R_1. Note that in this case it holds that $D < T - 1$. As σ increases, the point (T, D) moves along R_1 towards the right until σ reaches 1. At that point, T and D become infinite, which reflects the fact that for $\sigma = 1$ the system collapses into a one-dimensional difference equation. For $\sigma > 1$, the point (T, D) moves along R_2 in the negative orthant. For $\sigma < \bar{\sigma} := [2 + (1 + \alpha)\eta]/(1 - \alpha)$, it holds that $D < -T - 1$, whereas, for $\sigma > \bar{\sigma}$, we have $D > -T - 1$. For $\sigma \to +\infty$, the point (T, D) approaches the origin of the diagram. Using the terminology introduced in section 2.3, the system matrix corresponds to a point in area A_8 for all $\sigma \in (0, 1)$, to a point in area A_{10} for all $\sigma \in (1, \bar{\sigma})$, and to a point in area A_9 for $\sigma > \bar{\sigma}$.

To start our discussion, assume that $\sigma > \bar{\sigma}$. In this case, we know from section 2.3 that the system matrix has two stable eigenvalues. According to theorem 3.3, this implies that the fixed point is locally asymptotically stable.[7] Suppose now that the

---

[7] Because, in the present example, the linearization is precise on the set $\{(k, \ell) \mid k > 0, \ell > 0\}$, we can conclude that the basin of attraction is the interior of the system domain.

system is in the fixed point $(k^*, \ell^*)^\top$ when a shock hits the economy and changes the capital stock from k^* to a nearby value k_0. In terms of the local coordinates, the system is now at $x_0 = \ln k_0 - \ln k^*$. Because equation (3.8) has two stable eigenvalues, we know that for every value $y_0 \in \mathbb{R}$ the trajectory of (3.8) starting at $(x_0, y_0)^\top$ converges to $(0, 0)^\top$. In terms of the original variables k_t and ℓ_t, this means that there exists a continuum of equilibria with initial value k_0 all of which converge to the fixed point $(k^*, \ell^*)^\top$. Of course, this justifies to call the fixed point asymptotically stable. Note, however, that the fixed point exhibits a very strong form of non-uniqueness: in every neighbourhood of $(k^*, \ell^*)^\top$ there exist infinitely many equilibria different from the fixed point, even infinitely many ones starting at $k_0 = k^*$. Below, we shall introduce a specific terminology to describe this failure of local uniqueness, namely we shall call such a fixed point indeterminate.

Now let us turn to the case $\sigma \in (0, 1) \cup (1, \bar{\sigma})$. In this case, we know from the results presented in section 2.3 that the system matrix has one stable and one unstable real eigenvalue. Denoting these eigenvalues by λ_s and λ_u, respectively, and the corresponding eigenvectors by w_s and w_u, the general solution to (3.8) can be written in the form

$$\begin{pmatrix} x_t \\ y_t \end{pmatrix} = \beta_s \lambda_s^t w_s + \beta_u \lambda_u^t w_u,$$

where β_s and β_u are undetermined coefficients. Note that whenever $\beta_u = 0$, this solution converges to $(0, 0)^\top$. Thus, if $x_0 = \ln k_0 - \ln k^*$ is a perturbed initial value and if the first component of the eigenvector w_s, which we denote by $w_{s,1}$, is non-zero, then we can choose $\beta_s = x_0/w_{s,1}$ and $\beta_u = 0$ to get a particular solution which converges to the origin $(0, 0)^\top$ and which starts at the perturbed initial value of capital, x_0. Translating these observations back into the original variables, we see that there exists an equilibrium with initial capital stock k_0 that converges to the fixed point $(k^*, \ell^*)^\top$. Hence, it is again justified to call the fixed point asymptotically stable. However, in the present case where $\sigma \in (0, 1) \cup (1, \bar{\sigma})$, the particular solution to (3.8) that we constructed is the only one that converges to the fixed point from the initial value x_0. Hence, the equilibrium that leads back to the fixed point after a perturbation is locally unique. In this case, we call the fixed point determinate. Note that asymptotic stability and determinacy require two conditions to be satisfied: there must be a single stable eigenvalue and the eigenvector corresponding to this eigenvalue must not be parallel to the subspace spanned by the jump variable (that is, $w_{s,1} \neq 0$). We shall encounter both of these conditions in the ensuing discussion of the general theory of saddle points.

Let us summarize what we have learnt from the above example. If the system variable contains components that are jump variables, then the notions of stability or asymptotic stability of a fixed point, as they were introduced in section 3.3, are sufficient but not necessary for the robustness of the fixed point against perturbations of the system. Moreover, these stability notions imply that the fixed point fails to be a locally unique equilibrium. If the number of stable eigenvalues coincides with the number of pre-determined variables and if the subspace spanned by the stable eigenvectors is transversal to the subspace spanned by the jump variables, then the fixed point is also robust with respect to small perturbations and for every such perturbation there exists exactly one equilibrium that starts in the perturbed initial state and converges to the fixed point. The stable–unstable manifold theorem presented below shows that these properties generalize to arbitrary systems of autonomous difference equations that have a hyperbolic fixed point. In order to formulate the theorem, we first have to explain what a manifold is. For our purpose, the following definition will be sufficient: a manifold of dimension m is a set $W \subseteq \mathbb{R}^n$ such that for every point $x \in W$ there exists a set $U_x \subseteq W$ containing x such that U_x is homeomorphic to the open unit ball $B_1(0)$ in $\mathbb{R}^m$. Thus, a manifold of dimension m is a subset of $\mathbb{R}^n$ that is locally Euclidean of dimension m.

Theorem 3.6 Let the assumptions of theorem 3.2 be satisfied and assume that m eigenvalues of the Jacobian matrix J have absolute values smaller than 1 and the remaining $n - m$ eigenvalues have absolute values larger than 1. Denote by E_s the subspace of X spanned by the eigenvectors of J corresponding to the stable eigenvalues and by E_u the subspace of X spanned by the eigenvectors of J corresponding to unstable eigenvalues. Locally around the fixed point x^*, there exist an m-dimensional manifold W_s and an $(n - m)$-dimensional manifold W_u such that the following properties hold:

(a) W_s and W_u are differentiable manifolds and it holds that $x^* \in W_s \cap W_u$.
(b) At the fixed point x^*, W_s is tangential to the linear manifold $x^* + E_s$ and W_u is tangential to the linear manifold $x^* + E_u$.
(c) For all $x \in W_s$, it holds that $f(x) \in W_s$ and $\lim_{t \to +\infty} f^{(t)}(x) = x^*$.
(d) For all $x \in W_u$, it holds that $f(x) \in W_u$. The restriction of f to W_u is invertible, that is, there exists a function $f_u^{-1} : W_u \mapsto W_u$ such that $f(f_u^{-1}(x)) = f_u^{-1}(f(x)) = x$. Furthermore, for all $x \in W_u$ it holds that $\lim_{t \to +\infty} (f_u^{-1})^{(t)}(x) = x^*$.

It is common to refer to W_s as the *stable manifold* and to W_u as the *unstable manifold*. These manifolds exist locally around the fixed point x^*. According to part (c) of the theorem, every trajectory that starts on W_s converges to the fixed point as time t approaches $+\infty$. Part (d) shows that the restriction of f to W_u is locally invertible and that every trajectory of the inverted difference equation that starts on W_u approaches the fixed point as t goes to $+\infty$. In terms of the original (non-inverted) difference equation, this implies that from every $x \in W_u$ close to the fixed point we can construct a sequence of predecessors of x that converges to x^*. Parts (a) and (b) imply that the manifolds are differentiable and that their tangent hyperplanes are parallel to the eigenspaces spanned by the stable and unstable eigenvectors, respectively.

To proceed, let us write the system domain as $X = X_p + X_j$, where X_p is the subspace of X spanned by the pre-determined variables, X_j is the subspace spanned by the jump variables, and $X_p \cap X_j = \{0\}$. In other words, we can express every point $x \in X$ in a unique way as $x = x_p + x_j$ with $x_p \in X_p$ and $x_j \in X_j$. Assume that there are ℓ pre-determined variables and $n - \ell$ jump variables such that X_p is ℓ-dimensional and X_j is $(n - \ell)$-dimensional. Let $x^* = x_p^* + x_j^*$ be the fixed point and consider a perturbation of the system variables from x^* to $x_0 \in x^* + X_p$. Note that the condition $x_0 \in x^* + X_p$ means that only pre-determined variables are perturbed, but no jump variables. Because jump variables can adjust freely, the evolution of the system after the perturbation (assumed to occur in period 0) is described by a trajectory starting on the linear manifold $x_0 + X_j$. We can now formally define the concepts of local saddle point stability, determinacy, and indeterminacy.

If there exist $\varepsilon > 0$ and $\delta > 0$ such that for every $x_0 \in B_\delta(x^*) \cap [x^* + X_p]$ the set $B_\varepsilon(x^*) \cap W_s \cap [x_0 + X_j]$ is a singleton, then x^* is called *determinate* and *locally saddle point stable*.

If for all $\varepsilon > 0$ there exists $x_0 \in B_\varepsilon(x^*) \cap [x^* + X_p]$ such that the set $B_\varepsilon(x^*) \cap W_s \cap [x_0 + X_j]$ contains infinitely many elements, then x^* is called *indeterminate*.

If for all $\varepsilon > 0$ and for all $\delta > 0$ there exists $x_0 \in B_\delta(x^*) \cap [x^* + X_p]$ such that the set $B_\varepsilon(x^*) \cap W_s \cap [x_0 + X_j]$ is empty, then x^* is said to be *not locally saddle point stable*.

These definitions look more complicated than they are. Determinacy and local saddle point stability of a fixed point occur if, after every sufficiently small perturbation of the pre-determined components of the system variable, there is a unique way in which the jump variables can adapt such that the system is located on the stable manifold of the fixed point. If there are infinitely many such settings of the jump variables, then the fixed point is indeterminate, and if there are small perturbations of the pre-determined components such that it is not possible to jump to the stable manifold, then the fixed point lacks local saddle point stability.

Checking for local saddle point stability and determinacy versus indeterminacy, respectively, is greatly simplified by theorem 3.6(b), which states that the tangent hyperplane to W_s at the fixed point is given by $x^* + E_s$. As a matter of fact, we have the following theorem.

Theorem 3.7 Let the assumptions and notations of theorem 3.6 be satisfied. In particular, suppose that the Jacobian matrix has m stable eigenvalues. Furthermore, assume that the system variable has ℓ pre-determined components and $n - \ell$ components that are jump variables. Let X_j denote the subspace of X spanned by those system variables that are jump variables.

(a) The fixed point x^* is locally saddle point stable and determinate if $X_j + E_s = \mathbb{R}^n$ and $X_j \cap E_s = \{0\}$. This, in turn, is the case if and only if $m = \ell$ and if no non-zero vector of E_s is contained in X_j.

(b) The fixed point x^* is indeterminate if $X_j \cap E_s \neq \{0\}$. A sufficient condition for this is $m > \ell$.

(c) The fixed point x^* is not locally saddle point stable if $X_j + E_s \neq \mathbb{R}^n$. A sufficient condition for this is $m < \ell$.

Note that all the conditions stated in the above theorem are only sufficient but not necessary. Moreover, if $m = \ell$ and if X_j contains a non-zero element of E_s, then the theorem is inconclusive. We illustrate these remarks by the following example.

Example 3.8 Let the system domain be given by $X = \mathbb{R}^2$ and suppose that the system variable $x = (y, z)^\top$ has one pre-determined component y and one jump component z. That is, we have $\ell = 1$, $X_p = \{(y, 0)^\top \mid y \in \mathbb{R}\}$, and $X_j = \{(0, z)^\top \mid z \in \mathbb{R}\}$. Consider the difference equation

$$\begin{pmatrix} y_{t+1} \\ z_{t+1} \end{pmatrix} = \begin{pmatrix} (1/2)y_t \\ y_t + 2z_t \end{pmatrix}.$$

The unique fixed point is $x^* = (y^*, z^*)^\top = (0, 0)^\top$ and the eigenvalues of the Jacobian matrix J are $1/2$ and 2. The number of stable eigenvalues is therefore $m = 1$. An eigenvector corresponding to the stable eigenvalue $1/2$ is given by $(-3, 2)^\top$ such that the stable manifold W_s is given by the equation $z = -(2/3)y$. This is a one-dimensional linear manifold, and for every $y_0 \in \mathbb{R}$ there exists a unique value $z_0 \in \mathbb{R}$ such that $(y_0, z_0)^\top \in E_s = W_s$. Hence, the fixed point x^* is determinate and locally saddle point stable as predicted by theorem 3.7(a).

On the other hand, if the difference equation is given by

$$\begin{pmatrix} y_{t+1} \\ z_{t+1} \end{pmatrix} = \begin{pmatrix} 2y_t \\ y_t + (1/2)z_t \end{pmatrix},$$

then it follows that the eigenvalues are again given by $1/2$ and 2, but that an eigenvector corresponding to the stable eigenvalue is $(0, 1)^\top$. This vector is obviously contained in X_j so that theorem 3.7 is inconclusive. For this reason, let us check directly the definition of indeterminacy. We first observe that in this case it holds that $X_j = W_s$. Moreover, if we choose $y_0 = y^* = 0$, then it follows that $B_\varepsilon(x^*) \cap W_s \cap X_j$ is a one-dimensional manifold and, hence, contains infinitely many points. In other words, the fixed point x^* is indeterminate. As soon as we choose $y_0 \neq y^* = 0$, however, there is no corresponding z_0 such that $(y_0, z_0)^\top \in W_s$ and it follows that the fixed point is not locally saddle point stable. This example therefore demonstrates that the conditions $\ell < m$ and $\ell > m$ are not necessary for indeterminacy and for the failure of local saddle point stability, respectively. In other words, indeterminacy and lack of local saddle point stability can also occur if $\ell = m$, that is, if the Jacobian matrix has exactly as many stable eigenvalues as there are pre-determined system variables.

Now let us change the previous example to

$$\begin{pmatrix} y_{t+1} \\ z_{t+1} \end{pmatrix} = \begin{pmatrix} 2y_t + [y_t + (1/2)z_t]^3 - 2z_t^3 \\ y_t + (1/2)z_t \end{pmatrix}.$$

Apparently, we have only added terms of order 3 on the right-hand side. This shows that $x^* = (0, 0)^\top$ is still a fixed point, that the eigenvalues are still $1/2$ and 2, and that the eigenspace corresponding to the stable eigenvalue is still $E_s = X_j$. From theorem 3.6, it follows that there exists a one-dimensional stable manifold W_s that is tangential to E_s at the fixed point. However, since the difference equation is now non-linear, it no longer holds that $W_s = E_s$. It is easy to see that whenever $y_t = z_t^3$ it follows that $y_{t+1} = z_{t+1}^3$ and $z_{t+1} = z_t^3 + (1/2)z_t$. The latter equation is an autonomous non-linear first-order difference equation in z_t. It is straightforward to verify that $\lim_{t \to +\infty} y_t = \lim_{t \to +\infty} z_t = 0$ whenever $|z_0| < 1/\sqrt{2}$. To conclude, we have shown that the set $W_s = \{(y, z)^\top \in B_\varepsilon(x^*) \mid y = z^3\}$ is a one-dimensional stable manifold provided that ε is sufficiently small. Since the intersection of this manifold with the line $(y_0, 0)^\top + X_j$ is a singleton for every y_0, it follows that the fixed point x^* is determinate and locally saddle point stable. This example demonstrates therefore that the condition $X_j \cap E_s = \{0\}$ is not necessary for determinacy and/or local saddle point stability.

Whereas the previous example was simply meant to illustrate the fact that the conditions stated in theorem 3.7 are sufficient but not necessary, we conclude the section by an example demonstrating the economic relevance of these conditions.

Example 3.9 In example 1.6, we introduced the standard New-Keynesian model consisting of a Phillips curve, an IS-curve, and an interest rate rule. We have also shown that this model can be reduced to a system of two first-order linear difference equations for the rate of inflation π_t and the output gap y_t. Both of these variables are jump variables, that is, it holds that $n = 2$ and $\ell = 0$. Later on in example 2.5 we considered the special case in which the interest rate rule depends only on inflation and we used the (T, D)-diagram to show that there exist two unstable eigenvalues if the reaction coefficient b, which describes the sensitivity of the nominal interest rate with respect to the rate of inflation, is larger than 1. We called this condition the Taylor principle. The importance of the Taylor principle stems from the fact that it ensures that $m = 0 = \ell$. In order to be able to apply theorem 3.7(a), we need to prove that no non-zero vector of the stable eigenspace E_s is contained in the subspace X_j spanned by the jump variables. This is, however, trivial in the present case because $m = 0$ means that $E_s = \{0\}$ such that E_s does not contain any non-zero vector. Hence, the Taylor principle $b > 1$ ensures that the fixed point of the model is locally saddle point stable and determinate. Because the entire model consists of linear difference equations, local saddle point stability is in this situation equivalent to global saddle point stability.

The reader should be warned that the terminology 'saddle point stability' is not unanimously used in the literature. Quite often in economic applications it is used in the more restricted sense of a situation where exactly half of the eigenvalues of a Jacobian matrix are stable, that is, $m = n/2$. In these applications, however, it typically also holds that exactly half of the system variables are pre-determined, that is, $\ell = n/2$, so that saddle point stability is consistent with the condition $m = \ell$ referred to in theorem 3.7. The above example 3.9 is just one of many economic applications where the number of pre-determined components of the system variable differs from $n/2$. Examples like this one therefore suggest to interpret the terminology of saddle point stability in the broader sense that we have introduced in this section.

3.5 Sunspot equilibria

If a fixed point of a dynamic economic model is indeterminate, then there exist infinitely many different trajectories that stay in an arbitrarily small neighbourhood of the fixed point and converge to the latter. But this is not the entire story. There may also exist stochastic solutions of an (appropriately modified version) of the model that stay close to the fixed point. These solutions are called *sunspot equilibria*. Instead of stating theorems about the existence of sunspot equilibria, we illustrate their construction by means of examples.

Example 3.10 Consider a partial equilibrium model for a single market. Suppose that the supply on this market is constant and normalize this constant to 1. As for the demand in period t, we assume that it depends on the current market price p_t as well as on the expected future market price p_{t+1}^e. Hence, market demand in period t is given by $D(p_t, p_{t+1}^e)$, where $D : (0, +\infty)^2 \mapsto (0, +\infty)$ is a given function. Typically, it is assumed that $D(p_t, p_{t+1}^e)$ is decreasing with respect to the first argument and increasing with respect to the second one. This reflects the idea that an increase in the price p_t reduces the current demand, whereas an increase in the price forecasted for period $t + 1$ triggers an intertemporal substitution process that increases the demand in the current period t. Finally, we assume that the market participants have perfect foresight such that $p_{t+1}^e = p_{t+1}$. Hence, the market clearing condition is described by the implicit difference equation

$$D(p_t, p_{t+1}) = 1. \tag{3.9}$$

For concreteness, let us assume that $D(p, q) = p^{-\alpha} q^{\beta}$, where α and β are positive real numbers. Note that this specification satisfies the monotonicity assumption mentioned above. In this case, we can write equation (3.9) as the explicit difference equation

$$p_{t+1} = p_t^{\alpha/\beta}.$$

If $\alpha \neq \beta$, then it follows that $p^* = 1$ is a hyperbolic fixed point of this equation. The eigenvalue of the Jacobian matrix is equal to α/β. We can therefore conclude that the fixed point is stable if $\alpha < \beta$ and that it is unstable if $\alpha > \beta$.

What is the nature of the system variable p_t in this model? Since the price for goods in period t is determined in period t without any reference to events that have occurred before t, it must be the case that p_t is a jump variable. In other words, we have $n = 1$ and $\ell = 0$. As has been shown above, we have $m = 1$ if $\alpha < \beta$ and $m = 0$ if $\alpha > \beta$. From theorem 3.7, we can therefore infer that the fixed point is indeterminate if $\alpha < \beta$. Indeed, every sequence $(p_t)_{t=0}^{+\infty}$ with $p_t = p_0^{(\alpha/\beta)^t}$ and $p_0 > 0$ satisfies equation (3.9) and converges to $p^* = 1$.

We shall now show that in the indeterminate case $\alpha < \beta$, the model also admits stochastic solutions that stay close to p^*. If prices form a stochastic process, then we can obviously no longer assume that the agents have perfect foresight. The closest we can come to perfect foresight is that the agents know the probability distribution of future prices and that they form correct expectations. Thus, we assume that $p_{t+1}^e = \mathbb{E}_t(p_{t+1})$, where $\mathbb{E}_t$ is the expectations operator conditional on all the information that is available at time t. We therefore replace equation (3.9) by

$$D(p_t, \mathbb{E}_t(p_{t+1})) = p_t^{-\alpha} \left[\mathbb{E}_t(p_{t+1})\right]^{\beta} = 1. \tag{3.10}$$

Let $(\xi_t)_{t=0}^{+\infty}$ be any sequence of independent and identically distributed random variables with positive values and mean 1. That is, $\xi_t > 0$ and $\mathbb{E}_t(\xi_{t+1}) = 1$ for all $t \in \mathbb{N}_0$. Consider an arbitrary positive initial price p_0 and define the stochastic process $(p_t)_{t=0}^{+\infty}$ recursively by $p_{t+1} = p_t^{\alpha/\beta}\xi_{t+1}$. Taking logarithms, it follows that $\ln p_{t+1} = (\alpha/\beta)\ln p_t + \ln\xi_{t+1}$. This shows that the logarithms of the prices form an AR(1)-process with autocorrelation coefficient α/β. Because of the assumption $\alpha < \beta$ it follows that this process is stationary. Moreover, by the definition of p_{t+1} we have $\mathbb{E}_t(p_{t+1}) = p_t^{\alpha/\beta}$ and it follows that (3.10) holds identically for all t. Hence, we have constructed a non-trivial stationary stochastic process that satisfies the market clearing condition (3.10). Since $p_0 > 0$ was chosen arbitrarily and since the restrictions that were imposed on $(\xi_t)_{t=0}^{+\infty}$ are satisfied by many different stochastic processes, it is obvious that there exist infinitely many stochastic solutions of equation (3.10), in particular, infinitely many ones that stay arbitrarily close to the fixed point $p^* = 1$.

Before we consider other examples of sunspot equilibria, let us discuss a few points regarding example 3.10. First of all, difference equations like (3.9) occur frequently in economic models. We have already seen such equations in the cobweb model with naive expectations, example 1.5, and in the overlapping generations model in example 1.7. Whereas the system variable in the cobweb model under naive expectations is a pre-determined one, it is a jump variable in the overlapping generations economy of example 1.7. Our second remark concerns the nature of the stochastic solution to equation (3.10) that was constructed in example 3.10. Note that the stochastic process $(\xi_t)_{t=0}^{+\infty}$ has no relation to the fundamentals of the model, that is, to the specification of market supply or market demand. We call stochastic shocks that are completely unrelated to the fundamentals of the economy *extrinsic uncertainty*. The only reason why an equilibrium can depend on extrinsic uncertainty is that the agents in the economy can condition their expectations on these shock variables. This requires, of course, that the agents can observe the extrinsic shock process. The term 'sunspot equilibrium' derives from the fact that the sunspot activity on the Sun can be observed from the Earth but that it is not deemed to have any influence on the fundamentals of the economies on Earth.[8]

In the next example we briefly outline how the approach used in example 3.10 can be applied to the more complicated general equilibrium economy from example 3.7.

---

[8] The second claim can of course be disputed, but we could replace the term 'sunspot' by any other stochastic process that is observable by the economic agents and lacks a direct influence on the fundamentals of the economy.

Example 3.11 Let the basic assumptions of the overlapping generations model from example 3.7 be satisfied. If we want to allow that stochastic equilibria exist, we have to replace the assumption that the households in the model maximize their utility $-v(\ell_t) + u(c_{t+1})$ by the assumption that they maximize expected utility $-v(\ell_t) + \mathbb{E}_t u(c_{t+1})$. Here, $\mathbb{E}_t$ again denotes the expectation conditional on period-t information. It is straightforward to verify that this implies that the first-order condition is now

$$B\ell_t^{1+\eta} = \mathbb{E}_t c_{t+1}^{1-\sigma}$$

instead of $B\ell_t^{1+\eta} = c_{t+1}^{1-\sigma}$. All the other equations remain as in example 3.7. Performing operations analogous to those in example 3.7 we can show that equilibria are fully characterized by the two expectational difference equations

$$k_{t+1} = (1-\alpha)Ak_t^\alpha \ell_t^{1-\alpha}, \tag{3.11}$$

(which is identical to (3.6)) and

$$\mathbb{E}_t \ell_{t+1}^{(1-\alpha)(1-\sigma)} = C^{(1-\alpha)(1-\sigma)} k_t^{-\alpha^2(1-\sigma)} \ell_t^{1+\eta-\alpha(1-\alpha)(1-\sigma)}. \tag{3.12}$$

Now let k_0 and ℓ_0 be initial values close to the fixed point values k^* and ℓ^*, respectively, and let $(\xi_t)_{t=0}^{+\infty}$ be a sequence of independent and identically distributed random variables satisfying $\xi_t > 0$ and $\mathbb{E}_t \xi_{t+1} = 1$ for all $t \in \mathbb{N}_0$. Consider a trajectory of the stochastic difference equations (3.11) and

$$\ell_{t+1} = Ck_t^{-\alpha^2/(1-\alpha)} \ell_t^{(1+\eta)/[(1-\alpha)(1-\sigma)]-\alpha} \xi_{t+1}^{1/[(1-\alpha)(1-\sigma)]}. \tag{3.13}$$

Obviously, this trajectory is the realization of a non-trivial stochastic process. Moreover, by taking logarithms in (3.11) and (3.13) we can see that the process $(\ln k_t, \ln \ell_t)_{t=0}^{+\infty}$ is a stationary AR(1)-process if and only if the indeterminacy condition $\sigma > \bar{\sigma}$ holds. In that case, the original process $(k_t, \ell_t)_{t=0}^{+\infty}$ must also be stationary. Finally, by raising both sides in equation (3.13) to the power $(1-\alpha)(1-\sigma)$ and using $\mathbb{E}_t \xi_{t+1} = 1$ it is easily seen that this stochastic process also satisfies (3.12). Thus, it qualifies as an equilibrium.

Our final example of a sunspot equilibrium is based on a different construction. More specifically, we construct a sunspot equilibrium that takes the form of a finite Markov chain.

Example 3.12 Consider the monetary overlapping generations model introduced in example 1.7. In order to allow for stochastic equilibria, we assume that the agents maximize their expected utility $-v(y_t) + \mathbb{E}_t u(c_{t+1})$. Following the arguments from example 1.7, it is straightforward to verify that the equilibrium dynamics are completely described by the implicit expectational difference equation

$$V(y_t) = \mathbb{E}_t U(y_{t+1}),$$

where the only system variable y_t is a jump variable, that is, $n = 1$ and $\ell = 0$. For the purpose of the present example, let us choose the cost and utility functions $v(y) = \beta y^2 / 2$ and $u(y) = -e^{-\alpha y}$, where α and β are positive constants. This yields $V(y) = yv'(y) = \beta y^2$ and $U(y) = yu'(y) = \alpha y e^{-\alpha y}$, respectively. Moreover, to simplify the algebra we assume that $\beta = \alpha e^{-\alpha}$. Substituting these specifications into the equilibrium condition from above, we obtain

$$y_t^2 = \mathbb{E}_t y_{t+1} e^{\alpha(1-y_{t+1})}. \tag{3.14}$$

Before we construct sunspot equilibria, we need to check under which assumptions there exists an indeterminate fixed point of the deterministic model. Equilibria in the deterministic model are solutions of the implicit difference equation

$$y_t^2 = y_{t+1} e^{\alpha(1-y_{t+1})}.$$

It is easy to see that $y^* = 1$ is a fixed point of this equation. Suppose that the equation can be made explicit in the form $y_{t+1} = f(x_t)$ (at least locally around the fixed point). This will be the case if and only if the function f satisfies

$$y^2 = f(y) e^{\alpha[1-f(y)]}$$

for all y in a neighbourhood of the fixed point $y^* = 1$. By totally differentiating this equation with respect to y and using $f(y^*) = y^* = 1$, we obtain $f'(y^*) = 2/(1-\alpha)$. Due to the implicit function theorem, these calculations are correct and the function f is locally well-defined and differentiable as long as $\alpha \neq 1$, which we henceforth assume. Local asymptotic stability of y^* is ensured whenever $|f'(y^*)| < 1$, which is equivalent to $\alpha > 3$. In this case, we have $m = 1 > \ell = 0$ and it follows from theorem 3.7(b) that $y^* = 1$ is an indeterminate fixed point.

Let us now return to the stochastic difference equation (3.14). We want to show that whenever the indeterminacy condition $\alpha > 3$ is satisfied, there exists a finite Markov chain with state space $\{A, B\}$ and transition probabilities $\pi_{ij} = \mathbb{P}(y_{t+1} = j \mid y_t = i)$ for $\{i, j\} = \{A, B\}$ that satisfies equation (3.14). This amounts to verifying that there exist real numbers $A > 0$, $B > 0$, $\pi_A \in (0, 1)$, and $\pi_B \in (0, 1)$ with $A \neq B$ such that the two equations

$$A^2 = \pi_A A e^{\alpha(1-A)} + (1-\pi_A)B e^{\alpha(1-B)} \quad \text{and} \quad B^2 = \pi_B B e^{\alpha(1-B)} + (1-\pi_B)A e^{\alpha(1-A)}$$

$$\tag{3.15}$$

hold. Here, we have simplified the notation by writing π_i and $1 - \pi_i$ instead of π_{ii} and π_{ij}, respectively. We will first show that whenever $\alpha > 3$, there exist distinct positive

Difference equations

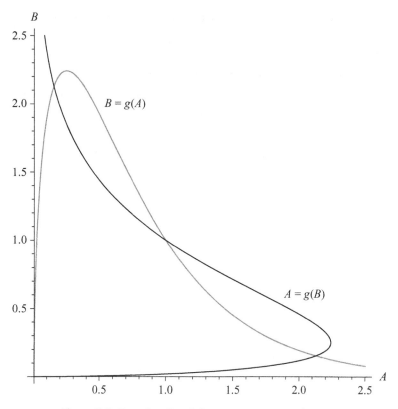

Figure 3.5 Equation (3.15) for $\pi_A = \pi_B = 0$ and $\alpha = 4$

numbers A and B that solve (3.15) when $\pi_A = \pi_B = 0$. Then we will show that this solution to (3.15) is robust against small perturbations of π_A and π_B.

If $\pi_A = \pi_B = 0$, equation (3.15) collapses to $A = g(B)$ and $B = g(A)$, where $g : \mathbb{R}_+ \mapsto \mathbb{R}_+$ is defined by $g(z) = e^{(\alpha/2)(1-z)}\sqrt{z}$. The graphs of these two curves are shown in figure 3.5 for $\alpha = 4$. They have three intersections: one is at the point $(A, B) = (1, 1)$, which corresponds to the deterministic fixed point of the model, and two further intersections occur at points where $A \neq B$. To show that the graphs intersect in that way whenever $\alpha > 3$, note that the slope of the curve $B = g(A)$ at the point $A = B = 1$ is given by $g'(1) = (1 - \alpha)/2$. This is smaller than -1 if and only if $\alpha > 3$. By symmetry, the slope of the curve $A = g(B)$ at $A = B = 1$ must be larger than -1 if and only if $\alpha > 3$. These properties imply that for $\alpha > 3$ the curve $B = g(A)$ intersects the curve $A = g(B)$ at the point $(A, B) = (1, 1)$ from above. Because both curves are continuous, start in the origin of the diagram, and approach the axes $B = 0$ and $A = 0$ as A, respectively, B approach $+\infty$, it is clear that there must be at least two intersections in addition to the one at $A = B = 1$.

Note that the assumption $\pi_A = \pi_B = 0$ implies that the Markov chain is degenerate and that the system variable y_t therefore alternates periodically between the two values A and B. In other words, what we have shown so far is that there exist deterministic but periodic equilibria. Let us now consider the case where π_A and π_B become positive. Because the right-hand sides of the equations in (3.15) are smooth functions of all variables A, B, π_A, and π_B, the diagram in figure 3.5 remains qualitatively the same if π_A and π_B are slightly perturbed to become positive. This proves that equation (3.15) has a solution as required above. This solution defines a non-degenerate Markov chain which satisfies equation (3.14) and, hence, it qualifies as a sunspot equilibrium.

3.6 EXERCISES

EXERCISE 3.1 Determine all fixed points and all periodic points of period 2 of the difference equation $x_{t+1} = f(x_t)$ on the system domain X:
(a) $X = \mathbb{R}$, $f(x) = 1 - x$.
(b) $X = \mathbb{R}$, $f(x) = 1 - x^2$.
(c) $X = [0, +\infty)$, $f(x) = A/(1 + x)$ with $A > 0$.
(d) $X = \mathbb{R}^2$, $f(x, y) = (1 - y, 1 - x^2)$.

EXERCISE 3.2 Consider the difference equation $x_{t+1} = f(x_t)$ on the system domain $X \subseteq \mathbb{R}^n$. The ω-limit set of $x \in X$ is the set of all points $y \in X$ for which there exists a strictly increasing sequence $(t_k)_{k=1}^{+\infty}$ with $\lim_{k \to +\infty} f^{(t_k)}(x) = y$. Prove that the ω-limit set of x is invariant under f provided that f is continuous.

EXERCISE 3.3 Consider the difference equation $x_{t+1} = x_t e^{\lambda - x_t}$, where the system domain is $X = [0, +\infty)$ and where λ is a positive parameter.
(a) Determine all fixed points of this difference equation.
(b) Linearize the difference equation in each of its fixed points.
(c) Prove that the difference equation has a periodic point of period 2 whenever $\lambda > 2$.

EXERCISE 3.4 Let the system domain be $X = (0, +\infty)^2$ and let a and λ be real numbers satisfying $a \in (0, 2)$ and $\lambda > 0$. Define the functions $f : X \mapsto (0, +\infty)$ and $g : X \mapsto (0, +\infty)$ by

$$f(x, y) = \frac{x(1 - y)}{(1 + x)(x + y)} \quad \text{and} \quad g(x, y) = \frac{(x - a)y + (1 - a)x}{(1 + y)(x + y)}$$

and consider the following system of difference equations defined on X:

$$x_{t+1} = x_t + \lambda f(x_t, y_t) \quad \text{and} \quad y_{t+1} = y_t + \lambda g(x_t, y_t).$$

(a) Determine the unique fixed point of the system and compute the Jacobian matrix J at that fixed point.

(b) Show that there exist functions $c : (0, 2) \mapsto \mathbb{R}$ and $d : (0, 2) \mapsto \mathbb{R}$ such that the trace and the determinant of J can be written as $T = 2 + c(a)\lambda$ and $D = 1 + c(a)\lambda + d(a)\lambda^2$. Show that $d(a) > 0$ holds for all $a \in (0, 2)$.

(c) Use the (T, D)-diagram to show that the fixed point is unstable whenever $a \in [1, 2)$ and that it is locally asymptotically stable whenever $a \in (0, 1)$ and λ is sufficiently small.

EXERCISE 3.5 Consider the two-player normal form game in which player 1 chooses $x \in \mathbb{R}$ to maximize $U(x, y) = axy - x^2/2$, whereas player 2 chooses $y \in \mathbb{R}$ so as to maximize $V(x, y) = bxy - y^2/2$. Here, a and b are non-zero constants satisfying $ab \neq 1$. Assume that in every period t both players choose the best response to the actions taken by their respective opponents in the previous period $t - 1$.

(a) Show that there exists a unique fixed point of the best response dynamics.

(b) Under which conditions for the parameters a and b is the fixed point stable with respect to the best response dynamics?

EXERCISE 3.6 Suppose that there exist two populations, one is a predator the other one the prey. The size of the predator population at time t is denoted by x_t and the size of the prey population by y_t. The gross growth rate of the predator population is a linearly increasing function of the prey population, namely

$$\frac{x_{t+1}}{x_t} = a + by_t,$$

where both a and b are positive parameters and where $a < 1$. The prey population is assumed to evolve according to

$$y_{t+1} = \frac{\sqrt{y_t}}{1 + x_t}.$$

(a) What happens to the predator population in the long run if there is no prey, that is, if $y_t = 0$ holds for all t? What happens to the prey population in the long run if there are no predators, that is, if $x_t = 0$ holds for all t?

(b) For which parameter constellations do there exist population levels $x^* > 0$ and $y^* > 0$ that can be sustained forever? Interpret this parameter assumption intuitively.

(c) For which parameter constellations is the fixed point (x^*, y^*) locally asymptotically stable?

EXERCISE 3.7 Consider the New-Keynesian model introduced in example 1.6 and assume that the central bank chooses a constant interest rate, that is, the reaction coefficients b and c are equal to 0.

(a) Determine the unique fixed point of the model and show that it is indeterminate. Is the Taylor principle satisfied?

(b) Now replace the forward-looking variables π_{t+1} and y_{t+1} in the IS-curve and the Phillips curve by their expected values $\mathbb{E}_t(\pi_{t+1})$ and $\mathbb{E}_t(y_{t+1})$, respectively. Furthermore, choose the parameter values $\alpha = 1/2$, $\beta = \gamma = 1$, and $a = 0$. Let $(\xi_t)_{t=0}^{+\infty}$ be an AR(1) process satisfying $\xi_{t+1} = \xi_t/2 + \varepsilon_{t+1}$, where $(\varepsilon_t)_{t=0}^{+\infty}$ is a sequence of independent and identically distributed random variables. Show that the stochastic processes $(\pi_t)_{t=0}^{+\infty}$ and $(y_t)_{t=0}^{+\infty}$ defined by $\pi_t = y_t = \xi_t$ satisfy the equilibrium conditions.

EXERCISE 3.8 Reconsider the model from exercise 2.4. Which of the two system variables π_t and y_t is pre-determined in this model and which one is a jump variable? For which values of b is the fixed point determinate and locally saddle point stable? What is the relevance of the Taylor principle $b > 1$ in this model?

3.7 COMMENTS AND REFERENCES

Fixed points, periodic points, and invariant sets are basic concepts from the topological theory of dynamical systems; see, for example, Brin and Stuck [14] or Katok and Hasselblatt [46]. The fixed point theorems by Brouwer and Banach that are referred to in the proof of theorem 3.1 are among the most useful results in mathematics and have numerous applications; see, for example, Agarwal *et al.* [2].

Local linearization methods are ubiquitous in economics. The Hartman–Grobman theorem, which forms the basis for many of them, is discussed, for example, in Katok and Hasselblatt [46]. The definitions of stability and asymptotic stability presented in section 3.3 are the standard definitions used in dynamical systems theory. As mentioned in section 3.4, they are appropriate only for systems in which all variables are pre-determined. In economics, we often encounter systems including jump variables for which the notion of saddle point stability is more appropriate. The stable–unstable manifold theorem (theorem 3.6) that we used to derive conditions for saddle point stability is also known as the Hadamard–Perron theorem; see Katok and Hasselblatt [46]. A standard reference for Lyapunov's direct method as described in theorems 3.4 and 3.5 is LaSalle and Lefschetz [56].

Early examples of sunspot equilibria (that is, equilibria depending on extrinsic uncertainty) can be found in Azariadis [4] and Cass and Shell [18]. Our presentation is closer to the paper by Azariadis [4], which uses the construction described in example 3.12. Azariadis and Guesnerie [6] show that this construction works whenever the deterministic model admits periodic equilibria close to the steady state. The relation between indeterminacy of a fixed point and the existence of stationary sunspot equilibria in the neighbourhood of such a fixed point is explored in great detail by Laitner [54] and Woodford [95]. The implications of the existence of indeterminate equilibria in the New-Keynesian model from example 3.9 and exercise 3.7 are discussed in Galí [34]; see also Bullard and Mitra [15].

4 One-dimensional maps

In this chapter, we return to the topic where we started our journey into the realm of dynamic economic analysis, namely to one-dimensional maps. Whereas we used this class of models in section 1.1 to introduce some of the basic concepts of difference equations, we shall now explore them in more detail.

There exist certain results which hold true for one-dimensional maps but fail to be true in higher-dimensional settings. For example, we can easily establish monotonicity properties of the trajectories of one-dimensional maps with a monotonic law of motion. We discuss these results in section 4.1. One-dimensional maps with non-monotonic system dynamics, on the other hand, can exhibit surprisingly complicated trajectories. A first hint at these properties will be provided in section 4.2, where we discuss local bifurcations of fixed points, that is, situations where an arbitrarily small variation of a model parameter changes the qualitative structure of the solutions. Finally, in section 4.3 we introduce the concept of deterministic chaos and state a number of results that can be used to prove that the solutions of a one-dimensional map are chaotic. The possible occurrence of all of these phenomena in economic models is illustrated by examples.

4.1 Monotonic maps

Let $X \subseteq \mathbb{R}$ be an interval on the real line and let $f : X \mapsto X$ be a given function. The autonomous difference equation

$$x_{t+1} = f(x_t) \tag{4.1}$$

on the system domain X is called a *one-dimensional map*. If the function f is monotonic, the dynamics generated by (4.1) cannot become very complicated. This is the essence of the following lemma.

Difference equations

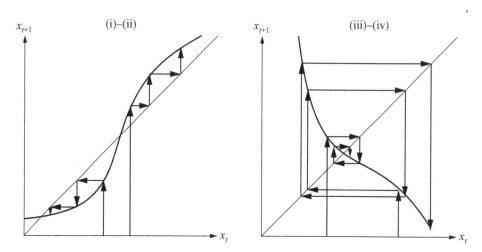

Figure 4.1 Dynamics of monotonic one-dimensional maps

Lemma 4.1 Let $(x_t)_{t=0}^{+\infty}$ be any trajectory of the difference equation (4.1).

(a) If f is non-decreasing on X, then it follows that the trajectory $(x_t)_{t=0}^{+\infty}$ is monotonic.

(b) If f is non-increasing on X, then it follows that the sequences $(x_{2t})_{t=0}^{+\infty}$ and $(x_{2t+1})_{t=0}^{+\infty}$ are monotonic. Moreover, if $(x_{2t})_{t=0}^{+\infty}$ is non-decreasing, then it follows that $(x_{2t+1})_{t=0}^{+\infty}$ is non-increasing and vice versa.

PROOF: (a) Assume first that $x_0 \leq x_1$. Since f is non-decreasing, this implies that $x_1 = f(x_0) \leq f(x_1) = x_2$. Continuing in this fashion, we can show that $x_t \leq x_{t+1}$ holds for all $t \in \mathbb{N}_0$ and it follows that the trajectory $(x_t)_{t=0}^{+\infty}$ is non-decreasing. Using analogous arguments, we can show that $x_0 \geq x_1$ implies that the trajectory starting at x_0 is non-increasing. Consequently, every trajectory has to be monotonic.

(b) Define $g : X \mapsto X$ by $g = f^{(2)}$. Since f is non-increasing, it follows that g is non-decreasing. Moreover, if $(x_t)_{t=0}^{+\infty}$ is a trajectory of (4.1), then it follows that both $(x_{2t})_{t=0}^{+\infty}$ and $(x_{2t+1})_{t=0}^{+\infty}$ are trajectories of the difference equation $y_{t+1} = g(y_t)$. Applying the result from part (a) to the latter difference equation yields the first result stated in part (b). If $(x_{2t})_{t=0}^{+\infty}$ is non-decreasing, then we have $x_{2t} \leq x_{2t+2}$ and, hence

$$x_{2t+1} = f(x_{2t}) \geq f(x_{2t+2}) = x_{2t+3},$$

where we have used the fact that f is non-increasing. This proves that $(x_{2t+1})_{t=0}^{+\infty}$ is non-increasing.

Lemma 4.1 allows only the following four types of trajectories for one-dimensional difference equations with a monotonic right-hand side: (i) non-decreasing trajectories, (ii) non-increasing trajectories, (iii) non-contracting period-two oscillations, and

(iv) non-expanding period-two oscillations. These four types of trajectories are illustrated in figure 4.1. Note that types (iii) and (iv) can only occur if the function f is non-increasing, and that a single difference equation of the form (4.1) can have trajectories of two different types simultaneously, namely either of types (i) and (ii) if f is non-decreasing or of types (iii) and (iv) if f is non-increasing. This is also shown in figure 4.1.

Note that lemma 4.1 does not require any assumptions on the law of motion f, except for its monotonicity. In the following result, we add more assumptions that allow us to prove the convergence of the trajectories.

Lemma 4.2   Let $(x_t)_{t=0}^{+\infty}$ be a trajectory of the difference equation (4.1), where f is a non-decreasing function on X. If X is compact, then it follows that $x^* = \lim_{t \to +\infty} x_t$ exists and that $x^* \in X$. If, in addition, f is continuous, then it follows that x^* is a fixed point of (4.1).

PROOF: From lemma 4.1, we know that the trajectory $(x_t)_{t=0}^{+\infty}$ is monotonic. Because this trajectory stays in the compact set X, it must have a limit $x^* \in X$. Furthermore, if f is continuous, then it follows that

$$x^* = \lim_{t \to +\infty} x_{t+1} = \lim_{t \to +\infty} f(x_t) = f(\lim_{t \to +\infty} x_t) = f(x^*),$$

which proves that x^* is a fixed point.

To see that the additional assumption of compactness is necessary for the validity of the first statement of the above lemma, consider, for example, the one-dimensional map $x_{t+1} = 1 + x_t$ on the non-compact system domain $X = \mathbb{R}_+$. The trajectory starting in $x_0 \in X$ is given by $x_t = x_0 + t$ and it is obvious that it does not converge. To see that continuity of f is required for the limit to be a fixed point, consider the difference equation

$$x_{t+1} = \begin{cases} \dfrac{1 + 2x_t}{4} & \text{if } x_t \in [0, 1/2), \\[2mm] \dfrac{1 + x_t}{2} & \text{if } x_t \in [1/2, 1], \end{cases}$$

defined on the system domain $X = [0, 1]$. Since X is compact and f is non-decreasing, every trajectory must converge to a limit in X. For example, if $x_0 = 0$, then we obtain $x_t = (1/2) - (1/2)^{t+1}$, which converges to $x^* = 1/2$ as t approaches infinity. However, $f(x^*) = f(1/2) = 3/4$ such that x^* does not qualify as a fixed point.

The next result is analogous to lemma 4.2, but it applies to non-increasing one-dimensional maps rather than to non-decreasing ones. Its proof is very similar to that of lemma 4.2 and is therefore left as an exercise.

Lemma 4.3 Let $(x_t)_{t=0}^{+\infty}$ be a trajectory of the difference equation (4.1), where f is a non-increasing function on X.

(a) If X is compact, then it follows that $x_e^* = \lim_{t \to +\infty} x_{2t}$ and $x_o^* = \lim_{t \to +\infty} x_{2t+1}$ exist and that $\{x_e^*, x_o^*\} \subseteq X$.

(b) Suppose in addition to compactness of X that f is continuous. If $x_e^* \neq x_o^*$, then it follows that $\{x_e^*, x_o^*\}$ is a periodic orbit of period 2 of the difference equation (4.1). If $x_e^* = x_o^*$, then it follows that x_e^* is a fixed point of (4.1).

We conclude this section by pointing out the wide applicability of the results presented above. All three examples of one-dimensional maps considered in section 1.1 are strictly increasing maps for which the results from lemma 4.1(a) and lemma 4.2 apply. This includes, in particular, the Solow–Swan growth model from example 1.1 and the replicator dynamics of the simple coordination game in example 1.2. Another example of an increasing one-dimensional map arises in the overlapping generations economy from example 1.7 when the elasticity of marginal utility of consumption, σ, is constant and smaller than 1; see figure 1.7. Examples of decreasing one-dimensional maps are the cobweb model under naive expectation (see equation (1.8) and figure 1.5) or the overlapping generations economy from example 1.7 when σ is constant and larger than 1 (see figure 1.6).

4.2 Local bifurcations

In this section, we consider parametric families of one-dimensional difference equations. We continue to denote the system variable by $x \in \mathbb{R}$ and we introduce a real-valued parameter $\mu \in \mathbb{R}$, which we call the *bifurcation parameter*. The difference equation under consideration is therefore

$$x_{t+1} = f(x_t, \mu). \tag{4.2}$$

We are interested in how the qualitative behaviour of the trajectories and orbits of (4.2) changes as the bifurcation parameter μ varies. In the overlapping generations economy from example 1.7, for instance, the role of the bifurcation parameter could be played by the elasticity of marginal utility σ because, as we have already seen, the equilibrium dynamics can exhibit qualitatively different patterns as σ is smaller than, equal to, or larger than 1.

In general, a *bifurcation* denotes a qualitative change of the orbit structure of a difference equation when the bifurcation parameter passes a critical value. We restrict the attention to *local* bifurcations, which occur when the trajectories in an arbitrarily small neighbourhood of a fixed point undergo such a change. Furthermore, we consider only those bifurcations that change the long-run behaviour of the trajectories.

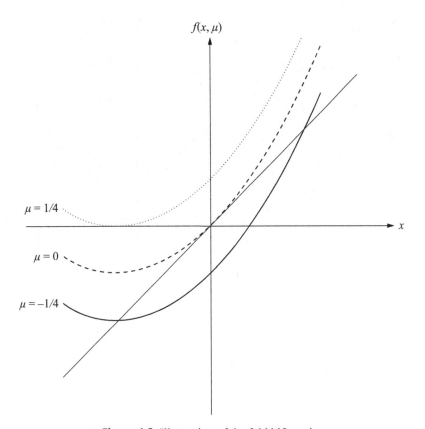

Figure 4.2 Illustration of the fold bifurcation

To simplify the presentation, we assume that a coordinate transformation has been performed such that equation (4.2) has the fixed point $x = 0$ when the parameter value is $\mu = 0$. In other words, we assume that $f(0, 0) = 0$. Moreover, we assume that the function f is continuously differentiable such that the stability of the fixed point 0 (when $\mu = 0$) is determined by the partial derivative $f_1(0, 0)$.[1] We know that the stability of the fixed point can only change when the partial derivative $f_1(0, 0)$ has the absolute value 1. Thus, there are only two possible cases in which a local bifurcation in the sense defined above can occur: it must either hold that $f_1(0, 0) = 1$ or that $f_1(0, 0) = -1$. Let us deal with these two cases in turn.

Consider, for example, the system dynamics $f(x, \mu) = \mu + x + x^2$. The graph of the function $x \mapsto f(x, \mu)$ is depicted in figure 4.2 for $\mu = -1/4$ (lower parabola), $\mu = 0$ (middle parabola), and $\mu = 1/4$ (upper parabola). The figure shows also the

---

[1] Recall that we denote partial derivatives by subscripts. Thus, $f_1(0, 0)$ is the partial derivative of the function $f(x, \mu)$ with respect to its first argument x evaluated at the point $(x, \mu) = (0, 0)$. Higher order partial derivatives will be denoted by multiple subscripts. For example, $f_{11}(a, b) = \partial^2 f(x, \mu)/\partial x^2|_{(x,\mu)=(a,b)}$, $f_{12}(a, b) = \partial^2 f(x, \mu)/(\partial x \partial \mu)|_{(x,\mu)=(a,b)}$, and $f_{111}(a, b) = \partial^3 f(x, \mu)/\partial x^3|_{(x,\mu)=(a,b)}$.

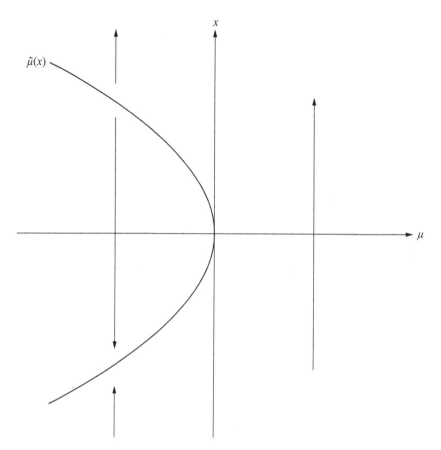

Figure 4.3 Bifurcation diagram for the fold bifurcation

45° diagonal so that fixed points of (4.2) can be determined as the intersection points of the graphs with the diagonal. It is clearly visible that there are two fixed points whenever $\mu < 0$. Graphical analysis also shows that the negative fixed point is locally asymptotically stable (at least for values of μ that are negative but sufficiently close to 0), whereas the positive one is unstable. As μ increases and becomes equal to 0, these two fixed points collapse into a single one. For parameter values $\mu > 0$, no fixed points exist. This scenario is called a *fold bifurcation*. Alternative names are saddle-node bifurcation or tangent bifurcation. It is quite obvious that the structure of the orbits changes dramatically as μ passes through its critical value 0. We can illustrate this also in a so-called *bifurcation diagram*. Such a diagram is drawn in (μ, x)-space, and shows how the fixed points depend on the bifurcation parameter. The bifurcation diagram for the fold bifurcation is shown in figure 4.3. The bold parabola is the set of all fixed points. Again we can see that there are two fixed points for negative values of μ, a single fixed point for $\mu = 0$, and no fixed points for $\mu > 0$. The vertical arrows in the figure indicate the direction of the trajectories, which can be derived from a graphical analysis in figure 4.2.

The following theorem states the conditions under which a fold bifurcation occurs in a general difference equation of the form (4.2).

Theorem 4.1 Consider the difference equation (4.2) with system domain $X \subseteq \mathbb{R}$ and bifurcation parameter $\mu \in \mathbb{R}$. Suppose that there exists an open set U such that $0 \in U \subseteq X$ and such that f is twice continuously differentiable on $U \times \mathbb{R}$. Assume furthermore that

$$f(0, 0) = 0, \quad f_1(0, 0) = 1, \quad f_2(0, 0) > 0, \quad f_{11}(0, 0) > 0.$$

Then there exist real numbers $\varepsilon > 0$, $\mu_1 < 0$, and $\mu_2 > 0$ such that the following properties hold:

(a) For all $\mu \in (\mu_1, 0)$, equation (4.2) has two fixed points in $(-\varepsilon, \varepsilon)$. One of these fixed points is negative and locally asymptotically stable, the other one is positive and unstable.

(b) For all $\mu \in (0, \mu_2)$, equation (4.2) has no fixed point in $(-\varepsilon, \varepsilon)$.

(c) If, instead of $f_{11}(0, 0) > 0$, it holds that $f_{11}(0, 0) < 0$, then the roles of the intervals $(\mu_1, 0)$ and $(0, \mu_2)$ are reversed: for $\mu \in (\mu_1, 0)$ there are no fixed points, whereas for $\mu \in (0, \mu_2)$ there exist a positive and locally asymptotically stable fixed point and a negative and unstable one.

PROOF: We only prove the theorem for the case where $f_{11}(0, 0) > 0$. The case where the converse inequality holds (part (c) of the theorem) can be proved analogously. Defining the function $g(x, \mu) = f(x, \mu) - x$, the fixed point condition can be written as $g(x, \mu) = 0$. Because of $g_2(0, 0) = f_2(0, 0) \neq 0$, the implicit function theorem implies the existence of $\varepsilon > 0$ and a twice continuously differentiable function $\tilde{\mu} : (-\varepsilon, \varepsilon) \mapsto \mathbb{R}$ such that $\tilde{\mu}(0) = 0$ and

$$g(x, \tilde{\mu}(x)) = 0 \tag{4.3}$$

for all $x \in (-\varepsilon, \varepsilon)$. The graph of the function $\tilde{\mu}$ is the parabolic curve shown in the bifurcation diagram in figure 4.3. Differentiating (4.3) with respect to x and evaluating at $x = 0$ yields

$$g_1(0, 0) + g_2(0, 0)\tilde{\mu}'(0) = 0.$$

Because of $g_1(0, 0) = f_1(0, 0) - 1 = 0$ and $g_2(0, 0) = f_2(0, 0) > 0$, this implies $\tilde{\mu}'(0) = 0$. Differentiating (4.3) twice with respect to x, evaluating at $x = 0$, and

Difference equations

using $\tilde{\mu}'(0) = 0$ yields

$$g_{11}(0, 0) + g_2(0, 0)\tilde{\mu}''(0) = 0.$$

Because of $g_{11}(0, 0) = f_{11}(0, 0) > 0$ and $g_2(0, 0) = f_2(0, 0) > 0$, it follows that $\tilde{\mu}''(0) < 0$. We conclude that the function $\tilde{\mu}$ has a local maximum at $x = 0$ and that it is strictly negative for all $x \in (-\varepsilon, \varepsilon) \setminus \{0\}$. This proves part (b) of the theorem as well as half of part (a).

It remains to determine the stability of the fixed points when $\mu \in (\mu_1, 0)$. Consider first the case of a positive fixed point, and denote this fixed point by x. Apparently, we must have $\tilde{\mu}'(x) < 0$. Differentiating the fixed point condition $f(x, \tilde{\mu}(x)) = x$ with respect to x yields

$$f_1(x, \tilde{\mu}(x)) + f_2(x, \tilde{\mu}(x))\tilde{\mu}'(x) = 1.$$

Because of $\tilde{\mu}'(x) < 0$ and $f_2(0, 0) > 0$, we must have $f_1(x, \tilde{\mu}(x)) > 1$ for all positive x that are sufficiently close to 0. This proves that the positive fixed point x is unstable. In a completely analogous way, we can show that the negative fixed point is stable.

Let us add some remarks on the conditions of this theorem. The assumption $f(0, 0) = 0$ ensures that $x = 0$ is a fixed point at the critical value of μ. This is simply a matter of normalization. The condition $f_1(0, 0) = 1$ implies that this fixed point is non-hyperbolic. In other words, a local linearization of (4.2) around its fixed point $x = 0$ is insufficient to determine the qualitative behaviour of its trajectories. This is the case because the orbit structure around the fixed point changes in a qualitative way as the bifurcation parameter μ passes through its critical value. The condition $f_2(0, 0) > 0$ is also mostly a normalization. What is important is that this partial derivative is non-zero. If the sign of $f_2(0, 0)$ were negative, we could simply consider $-\mu$ as the bifurcation parameter rather than μ, and the condition would hold as stated in the theorem. Finally, the sign of $f_{11}(0, 0)$ determines in which direction the parabolic curve in the bifurcation diagram in figure 4.3 points. In the situation described in parts (a) and (b) of the theorem, the parabola is open to the left and the two fixed points occur for negative values of μ. In the case dealt with in part (c) of the theorem, the parabola is open to the right and the fixed points exist for positive values of μ. In other words, changing the sign of $f_{11}(0, 0)$ does not affect the existence of the fold bifurcation but simply reverses the roles of the two intervals $(\mu_1, 0)$ and $(0, \mu_2)$.

The following example illustrates how a fold bifurcation occurs in a model of natural resource dynamics.

Example 4.1 Consider a fish population that evolves according to the dynamics

$$z_{t+1} = z_t^2(K - z_t), \tag{4.4}$$

where z_t is the population size and K is the carrying capacity of the habitat. It is straightforward to verify that whenever $K \in (0, (3/2)\sqrt{3}]$ and $z_0 \in [0, K]$, then $z_t \in [0, K]$ holds for all $t \in \mathbb{N}_0$. Let us specifically consider the parameter value $K = 2$, for which it is easy to see that $z^* = 1$ qualifies as a fixed point of the above difference equation. We shall now show that at $K = 2$ a fold bifurcation takes place.

To this end, we first rewrite the difference equation in the variables $x_t = z_t - 1$ and $\mu = K - 2$. This yields

$$x_{t+1} = f(x_t, \mu) = (1 + x_t)^2(1 + \mu - x_t) - 1.$$

Obviously, we have $f(0, 0) = 0$ and $f_1(0, 0) = 1$. Furthermore, it holds that $f_2(0, 0) = 1 > 0$ and $f_{11}(0, 0) = -2 < 0$. Hence, the conditions of theorem 4.1(c) are satisfied and it follows that a fold bifurcation occurs at the critical value $K = 2$. More specifically, for $K < 2$ (which corresponds to $\mu < 0$) there are no fixed points, whereas for $K > 2$ there are two of them with the larger one being locally asymptotically stable and the smaller one being unstable.

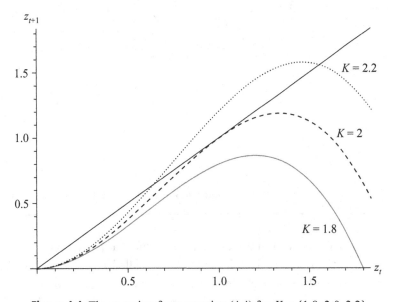

Figure 4.4 The mapping from equation (4.4) for $K \in \{1.8, 2.0, 2.2\}$

The effect of the fold bifurcation in this example is illustrated in figure 4.4, which depicts the dynamics of equation (4.4) for the three parameter values $K = 1.8$, $K = 2$, and $K = 2.2$. We see that for a carrying capacity K that is smaller than 2, there exists no positive fixed point and the population will become extinct from every initial value z_0. For $K > 2$, on the other hand, there exist two positive fixed points, as predicted by the fold bifurcation theorem. The smaller one, say z_1^*, is unstable and the larger one, z_2^*, is locally asymptotically stable. If the initial value z_0 is smaller than z_1^*, then the population size will converge to 0. If $z_0 > z_1^*$ (and if z_0 is not too large), however, then we obtain $\lim_{t \to +\infty} z_t = z_2^*$. Thus, the value of the smaller fixed point, z_1^*, serves as a threshold for the population size above which survival is possible.

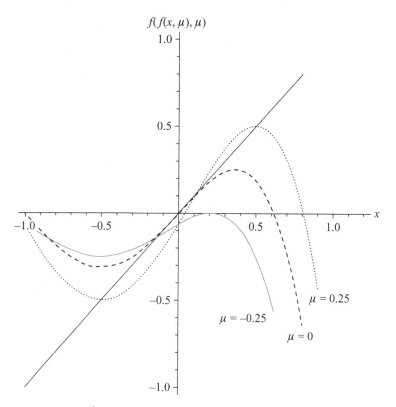

Figure 4.5 Illustration of the flip bifurcation

We now turn to the case in which a fixed point is non-hyperbolic because $f_1(0, 0) = -1$. This leads to the so-called *flip bifurcation*. We start again with an example. Consider the system dynamics $f(x, \mu) = \mu - x - x^2$. Drawing the graph of this function for different parameter values is not as helpful as it was in the case of the fold bifurcation. However, the nature of the flip bifurcation is easily revealed by drawing the graph of the second iterate of f, that is, the graph of the mapping $x \mapsto f^{(2)}(x, \mu) = f(f(x, \mu), \mu)$, for three different parameter values. This is done in figure 4.5 for $\mu \in \{-1/4, 0, 1/4\}$. To interpret this figure just recall that intersections of the graph of $f^{(2)}$ with the 45° line correspond to fixed points of the difference equation

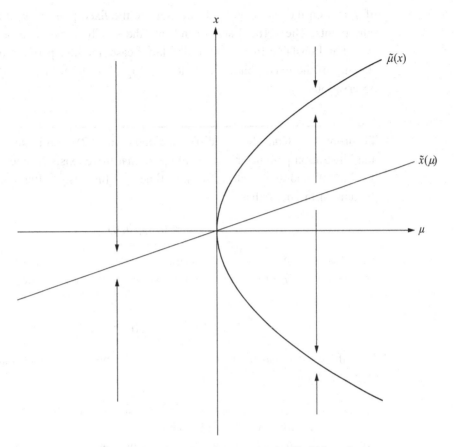

Figure 4.6 Bifurcation diagram for the flip bifurcation

$x_{t+1} = f^{(2)}(x_t, \mu)$. According to lemma 3.2(b), such a point must be a fixed point of the original difference equation (4.2) or it must be a periodic point of period 2 of (4.2). For $\mu = -1/4$, we see from figure 4.5 that the graph of $f^{(2)}$ intersects the 45° line at a single point, and that the slope of the graph at this intersection is smaller than 1 in absolute value. It is not difficult to show that this intersection corresponds to a locally asymptotically stable fixed point of (4.2). As μ increases towards the critical value 0, the slope of f at the fixed point approaches -1 and the slope of $f^{(2)}$ at this point approaches 1. At the critical value $\mu = 0$, the fixed point is therefore non-hyperbolic. When μ becomes positive, the graph of $f^{(2)}$ intersects the 45° line at two additional points. A careful examination reveals that these two intersections do not correspond to fixed points of (4.2). Appealing again to lemma 3.2(b), it follows that they form a pair of periodic points of period 2. Thus, the flip bifurcation generates a period-two cycle.

The bifurcation diagram for the flip bifurcation discussed above is shown in figure 4.6. On the left-hand side of this diagram, we can see the single fixed point of f and on the right-hand side we can see the fixed point as well as the two periodic points. The vertical arrows indicate the stability: the fixed point is stable for $\mu < 0$ and unstable for $\mu > 0$. In the latter case, the new periodic orbit inherits the stability of the fixed point. The following flip bifurcation theorem generalizes these observations.

Theorem 4.2 Consider the difference equation (4.2) with system domain $X \subseteq \mathbb{R}$ and bifurcation parameter $\mu \in \mathbb{R}$. Suppose that there exists an open set U such that $0 \in U \subseteq X$ and such that f is three times continuously differentiable on $U \times \mathbb{R}$. Assume furthermore that

$$f(0, 0) = 0, \quad f_1(0, 0) = -1.$$

Then there exist $\delta > 0$ and a unique function $\tilde{x} : (-\delta, \delta) \mapsto \mathbb{R}$ satisfying $\tilde{x}(0) = 0$ and $f(\tilde{x}(\mu), \mu) = \tilde{x}(\mu)$ for all $\mu \in (-\delta, \delta)$. Now define $h(\mu) = f_1(\tilde{x}(\mu), \mu)$ and assume that

$$h'(0) < 0, \quad f_{111}^{(2)}(0, 0) < 0.$$

Then there exist real numbers $\varepsilon > 0$, $\mu_1 < 0$, and $\mu_2 > 0$ such that the following properties hold:

(a) For all $\mu \in (\mu_1, 0)$, equation (4.2) has a unique fixed point in $(-\varepsilon, \varepsilon)$. This fixed point is locally asymptotically stable.

(b) For all $\mu \in (0, \mu_2)$, equation (4.2) has a unique fixed point and a unique periodic orbit of period 2 in $(-\varepsilon, \varepsilon)$. The fixed point is unstable and the periodic orbit is locally asymptotically stable.

(c) If instead of $f_{111}^{(2)}(0, 0) < 0$ it holds that $f_{111}^{(2)}(0, 0) > 0$, then the roles of the intervals $(\mu_1, 0)$ and $(0, \mu_2)$ as well as the stability properties of the periodic orbit are reversed: for $\mu \in (\mu_1, 0)$, there exist a locally asymptotically stable fixed point and an unstable orbit of period 2, and for $\mu \in (0, \mu_2)$, there exists an unstable fixed point.

PROOF: We prove the theorem under the assumption that $f_{111}^{(2)}(0, 0) < 0$. The converse case stated in part (c) of the theorem can be proved analogously. Defining the function $g(x, \mu) = f(x, \mu) - x$, the fixed point condition can be written as $g(x, \mu) = 0$. Because of $g_1(0, 0) = f_1(0, 0) - 1 = -2$, the implicit function theorem implies the existence of $\delta > 0$ and a unique three times continuously differentiable function $\tilde{x} : (-\delta, \delta) \mapsto \mathbb{R}$ such that $\tilde{x}(0) = 0$ and $g(\tilde{x}(\mu), \mu) = 0$ hold for all $\mu \in (-\delta, \delta)$. The graph of this function contains the fixed points mentioned in parts (a) and (b) of the theorem and is shown in figure 4.6 as an upward-sloping line. Furthermore, it holds that $\tilde{x}'(0) = (1/2)f_2(0, 0)$. Defining the function $G(x, \mu) = f(f(x, \mu), \mu) - x$, it follows that periodic points of period 2 must satisfy $G(x, \mu) = 0$ and $x \neq \tilde{x}(\mu)$. Moreover, we have $G_1(0, 0) = f_1(0, 0)^2 - 1 = 0$, $G_2(0, 0) = [f_1(0, 0) + 1]f_2(0, 0) = 0$, and $G_{11}(0, 0) = f_{11}(0, 0)f_1(0, 0)[f_1(0, 0) + 1] = 0$. It is therefore not possible to apply the implicit function theorem directly to the equation $G(x, \mu) = 0$. For this reason, we define

$$H(x, \mu) = \begin{cases} \dfrac{G(x, \mu)}{x - \tilde{x}(\mu)} & \text{if } x \neq \tilde{x}(\mu), \\ G_1(x, \mu) & \text{if } x = \tilde{x}(\mu). \end{cases}$$

Using the rule of de l'Hopital as well as the definition of the function h, we can show that H is twice continuously differentiable with

$$H(0, 0) = G_1(0, 0) = 0,$$

$$H_2(0, 0) = G_{12}(0, 0) = -2h'(0) > 0,$$

$$H_1(0, 0) = (1/2)G_{11}(0, 0) = 0,$$

$$H_{11}(0, 0) = (1/3)G_{111}(0, 0) = (1/3)f_{111}^{(2)}(0, 0) < 0,$$

where h is defined in the theorem. The first two of these conditions allow us to apply the implicit function theorem to the equation $H(x, \mu) = 0$ to get a unique function $\tilde{\mu} : (-\varepsilon, \varepsilon) \mapsto \mathbb{R}$ satisfying $\tilde{\mu}(0) = 0$ and $H(x, \tilde{\mu}(x)) = 0$ for all $x \in (-\varepsilon, \varepsilon)$. The derivative of this function at $x = 0$ is $\tilde{\mu}'(0) = 0$ such that $\tilde{x}(\tilde{\mu}(x)) \neq x$ holds for all $x \in (-\varepsilon, \varepsilon) \setminus \{0\}$. Thus, for all $x \in (-\varepsilon, \varepsilon) \setminus \{0\}$ it must hold that $G(x, \tilde{\mu}(x)) = 0$ and $f(x, \tilde{\mu}(x)) \neq x$. This proves that x is a periodic point of period 2 of the difference equation (4.2) whenever $\mu = \tilde{\mu}(x)$. Analogously to the proof of theorem 4.1, we can show that the function $\tilde{\mu}$ has a local minimum at $x = 0$ and that it is strictly positive for all $x \in (-\varepsilon, \varepsilon) \setminus \{0\}$. In the bifurcation diagram of figure 4.6, the graph of this function contains the periodic points of (4.2) that are mentioned in part (b) of the theorem.

It remains to determine the stability of the fixed points and periodic points. As $h'(0) < 0$ and $h(0) = -1$, it must hold that $f_1(\tilde{x}(\mu), \mu) \in (-1, 1)$ for all $\mu \in (\mu_1, 0)$. This shows that the fixed point is stable for $\mu \in (\mu_1, 0)$. Analogously, it follows that the fixed point is unstable for $\mu \in (0, \mu_2)$. The stability of the periodic points of period 2 will not be addressed here.

A few comments on the conditions of the theorem are appropriate. The key conditions are $f(0, 0) = 0$ and $f_1(0, 0) = -1$. If $h'(0) > 0$ holds, then we can simply change the bifurcation parameter from μ to $-\mu$ in order to get $h'(0) < 0$, as stated in the theorem. Thus, this condition is mostly a normalization of the bifurcation parameter. Finally, as is evident from a comparison of the cases (a) and (b), on the one hand, and case (c), on the other hand, the sign of $f_{111}^{(2)}(0, 0)$ determines whether the parabola depicting the periodic orbits in the bifurcation diagram of figure 4.6 points to the left or to the right.

Example 4.2 Consider the overlapping generations economy from example 1.7 with utility function $u(y) = -e^{-\alpha y}$ and cost function $v(y) = \beta y^2$, where α and β are positive parameters. As in our discussion of this model in example 3.12, we set $\beta = \alpha e^{-\alpha}$. We have seen that the equilibrium dynamics in this case are described by the implicit difference equation

$$y_t^2 = y_{t+1}e^{\alpha(1-y_{t+1})}.$$

We have also already pointed out that $y^* = 1$ is a fixed point of this equation and we have argued in example 3.12 that there exist periodic solutions of period 2 whenever $\alpha > 3$. In what follows, we confirm this finding by application of the flip bifurcation theorem 4.2.

We must first convert the difference equation into the normal form that we have used in theorem 4.2. To this end, we define the new variables $x_t = y_t - 1$ and $\mu = 3 - \alpha$. The above difference equation can then be rewritten in the form

$$(1 + x_t)^2 = (1 + x_{t+1})e^{(\mu-3)x_{t+1}}.$$

The system dynamics $f(x, \mu)$ is therefore implicitly defined by the equation

$$(1 + x)^2 = [1 + f(x, \mu)]e^{(\mu-3)f(x,\mu)}. \tag{4.5}$$

Setting $x = \mu = 0$, this implies $1 = [1 + f(0, 0)]e^{-3f(0,0)}$, which obviously has the solution $f(0, 0) = 0$.[2] Moreover, by differentiating equation (4.5) with respect to x and evaluating the resulting equation at $x = \mu = 0$ we obtain $f_1(0, 0) = -1$. For later use, we note that by continued implicit differentiation of equation (4.5) we obtain $f_{11}(0, 0) = 1/2$ and $f_{111}(0, 0) = -9/4$.

Theorem 4.2 guarantees that locally around $\mu = 0$ there exists a unique locus of fixed points $\tilde{x}(\mu)$ which is determined by the equation $f(\tilde{x}(\mu), \mu) = \tilde{x}(\mu)$. Because equation (4.5) holds for all values of μ whenever $x = 0$ and $f(x, \mu) = 0$, the function $\tilde{x}$ must be given by $\tilde{x}(\mu) = 0$ for all μ. Using implicit differentiation of (4.5) again, we therefore obtain $h(\mu) = f_1(\tilde{x}(\mu), \mu) = 2/(\mu - 2)$ and $h'(0) = -1/2 < 0$. Finally,

---

[2] There is a second solution $f(0, 0) \approx -0.94$, which does not concern us here. The flip bifurcation theorem uses only local information around a given fixed point, which we take to be $x^* = 0$ (and which corresponds to the fixed point $y^* = 1$ in the original variables).

we need to compute $f_{111}^{(2)}(0, 0)$. This can be accomplished by noting that

$$f_{111}^{(2)}(x, \mu) = f_{111}(f(x, \mu), \mu)f_1(x, \mu)^3 + 3 f_{11}(f(x, \mu), \mu)f_{11}(x, \mu)f_1(x, \mu)$$
$$+ f_1(f(x, \mu), \mu)f_{111}(x, \mu).$$

Substituting $x = \mu = f(0, 0) = 0$, $f_1(0, 0) = -1$, $f_{11}(0, 0) = 1/2$, and $f_{111}(0, 0) = -9/4$, this simplifies to $f_{111}^{(2)}(0, 0) = 15/4 > 0$. Hence, the conditions of theorem 4.2(c) are satisfied and it follows that for negative values of μ there exists an orbit of period 2. Note that negative values of μ correspond to values of α that are greater than 3.

The application of theorem 4.2 in the present example not only proves the existence of the periodic orbits, but also shows that they are unstable. Note, however, that this is what has to be expected. As has been shown in our discussion in example 3.12, the fixed point is determinate (and, hence, unstable) for $\alpha < 3$ and indeterminate (that is, stable) for $\alpha > 3$. The periodic orbit, which only exists for $\alpha > 3$, is determinate (that is, unstable): it inherits its determinacy from the fixed point as α passes the critical value 3.

The fold bifurcation and the flip bifurcation are the most common types of bifurcations occurring in one-dimensional difference equations. There are, however, also some other types of bifurcations that can occur in families of difference equations that display certain symmetries or other restrictions. We will now discuss two such cases for the situation in which $f_1(0, 0) = 1$.

Consider, for example, the difference equation (4.2) with $f(x, \mu) = (1 + \mu)x + x^2$. Note that this function has the property $f(0, \mu) = 0$ for all $\mu \in \mathbb{R}$, that is, the point $x = 0$ is a fixed point irrespective of the bifurcation parameter. Hence, it holds also that $f_2(0, \mu) = 0$, which contradicts the assumptions of theorem 4.1. The graph of the function $x \mapsto f(x, \mu)$ is depicted in figure 4.7 for the three values $\mu = -1/2$, $\mu = 0$, and $\mu = 1/2$. We see that the parabolic graph does not shift parallel as in the fold bifurcation, but that it sort of rotates around the fixed point. This gives rise to a scenario that is quite different from the fold bifurcation and which is referred to as a *transcritical bifurcation*. For $\mu < 0$, the difference equation has two fixed points with the smaller one, $x = 0$, being locally asymptotically stable and the larger one being unstable. As μ attains its critical value, the two fixed points coincide. For positive values of μ, there are again two fixed points – $x = 0$ and a negative one – with the latter being locally asymptotically stable and $x = 0$ being unstable.

The bifurcation diagram of the transcritical bifurcation is illustrated in figure 4.8, and the exact conditions generating this bifurcation are stated in theorem 4.3. The proof of this theorem uses similar methods as those employed to prove theorems 4.1 and 4.2 and will not be presented here.

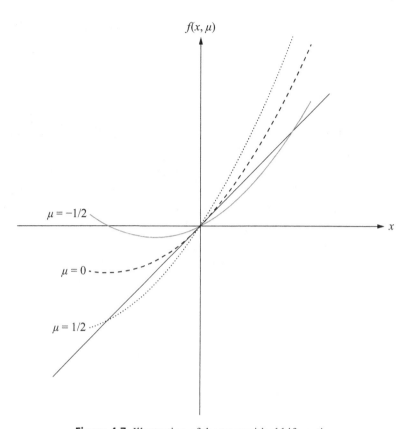

Figure 4.7 Illustration of the transcritical bifurcation

Theorem 4.3   Consider the difference equation (4.2) with system domain $X \subseteq \mathbb{R}$ and bifurcation parameter $\mu \in \mathbb{R}$. Suppose that there exists an open set U such that $0 \in U \subseteq X$ and such that f is twice continuously differentiable on $U \times \mathbb{R}$. Assume furthermore that the conditions

$$f(0, \mu) = 0, \quad f_1(0, 0) = 1, \quad f_{12}(0, 0) > 0, \quad f_{11}(0, 0) > 0$$

hold for all $\mu \in \mathbb{R}$. Then there exist real numbers $\varepsilon > 0$, $\mu_1 < 0$, and $\mu_2 > 0$ as well as a function $\tilde{x} : (\mu_1, \mu_2) \mapsto \mathbb{R}$ satisfying $\tilde{x}(0) = 0 \neq \tilde{x}(\mu) \in (-\varepsilon, \varepsilon)$ for all $\mu \neq 0$. For all $\mu \in (\mu_1, \mu_2)$, it holds that the only fixed points of (4.2) located in $(-\varepsilon, \varepsilon)$ are 0 and $\tilde{x}(\mu)$ and that these fixed points satisfy the following properties:

(a) For all $\mu \in (\mu_1, 0)$, the fixed point 0 is locally asymptotically stable and the fixed point $\tilde{x}(\mu)$ is positive and unstable.

(b) For all $\mu \in (0, \mu_2)$, the fixed point 0 is unstable and the fixed point $\tilde{x}(\mu)$ is negative and locally asymptotically stable.

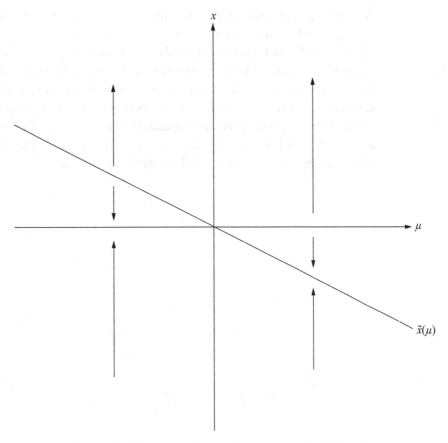

Figure 4.8 Bifurcation diagram for the transcritical bifurcation

(c) If instead of $f_{11}(0, 0) > 0$ it holds that $f_{11}(0, 0) < 0$, then the graph of $\tilde{x}$ in the bifurcation diagram 4.8 is upward sloping and the stability properties of the fixed points 0 and $\tilde{x}(\mu)$ are exactly opposite to those stated in parts (a) and (b) above.

The following example demonstrates how the transcritical bifurcation emerges in a model from population dynamics.

Example 4.3 Consider the following variation of the model from example 4.1. Let the natural growth of the fish population be given by

$$z_{t+1} = z_t(K - z_t),$$

which differs from equation (4.4) in that the growth factor z_{t+1}/z_t is not hump-shaped as in example 4.1 but linearly declining. The parameter K denotes again the carrying capacity of the habitat and we therefore choose the system domain to be given by

$X = [0, K]$.[3] Obviously, the system dynamics can also be written as $x_{t+1} = (1 + \mu)x_t + x_t^2$, where $x_t = -z_t$ and $\mu = K - 1$. Hence, the model has exactly the same structure as the motivating example that we discussed before the statement of theorem 4.3, and it follows that the fixed point $x = 0$ undergoes a transcritical bifurcation at the critical value $\mu = 0$. In terms of the original variables, this corresponds to a bifurcation of $z = 0$ at $K = 1$. If $K < 1$, the fixed point $z = 0$ is globally asymptotically stable, which implies that the fish population faces extinction from every given initial stock $z_0 \in [0, K]$. For $K \in (1, 4]$, on the other hand, there exists a strictly positive fixed point at $z = K - 1$, and it follows that extinction does not occur.

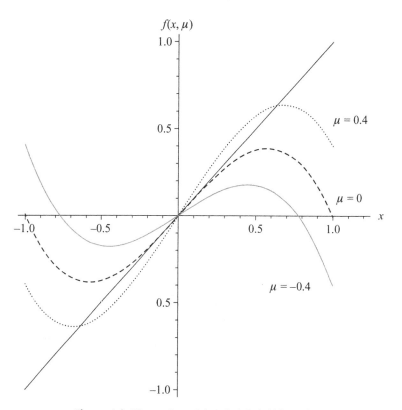

Figure 4.9 Illustration of the pitchfork bifurcation

Finally, let us consider the *pitchfork bifurcation*. A simple example in which this type of bifurcation occurs is the difference equation (4.2) with $f(x, \mu) = (1 + \mu)x - x^3$. Note that this function is an odd function, that is, it satisfies the symmetry property $f(-x, \mu) = -f(x, \mu)$ for all x and all μ. This implies in particular that $f(0, \mu) = 0$

[3] Choosing $X = [0, K]$ as the system domain makes sense as long as $K \in [0, 4]$.

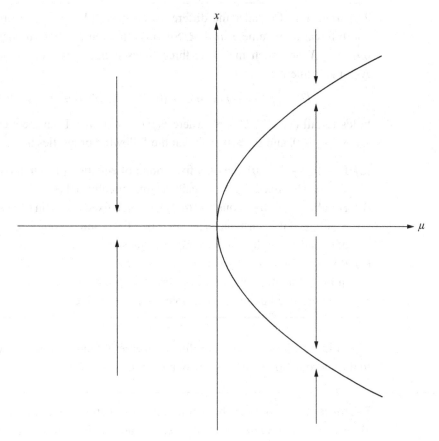

Figure 4.10 Bifurcation diagram for the pitchfork bifurcation

holds for all μ (as in the case of the transcritical bifurcation). Contrary to the transcritical bifurcation, however, it holds that $f_{11}(0, 0) = 0$. This follows simply from the fact that f is an odd function and implies that not only the third condition of theorem 4.1, but also the last one fails to hold. The graph of $x \mapsto f(x, \mu)$ for the present example is shown in figure 4.9 for the three parameter values $\mu \in \{-2/5, 0, 2/5\}$. We can see from this figure that two new fixed points are born as the bifurcation parameter μ passes through its critical value. While the single fixed point $x = 0$ is stable for $\mu < 0$, it loses its stability at the critical value when the two new fixed points emerge. Essentially, the graph of f undergoes the same changes in the pitchfork bifurcation as the graph of $f^{(2)}$ undergoes in the flip bifurcation. The bifurcation diagram of the pitchfork bifurcation is shown in figure 4.10 and the exact conditions generating the pitchfork bifurcation are stated in theorem 4.4. Again we omit the proof as it uses similar methods as those employed in the proofs of our previous bifurcation theorems.

Theorem 4.4 Consider the difference equation (4.2) with system domain $X \subseteq \mathbb{R}$ and bifurcation parameter $\mu \in \mathbb{R}$. Suppose that there exists an open set U such that $0 \in U \subseteq X$ and such that f is three times continuously differentiable on $U \times \mathbb{R}$. Assume furthermore that

$$f(-x, \mu) = -f(x, \mu), \quad f_1(0, 0) = 1, \quad h'(0) > 0, \quad f_{111}(0, 0) < 0$$

holds for all $(x, \mu) \in U \times \mathbb{R}$, where $h(\mu) = f_1(0, \mu)$. Then there exist real numbers $\varepsilon > 0$, $\mu_1 < 0$, and $\mu_2 > 0$ such that the following properties hold:

(a) For all $\mu \in (\mu_1, 0)$, the only fixed point of equation (4.2) in the interval $(-\varepsilon, \varepsilon)$ is $x = 0$. This fixed point is locally asymptotically stable.
(b) For all $\mu \in (0, \mu_2)$, equation (4.2) has three fixed points in $(-\varepsilon, \varepsilon)$. One of them is $x = 0$, and it is unstable. The other two fixed points are located on opposite sides of 0, and are both locally asymptotically stable.
(c) If instead of $f_{111}(0, 0) < 0$ it holds that $f_{111}(0, 0) > 0$, then the parabola depicted in the bifurcation diagram in figure 4.10 points in the opposite direction and the non-zero fixed points are unstable instead of stable.

To illustrate how a pitchfork bifurcation emerges in an economic example, we return to the coordination game first encountered in example 1.2.

Example 4.4 Consider the two-player coordination game from example 1.2. As an alternative to the replicator dynamics, we can use the logit model of discrete choice. Recall that an A-player in period t obtains on average the payoff ax_t, whereas a B-player in period t obtains on average $b(1 - x_t)$. The logit model postulates that the probability of any given player to choose strategy A in period $t + 1$ is given by

$$\frac{e^{\lambda ax_t}}{e^{\lambda ax_t} + e^{\lambda b(1-x_t)}},$$

where $\lambda > 0$ is a parameter measuring how strongly the probability of choosing a certain action is affected by the observed average payoffs from the previous round. If the choice of strategies occurs independently across agents, this implies that

$$x_{t+1} = g(x_t, \lambda) := \frac{e^{\lambda ax_t}}{e^{\lambda ax_t} + e^{\lambda b(1-x_t)}} = \frac{1}{1 + e^{\lambda[b-(a+b)x_t]}}. \tag{4.6}$$

An important difference between the logit model and the replicator dynamics is that the pure strategy Nash equilibria do not qualify as fixed points of the logit dynamics. Indeed, even if the entire population in period t plays strategy A, that is, if $x_t = 1$, there will be a positive fraction of B-players in period $t + 1$ because $g(1, \lambda) = 1/(1 + e^{-\lambda a}) < 1$. The reason is that the logit model allows for a considerable influence of chance on the strategy selection. This influence is a decreasing function of the parameter λ.

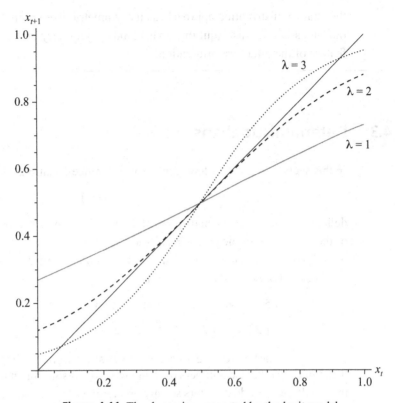

Figure 4.11 The dynamics generated by the logit model

For analytical convenience, we restrict ourselves from now on to the case of equal payoffs $a = b$, and without loss of generality we may even assume that $a = b = 1$. With this choice of parameters, it is easy to see that $g(1/2, \lambda) = 1/2$ holds for all $\lambda > 0$, which proves that $x^* = 1/2$ is a fixed point. Moreover, it holds that $g_1(1/2, \lambda) = \lambda/2$. If a pitchfork bifurcation occurs, it must therefore be at the critical value $\lambda = 2$. Let us therefore rewrite the dynamics in the variables $y_t = x_t - 1/2$ and $\mu = \lambda - 2$. This yields $y_{t+1} = f(y_t, \mu)$ with

$$f(y, \mu) = \frac{1}{1 + e^{-2(2+\mu)y}} - \frac{1}{2}.$$

It is straightforward to verify that $f(-y, \mu) = -f(y, \mu)$ holds and that $h(\mu) = f_1(0, \mu) = 1 + \mu/2$. The latter equation implies obviously that $h'(0) = 1/2 > 0$. Finally, we can compute $f_{111}(0, 0) = -8$. Hence, all conditions of theorem 4.4 are satisfied and it follows that a pitchfork bifurcation occurs at the critical value $\lambda = 2$.

The dynamics of equation (4.6) are illustrated in figure 4.11 for the parameter values $a = b = 1$ and $\lambda \in \{1, 2, 3\}$. For $\lambda < 2$, the fixed point $1/2$ is unique and globally asymptotically stable. In this case, the logit model does not give much weight to the average payoffs, and the eventual distribution of strategies is therefore mostly driven by chance. For $\lambda > 2$, however, the effect of differences in the payoffs is so strong that the strategy distribution approaches an asymmetric fixed point that is closer to one of the pure strategy Nash equilibria. This kind of symmetry breaking is the characteristic feature of the pitchfork bifurcation.

4.3   Deterministic chaos

In this section, we state a few results for difference equations of the form

$$x_{t+1} = f(x_t) \tag{4.7}$$

defined on a one-dimensional system domain $X \subseteq \mathbb{R}$, which allow us to catch a glimpse of the fascinating topic of deterministic chaos. We start with the remarkable theorem of Sarkovskii. To formulate it, let us define a complete order $\lhd$ on the positive integers, the so-called *Sarkovskii order*, as follows

$$3 \lhd 5 \lhd 7 \lhd \ldots \lhd 2 \times 3 \lhd 2 \times 5 \lhd \ldots \lhd 2^2 \times 3 \lhd 2^2 \times 5 \lhd \ldots$$

$$\ldots \lhd 2^3 \times 3 \lhd 2^3 \times 5 \lhd \ldots \lhd 2^3 \lhd 2^2 \lhd 2 \lhd 1.$$

In words, we start by writing all odd numbers strictly greater than 1 in ascending order, then multiply all these numbers by 2 and write the results again in ascending order. We then multiply the odd numbers strictly greater than 1 by 4 and write them in ascending order. Continuing in this way by using as multipliers all the powers of 2, we exhaust all positive integers, except for the powers of 2 themselves. The powers of 2 are then written at the end in descending order. The Sarkovskii theorem can now be stated as follows.

Theorem 4.5   Consider the system domain $X = \mathbb{R}$ and let $f : X \mapsto X$ be a continuous function. Suppose that the difference equation (4.7) has a periodic point of period p. For every positive integer q satisfying $p \lhd q$, it holds that the difference equation (4.7) admits a periodic point of period q.

We do not present the proof of this result, but restrict ourselves to discussing several of its implications. First, note that the theorem says that every one-dimensional difference equation with continuous right-hand side that admits a periodic point (of any period) must also have a fixed point. This is the case because 1 is the largest number according to the Sarkovskii order. A second important implication of theorem 4.5 is that every one-dimensional difference equation that admits a periodic point with a period that is not a power of 2 must have infinitely many periodic points of different periods. Finally, we would like to point out that the smallest number in the Sarkovskii order is the number 3. Whenever a one-dimensional difference equation with a continuous right-hand side has a periodic point of period 3, it follows that it has periodic points of all periods. The special role of periodic points of period 3 is further underlined by the following result.

Theorem 4.6 Let $X \subseteq \mathbb{R}$ be an interval on the real line and let $f : X \mapsto X$ be a continuous function. If there exists $x \in X$ such that either $f^{(3)}(x) \leq x < f(x) < f^{(2)}(x)$ or $f^{(3)}(x) \geq x > f(x) > f^{(2)}(x)$ holds, then the following properties are true:

(a) For every positive integer p, it holds that the difference equation (4.7) admits a periodic point of period p.

(b) There exists an uncountable set $S \subseteq X$ with the following properties:
   (i) S does not contain any periodic point.
   (ii) For any two elements y and z of S, it holds that

$$\limsup_{t \to +\infty} |f^{(t)}(y) - f^{(t)}(z)| > 0 \text{ and } \liminf_{t \to +\infty} |f^{(t)}(y) - f^{(t)}(z)| = 0.$$

   (iii) If $y \in S$ and z is a periodic point, then it holds that

$$\limsup_{t \to +\infty} |f^{(t)}(y) - f^{(t)}(z)| > 0.$$

It is obvious that the conditions of this theorem are satisfied whenever there exists a periodic point of period 3. Part (a) of the theorem follows then also from theorem 4.5. The set S is usually referred to as a scrambled set because it contains infinitely many points such that the trajectories emanating from these points become arbitrarily close without converging to each other. This is made precise in condition (ii) in part (b) of the theorem. Conditions (i) and (iii) together state that S does not contain any periodic points and that trajectories emanating from points in S are not even asymptotically periodic. If properties (a) and (b) of theorem 4.6 are satisfied, then we say that the difference equation (4.7) exhibits *Li–Yorke chaos*, named after the two mathematicians who first proved theorem 4.6. This definition of chaos is one of several that are nowadays used in dynamical systems theory. Using theorem 4.6, it is often quite easy to verify the existence of Li–Yorke chaos. This is illustrated in the following examples.

Example 4.5 Recall the population dynamics from example 4.1, which were given by the difference equation

$$x_{t+1} = x_t^2(K - x_t).$$

We have seen in the discussion of this example in section 4.2 that at the critical value $K = 2$ a fold bifurcation takes place and that for all values of K larger than this critical value the population can survive. Now let us choose $K = 5/2$ and note that this value still satisfies the constraint $K \in (0, (3/2)\sqrt{3}]$ that we imposed in example 4.1. If we choose the initial population size $x_0 = 1.1$, then we obtain $x_1 = 1.694$, $x_2 \approx 2.313$, and $x_3 \approx 1.001$. Hence, we have $x_3 \leq x_0 < x_1 < x_2$, and theorem 4.6 applies. The population dynamics can therefore display extremely complicated patterns.

Example 4.6 Now consider the overlapping generations economy that we have already discussed in examples 1.7, 3.12, and 4.2. Under the same assumptions on the functional forms that we imposed in examples 3.12 and 4.2, the backward equilibrium dynamics are given by

$$y_t = \sqrt{y_{t+1}}\, e^{(\alpha/2)(1-y_{t+1})}.$$

If we choose $\alpha = 6$ and $y_3 = 0.0003$, we obtain $y_2 \approx 0.348$, $y_1 \approx 4.174$, and $y_0 \approx 0.0001$. Hence, the backward dynamics satisfy the conditions of theorem 4.6, and it follows that there exist a scrambled set and periodic orbits of all periods for this difference equation. Every periodic orbit of the backward dynamics is obviously also a periodic orbit of the forward dynamics, and we know therefore that the forward equilibrium dynamics admit a cycle of period 3. Hence, theorems 4.5 and 4.6 apply also to the forward dynamics: perfect foresight equilibria in this example can display Li–Yorke chaos.

The concept of Li-Yorke chaos is widely used and due to theorem 4.6 its occurrence is easy to verify. However, it has also a serious drawback, namely that the set of initial conditions for which the trajectories display complicated dynamics can be very small. Although we know that the scrambled set S contains uncountably many points, it can still be the case that from almost all points of the system domain (that is, from a subset of X that has the same Lebesgue measure as X itself), rather simple dynamics emerge. For example, it could be the case that there exists a periodic orbit of period 3 with a basin of attraction that is a subset of X with a full Lebesque measure. In such a situation, the trajectory starting from a randomly drawn initial point will display regular (that is, asymptotically periodic) behaviour with probability 1. An alternative definition of chaos, which ensures that the complicated dynamics can actually be observed, is ergodic chaos. In order to formalize this concept, we need to introduce some preliminary definitions.

For simplicity, let us assume that the system domain X of equation (4.7) is a compact interval on the real line. A measure μ on the Borel subsets of X is said to be absolutely continuous if $\mu(A) = 0$ holds for every Borel subset A of X which has Lebesgue measure 0. This is equivalent to the existence of a Lebesgue integrable function $g : X \mapsto \mathbb{R}$, called the Radon–Nikodym derivative of μ such that $\mu(A) = \int_A g(x)\, d\lambda(x)$ holds for all Borel subsets $A \subseteq X$, where λ denotes the Lebesgue measure. Moreover, the measure μ is said to be invariant under the function $f : X \mapsto X$ if for all Borel sets $A \subseteq X$ it holds that $\mu(A) = \mu(\{x \in X \mid f(x) \in A\})$. This says that μ assigns the same measure to a Borel set A as to the pre-image of A under f. Finally, an invariant measure μ on the Borel subsets of X is said to be ergodic if for every Borel set $A \subseteq X$ which satisfies $A = \{x \in X \mid f(x) \in A\}$ it either holds that $\mu(A) = 0$ or

$\mu(A) = \mu(X)$. The difference equation (4.7) is said to exhibit *ergodic chaos* if there exists an absolutely continuous probability measure on the system domain X which is invariant and ergodic under f. We can now state a sufficient condition for the existence of ergodic chaos.

Theorem 4.7   Consider the one-dimensional map (4.7) on the system domain X, where $X = [a, b] \subset \mathbb{R}$ is a compact interval. Assume that there exists $\hat{x} \in X$ such that the restrictions of f to $(a, \hat{x})$ and to $(\hat{x}, b)$ are twice continuously differentiable and can be extended as twice continuously differentiable functions to the closed intervals $[a, \hat{x}]$ and $[\hat{x}, b]$, respectively. If it holds that

$$\inf\{|f'(x)| \mid x \in (a, \hat{x}) \cup (\hat{x}, b)\} > 1,$$

then there exists a unique probability measure on X which is invariant and ergodic under f. Hence, the difference equation (4.7) exhibits ergodic chaos.

It should be noted that the function f can be discontinuous at the point $\hat{x}$. The crucial condition of the theorem is that the absolute value of the derivative of f is uniformly greater than 1. The theorem actually holds under the weaker condition that there exists some integer $n \geq 1$ such that the absolute value of the derivative of the nth iterate $f^{(n)}$ is uniformly greater than 1. We illustrate this by the following example.

Example 4.7   Consider the difference equation (4.7) on the system domain $X = [0, 1]$, where the function f is defined by

$$f(x) = \begin{cases} (2/3)(1 + x) & \text{if } x \in [0, 1/2], \\ 2(1 - x) & \text{if } x \in [1/2, 1]. \end{cases}$$

This function is piecewise linear and its derivative is equal to $2/3 < 1$ on the interval $[0, 1/2]$. Consequently, theorem 4.7 does not apply. However, it is straightforward to check that the second iterate of f is given by

$$f^{(2)}(x) = \begin{cases} (2/3)(1 - 2x) & \text{if } x \in [0, 1/2], \\ 4(x - 1/2) & \text{if } x \in [1/2, 3/4], \\ (2/3)(3 - 2x) & \text{if } x \in [3/4, 1]. \end{cases}$$

This implies that the absolute value of the derivative of $f^{(2)}$ is bounded below by $4/3$. Because this bound is strictly larger than 1, there exists a unique probability measure on $[0, 1]$ which is invariant and ergodic under $f^{(2)}$, and it follows therefore that the difference equation (4.7) exhibits ergodic chaos.

We now turn to a third definition of complicated dynamics or chaos. More specifically, we want to define what it means that the solutions of the difference equation (4.7) display *sensitive dependence on initial conditions* on a certain subset S of the system domain X. This is the case if there exists $\delta > 0$ such that for all $x \in S$ and all $\varepsilon > 0$ we can find $y \in S$ and $t \in \mathbb{N}_0$ such that $|y - x| < \varepsilon$ and $|f^{(t)}(x) - f^{(t)}(y)| > \delta$. In words, for every point $x \in S$ we can find another point y (also in S) that is arbitrarily close to x such that the trajectories of (4.7) emanating from x and y, respectively, reach a distance from each other that exceeds the given number δ. Note that this is by no means a contradiction to the continuity of trajectories that we established in theorem 1.2. Furthermore, we would like to emphasize that sensitive dependence with respect of initial conditions by itself does not imply complicated dynamics. Indeed, the simple linear difference equation $x_{t+1} = ax_t$ with $|a| > 1$ displays this property on the entire domain $S = X = \mathbb{R}$. However, if the set S is bounded, then sensitive dependence on initial conditions on S can only occur if the structure of the trajectories is very complicated. The essence of the definition is that there exists a limit on the precision of predictions of the future behaviour of the system, and that arbitrarily small perturbations of the initial point of the system will lead to sizable differences in the course of its dynamic evolution.

Theorem 4.8 Consider the one-dimensional map (4.7) on the system domain $X \subseteq \mathbb{R}$.

(a) If the conditions of theorem 4.6 hold, then it follows that the difference equation (4.7) displays sensitive dependence on initial conditions on the scrambled set S.

(b) If the conditions of theorem 4.7 hold, then it follows that the difference equation (4.7) displays sensitive dependence on initial conditions on the entire system domain X.

We conclude this section by deriving a formal measure of the local convergence or divergence of trajectories. To this end, we assume from now on that the law of motion $f : X \mapsto X$ is continuously differentiable. Recall that in the neighbourhood of a hyperbolic fixed point x^* of equation (4.7), the behaviour of the trajectories is approximately described by the linear difference equation $x_{t+1} = x^* + f'(x^*)(x_t - x^*)$. Thus, the local rate of convergence to or divergence from the fixed point is given by $\ln |f'(x^*)|$. If this expression is negative, then nearby trajectories converge to the fixed point; if it is positive, they diverge from it. This observation translates easily to hyperbolic periodic orbits $\{x_0^*, x_1^*, \ldots, x_{p-1}^*\}$, around which the local rate of convergence or divergence is given by

$$\frac{1}{p} \ln |(f^{(p)})'(x_i^*)|) = \frac{1}{p} \sum_{t=0}^{p-1} \ln |f'(f^{(t)}(x_0^*))| \qquad (4.8)$$

for all $i \in \{0, 1, \ldots, p-1\}$. In analogy to these results, we can define the *Lyapunov exponent* of the trajectory emanating from x_0 by

$$\ell(x_0) = \lim_{T \to +\infty} \frac{1}{T} \sum_{t=0}^{T-1} \ln |f'(f^{(t)}(x_0))|.$$

If the Lyapunov exponent is positive on a set $A \subseteq X$ which is invariant under f, then we can conclude that the difference equation (4.7) exhibits sensitive dependence on initial conditions on A. The following lemma greatly facilitates the computation of Lyapunov exponents.

Lemma 4.4 Consider equation (4.7) defined on the system domain X, where X is an interval on the real line.

(a) If f is continuously differentiable and the trajectory emanating from x converges to the point x^*, then it follows that $\ell(x) = \ln |f'(x^*)|$.
(b) If f is continuously differentiable and the trajectory emanating from x converges to a periodic orbit $\{x_0^*, x_1^*, \ldots, x_{p-1}^*\}$, then it follows that $\ell(x)$ is given by the expression in (4.8).
(c) If the conditions of theorem 4.7 are satisfied, then there exist a set $S \subseteq [a, b]$ with Lebesgue measure $\lambda(S) = b - a$ and a number $L > 0$ such that the Lyapunov exponent $\ell(x)$ exists and satisfies $\ell(x) = L$ for all $x \in S$.

PROOF: Since $\lim_{t \to +\infty} x_t = x^*$ and since f is continuously differentiable, it follows that $\lim_{t \to +\infty} f'(x_t) = f'(x^*)$. Part (a) follows from this observation, the definition of the Lyapunov exponent, and from the well-known fact that whenever a sequence $(a_t)_{t=0}^{+\infty}$ converges to a limit a^*, then the limit of the averages $(a_0 + a_1 + \ldots + a_{t-1})/t$ exists and coincides with a^*. Part (b) can be proved analogously. The proof of part (c) is a consequence of the ergodic theorem and is omitted.

The application of this lemma is illustrated by the following example.

Example 4.8 Consider the difference equation

$$x_{t+1} = f(x_t) := \frac{4x_t^2}{3 + x_t^2} \qquad (4.9)$$

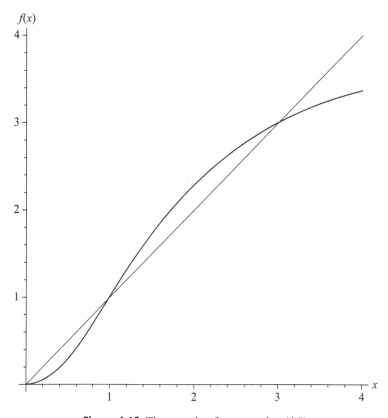

Figure 4.12 The mapping from equation (4.9)

on the system domain $X = [0, +\infty)$. It is easily checked that the function f is continuously differentiable and strictly increasing on X. Hence, equation (4.9) is a monotonic
one-dimensional map. Graphical analysis along the lines of section 1.1 as well as the
results from section 4.1 show that there exist three fixed points 0, 1, and 3, where
the one in the middle is unstable, whereas the other two are stable. Moreover, the
basin of attraction of the fixed point 0 is the interval $[0, 1)$ and the basin of attraction
of the fixed point 3 is the interval $(1, +\infty)$; see figure 4.12. Using lemma 4.4 and
$f'(x) = 24x/(3 + x^2)^2$, we therefore obtain

$$\ell(x) = \begin{cases} -\infty & \text{if } x \in [0, 1), \\ \ln 3 - \ln 2 & \text{if } x = 1, \\ -\ln 2 & \text{if } x \in (1, +\infty). \end{cases}$$

The Lyapunov exponent is a piecewise constant function, which takes negative values
in all points, except for the unstable fixed point.

4.4 EXERCISES

EXERCISE 4.1 Prove lemma 4.3.

EXERCISE 4.2 Consider the difference equation $x_{t+1} = e^{x_t - \mu} - 1$, where $x_t \in X = \mathbb{R}$ is the system variable and $\mu \in \mathbb{R}$ is a parameter.
(a) Prove that $x^* = 0$ is a fixed point if the parameter μ is equal to zero.
(b) Check whether a bifurcation occurs at the critical value $\mu = 0$. Which type of bifurcation is it?

EXERCISE 4.3 Repeat exercise 4.2 for the difference equation $x_{t+1} = e^{(1+\mu)x_t} - 1$.

EXERCISE 4.4 Consider the cobweb model with adaptive expectations introduced in example 1.5. It has been shown there that the dynamics of price forecasts follows the law

$$p_{t+1}^e = (1 - \gamma)p_t^e + \gamma D^{-1}(S(p_t^e)),$$

where $\gamma \in [0, 1]$ is a weight parameter and where $D : \mathbb{R}_+ \mapsto \mathbb{R}_+$ and $S : \mathbb{R}_+ \mapsto \mathbb{R}_+$ are the demand and the supply function, respectively. Throughout this exercise, assume that $D(p) = 1/\sqrt{p}$ and $S(p) = p$.
(a) Show that under the stated assumption the price forecasts satisfy the difference equation

$$p_{t+1}^e = (1 - \gamma)p_t^e + \frac{\gamma}{(p_t^e)^2}.$$

(b) Show that $p^* = 1$ is a fixed point for every feasible value of the weight parameter γ.
(c) Prove that a flip bifurcation occurs at the critical value $\gamma = 2/3$.

EXERCISE 4.5 Consider the logistic equation

$$x_{t+1} = \lambda x_t (1 - x_t)$$

defined on the system domain $X = [0, 1]$. Here, $\lambda \in [0, 4]$ is a parameter.
(a) Prove that at $\lambda = 1$ the logistic equation undergoes a transcritical bifurcation.
(b) Prove that at $\lambda = 3$ the logistic equation undergoes a flip bifurcation.
(c) Use theorem 4.6 to verify that the logistic equation generates Li–Yorke chaos if $\lambda = 4$.

EXERCISE 4.6   Consider the tent map defined on the set $X = [0, 1]$ by

$$f(x) = \begin{cases} 2x & \text{if } x \in [0, 1/2], \\ 2(1 - x) & \text{if } x \in [1/2, 1]. \end{cases}$$

Show that the tent map generates Li–Yorke chaos and ergodic chaos.

EXERCISE 4.7   Compute the Lyapunov exponent for the replicator dynamics in example 1.2 for the case $a = 2$ and $b = 1$ which is depicted in figure 1.3.

EXERCISE 4.8   Simulate the dynamics generated by the logistic map and the tent map from exercises 4.5 and 4.6.
(a) Choose $x_0 = 0.21$ and calculate at least 10 elements of the trajectory of the logistic difference equation with $\lambda = 4$ that emanates from that initial value. Now simulate the same difference equation for the slightly perturbed initial value $x_0 = 0.211$ and compare the two trajectories.
(b) Repeat the exercise with the tent map instead of the logistic map.

4.5   COMMENTS AND REFERENCES

One-dimensional maps have been thoroughly studied and many more results than those presented here are available in the literature. Two excellent books on this topic are Collet and Eckmann [23] and De Melo and Van Strien [26]. An authoritative treatment of bifurcation theory is provided by Kuznetsov [51]. Theorem 4.5 is due to Sarkovskii [81], theorem 4.6 was first proved by Li and Yorke [60], and theorem 4.7 combines results from Lasota and Yorke [57] and Li and Yorke [61]. The ergodic theorem mentioned in the proof of lemma 4.4 can be found in Katok and Hasselblatt [46].

Population dynamics similar to those discussed in example 4.1, 4.3, and 4.5 are very popular in biology; see, for example, Clark [22]. As has already been mentioned in the comments on chapter 1, the overlapping generations model with money from examples 4.2 and 4.6 and, in particular, the occurrence of complicated dynamics in this model have been discussed in Grandmont [37]. The logit model referred to in example 4.4 is a standard tool of discrete choice theory; see, for example, Train [91]. For further references on the occurrence of bifurcations and complicated dynamics in the cobweb model from exercise 4.4, see Hommes [41]. The logistic equation from exercise 4.5 and the tent map from exercise 4.6 are perhaps the best-known examples of chaotic one-dimensional maps and are discussed in virtually all books on chaos and one-dimensional maps. Example 4.3 is an application of the logistic equation.

II Dynamic optimization

5 Optimization techniques

Many models in economics are formulated as dynamic optimization problems in which the objective functional is a sum (often discounted) of the instantaneous utilities derived over infinitely many periods and in which the system variables of adjacent periods are linked via intertemporal constraints. In this chapter, we present different solution methods for this class of problems which we refer to as 'standard problems'.

We start in section 5.1 by describing the structure of the standard problem and by defining what we mean by its solution. After formulating the problem in primitive form (containing both state variables and control variables), we also present a reduced form that contains only state variables. In section 5.2, we discuss a solution method for the reduced form problem that is based on the Euler equation and the transversality condition. In section 5.3, we return to the primitive form of the dynamic optimization problem and show how it can be solved by a Lagrangian approach. Both approaches, the one based on the Euler equation and the transversality condition as well as the Lagrangian approach, are variational techniques that require differentiability assumptions. In section 5.4, we contrast these approaches to the technique of dynamic programming which can, in principle, be applied without any smoothness assumptions. Dynamic programming is a recursive solution technique, the heart of which is formed by the Bellman equation and the optimal value function. It is particularly powerful in the class of stationary discounted problems which will be discussed in section 5.5.

5.1 Model formulation and terminology

In the present section, we formulate a dynamic optimization problem that appears frequently in economics. As in part I of the book, we assume that the economic system under consideration is described by a finite set of system variables. In what follows, however, we shall distinguish between two kinds of system variables: state variables and control variables. The *state variables* describe the state of the system at the beginning of period t before the decision maker can make any choices. We denote the state of the economy in period t by $x_t \in X$, where X is an arbitrary non-empty set called the *state space* of the model.[1] The *initial state* in period 0, $x_0 \in X$, is exogenously given. In the terminology introduced in section 1.2, this can be expressed by saying that the state variables are pre-determined. The state of the system can change once in every period. A decision maker controls the state transitions by choosing a vector of *control variables* c_t in each period t. The set of feasible values of the controls when the state of the system in period t is equal to $x \in X$ is denoted by $\bar{G}(x, t)$, which is assumed to be non-empty for all $x \in X$ and all $t \in \mathbb{N}_0$. Since c_t can be chosen in period t, it is not a pre-determined variable but a jump variable.

Let us define the set $\bar{\Omega} = \{(x, c, t) \,|\, x \in X, t \in \mathbb{N}_0, c \in \bar{G}(x, t)\}$. Given the state and control in period t, x_t and c_t, respectively, the state in period $t + 1$ is determined by

$$x_{t+1} = f(x_t, c_t, t), \tag{5.1}$$

where $f : \bar{\Omega} \mapsto X$ is a given function. A state trajectory $(x_t)_{t=0}^{+\infty}$ together with a control path $(c_t)_{t=0}^{+\infty}$ is called a *feasible pair* from the given initial state x_0 if $x_t \in X$, $c_t \in \bar{G}(x_t, t)$, and equation (5.1) hold for all $t \in \mathbb{N}_0$. Finally, suppose that the decision maker derives utility $F(x_t, c_t, t)$ in period t, where $F : \bar{\Omega} \mapsto \mathbb{R}$ is called the instantaneous utility function. We assume that the decision maker seeks to choose an *optimal pair*, that is, a feasible pair which maximizes the objective functional

$$\sum_{t=0}^{+\infty} F(x_t, c_t, t) \tag{5.2}$$

over the set of all feasible pairs. In order for the objective functional to be well-defined, we assume that $\lim_{T \to +\infty} \sum_{t=0}^{T} F(x_t, c_t, t)$ exists as a finite number for all feasible pairs. We shall be more precise in the following section.

The version of the dynamic optimization problem described above is called the *primitive form* of the optimization problem. The fundamentals of the primitive form are the state space X, the set of feasible controls $\bar{G}$, the function describing state transitions f, the instantaneous utility function F, and the initial state x_0. Sometimes it is convenient to eliminate the control variables from the problem and to formulate the latter only in terms of the state variables. This is called the *reduced form* of the dynamic optimization problem. To convert the primitive form into the reduced form, we define

$$G(x, t) = \{f(x, c, t) \,|\, c \in \bar{G}(x, t)\}.$$

Obviously, this is the set of all states that can be reached in period $t + 1$ if the state in period t is x and if a feasible control is applied. In particular, it holds for all $x \in X$ and

---

[1] We hope that we use the symbols x_t and X to denote the state variables and the state space, respectively, does not cause confusion, although we used the same symbols for the system variables and the system domain in part I of the book.

all $t \in \mathbb{N}_0$ that $G(x, t) \subseteq X$. We refer to $G(x, t)$ as the set of feasible successor states of x or as the transition possibility set. With these definitions, condition (5.1) can be written as

$$x_{t+1} \in G(x_t, t). \tag{5.3}$$

Every state trajectory $(x_t)_{t=0}^{+\infty}$ that satisfies condition (5.3) and that starts in the given initial state x_0 is called a *feasible path* from x_0. The reduced-form utility function $U : \Omega \mapsto \mathbb{R}$ is defined on the set $\Omega = \{(x, y, t) \mid x \in X, t \in \mathbb{N}_0, y \in G(x, t)\}$ by

$$U(x, y, t) = \max\{F(x, c, t) \mid y = f(x, c, t), c \in \bar{G}(x, t)\},$$

where the maximization is with respect to the control variable c. Hence, $U(x, y, t)$ is the maximal value that the instantaneous utility function can take if the state in period t is equal to x, the state in period $t + 1$ is equal to y, and a feasible control is applied. For the moment, we simply assume that the maximum in the definition of $U(x, y, t)$ exists. This will be the case under appropriate continuity and compactness assumptions to be imposed in the following sections.

The objective functional in the reduced form of the optimization problem can be expressed as

$$\sum_{t=0}^{+\infty} U(x_t, x_{t+1}, t). \tag{5.4}$$

To summarize, the decision maker in the reduced form problem seeks to maximize (5.4) subject to (5.3) and a given initial state x_0. A feasible path which attains this maximum is called an *optimal path*. The fundamentals of the reduced form problem are X, G, U, and x_0.

In the remainder of this section, we discuss three related examples and illustrate in each case how the primitive form can be converted into the reduced form. All three examples describe the intertemporal trade-off between consumption (to obtain immediate satisfaction) and saving (to increase consumption possibilities in the future). This trade-off is paramount in dynamic economic theory.

Example 5.1 In this example, we discuss a simple saving problem that highlights the tradeoff between spending income for present consumption or saving it for future consumption. Consider an individual who faces the income stream $(I_t)_{t=0}^{+\infty}$ and the sequence $(R_t)_{t=0}^{+\infty}$ of gross rates of return on asset holdings.[2] It is assumed that $R_t > 0$

---

[2] More precisely, R_t denotes the gross rate of return on assets held from period t to period $t + 1$.

holds for all t and that

$$h_t = \sum_{s=t}^{+\infty} D_{s,t} I_s$$

is finite for all t, where $D_{s,t} = \prod_{j=t}^{s-1} R_j^{-1}$ is the discount factor used to compute the present value as of time t of income received in period s. Note that h_t is the present value as of time t of all the income earned from period t onwards, which can be interpreted as the value of the human capital of the individual.

Let us denote by c_t the consumption rate in period t and by x_t the asset holdings of the decision maker at the outset of period t. Then it follows that the flow budget equation (which describes the state transitions)

$$x_{t+1} = R_t(x_t + I_t - c_t)$$

must hold.[3] The initial asset holdings x_0 are assumed to be given. Furthermore, suppose that the individual has the instantaneous utility function $u : \mathbb{R}_+ \mapsto \mathbb{R}$ and the time-preference factor $\beta \in (0, 1)$, and that it seeks to maximize the total lifetime utility

$$\sum_{t=0}^{+\infty} \beta^t u(c_t)$$

subject to the flow budget constraint and a non-negativity constraint on consumption, $c_t \geq 0$.

Without further constraints on the ability to borrow, the agent can finance any (arbitrarily high) level of consumption by accumulating debt. Thus, the problem does not have an optimal solution. It is therefore essential to include a borrowing constraint. The literature considers various possibilities. For example, we could completely rule out debt accumulation by a non-negativity constraint on asset holdings, that is, by a borrowing constraint of the form $x_t \geq 0$ for all t. This is sometimes called a 'no-borrowing constraint'. A more general possibility is to allow for debt, but to limit it by some given amounts. This could be formulated by imposing the constraint $x_t \geq \underline{x}_t$ for a given sequence $(\underline{x}_t)_{t=0}^{+\infty}$ of lower bounds on asset holdings. In both of these cases, the optimization problem is of the form discussed at the outset of this section. Specifically, we have $X = \mathbb{R}$, $\bar{G}(x, t) = [0, x + I_t - \underline{x}_{t+1}/R_t]$, $f(x, c, t) = R_t(x + I_t - c)$, and $F(x, c, t) = \beta^t u(c)$. Of course, we can also rewrite the problem in reduced form. The state variable is the asset position x_t, the transition possibility set is $G(x, t) = [\underline{x}_{t+1}, R_t(x + I_t)]$, and the reduced-form utility function is given by $U(x, y, t) = \beta^t u(x + I_t - y/R_t)$.

---

[3] Here it is assumed that interest accrues after income is received and after consumption expenditures have been made. We could also use alternative timing assumptions.

An notable special case of the borrowing constraint arises if we choose $\underline{x}_t = -h_t$, where h_t is the human capital value introduced above. This is usually referred to as the natural borrowing constraint because it has two important consequences. The first one regards its interpretation. Recalling that h_t is the value of the human capital stock held by the agent at time t, we can interpret $z_t = x_t + h_t$ as the total wealth of the agent at the outset of period t, which consists of financial wealth x_t and human wealth h_t. The natural borrowing constraint requires total wealth to be non-negative at all times. This means that the agent is allowed to borrow but that he or she must be able to repay the debt with future earnings.

The second important consequence of the natural borrowing constraint is that we can rewrite the model in terms of total wealth in a very simple form. To this end, just note that $h_{t+1} = R_t(h_t - I_t)$. Combining this observation with the state transition equation, we obtain

$$z_{t+1} = x_{t+1} + h_{t+1} = R_t(x_t + h_t - c_t) = R_t(z_t - c_t).$$

By choosing z_t instead of x_t as the state variable, we can therefore specify the optimization problem by the state space $X = \mathbb{R}_+$, the transition possibility set $G(z, t) = [0, R_t z]$, and the reduced-form utility function $U(z, y, t) = \beta^t u(z - y/R_t)$.

Example 5.2 Next consider the one-sector optimal growth model with Harrod-neutral technological progress. The instantaneous utility function is $u : \mathbb{R}_+ \mapsto \mathbb{R}$, the time-preference factor is β, exogenous labour efficiency is given by $(A_t)_{t=0}^{+\infty}$, and the technology is described by the intensive production function $\bar{f} : \mathbb{R}_+^2 \mapsto \mathbb{R}_+$, where $\bar{f}(k_t, A_t)$ denotes the output plus undepreciated capital that is available for consumption and investment in period t, given that the capital stock at the beginning of the period is k_t and that labour efficiency is A_t. The optimal growth problem can be formulated as

$$\text{maximize} \quad \sum_{t=0}^{+\infty} \beta^t u(c_t)$$

$$\text{subject to} \quad c_t + k_{t+1} = \bar{f}(k_t, A_t)$$

$$\text{and} \quad c_t \geq 0, k_{t+1} \geq 0, k_0 \text{ given.}$$

The primitive form of this problem has the state variable k, the state space $X = [0, +\infty)$, and the control variable c. Moreover, by using the notation from the general model formulation, we have $\bar{G}(k, t) = [0, \bar{f}(k, A_t)]$, $f(k, c, t) = \bar{f}(k, A_t) - c$, and $F(k, c, t) = \beta^t u(c)$. This problem can be rewritten in reduced form by using the transition possibility set $G(k, t) = [0, \bar{f}(k, A_t)]$ and the reduced-form utility function $U(k, k', t) = \beta^t u(\bar{f}(k, A_t) - k')$.

Example 5.3 Finally, consider a two-sector optimal growth model without techno-logical progress. The instantaneous utility function is $u : \mathbb{R}_+ \mapsto \mathbb{R}$, the time-preference factor is β, capital depreciates at the rate δ, the labour force in period t is assumed to be equal to L_t, and the production functions for consumption and investment goods are $\bar{f} : \mathbb{R}_+^2 \mapsto \mathbb{R}_+$ and $\bar{g} : \mathbb{R}_+^2 \mapsto \mathbb{R}_+$, respectively. Denoting by k_t^i and ℓ_t^i the period-t factor inputs of capital and labour in the consumption goods sector (indicated by the superscript $i = c$) and the investment goods sector (superscript $i = k$) and by K_t the aggregate capital stock available in period t, the optimization problem can be formulated as

$$\text{maximize} \quad \sum_{t=0}^{+\infty} \beta^t u(c_t)$$

$$\text{subject to} \quad c_t = \bar{f}\left(k_t^c, \ell_t^c\right)$$

$$K_{t+1} = (1 - \delta)K_t + \bar{g}\left(k_t^k, \ell_t^k\right)$$

$$k_t^c + k_t^k = K_t,$$

$$\ell_t^c + \ell_t^k = L_t,$$

$$k_t^c \geq 0, k_t^k \geq 0, \ell_t^c \geq 0, \ell_t^k \geq 0,$$

$$K_0 \text{ given.}$$

As in the previous example, the aggregate capital stock K_t serves as the state variable. In the present case, however, there are five control variables: $c_t, k_t^c, k_t^k, \ell_t^c$, and ℓ_t^k. The set of feasible controls $\bar{G}(K, t)$ contains all 5-tuples $(c, k^c, k^k, \ell^c, \ell^k)$ which satisfy the constraints

$$c = \bar{f}(k^c, \ell^c), \quad k^c + k^k = K, \quad \ell^c + \ell^k = L_t,$$

$$k^c \geq 0, k^k \geq 0, \ell^c \geq 0, \ell^k \geq 0.$$

The functions $f(K, c, k^c, k^k, \ell^c, \ell^k, t)$ and $F(K, c, k^c, k^k, \ell^c, \ell^k, t)$ are given by $(1 - \delta)K + \bar{g}(k^k, \ell^k)$ and $\beta^t u(c)$, respectively.

The two-sector optimal growth problem can be rewritten in reduced form as follows. The transition possibility set is defined by

$$G(K, t) = [(1 - \delta)K, (1 - \delta)K + \bar{g}(K, L_t)].$$

Note that the upper boundary of the transition possibility set corresponds to a situation in which both factor inputs are entirely allocated to the investment goods sector. The reduced-form utility function is given by

$$U(K, K', t) = \max\{\beta^t u(\bar{f}(k^c, \ell^c)) \mid K' = (1 - \delta)K + \bar{g}(k^k, \ell^k), k^c + k^k$$

$$= K, \ell^c + \ell^k = L_t, k^c \geq 0, k^k \geq 0, \ell^c \geq 0, \ell^k \geq 0\},$$

where the maximization is with respect to the variables k^c, k^k, ℓ^c, and ℓ^k. In words, the value of the reduced form utility function is the maximal utility that can be achieved by allocating the factor inputs capital and labour to the two sectors given the aggregate capital stock K that is available at the start of the period t and the aggregate capital stock K' that is desired for period $t + 1$.

5.2 Euler equation and transversality condition

In this section, we present the first-order optimality conditions for the standard problem in reduced form. We start by deriving the Euler equation, a necessary optimality condition for an interior optimal path. Then we show that under some additional assumptions a limiting transversality condition must also be satisfied by every optimal path. Finally, we prove that under the additional assumptions the Euler equation and the transversality condition together constitute a set of sufficient optimality conditions.

The optimality conditions discussed in the present section are derived under two important assumptions: differentiability of the utility function and interiority of the optimal path. Both of these assumptions are most easily formulated when the state space X is a subset of a Euclidean space. Since this is the case anyway in most economic applications, we assume throughout this section that there exists a positive integer n such that $X \subseteq \mathbb{R}^n$. In order to be able to speak of an interior path, we assume furthermore that the state space X itself has a non-empty interior and that for all pairs $(x, t) \in X \times \mathbb{N}_0$ it holds that the transition possibility set $G(x, t)$ has a non-empty interior as well.[4] A feasible path $(x_t)_{t=0}^{+\infty}$ is said to be an *interior path* if x_{t+1} is in the interior of $G(x_t, t)$ for all $t \in \mathbb{N}_0$. Under the stated assumptions, it is easy to see that an interior path exists for all initial states $x_0 \in X$.

Our next assumption ensures that the infinite sum in the objective functional (5.4) is well defined and that we can compare its values across different feasible paths. More specifically, we assume that the limit

$$\lim_{T \to +\infty} \sum_{t=0}^{T} U(x_t, x_{t+1}, t) \tag{5.5}$$

exists (as a finite number) for all feasible paths $(x_t)_{t=0}^{+\infty}$. Given this assumption, we can say that a feasible path $(x_t)_{t=0}^{+\infty}$ is an optimal path if

$$\lim_{T \to +\infty} \sum_{t=0}^{T} U(x_t, x_{t+1}, t) \geq \lim_{T \to +\infty} \sum_{t=0}^{T} U(\tilde{x}_t, \tilde{x}_{t+1}, t)$$

holds for all feasible paths $(\tilde{x}_t)_{t=0}^{+\infty}$ emanating from x_0.

---

[4] Here, the term 'non-empty interior' has to be understood relative to $\mathbb{R}^n$.

Finally, let us define for all $t \in \mathbb{N}_0$ the set $\Omega_t = \{(x, y) \,|\, x \in X, y \in G(x, t)\} \subseteq X^2$. We assume that for all $t \in \mathbb{N}_0$ it holds that the function $(x, y) \mapsto U(x, y, t)$ is continuous on Ω_t and continuously differentiable on the interior of Ω_t.

We are now ready to derive the Euler equation. To this end, we write the objective functional from (5.4) or (5.5) as

$$\sum_{t=0}^{+\infty} U(x_t, x_{t+1}, t) = \ldots + U(x_t, x_{t+1}, t) + U(x_{t+1}, x_{t+2}, t+1) + \ldots$$

Note that the two displayed terms on the right-hand side of this equation are the only ones that involve the variable x_{t+1}. The only constraints that involve x_{t+1} are $x_{t+1} \in G(x_t, t)$ and $x_{t+2} \in G(x_{t+1}, t+1)$. It follows therefore that if $(x_t)_{t=0}^{+\infty}$ is an optimal path, then it must hold that $y = x_{t+1}$ solves the optimization problem

$$\text{maximize} \quad U(x_t, y, t) + U(y, x_{t+2}, t+1)$$

$$\text{subject to} \quad y \in G(x_t, t) \text{ and } x_{t+2} \in G(y, t+1),$$

where the maximization is with respect to y, whereas x_t and x_{t+2} are fixed. Otherwise, it would be possible to improve the objective value by choosing a state $\tilde{x}_{t+1}$ that differs from x_{t+1}. Since the above problem is a standard static optimization problem with constraints, we can apply the usual optimality conditions from calculus to solve it. In particular, if $(x_t)_{t=0}^{+\infty}$ is an interior optimal path and if the utility function is continuously differentiable on the interior of Ω_t, as we have assumed, then it follows necessarily that[5]

$$U_2(x_t, x_{t+1}, t) + U_1(x_{t+1}, x_{t+2}, t+1) = 0. \tag{5.6}$$

Equation (5.6) is called the *Euler equation*. It is simply the first-order condition for an interior optimum of the static optimization problem displayed above. We summarize these observations in the following theorem.

Theorem 5.1 Consider the dynamic optimization problem in reduced form and assume that X and $G(x, t)$ are subsets of $\mathbb{R}^n$ with non-empty interiors whenever $x \in X$ and $t \in \mathbb{N}_0$. Furthermore, assume that the utility function $U : \Omega \mapsto \mathbb{R}$ is continuously differentiable with respect to its first two arguments on the interior of Ω_t and that the limit in (5.5) exists for all feasible paths. If $(x_t)_{t=0}^{+\infty}$ is an interior optimal path, then it follows that the Euler equation (5.6) holds for all $t \in \mathbb{N}_0$.

---

[5] Recall that we indicate partial derivatives by subscripts (for example, U_1 is the first-order partial derivative of the function U with respect to its first argument, U_{12} is the cross partial derivative of U with respect to its first two arguments etc.).

Recall that we have assumed that the state space is a subset of $\mathbb{R}^n$. Thus, the Euler equation (5.6) is an implicit second-order difference equation in the n state variables. We know from section 1.2 that such an equation can equivalently be written as a first-order difference equation in $2n$ variables. We also know (see theorem 1.1 and the ensuing discussion) that the n initial conditions given by x_0 are typically not sufficient to pin down a unique solution to the Euler equation, but that this is only the case if we have n additional boundary conditions. Our next result often helps to obtain these additional boundary conditions in the form of the so-called *transversality condition*. This optimality condition holds provided that the state space contains only non-negative elements and that the reduced-form utility function satisfies some monotonicity and concavity assumptions.

Theorem 5.2 Consider the dynamic optimization problem in reduced form and assume that the conditions stated in theorem 5.1 are satisfied. In addition, suppose that X is a convex subset of $\mathbb{R}^n_+$ and that for all $t \in \mathbb{N}_0$ the set Ω_t is a convex subset of $\mathbb{R}^{2n}_+$ which contains the origin $(0, 0)$. Finally, suppose that for all $t \in \mathbb{N}_0$ it holds that $U(x, y, t)$ is concave with respect to (x, y). If $(x_t)_{t=0}^{+\infty}$ is an interior optimal path such that $U_2(x_t, x_{t+1}, t) \leq 0$ holds for all $t \in \mathbb{N}_0$, then it follows that

$$\lim_{t \to +\infty} U_2(x_t, x_{t+1}, t)x_{t+1} = 0. \tag{5.7}$$

PROOF: Fix any $T \in \mathbb{N}_0$. From the interiority of the given path $(x_t)_{t=0}^{+\infty}$, the convexity of Ω_t for all $t \in \mathbb{N}_0$, and the fact that $(0, 0) \in \Omega_t$ holds for all $t \in \mathbb{N}_0$, it follows that the path $(\tilde{x}_t^T)_{t=0}^{+\infty}$ defined by

$$\tilde{x}_t^T = \begin{cases} x_t & \text{if } t \leq T, \\ (1 - \alpha)x_t & \text{if } t \geq T + 1 \end{cases}$$

is feasible if α is a sufficiently small positive number. Hence, because of the optimality of $(x_t)_{t=0}^{+\infty}$ it follows that

$$\sum_{t=0}^{+\infty}[U(x_t, x_{t+1}, t) - U(\tilde{x}_t^T, \tilde{x}_{t+1}^T, t)] \geq 0.$$

Using the definition of $(\tilde{x}_t^T)_{t=0}^{+\infty}$, we can rewrite this inequality as

$$U(x_T, x_{T+1}, T) - U(x_T, x_{T+1} - \alpha x_{T+1}, T)$$
$$\geq \sum_{t=T+1}^{+\infty}[U((1 - \alpha)x_t, (1 - \alpha)x_{t+1}, t) - U(x_t, x_{t+1}, t)]. \tag{5.8}$$

The concavity of U with respect to its first two arguments implies furthermore that

$$U((1-\alpha)x_t, (1-\alpha)x_{t+1}, t)) \geq \alpha U(0, 0, t) + (1-\alpha)U(x_t, x_{t+1}, t)$$

which, in turn, yields

$$U((1-\alpha)x_t, (1-\alpha)x_{t+1}, t)) - U(x_t, x_{t+1}, t) \geq \alpha[U(0, 0, t) - U(x_t, x_{t+1}, t)].$$

Combining this inequality with (5.8) and dividing by α, we obtain

$$\frac{U(x_T, x_{T+1}, T) - U(x_T, x_{T+1} - \alpha x_{T+1}, T)}{\alpha} \geq \sum_{t=T+1}^{+\infty} [U(0, 0, t) - U(x_t, x_{t+1}, t)].$$

In the limit as α approaches 0, this inequality becomes

$$U_2(x_T, x_{T+1}, T)x_{T+1} \geq \sum_{t=T+1}^{+\infty} [U(0, 0, t) - U(x_t, x_{t+1}, t)].$$

The left-hand side of this inequality is non-positive because it was assumed that $U_2(x_t, x_{t+1}, t) \leq 0$ holds for all $t \in \mathbb{N}_0$ and because the state space is a subset of the non-negative orthant $\mathbb{R}^n_+$. Hence, letting T approach $+\infty$ and making use of the assumption that the limit in (5.5) exists along every feasible path, it follows that condition (5.7) holds.

Note that the transversality condition is automatically satisfied if $(x_t)_{t=0}^{+\infty}$ is a bounded path and if the partial derivative $U_2(x_t, x_{t+1}, t)$ converges to 0 as t approaches $+\infty$. The latter property is trivially true if U has the form $U(x, y, t) = \beta^t u(x, y)$ with a time-preference factor $\beta \in (0, 1)$ and a continuously differentiable function u with bounded first-order partial derivatives. We would also like to emphasize that in general the additional assumptions required in theorem 5.2 (relative to those of theorem 5.1) cannot be dispensed with. The following example demonstrates for instance that the transversality condition may fail to hold if the requirement $(0, 0) \in \Omega_t$ is not satisfied.

Example 5.4 Consider the reduced-form problem with $X = [0, 1]$

$$G(x, t) = [1/2 - 1/(t+2), 1/2 + 1/(t+2)],$$

$U(x, y, t) = x - y$, and $x_0 = 1/2$. Note that the feasibility of a path $(x_t)_{t=0}^{+\infty}$ implies that $1/2 - 1/(t+2) \leq x_{t+1} \leq 1/2 + 1/(t+2)$ holds for all $t \in \mathbb{N}_0$ and, consequently, that $\lim_{t \to +\infty} x_t = 1/2$ must be satisfied. This, in turn, shows that

$$\sum_{t=0}^{+\infty} U(x_t, x_{t+1}, t) = \lim_{T \to +\infty} \sum_{t=0}^{T} U(x_t, x_{t+1}, t) = x_0 - \lim_{T \to +\infty} x_{T+1} = 0$$

holds for all feasible paths. It follows therefore that every feasible path is optimal. Moreover, there exist interior optimal paths such as the constant one defined by $x_t = 1/2$ for all $t \in \mathbb{N}_0$. On the other hand, we have $\lim_{t \to +\infty} U_2(x_t, x_{t+1}, t)x_{t+1} = -1/2$ such that the transversality condition (5.7) is violated along every optimal path. It is straightforward to verify that the optimization problem of this example satisfies all assumptions of theorem 5.2, except for $(0, 0) \in \Omega_t$ because $\Omega_t = [0, 1] \times [1/2 - 1/(t + 2), 1/2 + 1/(t + 2)]$.

The next example shows that the interiority assumption on the optimal path is also necessary for theorem 5.2 to hold.

Example 5.5 Consider the primitive-form optimization problem of maximizing

$$\sum_{t=0}^{+\infty} \beta^t c_t$$

subject to the state equation

$$x_{t+1} = (x_t - c_t)/\beta$$

as well as the constraints $-1 \leq c_t \leq 0$ and $x_{t+1} \geq 0$ for all $t \in \mathbb{N}_0$. An initial state $x_0 \geq 0$ is assumed to be given. The state space is $X = \mathbb{R}_+$. Because c_t must be non-positive for all t, it follows from the state equation that $x_{t+1} \geq 0$ holds automatically for every feasible sequence of controls. Obviously, this implies that the unique optimal control path is the one in which $c_t = 0$ and

$$x_t = x_0 \beta^{-t} \tag{5.9}$$

hold for all $t \in \mathbb{N}_0$.

The reduced form of this problem can easily be obtained by solving the state equation for c_t and substituting the result into the objective functional and into the constraints. This yields $U(x, y, t) = \beta^t(x - \beta y)$, $G(x, t) = [x/\beta, (x + 1)/\beta]$, and $\Omega_t = \{(x, y) \mid 0 \leq x/\beta \leq y \leq (x + 1)/\beta\}$. Hence, we have $U_2(x, y, t) = -\beta^{t+1}$. Together with (5.9), this implies that along the unique optimal path it holds that

$$\lim_{t \to +\infty} U_2(x_t, x_{t+1}, t)x_{t+1} = -x_0$$

such that the transversality condition is violated for every initial state $x_0 \neq 0$. It is easy to check that the only assumption of theorem 5.2 that is not satisfied in this example is the interiority of the optimal path.

Theorems 5.1 and 5.2 prove that the Euler equation and the transversality condition are necessary for the optimality of a given interior path. The next result shows that under the assumptions of theorem 5.2 these two conditions are also sufficient for optimality.

Theorem 5.3 Consider the dynamic optimization problem in reduced form and let the assumptions of theorem 5.2 be satisfied. If $(x_t)_{t=0}^{+\infty}$ is a feasible path which satisfies the Euler equation (5.6), the transversality condition (5.7), and $U_2(x_t, x_{t+1}, t) \leq 0$ for all $t \in \mathbb{N}_0$, then it follows that $(x_t)_{t=0}^{+\infty}$ is an optimal path.

PROOF: Consider the given path $(x_t)_{t=0}^{+\infty}$ and an alternative feasible path $(\tilde{x}_t)_{t=0}^{+\infty}$ starting at x_0. We have

$$\lim_{T\to+\infty} \sum_{t=0}^{T} [U(x_t, x_{t+1}, t) - U(\tilde{x}_t, \tilde{x}_{t+1}, t)]$$

$$\geq \lim_{T\to+\infty} \sum_{t=0}^{T} [U_1(x_t, x_{t+1}, t)(x_t - \tilde{x}_t) + U_2(x_t, x_{t+1}, t)(x_{t+1} - \tilde{x}_{t+1})]$$

$$= U_1(x_0, x_1, 0)(x_0 - \tilde{x}_0) + \lim_{T\to+\infty} U_2(x_T, x_{T+1}, T)(x_{T+1} - \tilde{x}_{T+1})$$

$$\geq 0,$$

where the first inequality follows from the concavity and differentiability of the utility function U with respect to its first two arguments, the second one from the Euler equation (5.6), and the last one from the feasibility of the two paths (which implies $\tilde{x}_0 - x_0$), the assumptions $U_2(x_t, x_{t+1}, t) \leq 0$ and $X \subseteq \mathbb{R}_+^n$ (which together imply $-U_2(x_T, x_{T+1}, T)\tilde{x}_{T+1} \geq 0$), and the transversality condition (5.7).

The alert reader will have noticed that we do not really need all assumptions of theorem 5.2 for the proof of theorem 5.3. In particular, it is neither necessary that $(0,0) \in \Omega_t$ holds for all $t \in \mathbb{N}_0$ nor that the given path is an interior one (as long as all first-order derivatives of the utility function exist along this path). We illustrate the application of the Euler equation approach in the following example.

Example 5.6 Consider the simple saving problem from example 5.1 with the natural borrowing constraint. Suppose furthermore that the utility function is given by $u(c) = c^\alpha$, where $\alpha \in (0, 1)$, and that the gross rate of return is constant and equal to $R \in (0, \beta^{-1/\alpha})$. As we have seen in example 5.1, this problem can be written in reduced form with $X = \mathbb{R}_+$, $G(x, t) = [0, Rx]$, and $U(x, y, t) = \beta^t u(x - y/R)$, where the state variable x denotes the total wealth of the agent (financial assets plus human capital). All assumptions of theorem 5.1, except for the existence of the limit in (5.5), are trivially satisfied. To verify also the latter assumption just note that the state equation $x_{t+1} = R(x_t - c_t)$ implies that $x_t \leq x_0 R^t$. Moreover, from the natural borrowing constraint we obtain $c_t \leq x_t$ such that $c_t \leq x_0 R^t$ must also hold. From this property, we obtain

$$0 \leq \beta^t u(c_t) = \beta^t c_t^\alpha \leq x_0^\alpha (\beta R^\alpha)^t.$$

Using the assumption $R < \beta^{-1/\alpha}$, it follows from a direct comparison test that the limit in (5.5) exists as a finite number for all feasible paths. Hence, theorem 5.1 applies and an interior optimal path must satisfy the Euler equation

$$-(\beta^t \alpha / R) \left(x_t - \frac{x_{t+1}}{R} \right)^{\alpha-1} + \beta^{t+1} \alpha \left(x_{t+1} - \frac{x_{t+2}}{R} \right)^{\alpha-1} = 0.$$

Note that this equation can also be written in terms of consumption as

$$c_{t+1} = (\beta R)^{1/(1-\alpha)} c_t.$$

In combination with the asset accumulation equation

$$x_{t+1} = R(x_t - c_t),$$

this forms a system of two linear first-order difference equations. Applying the methods developed in chapter 2, we can show that the general solution to this system satisfying the initial condition x_0 is given by

$$c_t = c_0 (\beta R)^{t/(1-\alpha)} \text{ and } x_t = x_0 R^t - \frac{c_0 R^t [1 - (\beta R^\alpha)^{t/(1-\alpha)}]}{1 - (\beta R^\alpha)^{1/(1-\alpha)}}, \tag{5.10}$$

where c_0 is a real number that still needs to be determined. As the Euler equation does not help us to pin down c_0, we need the transversality condition. It is easy to verify that the additional convexity and monotonicity assumptions of theorem 5.2 hold. Note also that $(0, 0) \in \Omega_t = \{(x, y) \mid 0 \leq y \leq Rx\}$. In the present example, the transversality condition (5.7) is equivalent to

$$\lim_{t \to +\infty} \beta^t c_t^{-(1-\alpha)} x_{t+1} = 0.$$

Substituting from (5.10) into this condition, the latter simplifies to $c_0 = [1 - (\beta R^\alpha)^{1/(1-\alpha)}] x_0$. Substituting this result into the expression for x_t stated in (5.10), we see that $x_t = x_0 (\beta R)^{t/(1-\alpha)}$ and, hence, $c_t = [1 - (\beta R^\alpha)^{1/(1-\alpha)}] x_t$ hold for all $t \in \mathbb{N}_0$.

To summarize, we have found a unique feasible path which satisfies both the Euler equation and the transversality condition. Application of theorem 5.3 establishes that this path is indeed an optimal one. It follows that under the stated assumptions it is optimal for the individual to consume the fixed fraction $1 - (\beta R^\alpha)^{1/(1-\alpha)}$ of its total wealth in every period. This generates a geometrically increasing or declining (depending on whether $\beta R > 1$ or $\beta R < 1$) consumption path.

An explicit closed form solution to the Euler equation and the transversality condition as in the above example is often not available. In such a situation, we have two options. Either we employ numerical solution techniques or try to characterize the behaviour of the solution qualitatively using methods such as those presented in part I of this book.

Although the assumptions of theorem 5.3 are satisfied in many economic applications, they are not innocuous. In linear-quadratic models, for example, the instantaneous utility function $U(x, y, t)$ is a quadratic polynomial in the variables x and y and the state space X as well as the transition possibility sets $G(x, t)$ are typically unbounded. This implies that neither the restriction $X \subseteq \mathbb{R}_+^n$ nor the non-positivity of $U_2(x_t, x_{t+1}, t)$ is satisfied. Consequently, theorem 5.3 is not applicable. Fortunately, an approach based on finite-horizon approximations can be used to derive sufficient optimality conditions for this case as well. This is the content of the following theorem.

Theorem 5.4   Consider the dynamic optimization problem in reduced form and let the assumptions of theorem 5.1 be satisfied. In addition, suppose that X is a convex subset of $\mathbb{R}^n$ and that for all $t \in \mathbb{N}_0$ the set Ω_t is a convex subset of $\mathbb{R}^{2n}$ and the function $U(x, y, t)$ is concave with respect to $(x, y) \in \Omega_t$. Let $(x_t)_{t=0}^{+\infty}$ be a feasible path that satisfies the Euler equation (5.6) as well as the transversality condition (5.7). This path is an optimal path provided that the following two conditions hold:

(a) For every $T \in \mathbb{N}_0$, there exists a finite path $(x_t^T)_{t=0}^{T+1}$ satisfying the feasibility constraints $x_0^T = x_0$ and $x_{t+1}^T \in G(x_t^T, t)$, the Euler equation $U_2(x_t^T, x_{t+1}^T, t) + U_1(x_{t+1}^T, x_{t+2}^T, t + 1) = 0$, and the terminal condition $U_2(x_T^T, x_{T+1}^T, T) = 0$.
(b) It holds that $\lim_{T \to +\infty} U_2(x_T, x_{T+1}, T) x_{T+1}^T = 0$.

PROOF: Using the same arguments as in the proof of theorem 5.3, it can be shown that for every feasible path $(\tilde{x}_t)_{t=0}^{+\infty}$ that emanates from x_0 and for every $T \in \mathbb{N}_0$ it holds that

$$\sum_{t=0}^{T} \left[U(x_t, x_{t+1}, t) - U\left(x_t^T, x_{t+1}^T, t\right) \right] \geq U_2(x_T, x_{T+1}, T)\left(x_{T+1} - x_{T+1}^T\right)$$

and

$$\sum_{t=0}^{T} \left[U\left(x_t^T, x_{t+1}^T, t\right) - U(\tilde{x}_t, \tilde{x}_{t+1}, t) \right] \geq 0. \tag{5.11}$$

Adding these inequalities and letting T approach infinity, we get

$$\sum_{t=0}^{+\infty} [U(x_t, x_{t+1}, t) - U(\tilde{x}_t, \tilde{x}_{t+1}, t)] \geq \lim_{T \to +\infty} U_2(x_T, x_{T+1}, T)\left(x_{T+1} - x_{T+1}^T\right) = 0,$$

where the last equality follows from the transversality condition (5.7) and condition
(b) of the theorem. This completes the proof.

A couple of comments on the assumptions of theorem 5.4 are in order. First, theorem 5.4 imposes the same convexity conditions on the dynamic optimization problem
as theorem 5.3 but neither the non-negativity constraints on the state variables nor
the non-positivity of $U_2(x_t, x_{t+1}, t)$. Second, as in theorem 5.3 it is assumed that
the candidate path $(x_t)_{t=0}^{+\infty}$ satisfies the Euler equation and the transversality condition. Finally, instead of the non-negativity of the state variables and the condition
$U_2(x_t, x_{t+1}, t) \leq 0$, we now assume conditions (a) and (b). Condition (a) requires that
for every $T \in \mathbb{N}_0$ there exists an auxiliary path $(x_t^T)_{t=0}^{T+1}$ satisfying the Euler equation as
well as the finite-horizon version of the transversality condition, $U_2(x_T^T, x_{T+1}^T, T) = 0$.
As is shown in inequality (5.11) of the proof of the theorem, this auxiliary path is
optimal for the optimization problem when it is truncated at period T. Condition
(b) of theorem 5.4, on the other hand, is sort of a transversality condition that links
the original candidate path with the optimal paths of the truncated problems. The
following example demonstrates the application of theorem 5.4 to a linear-quadratic
problem.

Example 5.7   Consider the problem of maximizing

$$-(1/2) \sum_{t=0}^{+\infty} \beta^t \left[(x_t - 1)^2 + u_t^2 \right]$$

subject to the constraints $x_0 = 0$ and $x_{t+1} = u_t + \delta x_t$ for all $t \in \mathbb{N}_0$. A possible interpretation of this problem is as follows. The state x_t describes the stock of goodwill
available to a firm in period t. There is an optimal value of the goodwill stock which
is here normalized to 1. Without any effort by the firm ($u_t = 0$), the stock of goodwill approaches 0, the speed of convergence depending on the parameter $\delta \in (0, 1)$.
However, by exerting costly effort u_t the firm can maintain a higher stock of goodwill.

The goal of the firm is to balance the costs of effort against the costs of not having the optimal goodwill stock (both cost functions are assumed to be quadratic). The time-preference factor of the firm is equal to $\beta \in (0, 1)$.

The reduced form of this problem is given by $X = \mathbb{R}$, $G(x, t) = \mathbb{R}$ for all $x \in X$ and all $t \in \mathbb{N}_0$, and $U(x, y, t) = -(1/2)\beta^t[(x - 1)^2 + (y - \delta x)^2]$. The Euler equation is

$$\delta x_t - (1 + \beta + \beta \delta^2)x_{t+1} + \beta \delta x_{t+2} + \beta = 0.$$

The eigenvalues of this difference equation are

$$\sigma_{1,2} = \frac{1 + \beta + \beta \delta^2 \pm \sqrt{D}}{2\beta\delta},$$

where $D = 1 + \beta^2(1 + \delta^2)^2 + 2\beta(1 - \delta^2) > 0$. Hence, both eigenvalues are real and it is straightforward to verify that $0 < \sigma_1 < 1 < 1/\beta < \sigma_2$. The general solution to the Euler equation under the initial condition $x_0 = 0$ is given by

$$x_t = x_t^* + A\left(\sigma_2^t - \sigma_1^t\right), \tag{5.12}$$

where A is a constant and

$$x_t^* = \frac{\beta\left(1 - \sigma_1^t\right)}{(1 + \beta)(1 - \delta) + \beta\delta^2}.$$

The transversality condition (5.7) requires that

$$\lim_{t \to +\infty} \beta^t(\delta x_t - x_{t+1})x_{t+1} = 0.$$

Clearly, this transversality condition can hold along the solution stated in (5.12) only if $A = 0$, because otherwise the terms involving σ_2^t would grow without bound.[6] The unique solution to the Euler equation and the transversality condition is therefore given by $x_t = x_t^*$ for all $t \in \mathbb{N}_0$.

In order to prove the optimality of this path, we verify the conditions of theorem 5.4. The general convexity assumptions of that theorem are obviously satisfied. It remains to verify conditions (a) and (b). To this end, first note that

$$\lim_{t \to +\infty} x_t^* = x^* := \frac{\beta}{(1 + \beta)(1 - \delta) + \beta\delta^2}, \tag{5.13}$$

that is, this limit exists as a finite number. Next consider the solutions $(x_t^T)_{t=0}^{+\infty}$ of the Euler equation starting in $x_0^T = 0$ and satisfying the finite-horizon transversality condition

$$U_2\left(x_T^T, x_{T+1}^T, T\right) = \beta^T\left(\delta x_T^T - x_{T+1}^T\right) = 0. \tag{5.14}$$

---

[6] Recall that $\beta\sigma_2 > 1$.

Because of $x_0^T = 0$, these solutions must be of the form (5.12) for some appropriately chosen coefficient $A = A_T$. This coefficient can be determined by combining (5.12) and (5.14), which yields

$$A_T = \frac{\delta x_T^* - x_{T+1}^*}{(\sigma_2 - \delta)\sigma_2^T - (\sigma_1 - \delta)\sigma_1^T}.$$

Hence, condition (a) of theorem 5.4 holds for the path $x_t^T = x_t^* + A_T(\sigma_2^t - \sigma_1^t)$, where x_t^* and A_T are specified above.

Taking the limit as T approaches infinity of x_{T+1}^T, we can show that

$$\lim_{T \to +\infty} x_{T+1}^T = \frac{\delta x^*(\sigma_2 - 1)}{\sigma_2 - \delta}.$$

Since $\beta \in (0, 1)$ it follows that

$$\lim_{T \to +\infty} U_2(x_T, x_{T+1}, T) x_{T+1}^T = -\frac{\delta(1 - \delta)(x^*)^2(\sigma_2 - 1)}{\sigma_2 - \delta} \lim_{T \to +\infty} \beta^T = 0.$$

This shows that condition (b) of theorem 5.4 is satisfied as well, and it follows that the path $(x_t^*)_{t=0}^{+\infty}$ is indeed optimal.

5.3 The Lagrangian approach

Let us now return to the standard problem in its primitive (non-reduced) form first introduced in section 5.1. A popular way to solve that problem, without translating it first into its reduced form, is the Lagrangian approach. In the present section, we illustrate this approach under the assumption that the state space X is a subset of $\mathbb{R}^n$ and that the control sets $\bar{G}(x, t)$ are subsets of $\mathbb{R}^m$ for some positive integers n and m. Moreover, we assume throughout this section that the functions F and f are continuously differentiable with respect to x and c.

According to the Lagrangian approach, we adjoin the state equation (5.1) to the objective functional (5.2) to form the *Lagrangian function*

$$L\left((x_t)_{t=0}^{+\infty}, (c_t)_{t=0}^{+\infty}, (\lambda_t)_{t=0}^{+\infty}\right) = \sum_{t=0}^{+\infty} \{F(x_t, c_t, t) + \lambda_t[f(x_t, c_t, t) - x_{t+1}]\},$$

where $(\lambda_t)_{t=0}^{+\infty}$ is a sequence of *Lagrange multipliers* satisfying $\lambda_t \in \mathbb{R}^n$ for all $t \in \mathbb{N}_0$.

We note that, whenever $(x_t)_{t=0}^{+\infty}$ and $(c_t)_{t=0}^{+\infty}$ form a feasible pair, the value of the Lagrangian function $L((x_t)_{t=0}^{+\infty}, (c_t)_{t=0}^{+\infty}, (\lambda_t)_{t=0}^{+\infty})$ must coincide with the value of the objective functional in (5.2). This shows in particular that

$$L\left((\tilde{x}_t)_{t=0}^{+\infty}, (\tilde{c}_t)_{t=0}^{+\infty}, (\lambda_t)_{t=0}^{+\infty}\right) \leq L\left((x_t)_{t=0}^{+\infty}, (c_t)_{t=0}^{+\infty}, (\lambda_t)_{t=0}^{+\infty}\right)$$

holds for all sequences of Lagrange multipliers $(\lambda_t)_{t=0}^{+\infty}$ and all feasible pairs $((\tilde{x}_t)_{t=0}^{+\infty}, (\tilde{c}_t)_{t=0}^{+\infty})$ provided that $((x_t)_{t=0}^{+\infty}, (c_t)_{t=0}^{+\infty})$ is an optimal pair. In other words, the optimal pair $((x_t)_{t=0}^{+\infty}, (c_t)_{t=0}^{+\infty})$ maximizes the Lagrangian function irrespective of the values of the Lagrange multipliers. This observation suggests to apply the first-order optimality conditions for the maximization of the Lagrangian with respect to the choice variables $(c_t)_{t=0}^{+\infty}$ and $(x_{t+1})_{t=0}^{+\infty}$.[7] These conditions are given by

$$F_2(x_t, c_t, t) + \lambda_t f_2(x_t, c_t, t) = 0 \tag{5.15}$$

and

$$F_1(x_{t+1}, c_{t+1}, t+1) + \lambda_{t+1} f_1(x_{t+1}, c_{t+1}, t+1) - \lambda_t = 0, \tag{5.16}$$

respectively. It is important to emphasize, however, that the control and state variables cannot be varied independently of each other as they are linked by the state equation (5.1). The following theorem, which shows that conditions (5.15)–(5.16) must hold along an interior optimal pair, is therefore a non-trivial result. It requires an additional regularity assumption and establishes the existence of Lagrange multipliers such that conditions (5.15)–(5.16) are satisfied.

Theorem 5.5 Let $((x_t)_{t=0}^{+\infty}, (c_t)_{t=0}^{+\infty})$ be a feasible pair for problem (5.1)–(5.2) and suppose that for all $t \in \mathbb{N}_0$ it holds that x_t is in the interior of X and that c_t is in the interior of $\bar{G}(x_t, t)$. If $((x_t)_{t=0}^{+\infty}, (c_t)_{t=0}^{+\infty})$ is an optimal pair and if the matrix $f_2(x_t, c_t, t) \in \mathbb{R}^{n \times m}$ has rank m for all t, then it follows that there exists a sequence of Lagrange multipliers $(\lambda_t)_{t=0}^{+\infty}$ such that conditions (5.15)–(5.16) are satisfied.

PROOF: The assumption that the $n \times m$ matrix $f_2(x_t, c_t, t)$ has rank m implies that $m \leq n$ and that $f_2(x_t, c_t, t)$ has full rank. It follows therefore that (5.15) is a system of m linearly independent linear equations in the n components of the vector λ_t. Hence, there exists a vector λ_t satisfying (5.15). The full rank assumption on $f_2(x_t, c_t, t)$ also implies that locally around the optimal pair we can solve (5.1) uniquely for c_t, say $c_t = g(x_{t+1}, x_t, t)$ where g is a smooth function. Furthermore, implicit differentiation of $x_{t+1} = f(x_t, g(x_{t+1}, x_t, t), t)$ yields

$$f_2(x_t, c_t, t)g_1(x_{t+1}, x_t, t) = I_n \text{ and } f_1(x_t, c_t, t) + f_2(x_t, c_t, t)g_2(x_{t+1}, x_t, t) = 0_n,$$

---

[7] Note that x_0 is not a choice variable because it is fixed by the initial condition.

where I_n is the $n \times n$ unit matrix and 0_n is the $n \times n$ zero matrix. Multiplying these equations from the left by $-\lambda_t$ and using (5.15), we get

$$F_2(x_t, c_t, t)g_1(x_{t+1}, x_t, t) = -\lambda_t \text{ and } F_2(x_t, c_t, t)g_2(x_{t+1}, x_t, t) - \lambda_t f_1(x_t, c_t, t) = 0.$$
(5.17)

Finally, by using $c_t = g(x_{t+1}, x_t, t)$, the objective functional can be written (locally around the optimal pair) as

$$\sum_{t=0}^{+\infty} F(x_t, g(x_{t+1}, x_t, t), t).$$

The maximization of this objective functional is a reduced-form problem with reduced-form utility function $U(x, y, t) = F(x, g(y, x, t), t)$. Given the smoothness and interiority assumptions stated above, it follows that the Euler equation must hold, which is given by

$$F_2(x_t, c_t, t)g_1(x_{t+1}, x_t, t) + F_1(x_{t+1}, c_{t+1}, t+1)$$
$$+ F_2(x_{t+1}, c_{t+1}, t+1)g_2(x_{t+2}, x_{t+1}, t+1) = 0.$$

Combining this equation with (5.17), we obtain (5.16).

The requirement that the matrix $f_2(x_t, c_t, t)$ has full rank is the regularity assumption that we have mentioned above, and it is usually referred to as a *constraint qualification*. Without such a regularity assumption, it is not possible to establish the existence of Lagrange multipliers satisfying conditions (5.15)–(5.16). However, the constraint qualification that we have postulated is not the only possible regularity condition. We have chosen the present form as it is easy to verify and because it allows a rather intuitive proof of the theorem. This proof is based on a conversion of the primitive form of the problem into its reduced form with utility function $U(x, y, t) = F(x, g(y, x, t), t)$. This approach helps also to find the appropriate form of the transversality condition for the Lagrangian approach. Recall that the transversality condition for the reduced-form problem is given by (5.7). In the present case, we have

$$U_2(x_t, x_{t+1}, t) = F_2(x_t, c_t, t)g_1(x_{t+1}, x_t, t) = -\lambda_t,$$

where the first equality follows from $U(x, y, t) = F(x, g(y, x, t), t)$ and the second one from (5.17). This shows that the transversality condition (5.7) can be rewritten as

$$\lim_{t \to +\infty} \lambda_t x_{t+1} = 0.$$
(5.18)

We do not formally state a theorem that proves the necessity of the transversality condition for the primitive form of the standard problem but simply note that as in the case of the reduced-form model such a theorem would require additional assumptions such as convexity; see theorem 5.2. These additional assumptions are also required in the following result, which is the analogue to theorem 5.3.

Theorem 5.6 Let $X \subseteq \mathbb{R}^n_+$ and $\bar{\Omega}_t = \{(x, c) \mid x \in X, c \in \bar{G}(x, t)\}$ be convex sets for all $t \in \mathbb{N}_0$. Suppose that there exists a feasible pair $((x_t)^{+\infty}_{t=0}, (c_t)^{+\infty}_{t=0})$ as well as a sequence of non-negative Lagrange multipliers $(\lambda_t)^{+\infty}_{t=0}$ such that conditions (5.15)–(5.16) hold for all t. If the function $F(x, c, t) + \lambda_t f(x, c, t)$ is concave with respect to (x, c) for all t and if the transversality condition (5.18) is satisfied, then it follows that $((x_t)^{+\infty}_{t=0}, (c_t)^{+\infty}_{t=0})$ is an optimal pair.

PROOF: Let $((x_t)^{+\infty}_{t=0}, (c_t)^{+\infty}_{t=0})$ be the given pair and consider an alternative feasible pair, say $((\tilde{x}_t)^{+\infty}_{t=0}, (\tilde{c}_t)^{+\infty}_{t=0})$. Furthermore, define $M(x, c, t) = F(x, c, t) + \lambda_t f(x, c, t)$. We have

$$\lim_{T \to +\infty} \sum_{t=0}^{T} [F(x_t, c_t, t) - F(\tilde{x}_t, \tilde{c}_t, t)]$$

$$= \lim_{T \to +\infty} \sum_{t=0}^{T} [M(x_t, c_t, t) - M(\tilde{x}_t, \tilde{c}_t, t) - \lambda_t(x_{t+1} - \tilde{x}_{t+1})]$$

$$\geq \lim_{T \to +\infty} \sum_{t=0}^{T} [M_1(x_t, c_t, t)(x_t - \tilde{x}_t) + M_2(x_t, c_t, t)(c_t - \tilde{c}_t) - \lambda_t(x_{t+1} - \tilde{x}_{t+1})]$$

$$= M_1(x_0, c_0, 0)(x_0 - \tilde{x}_0) - \lim_{T \to +\infty} \lambda_T(x_{T+1} - \tilde{x}_{T+1})$$

$$\geq 0,$$

where the first step follows from the definition of the function M, the second one from the convexity assumptions stated in the theorem, the third one from the first-order conditions (5.15)–(5.16), and the last one from the feasibility of both pairs (which implies $x_0 = \tilde{x}_0$), the transversality condition (5.18), and the non-negativity of $\tilde{x}_{T+1}$ and λ_T.

The Lagrangian approach to solve dynamic optimization problems is very versatile. It can be used not only to solve the standard problem formulated in section 5.1, but also many problems with non-standard features. We will see several examples of its applicability in the following chapters. Here we illustrate the application of the Lagrangian approach by means of a growth model.

Example 5.8 The state variable in the optimal growth model from example 5.2 is the aggregate capital stock k. The capital accumulation equation is given by

$$k_{t+1} = \bar{f}(k_t, A_t) - c_t. \tag{5.19}$$

The fundamentals of the problem are $X = [0, +\infty)$, $\bar{G}(k, t) = [0, \bar{f}(k, A_t)]$, $f(k, c, t) = \bar{f}(k, A_t) - c$, and $F(k, c, t) = \beta^t u(c)$. We assume that the utility function u is non-decreasing and concave, and that the production function $\bar{f}(k, A)$ is non-negative and concave with respect to the capital stock k. The latter assumption implies in particular that $\bar{\Omega}_t$ is convex as required by theorem 5.6. Note furthermore that $f_2(k, c, t) = -1$ such that the constraint qualification is trivially satisfied. The first-order condition (5.15) is given by

$$\beta^t u'(c_t) - \lambda_t = 0, \tag{5.20}$$

which shows that the Lagrange multiplier for period t is equal to the present value of marginal utility in period t. Because the utility function is non-decreasing, it follows that λ_t is non-negative as required in theorem 5.6. Moreover, because both $F(k, c, t) = \beta^t u(c)$ and $f(k, c, t) = \bar{f}(k, A) - c$ are concave with respect to (k, c) and because λ_t is non-negative for all t, it holds that $F(k, c, t) + \lambda_t f(k, c, t)$ is a concave function of (k, c). To summarize, all assumptions of theorem 5.6 are satisfied, and it follows that the first-order conditions (5.15)–(5.16) plus the transversality condition (5.18) are sufficient for optimality.

We have already shown that in the present example condition (5.15) is equivalent to (5.20). Combining equation (5.20) with condition (5.16), we obtain after division by β^t

$$u'(c_t) = \beta u'(c_{t+1}) \bar{f}_1(k_{t+1}, A_{t+1}). \tag{5.21}$$

This demonstrates that the marginal rate of substitution between consumption in two consecutive periods t and $t + 1$, $u'(c_t)/[\beta u'(c_{t+1})]$, must be equal to the marginal return on holding capital from period t to period $t + 1$, $\bar{f}_1(k_{t+1}, A_{t+1})$. Equations (5.19) and (5.21) form a system of two implicit non-linear difference equations in the system variables (k_t, c_t).[8] Every trajectory of this system, which starts at the given initial stock of capital k_0 and which satisfies the transversality condition

$$\lim_{t \to +\infty} \beta^t u'(c_t) k_{t+1} = 0, \tag{5.22}$$

must be an optimal pair. Note in particular that every trajectory of (5.19) and (5.21), which remains bounded and for which there exists $\varepsilon > 0$ such that $c_t \geq \varepsilon$ holds for all $t \in \mathbb{N}_0$, automatically satisfies (5.22).

---

[8] Recall that the productivity process $(A_t)_{t=0}^{+\infty}$ is assumed to be exogenously given.

The solution of the one-sector growth model can be described in closed form if the utility function is logarithmic, that is, $u(c) = \ln c$, and if the production function takes the Cobb-Douglas form $\bar{f}(k, A) = \psi(A)k^\alpha$. Here $\alpha \in (0, 1)$ is a parameter and ψ is an arbitrary strictly positive function. In this special case, it turns out that the optimal saving rate is a constant $s \in (0, 1)$. To determine this value s, we substitute the conjectured relation $c_t = (1 - s)\bar{f}(k_t, A_t)$ into (5.19) and (5.21). Because of the assumed functional forms, this yields

$$k_{t+1} = s\psi(A_t)k_t^\alpha$$

and

$$\left[(1 - s)\psi(A_t)k_t^\alpha\right]^{-1} = \beta\left[(1 - s)\psi(A_{t+1})k_{t+1}^\alpha\right]^{-1}\alpha\psi(A_{t+1})k_{t+1}^{\alpha-1}.$$

Substituting the expression for k_{t+1} from the former equation into the latter yields, after some simplifications, $s = \alpha\beta$. The capital accumulation equation therefore takes the form

$$k_{t+1} = \alpha\beta\psi(A_t)k_t^\alpha.$$

Defining $z_t = \ln k_t$, this equation can be rewritten as

$$z_{t+1} = b(t) + \alpha z_t,$$

with $b(t) = \ln\alpha + \ln\beta + \ln\psi(A_t)$. Applying the methods introduced in section 2.4, this non-homogeneous linear difference equation can be shown to have the solution

$$z_t = \alpha^t\left[\ln k_0 + \sum_{s=1}^t \alpha^{-s}b(s - 1)\right].$$

Now consider the transversality condition (5.22) for the present specification. It becomes

$$\lim_{t\to+\infty}\beta^t u'(c_t)k_{t+1} = \lim_{t\to+\infty}\beta^t\left[(1 - s)\psi(A_t)k_t^\alpha\right]^{-1}s\psi(A_t)k_t^\alpha = \lim_{t\to+\infty}\beta^t s/(1 - s) = 0,$$

where $c_t = (1 - s)\psi(A_t)k_t^\alpha$ and $k_{t+1} = s\psi(A_t)k_t^\alpha$ have been used. Obviously, this holds independently of the specification of the process $(A_t)_{t=0}^{+\infty}$. We conclude that for a logarithmic utility function and Cobb–Douglas technology a constant saving rate equal to $s = \alpha\beta$ is optimal.

For general utility and production functions, an analytical solution to the one-sector growth model is not available. However, it is often possible to derive the qualitative properties of the optimal solution from the difference equations (5.19) and (5.21) and the transversality condition (5.22). For example, if the production function $\bar{f}$ is homogeneous of degree 1, if marginal utility takes the form $u'(c) = c^{-\sigma}$ for some constant $\sigma > 0$, and if the gross rate of technological progress A_{t+1}/A_t is a constant

$g > 0$, then we can rewrite the two difference equations in terms of the transformed variables $\tilde{k}_t = k_t/A_t$ and $\tilde{c}_t = c_t/A_t$ as

$$\tilde{k}_{t+1} = [\bar{f}(\tilde{k}_t, 1) - \tilde{c}_t]/g, \tag{5.23}$$

$$u'(\tilde{c}_t) = \beta g^{-\sigma} u'(\tilde{c}_{t+1}) \bar{f}_1(\tilde{k}_{t+1}, 1) \tag{5.24}$$

and the transversality condition becomes

$$\lim_{t \to +\infty} \beta^t g^{(1-\sigma)t} u'(\tilde{c}_t)\tilde{k}_{t+1} = 0. \tag{5.25}$$

Note that the difference equations (5.23)–(5.24) are autonomous, which suggests to identify their fixed points. From (5.24), it is clear that in a fixed point $(\tilde{k}^*, \tilde{c}^*)$ it must be the case that $\bar{f}_1(\tilde{k}^*, 1) = g^\sigma/\beta$. Substituting this value into (5.23) yields a unique value for $\tilde{c}^*$. Hence, there exists a unique fixed point of (5.23)–(5.24). The Jacobian matrix of these two difference equations evaluated at the fixed point is given by

$$J = \begin{pmatrix} (\beta g^{1-\sigma})^{-1} & -g^{-1} \\ \tilde{c}^* \bar{f}_{11}(\tilde{k}^*, 1)(\sigma g)^{-1} & 1 - \beta \tilde{c}^* \bar{f}_{11}(\tilde{k}^*, 1)(\sigma g^{1+\sigma})^{-1} \end{pmatrix}.$$

The determinant of this matrix is given by $D = (\beta g^{1-\sigma})^{-1}$ and its trace is $T = D + 1 - \beta \tilde{c}^* \bar{f}_{11}(\tilde{k}^*, 1)(\sigma g^{1+\sigma})^{-1}$. Assuming $\beta g^{1-\sigma} < 1$ and $\bar{f}_{11}(\tilde{k}^*, 1) < 0$, it follows therefore that $1 < D < T - 1$. According to the results from section 2.3, this implies that the Jacobian matrix has one stable and one unstable eigenvalue, and the stable-unstable manifold theorem 3.6 tells us that there exists a one-dimensional stable manifold locally around the fixed point. We can therefore conclude that for all initial values $\tilde{k}_0$ sufficiently close to the fixed point there exists a unique trajectory of the system (5.23)–(5.24) that converges to the fixed point. Because we have assumed that $\beta g^{1-\sigma} < 1$, it is obvious that the transversality condition (5.25) holds along this trajectory and it follows finally from theorem 5.6 that this trajectory is an optimal pair.

5.4 The recursive approach

The recursive approach to dynamic optimization (also called the dynamic programming approach) is conceptually quite different from the Euler equation approach or the Lagrangian approach. Whereas the latter methods are based on variational arguments and yield necessary optimality conditions for interior optima or, in the presence of additional convexity properties, sufficient optimality conditions, the recursive approach does not require any variational arguments or interiority assumptions and yields necessary and sufficient optimality conditions without convexity assumptions.

Recall the standard problem in reduced form as introduced in equations (5.3)–(5.4) of section 5.1. The state space X is some arbitrary non-empty set and the transition possibility set $G(x, t) \subseteq X$ is non-empty for all $x \in X$ and all $t \in \mathbb{N}_0$. This ensures that for every initial time $s \in \mathbb{N}_0$ and for every initial state $x \in X$ there exists at least one sequence $(x_t)_{t=s}^{+\infty}$ satisfying $x_s = x$ and $x_{t+1} \in G(x_t, t)$ for all $t \geq s$. In other words, there exists at least one feasible path for problem $\mathbf{P}(x, s)$, where $\mathbf{P}(x, s)$ is defined as the maximization of

$$J((x_t)_{t=s}^{+\infty}, s) = \sum_{t=s}^{+\infty} U(x_t, x_{t+1}, t)$$

subject to $x_s = x$ and $x_{t+1} \in G(x_t, t)$ for all $t \geq s$. Let us denote the set of all feasible paths for problem $\mathbf{P}(x, s)$ by $\mathcal{F}(x, s)$. Furthermore, we maintain the assumption that

$$\lim_{T \to +\infty} \sum_{t=s}^{T} U(x_t, x_{t+1}, t)$$

exists for all feasible paths, which ensures that the objective functional $J((x_t)_{t=s}^{+\infty}, s)$ is a well defined real number whenever $(x_t)_{t=s}^{+\infty} \in \mathcal{F}(x, s)$. At the heart of the recursive approach to dynamic optimization are the *optimal value function* $V : X \times \mathbb{N}_0 \mapsto \mathbb{R}$ defined by

$$V(x, s) = \sup \left\{ J((x_t)_{t=s}^{+\infty}, s) \,|\, (x_t)_{t=s}^{+\infty} \in \mathcal{F}(x, s) \right\}$$

and the *Bellman equation*

$$V(x, s) = \sup \left\{ U(x, y, s) + V(y, s + 1) \,|\, y \in G(x, s) \right\}. \tag{5.26}$$

The remainder of this section is devoted to establishing the connection between the dynamic optimization problem (5.3)–(5.4) and the Bellman equation (5.26).

Theorem 5.7 The optimal value function satisfies the Bellman equation.

PROOF: Let $(x_t)_{t=s}^{+\infty} \in \mathcal{F}(x, s)$ be any feasible path for $\mathbf{P}(x, s)$. Note that

$$J((x_t)_{t=s}^{+\infty}, s) = \sum_{t=s}^{+\infty} U(x_t, x_{t+1}, t) = U(x, x_{s+1}, s) + J((x_t)_{t=s+1}^{+\infty}, s + 1)$$

and that $(x_t)_{t=s+1}^{+\infty} \in \mathcal{F}(x_{s+1}, s + 1)$. Thus, we have

$$V(x, s) = \sup \left\{ J((x_t)_{t=s}^{+\infty}, s) \,\big|\, (x_t)_{t=s}^{+\infty} \in \mathcal{F}(x, s) \right\}$$

$$= \sup \left\{ U(x, y, s) + J((x_t)_{t=s+1}^{+\infty}, s + 1) \,\big|\, y \in G(x, s), (x_t)_{t=s+1}^{+\infty} \in \mathcal{F}(y, s+1) \right\}$$

$$= \sup \{ U(x, y, s) + V(y, s + 1) \,|\, y \in G(x, s) \}.$$

This completes the proof of the theorem.

Having shown that the optimal value function is a solution to the Bellman equation, we want to know whether it is the unique solution. The following example demonstrates that this is in general not the case.

Example 5.9 Let us reconsider the optimization problem from example 5.5. Its reduced form is

$$\text{maximize} \quad \sum_{t=0}^{+\infty} \beta^t (x_t - \beta x_{t+1})$$

$$\text{subject to} \quad x_{t+1} \in [x_t/\beta, (x_t + 1)/\beta]$$

and the state space is $X = \mathbb{R}_+$. From the discussion in example 5.5, we know that the unique optimal path is given by $x_t = x_0 \beta^{-t}$ and that the corresponding optimal value is equal to $V(x, s) = 0$ for all $x \in X$ and all $s \in \mathbb{N}_0$. The Bellman equation for this problem is given by

$$V(x, s) = \sup\{\beta^s(x - \beta y) + V(y, s + 1) \mid x/\beta \le y \le (x + 1)/\beta\}. \tag{5.27}$$

In accordance with theorem 5.7, we see that the optimal value function $V(x, s) = 0$ indeed satisfies this equation, where the supremum on the right-hand side of (5.27) is obtained for $y = x/\beta$. We claim, however, that every function

$$\tilde{V}(x, s) = \beta^s(Px + Q) \tag{5.28}$$

with $P \in \mathbb{R}$ and

$$Q = \begin{cases} 0 & \text{if } P \le 1, \\ (P - 1)/(1 - \beta) & \text{if } P > 1 \end{cases}$$

satisfies the Bellman equation. Indeed, if we replace $V(y, s + 1)$ on the right-hand side of (5.27) by $\tilde{V}(y, s + 1) = \beta^{s+1}(Py + Q)$, then the supremum is attained at $y = x/\beta$ if $P < 1$, at any value $y \in [x/\beta, (x + 1)/\beta]$ if $P = 1$, and at $y = (x + 1)/\beta$ if $P > 1$. The supremum itself is easily seen to be equal to $\tilde{V}(x, s)$ as specified in (5.28) such that our claim is verified.

This simple example shows that the Bellman equation does not necessarily have a unique solution. The following theorem, however, proves that it can only have a single solution for which the condition

$$\lim_{t \to +\infty} V(x_t, t) = 0 \tag{5.29}$$

holds for all feasible paths $(x_t)_{t=0}^{+\infty} \in \mathcal{F}(x, 0)$ and all $x \in X$.

Theorem 5.8 Suppose that the function $V : X \times \mathbb{N}_0 \mapsto \mathbb{R}$ satisfies the Bellman equation and that condition (5.29) holds for all feasible paths $(x_t)_{t=0}^{+\infty} \in \mathcal{F}(x, 0)$ and all $x \in X$. Then it follows that V is the optimal value function.

PROOF: Let $V : X \times \mathbb{N}_0 \mapsto \mathbb{R}$ be an arbitrary solution to the Bellman equation and let $(x_t)_{t=s}^{+\infty} \in \mathcal{F}(x, s)$ be an arbitrary feasible path. We have

$$V(x, s) \geq U(x_s, x_{s+1}, s) + V(x_{s+1}, s + 1)$$

$$\geq U(x_s, x_{s+1}, s) + U(x_{s+1}, x_{s+2}, s + 1) + V(x_{s+2}, s + 2)$$

$$\vdots$$

$$\geq \sum_{t=s}^{T-1} U(x_t, x_{t+1}, t) + V(x_T, T).$$

By taking the limit $T \to +\infty$, this inequality together with (5.29) implies that $V(x, s) \geq J((x_t)_{t=s}^{+\infty}, s)$ holds. Because the path $(x_t)_{t=s}^{+\infty}$ was chosen arbitrarily from $\mathcal{F}(x, s)$, it follows that

$$V(x, s) \geq \sup \left\{ J((x_t)_{t=s}^{+\infty}, s) \mid (x_t)_{t=s}^{+\infty} \in \mathcal{F}(x, s) \right\}.$$

This demonstrates that $V(x, s)$ is at least as large as the optimal value of the dynamic optimization problem. In order to complete the proof, it is therefore sufficient to show that $V(x, s)$ cannot be strictly larger than the optimal value. Suppose that this property is not true, that is, that there exists a state $x_s \in X$ and a positive real number ε such that for all feasible paths $(x_t)_{t=s}^{+\infty} \in \mathcal{F}(x_s, s)$ it holds that

$$V(x_s, s) \geq \sum_{t=s}^{+\infty} U(x_t, x_{t+1}, t) + \varepsilon. \tag{5.30}$$

In particular, this has to hold for the feasible path $(x_t)_{t=s}^{+\infty} \in \mathcal{F}(x_s, s)$ that is constructed in the following way. Let $(\delta_t)_{t=s}^{+\infty}$ be a sequence of positive numbers such that

$$\sum_{t=s}^{+\infty} \delta_t \leq \varepsilon/2. \tag{5.31}$$

Because V is a solution to the Bellman equation and because δ_t is positive, there exists $x_{t+1} \in G(x_t, t)$ such that

$$V(x_t, t) \leq U(x_t, x_{t+1}, t) + V(x_{t+1}, t + 1) + \delta_t. \tag{5.32}$$

Now we set $t = s$ in inequality (5.32) and combine this result with (5.30) to obtain

$$U(x_s, x_{s+1}, s) + V(x_{s+1}, s + 1) + \delta_s \geq \sum_{t=s}^{+\infty} U(x_t, x_{t+1}, t) + \varepsilon.$$

Subtracting $U(x_s, x_{s+1}, s)$ from both sides, we get

$$V(x_{s+1}, s+1) + \delta_s \geq \sum_{t=s+1}^{+\infty} U(x_t, x_{t+1}, t) + \varepsilon.$$

In an analogous way, we can set $t = s + 1$ in (5.32) and combine this with the above inequality to get

$$V(x_{s+2}, s+2) + \delta_s + \delta_{s+1} \geq \sum_{t=s+2}^{+\infty} U(x_t, x_{t+1}, t) + \varepsilon.$$

Proceeding in this fashion, it follows for all $T \in \mathbb{N}_0$ that

$$V(x_T, T) + \sum_{t=s}^{T-1} \delta_t \geq \sum_{t=T}^{+\infty} U(x_t, x_{t+1}, t) + \varepsilon.$$

Now we let T approach $+\infty$. Because of (5.29) and (5.31) and because of the fact that $\sum_{t=0}^{+\infty} U(x_t, x_{t+1}, t)$ is a finite number, it follows that $\varepsilon/2 \geq \varepsilon$ which is obviously a contradiction. This completes the proof of the theorem.

In theorems 5.7–5.8, we have established a link between the optimal value function of the dynamic optimization problem (5.3)–(5.4) and the solutions of the Bellman equation. Now we use the optimal value function to characterize optimal paths. We start by a result which is known as the *principle of optimality* and which basically says that every part of an optimal path must itself be optimal.

Lemma 5.1 Let $(x_t)_{t=s}^{+\infty}$ be an optimal path for problem $\mathbf{P}(x_s, s)$. For all $\tilde{s} \geq s$, it holds that $(x_t)_{t=\tilde{s}}^{+\infty}$ is an optimal path for problem $\mathbf{P}(x_{\tilde{s}}, \tilde{s})$.

PROOF: Suppose to the contrary that $(x_t)_{t=\tilde{s}}^{+\infty}$ is not an optimal path for problem $\mathbf{P}(x_{\tilde{s}}, \tilde{s})$. Then there exists a feasible path $(\tilde{x}_t)_{t=\tilde{s}}^{+\infty} \in \mathcal{F}(x_{\tilde{s}}, \tilde{s})$ such that

$$\sum_{t=\tilde{s}}^{+\infty} U(\tilde{x}_t, \tilde{x}_{t+1}, t) > \sum_{t=\tilde{s}}^{+\infty} U(x_t, x_{t+1}, t).$$

Consider the path $(\hat{x}_t)_{t=s}^{+\infty}$ defined by

$$\hat{x}_t = \begin{cases} x_t & \text{if } t \leq \tilde{s}, \\ \tilde{x}_t & \text{if } t \geq \tilde{s}. \end{cases}$$

This definition makes sense because it follows from the feasibility of $(\tilde{x}_s)_{t=\tilde{s}}^{+\infty}$ for $\mathbf{P}(x_{\tilde{s}}, \tilde{s})$ that $\tilde{x}_{\tilde{s}} = x_{\tilde{s}}$. Obviously, it holds that $(\hat{x}_t)_{t=s}^{+\infty} \in \mathcal{F}(x_s, s)$ and that

$$
\sum_{t=s}^{+\infty} U(\hat{x}_t, \hat{x}_{t+1}, t) = \sum_{t=s}^{\tilde{s}-1} U(x_t, x_{t+1}, t) + \sum_{t=\tilde{s}}^{+\infty} U(\tilde{x}_t, \tilde{x}_{t+1}, t)
$$

$$
> \sum_{t=s}^{\tilde{s}-1} U(x_t, x_{t+1}, t) + \sum_{t=\tilde{s}}^{+\infty} U(x_t, x_{t+1}, t)
$$

$$
= \sum_{t=s}^{+\infty} U(x_t, x_{t+1}, t).
$$

This is a contradiction to the optimality of $(x_t)_{t=s}^{+\infty}$ for $\mathbf{P}(x_s, s)$, which proves the lemma.

The next theorem says that along an optimal path the successor state of x_t attains the supremum in the Bellman equation, provided that V is the optimal value function. This property, formally stated as equation (5.33) below, is therefore a necessary optimality condition. Note that it holds without any differentiability assumptions such as those imposed throughout sections 5.2 and 5.3.

Theorem 5.9   If $V : X \times \mathbb{N}_0 \mapsto \mathbb{R}$ is the optimal value function of problem (5.3)–(5.4) and if $(x_t)_{t=s}^{+\infty} \in \mathcal{F}(x_s, s)$ is an optimal path, then it follows that the equation

$$
V(x_t, t) = U(x_t, x_{t+1}, t) + V(x_{t+1}, t + 1) \tag{5.33}
$$

holds for all $t \geq s$.

PROOF: Since V is the optimal value function and because $(x_t)_{t=s}^{+\infty}$ is an optimal path, we have

$$
V(x_s, s) = J\big((x_t)_{t=s}^{+\infty}, s\big) = U(x_s, x_{s+1}, s) + J\big((x_t)_{t=s+1}^{+\infty}, s + 1\big).
$$

From the principle of optimality (lemma 5.1), it follows that $(x_t)_{t=s+1}^{+\infty}$ is an optimal path for $\mathbf{P}(x_{s+1}, s + 1)$ such that

$$
J\big((x_t)_{t=s+1}^{+\infty}, s + 1\big) = V(x_{s+1}, s + 1).
$$

Combining the above two equations proves the theorem for $t = s$. Moreover, because $(x_t)_{t=s+1}^{+\infty}$ is optimal for $\mathbf{P}(x_{s+1}, s + 1)$, we can repeat the whole argument with s replaced by $s + 1$. Continuing this way, equation (5.33) can be proved for all $t \geq s$.

The converse of theorem 5.9 is true provided that condition (5.29) holds along the path under consideration. This is formally proved in the following theorem.

Theorem 5.10 If $V : X \times \mathbb{N}_0 \mapsto \mathbb{R}$ is the optimal value function of problem (5.3)–(5.4) and if $(x_t)_{t=s}^{+\infty}$ is a feasible path for that problem which satisfies conditions (5.29) and (5.33), then it follows that $(x_t)_{t=s}^{+\infty}$ is an optimal path.

PROOF: From (5.33), we obtain for all T that

$$V(x_s, s) = \sum_{t=s}^{T-1} U(x_t, x_{t+1}, t) + V(x_T, T).$$

Taking the limit as T approaches $+\infty$ and using (5.29), we obtain $V(x_s, s) = J((x_t)_{t=s}^{+\infty}, s)$. Since V is the optimal value function, this implies that $(x_t)_{t=s}^{+\infty}$ is an optimal path for problem $\mathbf{P}(x_s, s)$.

The above theorem shows that (5.29) and (5.33) together are sufficient for optimality. Note that these sufficient optimality conditions do not require that the optimization problem satisfies any convexity properties such as those we imposed in the corresponding results in sections 5.2 and 5.3.

We define the *optimal policy correspondence h*, a set-valued mapping from $X \times \mathbb{N}_0$ to X, by

$$h(x, s) = \{y \in G(x, s) \mid V(x, s) = U(x, y, s) + V(y, s + 1)\}.$$

Using this notation, we can restate the necessary optimality condition from theorem 5.9, equation (5.33), as the requirement that an optimal path must satisfy the condition

$$x_{t+1} \in h(x_t, t) \tag{5.34}$$

for all $t \in \mathbb{N}_0$. Analogously, the sufficient optimality conditions from theorem 5.10 require that the candidate path $(x_t)_{t=0}^{+\infty}$ must satisfy condition (5.34) along with the terminal condition at infinity (5.29).

We conclude this section with a simple example demonstrating some important aspects of the dynamic programming approach.

Example 5.10 Consider the reduced-form optimization problem defined by $X = [0, 1]$, $G(x, t) = [0, 1]$ for all $x \in X$ and all $t \in \mathbb{N}_0$, and

$$U(x, y, t) = 2^{-t}[x^3 - x^2 y + 2xy^2 - (3/2)y^3].$$

The Bellman equation is given by

$$V(x,s) = \sup\{2^{-s}[x^3 - x^2y + 2xy^2 - (3/2)y^3] + V(y, s+1) \mid y \in [0, 1]\}.$$

We claim that the function $V(x, s) = 2^{-s}x^3$ is a solution to this equation. To verify this claim, we substitute $V(y, s+1) = 2^{-s-1}y^3$ on the right-hand side of the equation to get $V(x, s) = \sup\{Z(y; x, s) \mid y \in [0, 1]\}$, where

$$Z(y; x, s) = 2^{-s}(x^3 - x^2y + 2xy^2 - y^3).$$

The function $Z(y; x, s)$ is a cubic polynomial in y. If it has an interior maximum $\tilde{y}$, then the first-order condition $Z_1(\tilde{y}; x, s) = 2^{-s}(3\tilde{y} - x)(x - \tilde{y}) = 0$ and the second-order condition $Z_{11}(\tilde{y}; x, s) = 2^{-s+1}(2x - 3\tilde{y}) \le 0$ must hold. The first-order condition has the two solutions $\tilde{y} = x$ and $\tilde{y} = x/3$. The second-order condition shows that only $\tilde{y} = x$ is a maximum. The function $Z(y; x, s)$ could also have maxima at the boundaries 0 or 1, respectively. We have $Z(0; x, s) = 2^{-s}x^3$ and $Z(1; x, s) = 2^{-s}[x^3 - (x - 1)^2] \le Z(0; x, s)$ with equality holding if and only if $x = 1$. Comparison of the values $Z(x; x, s)$, $Z(0; x, s)$, and $Z(1; x, s)$ therefore shows that for every $x \in X$, $Z(y; x, s)$ has two maxima at $y = x$ and $y = 0$ (for $x = 0$ the two maximizers coincide). The maximum is in any case equal to $2^{-s}x^3$ such that the maximized right-hand side of the Bellman equation is indeed equal to the proposed function $V(x, s) = 2^{-s}x^3$. This completes the proof that this function solves the Bellman equation.

Because the state space is a compact interval, every feasible path $(x_t)_{t=0}^{+\infty}$ remains bounded. This implies of course that $\lim_{t \to +\infty} V(x_t, t) = 2^{-t}x_t^3 = 0$ holds along all feasible paths $(x_t)_{t=0}^{+\infty}$, and it follows from theorem 5.8 that $V(x, s) = 2^{-s}x^3$ is indeed the optimal value function. As we have shown above, the right-hand side of the Bellman equation is maximized at $y = x$ and $y = 0$ such that the optimal policy correspondence is given by $h(x, s) = \{0, x\}$. Every path $(x_t)_{t=0}^{+\infty}$ that satisfies $x_{t+1} \in \{0, x_t\}$ is therefore an optimal path (see theorem 5.10). Because the optimal policy correspondence is not a singleton, there are infinitely many such paths starting from any given initial state $x_0 > 0$. For the initial state $x_0 = 0$, there exists a unique optimal path, namely the constant path $x_t = 0$ for all $t \in \mathbb{N}_0$.

Note that the utility function $U(x, y, s)$ in the above example is neither concave in x nor in y. Nevertheless, we could apply the sufficient optimality condition from theorem 5.10 to characterize the optimal policy correspondence. This is one of the strengths of the dynamic programming approach which distinguishes it from the variational approaches discussed in sections 5.2 and 5.3. Another distinguishing feature is that dynamic programming leads to a representation of the optimal solutions in the form $x_{t+1} \in h(x_t, t)$, which is a first-order difference equation (or, if h is set-valued, a difference inclusion), whereas the variational approaches lead to optimality conditions in the form of second-order difference equations. In many applications, the representation in the form of the optimal policy correspondence is more useful and easier to analyze. On the other hand, the dynamic programming approach has the major drawback that it is often impossible to solve the Bellman equation analytically simply because no closed-form solution exists. Fortunately, there exist some efficient techniques to solve the equation numerically (one of them will be discussed in the next section). In some cases, a guess-and-verify approach can be applied to obtain an analytical solution.

5.5 Stationary discounted problems

In this section, we restrict attention to a special class of standard problems which arises particularly often in economic applications. Dynamic optimization problems belonging to this class are characterized by a transition possibility set which is independent of t and a utility function that depends on time t only via a discounting term β^t, where $\beta \in (0, 1)$ is a time-preference factor. Thus, instead of the time-dependent transition possibility set $G(x, t)$ we now simply write $G(x)$, and instead of the utility function $U(x, y, t)$ we now write $\beta^t U(x, y)$. To summarize, we consider the maximization of

$$\sum_{t=0}^{+\infty} \beta^t U(x_t, x_{t+1}) \tag{5.35}$$

subject to the constraint

$$x_{t+1} \in G(x_t) \tag{5.36}$$

for all $t \in \mathbb{N}_0$ and a given initial state x_0. This class of problems is usually referred to as *stationary discounted problems*.

The reader should note that in the preceding sections $U(x_t, x_{t+1}, t)$ described the present value of utility as of time 0. In the framework to be considered now, this present value utility is given by $\beta^t U(x_t, x_{t+1})$, whereas $U(x_t, x_{t+1})$ is the current value of period-t utility, that is, the utility derived in period t evaluated at time t. In an analogous way, we can distinguish between a present value and a current value formulation of the optimal value function. Whereas the former is given by

$$V(x, s) = \sup \left\{ \sum_{t=s}^{+\infty} \beta^t U(x_t, x_{t+1}) \,\middle|\, (x_t)_{t=s}^{+\infty} \in \mathcal{F}(x, s) \right\},$$

the latter one is equal to

$$V(x) = \sup \left\{ \sum_{t=s}^{+\infty} \beta^{t-s} U(x_t, x_{t+1}) \,\middle|\, (x_t)_{t=s}^{+\infty} \in \mathcal{F}(x, s) \right\}.$$

Note that the only difference between these two formulations is the discounting term β^{-s} and note furthermore that the current value form of the optimal value function of a stationary discounted problem is independent of the time variable.[9] From now onwards whenever we deal with a stationary discounted problem, we will use the current value formulation because it leads to simpler formulas.

Let us start the discussion with a brief look at the Euler equation, which was stated in present value form in equation (5.6). Rewriting this equation in terms of the current value utility function yields

$$U_2(x_t, x_{t+1}) + \beta U_1(x_{t+1}, x_{t+2}) = 0. \tag{5.37}$$

This is an implicit and autonomous second-order difference equation. Due to its special structure, it has some properties that deserve to be emphasized. One of them regards the eigenvalues of the Jacobian matrix at a fixed point and is formally stated in the following theorem.

Theorem 5.11   Let $x \in X \subseteq \mathbb{R}^n$ be a fixed point of equation (5.37) and assume that the current value utility function $U : \Omega \mapsto \mathbb{R}$ is twice continuously differentiable locally around the fixed point. Moreover, assume that $U_{21}(x, x)$ is non-singular. Whenever λ is an eigenvalue of the Jacobian matrix of equation (5.37) evaluated at the fixed point x, then it follows that $\lambda \neq 0$ and that $1/(\beta\lambda)$ is an eigenvalue, too.

PROOF: The linearization of equation (5.37) around the fixed point x is given by

$$U_{21}(x, x)(x_t - x) + [U_{22}(x, x) + \beta U_{11}(x, x)](x_{t+1} - x) + \beta U_{12}(x, x)(x_{t+2} - x) = 0. \tag{5.38}$$

If λ is an eigenvalue of the Jacobian matrix, then it must be the case that $x_t = x + \lambda^t z$ is a solution to the linearized equation (5.38) for some non-zero vector $z \in \mathbb{R}^n$. Substituting this solution into (5.38), we obtain the characteristic equation

$$f(\lambda) = \det\{U_{21}(x, x) + \lambda[U_{22}(x, x) + \beta U_{11}(x, x)] + \beta\lambda^2 U_{12}(x, x)\} = 0.$$

Since $U_{21}(x, x)$ is non-singular, it follows that $f(0) \neq 0$ and, hence, that λ cannot be equal to 0. Moreover, because of twice continuous differentiability of U it follows that $U_{21}(x, x) = U_{12}(x, x)$. This shows that $f(1/(\beta\lambda)) = f(\lambda)/(\beta\lambda^2)$. It is now obvious that $f(\lambda) = 0$ implies $f(1/(\beta\lambda)) = 0$, which proves the theorem.

---

[9] This follows from the fact that $\mathcal{F}(x, s)$ is independent of s.

The relevance of this result derives from the following observation. Suppose that the Jacobian matrix has an eigenvalue λ satisfying $|\lambda| \leq 1$. Then it follows from theorem 5.11 that there exists another eigenvalue, namely $1/(\beta\lambda)$, which has absolute value $1/(\beta|\lambda|) \geq 1/\beta > 1$. Specifically, for every stable eigenvalue of the Jacobian matrix there must exist a corresponding unstable one. An obvious consequence of this result is that the number of stable eigenvalues cannot exceed n, the dimension of the state space X. Now recall that the Euler equation (5.37) is a second-order difference equation for the n state variables collected in the vector x_t. Introducing the auxiliary variable $y_t = x_{t+1}$, equation (5.37) can be rewritten as a first-order difference equation in (x_t, y_t). Since initial values are given only in the form of x_0 but not for $y_0 = x_1$, the n components of x_t are pre-determined, whereas the n components of y_t are jump variables. We conclude that, under the assumptions of theorem 5.11, the sufficient condition for the indeterminacy of the fixed point that is stated in theorem 3.7(b) cannot be satisfied.

Theorem 5.11 states that the Jacobian matrix of an optimal fixed point can have at most as many stable eigenvalues as there are state variables. There also exist results in the literature proving that the number of stable eigenvalues is equal to n (or, more precisely, that the fixed point is locally saddle point stable) provided that the time-preference factor β is sufficiently close to 1. These results are known as *turnpike theorems* and they hold for stationary discounted problems satisfying certain convexity properties. To understand the intuition for these results, we discuss the case of a one-dimensional state space.

Let X be an interval on the real line and suppose that $x^* \in X$ is a fixed point of the Euler equation (5.37), that is, $U_2(x^*, x^*) + \beta U_1(x^*, x^*) = 0$. Of course, the value of the fixed point depends in general on the time-preference factor β, which we shall indicate by the notation $x^*(\beta)$. In what follows, we assume for simplicity that there exists $\underline{\beta} \in (0, 1)$ such that for all $\beta \in (\underline{\beta}, 1]$ there exists a fixed point $x^*(\beta)$ and that the mapping $\beta \mapsto x^*(\beta)$ is continuous.[10] We can now state the following result.

Lemma 5.2 Consider a stationary discounted dynamic optimization problem on the state space $X \subseteq \mathbb{R}$ and assume that the properties mentioned in the preceding paragraph are satisfied. Assume furthermore that the set $\Omega = \{(x, y) \mid x \in X, y \in G(x)\}$ is a convex and compact set and that the utility function $U : \Omega \mapsto \mathbb{R}$ is concave and twice continuously differentiable. Finally, assume that $U_{12}(x, x) \neq 0$ and $U_{11}(x, x)U_{22}(x, x) - U_{12}^2(x, x) > 0$ hold for all $x \in X$ which satisfy $(x, x) \in \Omega$. There exists $\bar{\beta} \in (\underline{\beta}, 1)$ such that for all $\beta \in (\bar{\beta}, 1)$ the Jacobian matrix evaluated at the fixed point $x^*(\beta)$ has one stable and one unstable eigenvalue.

---

[10] This will hold under appropriate regularity conditions on the utility function U.

PROOF: Since we already know from theorem 5.11 that there is at least one unstable eigenvalue, it suffices to prove that there exists at least one stable eigenvalue. Because U is twice continuously differentiable and Ω is compact, it follows from the assumptions of the lemma that there exist $\varepsilon > 0$ and $M > 0$ such that $\Delta(x) := U_{11}(x, x)U_{22}(x, x) - U_{12}^2(x, x) > \varepsilon$ and $|U_{12}(x, x)| < M$ hold for all $x \in X$ which satisfy $(x, x) \in \Omega$. It has been shown in the proof of theorem 5.11 that the characteristic equation of the Jacobian matrix is given by

$$f_\beta(\lambda) = \{U_{21}(x, x) + \lambda[U_{22}(x, x) + \beta U_{11}(x, x)] + \beta\lambda^2 U_{12}(x, x)\}|_{x=x^*(\beta)} = 0.$$

Using $U_{12}(x, x) = U_{21}(x, x) \neq 0$, we can rewrite this equation also as

$$\lambda^2 - A(\beta)\lambda + 1/\beta = 0, \tag{5.39}$$

where

$$A(\beta) = -\left.\frac{U_{22}(x, x) + \beta U_{11}(x, x)}{\beta U_{12}(x, x)}\right|_{x=x^*(\beta)}.$$

For $\beta = 1$, we obtain

$$A(1)^2 - 4 = \left.\left[\frac{U_{11}(x, x) + U_{22}(x, x)}{U_{12}(x, x)}\right]^2\right|_{x=x^*(1)} - 4$$

$$= \frac{[U_{11}(x, x) - U_{22}(x, x)]^2 + 4\Delta(x)}{U_{12}^2(x, x)} > \frac{4\varepsilon}{M^2}.$$

Hence, we must have $A(1) > 2$ or $A(1) < -2$. For $\beta = 1$, it follows therefore that the two solutions of equation (5.39) are real and are given by

$$\lambda_{1,2} = \frac{A(1) \pm \sqrt{A(1)^2 - 4}}{2}.$$

If $A(1) > 2$, then we get

$$\lambda_1 = \frac{A(1) - \sqrt{A(1)^2 - 4}}{2} \in (0, 1).$$

Analogously, we can show that $A(1) < -2$ implies $\lambda_2 \in (-1, 0)$. Thus, if $\beta = 1$ there exists at least one stable eigenvalue. From the continuity of the coefficients in equation (5.39), it follows that this property holds also for all β that are sufficiently close to 1, say for all $\beta \in (\bar{\beta}, 1]$.

Let us now turn to the recursive approach for stationary discounted problems. To this end, we assume in addition to $X \subseteq \mathbb{R}^n$, stationarity, and discounting that the set $G(x)$ is non-empty and compact for all $x \in X$ and that the correspondence $x \mapsto G(x)$

is continuous.[11] Finally, we assume that the utility function $U : \Omega \mapsto \mathbb{R}$ is bounded and continuous on its domain $\Omega = \{(x, y) \mid x \in X, y \in G(x)\}$.

It is obvious that the above assumptions imply that the set of feasible paths for problem (5.35)–(5.36), $\mathcal{F}(x, s)$, is non-empty for all $x \in X$ and all $s \in \mathbb{N}_0$, and that the limit as T approaches $+\infty$ of $\sum_{t=0}^{T} \beta^t U(x_t, x_{t+1})$ exists as a finite number. Thus, all results from the previous section remain valid. In addition, we have the following theorem.

Theorem 5.12 There exists a unique bounded and continuous function $V : X \mapsto \mathbb{R}$ which satisfies the Bellman equation

$$V(x) = \max\{U(x, y) + \beta V(y) \mid y \in G(x)\} \tag{5.40}$$

for all $x \in X$. This function V is the (current value) optimal value function. Every path satisfying $x_{t+1} \in h(x_t)$ is an optimal path, where

$$h(x) = \text{argmax}\{U(x, y) + \beta V(y) \mid y \in G(x)\}.$$

PROOF: Let $C(X)$ be the set of bounded and continuous functions defined on X and let the Bellman operator $T : C(X) \mapsto C(X)$ be defined by

$$Tf(x) = \max\{U(x, y) + \beta f(y) \mid y \in G(x)\}. \tag{5.41}$$

Because $G(x)$ is compact and both U and f are continuous, the maximum on the right-hand side of this equation is indeed attained such that the definition makes sense. Furthermore, it follows from the maximum theorem that $Tf \in C(X)$. Denoting by $\|\cdot\|$ the supremum norm on $C(X)$, it holds for all functions $f \in C(X)$ and $g \in C(X)$ that $f \leq g + \|f - g\|$. From the definition of T, we therefore obtain

$$Tf \leq T(g + \|f - g\|) \leq Tg + \beta\|f - g\|$$

and, analogously

$$Tg \leq T(f + \|f - g\|) \leq Tf + \beta\|f - g\|.$$

Combining these two inequalities, it follows that

$$\|Tf - Tg\| \leq \beta\|f - g\|, \tag{5.42}$$

which shows that $T : C(X) \mapsto C(X)$ is a contraction mapping. Banach's fixed point theorem (also called the contraction mapping theorem) therefore implies that there

---

[11] The correspondence $x \mapsto G(x)$ is continuous at $x \in X$ if $G(x)$ is non-empty and if for every sequence $(x_n)_{n=0}^{+\infty}$ with $x_n \in X$ and $\lim_{n \to +\infty} x_n = x$ the following two properties hold: (i) for every $y \in G(x)$ there exists a sequence $(y_n)_{n=0}^{+\infty}$ converging to y and satisfying $y_n \in G(x_n)$ and (ii) every sequence $(y_n)_{n=0}^{+\infty}$ satisfying $y_n \in G(x_n)$ has a subsequence that has a limit in $G(x)$.

exists a unique function $V \in C(X)$ for which $TV = V$ holds. This proves the first statement of the theorem. Now consider condition (5.29) from the previous section. In current value formulation, it reads as $\lim_{t \to +\infty} \beta^t V(x_t) = 0$. Because V is a bounded function and $\beta \in (0, 1)$, it follows that this condition holds true. Hence, we can conclude from theorem 5.8 that V is the optimal value function. For the same reason, theorem 5.10 implies that every path generated by the optimal policy correspondence is an optimal path.

The above theorem shows that, under the present assumptions, the optimal value function is the only bounded and continuous function that satisfies the Bellman equation. Furthermore, it characterizes the set of optimal paths as the set of all trajectories of the optimal policy correspondence. Note that this result also proves the existence of optimal paths.

Banach's fixed point theorem that was used in the proof of theorem 5.12 does not only yield the existence of a fixed point, but it also provides an efficient algorithm to approximate this fixed point. In the present framework, this approximation is known as the *value iteration* algorithm. We start from an arbitrary initial guess $V_0 \in C(X)$ for the value function V and compute iteratively the functions $V_m \in C(X)$ via the formula

$$V_{m+1} = T V_m \tag{5.43}$$

for all $m \in \mathbb{N}_0$, where T is the Bellman operator defined in (5.41). The following lemma shows that the sequence $(V_m)_{m=0}^{+\infty}$ converges uniformly to the optimal value function V.

Lemma 5.3 Let $V_0 : X \mapsto \mathbb{R}$ be an arbitrary bounded and continuous function and define the sequence $(V_m)_{m=0}^{+\infty}$ by (5.43). Then it holds for all $m \in \mathbb{N}_0$ that

$$\| V_m - V \| \le \beta^m \| V_0 - V \|,$$

where $V : X \mapsto \mathbb{R}$ is the optimal value function. The sequence $(V_m)_{m=0}^{+\infty}$ converges uniformly to V.

PROOF: Combining the fixed point property $TV = V$ with equations (5.42)–(5.43), it follows that

$$\| V_{m+1} - V \| = \| T V_m - T V \| \le \beta \| V_m - V \|.$$

Obviously, this implies that $\| V_m - V \| \le \beta^m \| V_0 - V \|$ holds for all $m \in \mathbb{N}_0$. This proves the uniform convergence of V_m to the optimal value function V.

The lemma shows that the approximation error of the value iteration algorithm decreases exponentially, that is, at least as quickly as the geometric sequence $(\beta^m)_{m=0}^{+\infty}$. Although the value iteration method is primarily applied for the numerical solution to the Bellman equation, it is also very helpful in obtaining analytical solutions to the Bellman equation. Let us illustrate this by an example.

Example 5.11 Consider a person who likes to eat cake. Cake lasts for two periods only. Cake that has been produced in period t is called 'fresh' in period t and 'old' in period $t + 1$. The person is endowed with $x_0 \in [0, 1]$ units of old cake in period 0, and gets one unit of fresh cake in every period $t \geq 0$. Denote by x_t the amount of old cake that is available to the cake-eater in period t and by c_t and d_t the amounts of old cake and fresh cake, respectively, consumed in period t. The current value utility function of the cake-eater is assumed to be $u(c_t, d_t) = \sqrt{c_t d_t}$. Since old cake cannot be stored anymore, it is obvious that the decision maker consumes all available old cake, that is, $c_t = x_t$ for all t. Moreover, since fresh cake in period t becomes old in period $t + 1$ it follows that $x_{t+1} = 1 - d_t$. Consequently, we can write the reduced-form current value utility function as

$$U(x_t, x_{t+1}) = \sqrt{x_t(1 - x_{t+1})}.$$

The time-preference factor is equal to $\beta \in (0, 1)$. The optimization problem consists of maximizing

$$\sum_{t=0}^{+\infty} \beta^t \sqrt{x_t(1 - x_{t+1})}$$

subject to the constraint $x_{t+1} \in [0, 1]$ for all $t \in \mathbb{N}_0$ and a given initial value x_0.

In order to solve this problem by the value iteration method, we start with the function $V_0(x) = 0$. Applying the Bellman operator T yields

$$V_1(x) = TV_0(x) = \max\{\sqrt{x(1 - y)} + \beta V_0(y) \mid y \in [0, 1]\}$$
$$= \max\{\sqrt{x(1 - y)} \mid y \in [0, 1]\}.$$

Obviously, the maximizer is $y = 0$ for all x and, hence, $V_1(x) = \sqrt{x}$ holds for all $x \in [0, 1]$. The second step of the value iteration requires the solution

$$V_2(x) = TV_1(x) = \max\{\sqrt{x(1 - y)} + \beta V_1(y) \mid y \in [0, 1]\}$$
$$= \max\{\sqrt{x(1 - y)} + \beta \sqrt{y} \mid y \in [0, 1]\}.$$

It is straightforward to verify that the expression on the right-hand side is maximized at $y = \beta^2/(x + \beta^2)$, which implies that $V_2(x) = \sqrt{x + \beta^2}$. In the third iteration, we solve

$$V_3(x) = \max\{\sqrt{x(1-y)} + \beta V_2(y) \mid y \in [0, 1]\}$$
$$= \max\{\sqrt{x(1-y)} + \beta\sqrt{y + \beta^2} \mid y \in [0, 1]\},$$

which leads to $y = \beta^2(1-x)/(x + \beta^2)$ and $V_3(x) = \sqrt{(1 + \beta^2)(x + \beta^2)}$. Thus, a pattern emerges: in all iterations so far, the value function takes the form $V_m(x) = \sqrt{a_m(x + b_m)}$ with $0 \le a_m \le 1 + b_m$ and $0 \le b_m \le \beta^2 a_m$. We conjecture that this holds for all $m \in \mathbb{N}_0$ and prove the conjecture by induction. All we have to show is that the function

$$V_{m+1}(x) = \max\{\sqrt{x(1-y)} + \beta V_m(y) \mid y \in [0, 1]\}$$
$$= \max\{\sqrt{x(1-y)} + \beta\sqrt{a_m(y + b_m)} \mid y \in [0, 1]\}$$

is of the form $V_{m+1}(x) = \sqrt{a_{m+1}(x + b_{m+1})}$ with $0 \le a_{m+1} \le 1 + b_{m+1}$ and $0 \le b_{m+1} \le \beta^2 a_{m+1}$. The first-order condition for the maximization on the right-hand side is

$$\sqrt{\frac{x}{1-y}} = \beta\sqrt{\frac{a_m}{y + b_m}},$$

which yields

$$y = \frac{\beta^2 a_m - b_m x}{x + \beta^2 a_m}. \tag{5.44}$$

Because of $a_m \ge 0, 0 \le b_m \le \beta^2 a_m$, and $x \in [0, 1]$, we see that $y \in [0, 1]$. Because the right-hand side of the Bellman equation is strictly concave with respect to y, the first-order condition is sufficient for optimality. Hence, $y = (\beta^2 a_m - b_m x)/(x + \beta^2 a_m)$ is the maximizer. Substituting this value into the right-hand side of the Bellman equation, we obtain

$$V_{m+1}(x) = \sqrt{(1 + b_m)(x + \beta^2 a_m)},$$

which confirms our conjecture provided that

$$a_{m+1} = 1 + b_m \text{ and } b_{m+1} = \beta^2 a_m. \tag{5.45}$$

It is straightforward to see that these relations imply that $0 \le a_{m+1} \le 1 + b_{m+1}$ and $0 \le b_{m+1} \le \beta^2 a_{m+1}$. Combining the two equations in (5.45), we obtain $b_{m+1} = \beta^2(1 + b_{m-1})$. Noting that $b_0 = b_1 = 0$, we can solve this linear difference equation for the coefficients b_m to get $b_{2m} = b_{2m+1} = \beta^2(1 - \beta^{2m})/(1 - \beta^2)$. Obviously, this implies that $b := \lim_{m \to +\infty} b_m = \beta^2/(1 - \beta^2)$. From the formula for the coefficient a_m, we therefore obtain that $a := \lim_{m \to +\infty} a_m = 1 + b = 1/(1 - \beta^2)$. Application of lemma 5.3 therefore shows that the optimal value function is given by

$$V(x) = \sqrt{a(x+b)} = \frac{\sqrt{x + \beta^2(1-x)}}{1 - \beta^2}. \tag{5.46}$$

The corresponding optimal policy function can be obtained by computing the limit as m approaches $+\infty$ in (5.44). This yields

$$h(x) = \frac{\beta^2(1-x)}{x + \beta^2(1-x)}. \tag{5.47}$$

This completes the solution to this example via the value iteration method. It is interesting to note that the difference equation $x_{t+1} = h(x_t)$ has a unique fixed point $x^* = \beta/(1+\beta)$ and that for all $x \in [0, 1]$ it holds that $h(h(x)) = x$.[12] This implies that the optimal path from every initial state $x_0 \neq x^*$ is periodic of period 2.

All assumptions of theorem 5.12 and lemma 5.3 are satisfied in the above example. The value iteration algorithm, however, can also be applied to problems in which not all of these assumptions hold. In such a case, there is no guarantee that the algorithm converges to the true optimal value function, but in many cases it does. You will be asked to follow this approach in exercise 5.7 below.

In addition to providing an efficient method to approximate the optimal value function of a dynamic optimization problem, the value iteration algorithm has another useful consequence. If a certain property of the initial guess V_0 is preserved by the Bellman operator T, then it follows from (5.43) that V_1 has this property as well. Repeating this argument, it follows that the function V_m shares this property for all $m \in \mathbb{N}_0$. If the property is also preserved by the limit operation, then it follows that the optimal value function must have this property, because it is the limit of the functions V_m. To illustrate this argument, let us define the following properties of stationary discounted dynamic optimization problems.

M: For all $(x, x') \in X^2$ satisfying $x \leq x'$ and for all $y \in G(x)$, it holds that $G(x) \subseteq G(x')$ and $U(x, y) \leq U(x', y)$.

C0: The states space X and the domain Ω are convex sets, and the utility function $U : \Omega \mapsto \mathbb{R}$ is concave.

C1: It holds that

$$(1 - \alpha)U(x, y) + \alpha U(x', y') < U(x'', y'') \tag{5.48}$$

whenever x and x' are different elements of X, $y \in G(x)$ and $y' \in G(x')$ are feasible successor states, $\alpha \in (0, 1)$, $x'' = (1 - \alpha)x + \alpha x'$ and $y'' = (1 - \alpha)y + \alpha y'$.

---

[12] The reader will be asked to verify this claim in exercise 5.5 below.

Note that condition **C1** is trivially satisfied if U is a strictly concave function, but that it holds also for functions U that are not strictly concave. An example of a utility function that is not strictly concave but which does satisfy condition **C1** is $U(x, y) = -x^2 + y$. In many economic applications, strict concavity of U is not satisfied, whereas condition **C1** typically holds.

Theorem 5.13　Consider the stationary discounted dynamic optimization problem (5.35)–(5.36) under the general assumptions of this section. Assume in addition that $G(x)$ is non-empty and compact for all $x \in X$, that the correspondence $x \mapsto G(x)$ is continuous, and that the utility function U is bounded and continuous.

(a) If property **M** holds, then it follows that the optimal value function V is non-decreasing. If, in addition, the utility function U is strictly increasing with respect to its first argument, then the optimal value function is also strictly increasing.

(b) If property **C0** holds, then it follows that the optimal value function V is concave. If, in addition, condition **C1** holds, then V is strictly concave and the optimal policy correspondence is single-valued and continuous.

PROOF: (a) It holds for all $x \le x'$ that

$$Tf(x) = \max\{U(x, y) + \beta f(y) \,|\, y \in G(x)\} \le \max\{U(x', y) + \beta f(y) \,|\, y \in G(x')\}$$
$$= Tf(x'),$$

where we have used the definition of T, the monotonicity of U with respect to its first argument, and the fact that $G(x) \subseteq G(x')$ holds for all $x \le x'$. Now consider the sequence $(V_m)_{m=0}^{+\infty}$ constructed by the value iteration method. Because of $V_{m+1} = TV_m$, it follows from the above argument that V_m is non-decreasing for all $m \ge 1$. Since monotonicity is preserved under the limit operation, this implies that $V = \lim_{m \to +\infty} V_m$ is non-decreasing as well. Next suppose that U is strictly increasing. Using the same chain of arguments as above, it can be shown that Tf is strictly increasing. Because we know that $V = TV$ holds, it follows that V must be strictly increasing.

(b) We first show that concavity is preserved by the Bellman operator T. To this end, assume that V_m is a continuous and concave function and define $h_m(x) = \operatorname{argmax}\{U(x, y) + \beta V_m(y) \,|\, y \in G(x)\}$. Since the continuous function $U(x, y) + \beta V_m(y)$ attains its maximum over the compact set $G(x)$, it follows that $h_m(x)$ is well-defined. Now let x and x' be arbitrary feasible states, and let $\alpha \in [0, 1]$ be a fixed number. Furthermore, define $x'' = (1 - \alpha)x + \alpha x'$, $y = h_m(x)$, $y' = h_m(x')$, and $y'' = (1 - \alpha)y + \alpha y'$. Convexity of X and Ω implies that $x'' \in X$ and $(x'', y'') \in \Omega$. It follows from these properties and the concavity of U and V_m that

$$V_{m+1}(x'') = \max\{U(x'', z) + \beta V_m(z) \mid z \in G(x'')\}$$
$$\geq U(x'', y'') + \beta V_m(y'')$$
$$\geq [(1 - \alpha)U(x, y) + \alpha U(x', y')] + \beta[(1 - \alpha)V_m(y) + \alpha V_m(y')]$$
$$= (1 - \alpha)V_{m+1}(x) + \alpha V_{m+1}(x').$$

This proves concavity of V_{m+1}. Since the limit of a sequence of concave functions is also concave, it follows that the optimal value function must be concave. In an analogous way, we can show that properties **C0** and **C1** together imply that Tf is strictly concave whenever f is concave. Because the optimal value function satisfies $V = TV$, it follows that V is a strictly concave function whenever properties **C0** and **C1** are satisfied.

Finally, because under conditions **C0** and **C1** the right-hand side of the Bellman equation (5.40) is a strictly concave function of y, it follows that for every state $x \in X$ there exists a unique optimal successor state $h(x)$. This proves that the optimal policy correspondence is a single-valued function. The continuity of that function will not be proved here.

Part (b) of the theorem shows that in the case where both conditions **C0** and **C1** hold the optimal policy correspondence h is a single-valued function. We shall refer to this function as the *optimal policy function*. Optimal paths are therefore completely characterized as the trajectories of the autonomous difference equation

$$x_{t+1} = h(x_t).$$

This difference equation can be studied by the methods discussed in part I of the book in order to derive the qualitative properties of optimal paths. Note that the recursive approach leads to a first-order difference equation in the state variables of the problem, whereas the variational approaches discussed in sections 5.2 and 5.3 describe optimal paths by means of second-order equations.

Our last result in this section has a similar flavor as theorem 5.13, although its proof takes a different approach. Specifically, the theorem shows that differentiability of the utility function is another property that is inherited by the optimal value function.

Theorem 5.14 Consider the stationary discounted dynamic optimization problem (5.35)–(5.36) under the assumptions stated in theorem 5.13. Suppose that the convexity assumptions **C0** and **C1** hold and that the utility function U is continuously differentiable on the interior of its domain Ω. If x is in the interior of X and $h(x)$ is in the interior of $G(x)$, then it follows that the optimal value function U is continuously differentiable at x and that

$$V'(x) = U_1(x, h(x)).\tag{5.49}$$

PROOF: From theorem 5.13(b), it follows that h is a single valued function and that V is strictly concave. By assumption, it holds that x and $h(x)$ are in the interior of X and $G(x)$, respectively. We have also assumed that the correspondence $z \mapsto G(z)$ is continuous and it follows from theorem 5.13(b) that the optimal policy function is continuous. Taking these properties together, we see that $h(z)$ is in the interior of $G(z)$ for all z sufficiently close to x. Defining the function $W : X \mapsto \mathbb{R}$ by $W(z) = U(z, h(x)) + \beta V(h(x))$, where V is the optimal value function, it follows that W is concave and continuously differentiable, that $W(z) \leq V(z)$ holds for all z sufficiently close to x, and that $W(x) = V(x)$. In other words, the concave function V dominates the concave function W locally around x and coincides with it at the point x. Since the latter function is continuously differentiable at x, it can easily be seen that the same must be true for V and that both functions must have the same derivative.

Condition (5.49) is called the *envelope condition* for the Bellman equation (5.40). It relates the derivative of the optimal value function to the partial derivative (with respect to the first argument) of the utility function evaluated at the optimal successor state. Note in this regard that in the case where both the utility function U and the optimal value function V are concave and differentiable the maximization problem on the right-hand side of the Bellman equation (5.40) gives rise to the first-order optimality condition

$$U_2(x, h(x)) + \beta V'(h(x)) = 0,\tag{5.50}$$

provided that $h(x)$ is in the interior of $G(x)$. Combining (5.49) and (5.50) we obtain

$$U_2(x, h(x)) + \beta U_1(h(x), h(h(x))) = 0,$$

which is, of course, the Euler equation.

5.6   EXERCISES

EXERCISE 5.1 Consider the following variant of the basic one-sector optimal growth model. Instantaneous utility in period t, which is denoted by $u(c_t, \ell_t)$, depends on consumption $c_t \geq 0$ and on labour supply $\ell_t \in [0, 1]$ (that is, the maximal supply of labour is equal to 1). Future utilities are discounted using the time-preference factor $\beta \in (0, 1)$. The single output good is produced from capital input k_t and labour input ℓ_t according to the production technology $y_t = f(k_t, \ell_t)$. Output can be used for consumption or for investment. Capital, once installed, cannot be consumed but depreciates at the rate $\delta \in [0, 1]$. Formulate the optimal growth problem in primitive form and in reduced form. Clearly identify the state space, the transition possibility set, and the reduced-form utility function.

EXERCISE 5.2 This exercise elaborates on the model of a tree farm, which was introduced in exercise 1.2. Instead of assuming that the farmer cuts down a fixed fraction z of young trees in every period, we assume now that the farmer clears an area $z_t \in [0, 1]$ of young trees, where z_t is a control variable chosen optimally. The timing within period t is as in exercise 1.2. First, all old trees are cut down, then the farmer cuts down young trees on an area of size z_t, and finally the farmer plants new trees of age 0 on the entire area that is available after tree-cutting. An area x of old trees yields an amount x of timber. An area y of young trees yields an amount αy of timber, where $\alpha \in (0, 1)$ is a given parameter. The farmer derives instantaneous utility $u(c_t)$ if he or she produces c_t units of timber in period t. The utility function u is assumed to be twice continuously differentiable, strictly increasing, and strictly concave. The time-preference factor of the farmer is $\beta \in (0, 1)$ and the area that is initially covered with old trees has size x_0.

(a) Formulate the farmer's utility maximization problem over an infinite time-horizon with x_t as the state variable. Clearly identify the state space, the transition possibility set, and the reduced-form utility function.

(b) Derive the Euler equation for this problem. Under which parameter condition does the Euler equation have a fixed point? Prove that under this parameter condition every $x \in [0, 1]$ is a fixed point of the Euler equation. Which of these fixed points of the Euler equation correspond to constant optimal paths of the optimization problem?

EXERCISE 5.3 Consider the reduced-form dynamic optimization problem on the state space $X = \mathbb{R}$ with $G(x, t) = \mathbb{R}$, $U(x, y, t) = (-\beta^t/2)(2x^2 + 2xy + y^2)$, and $x_0 \in X$.

(a) Derive the Euler equation and rewrite it as an autonomous linear difference equation.

(b) For this part, assume that $\beta = 3/8$. Find all feasible paths from x_0 that satisfy the Euler equation. Which of these paths satisfies the transversality condition?

EXERCISE 5.4 Consider an infinitely lived individual who wants to maximize total lifetime utility. The individual is endowed with one unit of time per period which can be used in two different ways: either for work or to accumulate human capital for the next period. We denote by $u_t \in [0, 1]$ the fraction of time spent for work and by $1 - u_t$ the fraction of time used to learn (that is, to form human capital). Furthermore, we denote by $x_t \geq 0$ the human capital of the individual at the beginning of period t. Human capital accumulates according to

$$x_{t+1} = \alpha x_t (1 - u_t),$$

where $\alpha > 0$ is an exogenous parameter and x_0 is a given initial stock of human capital. If the individual in period t has human capital x_t and spends the fraction u_t of its time in the production process, it earns and consumes $c_t = u_t x_t$ and derives the instantaneous utility $\sqrt{c_t}$. The individual discounts future utility with the time-preference factor β. Assume that $\alpha \beta^2 < 1$.

(a) Formulate the utility maximization problem of the individual as a stationary discounted dynamic optimization problem.

(b) Solve the optimization problem using the Euler equation approach or the Lagrangian approach (hint: you may restrict yourself to interior solutions).

(c) Show that it is optimal to spend a constant fraction $\bar{u}$ of time for work. Calculate $\bar{u}$ and interpret its dependence on α and β.

EXERCISE 5.5 Consider the cake-eating problem from example 5.11. Prove that $h(h(x)) = x$ holds for all $x \in [0, 1]$, where $h : [0, 1] \mapsto [0, 1]$ is defined in (5.47). Verify that every solution to the difference equation $x_{t+1} = h(x_t)$ that starts in the interior of the state space $X = [0, 1]$ satisfies the Euler equation and the transversality condition.

EXERCISE 5.6 Consider the stationary discounted problem of maximizing

$$\sum_{t=0}^{+\infty} \beta^t [x_{t+1} - (\gamma/2)(x_{t+1} - x_t)^2],$$

where β and γ are positive numbers with $\beta < 1$. The state space is $X = \mathbb{R}_+$ and there are no further constraints.

(a) Find a linear function of the form $V(x) = A + Bx$ that satisfies the (current value) Bellman equation.

(b) Assuming that the function derived in part (a) is the (current value) optimal value function, determine the corresponding optimal policy function as well as an optimal path starting in the initial state x_0.

EXERCISE 5.7 Consider the optimal growth model from example 5.2 without technological progress (that is, $A_t = A$ for some $A > 0$ and all $t \in \mathbb{N}_0$), logarithmic utility function $u(c) = \ln c$, and Cobb–Douglas technology $\bar{f}(k, A) = Ak^\alpha$, where $\alpha \in (0, 1)$ is a parameter.

(a) Rewrite the problem as a stationary discounted optimization problem in reduced form.

(b) As in example 5.11, carry out the first steps of the value iteration method starting with the function V_0 defined by $V_0(k) = 0$ for all $k \in X$. Try to conjecture the form of the functions V_m and verify your conjecture. Compute the limit $V^* = \lim_{m \to +\infty} V_m$ and verify that this function indeed satisfies the Bellman equation. Why are theorem 5.12 and lemma 5.3 not applicable?

(c) Assuming that V^* as computed in part (b) is indeed the optimal value function, derive the optimal policy function.

EXERCISE 5.8 Solve the problem from example 5.6 by the recursive approach. Start with a conjecture that the optimal value function has the form $V(x) = Ax^\alpha$.

5.7 COMMENTS AND REFERENCES

The Euler equation, the Lagrangian approach, and the recursive approach are the most commonly used methods to solve discrete-time dynamic optimization problems. Very good treatments that focus on the recursive approach are contained in Stokey and Lucas [86] or Ljungqvist and Sargent [62].

The simple saving problem from example 5.1 as well as various forms of borrowing constraints are discussed extensively in Ljungqvist and Sargent [62]. The model from examples 5.2 and 5.8 is the standard neoclassical optimal growth model originating from Ramsey [77]. Multisector growth models like the one discussed in example 5.3 can be found in Sutherland [88] or Stokey and Lucas [86]. An authoritative survey of economic growth models is Acemoglu [1].

The transversality condition has been derived under different sets of assumptions; the version presented in theorem 5.2 originates from Kamihigashi [45] where further references are provided. There exist several examples similar to examples 5.4 and 5.5 which show that the transversality condition is a necessary optimality condition only under rather strong assumptions. The most famous such example was presented by Halkin [39] in a continuous-time framework. Theorem 5.4 is taken from Carlson and Haurie [16]. Example 5.7 is based on Nerlove and Arrow [72].

Dynamic programming was invented by Bellman [11]; an up-to-date presentation, on which most of the material in sections 5.4 and 5.5 is based, is Stokey and Lucas [86]. The result presented in theorem 5.11 originates from Kurz [50] and Levhari and Liviatan [58]. For a very comprehensive survey of turnpike theorems, we refer the reader to McKenzie [66]. The optimization problem from example 5.11 and exercise 5.5 is due to Weitzman and was first reported in Samuelson [80]. Theorem 5.14 stems from Beneviste and Scheinkman [12]. Exercise 5.2 is based on Mitra and Wan [69, 70].

6 Dynamic inconsistency and commitment

So far, we have assumed that the decision maker solves a dynamic optimization problem once and for all at the outset of the time horizon. In the present chapter, we address the questions of whether there exist incentives for the decision maker to deviate from the optimal solution in the course of time and, if so, how to model the behaviour of such a decision maker.

In section 6.1, we introduce the phenomenon of dynamic inconsistency in an abstract setting and we illustrate how it can emerge by means of three economic examples. The examples are chosen such as to illustrate different possible causes of dynamic inconsistency. We argue that a dynamically inconsistent solution can only be implemented if the decision maker has the ability to commit himself or herself to carry out future actions even in the case that his or her incentives change over time. In section 6.2, we discuss two solution concepts for problems in which the decision maker lacks commitment power. Such a decision maker is often said to act under discretion. Finally, in section 6.3 we briefly deal with intermediate situations in which the decision maker possesses partial commitment power. This is the case if the decision maker can pre-commit his or her actions in the near future but cannot pre-commit to a control path over the entire time horizon.

6.1 Dynamic inconsistency

Suppose that a decision maker not only faces a dynamic optimization problem in period 0, but that he or she faces a separate optimization problem in every period $t \in \mathbb{N}_0$. Let us denote the sequence of optimization problems by $(\mathbf{P}_t)_{t=0}^{+\infty}$. That is, in period t, the decision maker seeks to act optimally according to problem $\mathbf{P}_t$. Let us furthermore suppose that a feasible solution to $\mathbf{P}_t$ is a sequence of variables $(z_s)_{s=t}^{+\infty}$, where $z_s \in Z$ is the system variable for period s and where Z is a non-empty system domain. This means that in every period $t \in \mathbb{N}_0$ the decision maker can decide upon the entire path of system variables from period t onwards. Now consider a feasible path $(z_t)_{t=0}^{+\infty}$ and assume that it is an optimal solution to problem $\mathbf{P}_0$. We say that this optimal solution is *dynamically consistent* (or *time-consistent*) relative to the sequence of optimization problems $(\mathbf{P}_t)_{t=0}^{+\infty}$ if for all $t \in \mathbb{N}_0$ the subsequence $(z_s)_{s=t}^{+\infty}$ is an optimal solution to problem $\mathbf{P}_t$. In words, the optimal solution $(z_t)_{t=0}^{+\infty}$ is dynamically consistent if the truncation of this solution that starts at any later period t is optimal also from the point of view of that period. If an optimal solution is not dynamically consistent, we call it *dynamically inconsistent*.

To understand how the issue of dynamic inconsistency arises, let us first recall the standard problem in reduced form that we introduced in section 5.1. More specifically, we denoted by $\mathbf{P}(x, t)$ the problem of maximizing

$$\sum_{s=t}^{+\infty} U(x_s, x_{s+1}, s)$$

subject to

$$x_{s+1} \in G(x_s, s)$$

and the initial condition $x_t = x$. The fact that an initial value for the variable x_t is given qualifies this variable as a state variable, that is, a pre-determined variable. In other words, the variable x_t is not under the control of the decision maker when he or she solves problem $\mathbf{P}(x, t)$. Now suppose that $(x_t)_{t=0}^{+\infty}$ is an optimal path for $\mathbf{P}(x, 0)$ and that the decision maker who has chosen this optimal path reconsiders his or her choice at the beginning of period $t > 0$. Note that at that point in time the decision maker faces the problem $\mathbf{P}(x_t, t)$, because the utility derived through periods $\{0, 1, \ldots, t-1\}$ is already bygone and because the value x_t is not under his or her control anymore. In other words, given a reduced-form dynamic optimization problem $\mathbf{P}(x, 0)$ and an optimal solution $(x_t)_{t=0}^{+\infty}$ of that problem, we can define a sequence of optimization problems $(\mathbf{P}_t)_{t=0}^{+\infty}$ via $\mathbf{P}_t = \mathbf{P}(x_t, t)$. From the principle of optimality proved in lemma 5.1, we know that $(x_s)_{s=t}^{+\infty}$ is an optimal path for $\mathbf{P}(x_t, t)$. It follows therefore that the optimal solution $(x_t)_{t=0}^{+\infty}$ is dynamically consistent relative to the sequence $(\mathbf{P}_t)_{t=0}^{+\infty}$ and, consequently, that the decision maker has no incentives to deviate from his or her original plan made at the outset of period 0. Thus, it does not make a difference whether we assume that the decision maker makes his or her choice once and for all at the beginning of the time horizon or whether we assume that he or she makes choices sequentially throughout the time horizon, because the resulting optimal behaviour is exactly the same in both cases.

Now let us consider the dynamic optimization problem $\mathbf{Q}(t)$ that differs from $\mathbf{P}(x, t)$ in a small but crucial detail. More specifically, the problem $\mathbf{Q}(t)$ consists of the maximization of

$$\sum_{s=t}^{+\infty} U(c_s, c_{s+1}, s)$$

subject to

$$c_{s+1} \in G(c_s, s). \tag{6.1}$$

Note that the only difference between the two problems $\mathbf{Q}(t)$ and $\mathbf{P}(x, t)$ is that no initial value for c_t is given in $\mathbf{Q}(t)$, whereas an initial value for x_t is given in $\mathbf{P}(x, t)$. This reflects the fact that c_t is a control variable in problem $\mathbf{Q}(t)$, that is, a jump variable, whereas x_t is a pre-determined state variable in problem $\mathbf{P}(x, t)$. In order to emphasize this difference, we denote the system variable in problem $\mathbf{Q}(t)$ by c_t rather than by x_t.

We conduct the same thought experiment as before and suppose that in each period $t \in \mathbb{N}_0$ the decision maker chooses a path $(c_s)_{s=t}^{+\infty}$ which is optimal according to problem $\mathbf{Q}(t)$. In exactly the same way that we derived the Euler equation (5.6) for the standard problem $\mathbf{P}(x_0, 0)$, we can see that the optimality of $(c_t)_{t=0}^{+\infty}$ for problem $\mathbf{Q}(0)$ requires that for every $t \geq 1$ the value $y = c_t$ must be the solution to the static optimization problem of maximizing

$$U(c_{t-1}, y, t-1) + U(y, c_{t+1}, t)$$
$$\text{subject to} \quad y \in G(c_{t-1}, t-1) \quad \text{and} \quad c_{t+1} \in G(y, t), \tag{6.2}$$

where the maximization is with respect to y and where c_{t-1} and c_{t+1} are considered as fixed. When the decision maker reconsiders the choice of $(c_s)_{s=t}^{+\infty}$ in period t, however, he or she faces problem $\mathbf{Q}(t)$. By our assumptions, the variable c_t is a choice variable in that problem, and using the same reasoning as above it follows that the value $y = c_t$ must maximize

$$U(y, c_{t+1}, t)$$
$$\text{subject to} \quad c_{t+1} \in G(y, t). \tag{6.3}$$

Note that problem (6.3) does neither contain the term $U(c_{t-1}, y, t-1)$ in the objective function nor the restriction $y \in G(c_{t-1}, t-1)$ among its constraints. The optimal solution to problem (6.3) is therefore typically different from the optimal solution to problem (6.2). This implies in turn that, given the opportunity to deviate in period t from the original plan set up in period 0, the decision maker may have incentives do so. The optimal solution to problem $\mathbf{Q}(0)$ is therefore in general dynamically inconsistent relative to the sequence $(\mathbf{Q}(t))_{t=0}^{+\infty}$.

To understand the reasons underlying the dynamic inconsistency arising in problem $\mathbf{Q}(0)$, notice that, in the standard problem $\mathbf{P}(x, 0)$ the decision maker decides about $(x_t)_{t=1}^{+\infty}$ but not about x_0, because the latter variable is pre-determined by the initial condition $x_0 = x$. The choice of x_t affects the instantaneous utilities in periods $t-1$ and t, but when period t comes around this choice cannot be revised anymore due to the nature of x_t as a pre-determined variable for problem $\mathbf{P}(x_t, t)$. In contrast, in problem $\mathbf{Q}(t)$ the decision maker in period t still has control over c_t, a variable that affects the instantaneous utilities in periods $t - 1$ and t. In period t, however, the utility from period $t - 1$ has already materialized, so that the decision maker's incentives for choosing c_t in period t are different from what they were in period 0.

It is clear that a dynamically inconsistent solution can only be implemented if the decision maker has commitment power or some technology that allows him or her to commit to the decisions made in period 0. Otherwise, he or she would give in to the incentives to deviate from the announced solution when they arise in the course of time. In the following example about optimal monetary policy, a dynamically inconsistent solution arises for the reason that has been outlined in the above discussion.

Example 6.1   Consider the New Keynesian model from example 1.6 but assume now that the instrument variable of the central bank, that is, the nominal interest rate i_t, is chosen optimally instead of being determined by an interest rate rule. The objective functional of the central bank is assumed to be given by

$$\sum_{t=0}^{+\infty} \beta^t [-\pi_t^2 - \kappa(y_t - \bar{y})^2], \tag{6.4}$$

where κ and $\bar{y}$ are positive constants and where $\beta \in (0, 1)$ is the time-preference factor. Recall from our discussion of example 1.6 that both π_t and y_t are jump variables.

Since the objective functional contains only the inflation rates $(\pi_t)_{t=0}^{+\infty}$ and the output gaps $(y_t)_{t=0}^{+\infty}$ but not the interest rates $(i_t)_{t=0}^{+\infty}$, we can apply the following stepwise solution technique. In the first step, the above objective functional is maximized with respect to $(\pi_t)_{t=0}^{+\infty}$ and $(y_t)_{t=0}^{+\infty}$ and subject to the Phillips curve

$$\pi_t = \beta \pi_{t+1} + \alpha y_t. \tag{6.5}$$

Once the optimal paths $(\pi_t)_{t=0}^{+\infty}$ and $(y_t)_{t=0}^{+\infty}$ are determined, we can simply solve the IS-curve

$$y_t = y_{t+1} - \gamma(i_t - \pi_{t+1})$$

for the nominal interest rates in order to find the optimal sequence $(i_t)_{t=0}^{+\infty}$. In what follows, we consider only step one of this procedure, because this will be sufficient to illustrate the dynamic inconsistency of the solution.

Using the Phillips curve (6.5), we can eliminate the output gap from the welfare function and rewrite the above problem in reduced form with inflation as the only system variable. The objective functional to be maximized becomes

$$\sum_{t=0}^{+\infty} \beta^t \left[-\pi_t^2 - \frac{\kappa}{\alpha^2}(\pi_t - \beta \pi_{t+1} - \alpha \bar{y})^2 \right].$$

We can see that the optimization problem has the standard (reduced) form but that the system variable is the jump variable π_t. Hence, the arguments from the

Dynamic optimization

general discussion above suggest that the optimal solution is dynamically inconsistent.

In order to verify this formally and for later reference, we will now characterize the optimal solution in more detail. To do that, we apply the Lagrangian approach to the original (non-reduced) form of the optimization problem consisting of equations (6.4) and (6.5). The Lagrangian function is given by

$$L = \sum_{t=0}^{+\infty} \beta^t \left[-\pi_t^2 - \kappa(y_t - \bar{y})^2 + \lambda_t(\beta\pi_{t+1} + \alpha y_t - \pi_t) \right],$$

where $(\lambda_t)_{t=0}^{+\infty}$ is a sequence of Lagrange multipliers. Note that the Lagrangian can also be written as

$$L = -\pi_0^2 - \kappa(y_0 - \bar{y})^2 + \lambda_0(\alpha y_0 - \pi_0)$$

$$+ \sum_{t=1}^{+\infty} \beta^t \left[-\pi_t^2 - \kappa(y_t - \bar{y})^2 + \lambda_t(\alpha y_t - \pi_t) + \lambda_{t-1}\pi_t \right].$$

The first-order conditions for the optimal choice of π_0 and y_0 are $-2\pi_0 - \lambda_0 = 0$ and $-2\kappa(y_0 - \bar{y}) + \alpha\lambda_0 = 0$. Eliminating λ_0 from these two equations yields

$$\pi_0 = (\kappa/\alpha)(\bar{y} - y_0). \tag{6.6}$$

The first-order conditions for the maximization of the Lagrangian with respect to π_t and y_t for $t \geq 1$, on the other hand, are $-2\pi_t + \lambda_{t-1} - \lambda_t = 0$ and $-2\kappa(y_t - \bar{y}) + \alpha\lambda_t = 0$. Elimination of the Lagrange multipliers implies that

$$\pi_t = (\kappa/\alpha)(y_{t-1} - y_t) \tag{6.7}$$

holds for all $t \geq 1$. We can rewrite the Phillips curve (6.5) and equation (6.7) as the following system of two homogeneous first-order linear difference equations

$$\begin{pmatrix} \pi_{t+1} \\ y_{t+1} \end{pmatrix} = \begin{pmatrix} 1/\beta & -\alpha/\beta \\ -\alpha/(\beta\kappa) & 1 + \alpha^2/(\beta\kappa) \end{pmatrix} \begin{pmatrix} \pi_t \\ y_t \end{pmatrix}. \tag{6.8}$$

The system matrix has the trace

$$T = 1 + \frac{1}{\beta} + \frac{\alpha^2}{\beta\kappa}$$

and the determinant $D = 1/\beta$. It holds that $1 < D < T - 1$, which shows that the eigenvalues of the system matrix satisfy $0 < \sigma_1 < 1 < \sigma_2$.[1] It follows that the general solution to equation (6.8) takes the form

$$\begin{pmatrix} \pi_t \\ y_t \end{pmatrix} = A\sigma_1^t w_1 + B\sigma_2^t w_2,$$

---

[1] See the discussion in section 2.3.

where A and B are undetermined coefficients, and where w_1 and w_2 are the eigenvectors of the system matrix corresponding to σ_1 and σ_2, respectively. Because the product of the two eigenvalues must be equal to the determinant D and because of $0 < \sigma_1 < 1$, it follows that $\sigma_2 > 1/\beta$. We can therefore conclude that solutions of (6.8) with $B \neq 0$ cannot satisfy the transversality condition for the central bank's optimization problem.[2] Let us therefore set $B = 0$. The eigenvector $w_1 = (w_{1,\pi}, w_{1,y})$ satisfies $w_{1,\pi} - \alpha w_{1,y} = \beta \sigma_1 w_{1,\pi}$ and it follows therefore from $B = 0$ that

$$y_0 = A w_{1,y} = \frac{1 - \beta \sigma_1}{\alpha} A w_{1,\pi} = \frac{(1 - \beta \sigma_1)\pi_0}{\alpha}. \tag{6.9}$$

The unique solution to the first-order condition (6.8) that satisfies the transversality condition is therefore given by $\pi_t = \pi_0 \sigma_1^t$ and $y_t = y_0 \sigma_1^t$, where π_0 and y_0 are related by (6.9).

Finally, by combining (6.6) and (6.9) it follows that

$$\pi_0 = \frac{\alpha \kappa \bar{y}}{\alpha^2 + \kappa(1 - \beta \sigma_1)} \quad \text{and} \quad y_0 = \frac{\kappa(1 - \beta \sigma_1)\bar{y}}{\alpha^2 + \kappa(1 - \beta \sigma_1)}.$$

The determination of the optimal policy is now complete. It shows that the central bank chooses a strictly positive initial inflation rate π_0 (recall that $\bar{y}$ was assumed to be positive) and commits to reducing inflation down to 0 following a geometric sequence $\pi_t = \pi_0 \sigma_1^t$.

To see why this solution is not dynamically consistent, suppose that the central bank would reconsider its original plan in some period $t > 0$. The original plan stipulates that $\pi_t = \pi_0 \sigma_1^t$ and $y_t = y_0 \sigma_1^t$. However, the central bank's problem from period t onwards is identical to the original problem that it faced in period 0. Thus, if the central bank were able to re-optimize in period t it would choose the values π_0 and y_0 for period t instead of the values $\pi_t = \pi_0 \sigma_1^t$ and $y_t = y_0 \sigma_1^t$. In other words, in every period $t > 0$, the central bank faces an incentive to deviate from the original plan and to generate higher inflation than originally planned.

In the above example, dynamic inconsistency arises because the Phillips curve (6.5) forms a constraint (involving π_t and π_{t+1}) that is relevant for the central bank's optimization problem in period t but no longer relevant for the optimization problem in period $t + 1$. This has the consequence that the central bank in period $t + 1$ is less restricted in its choice of π_{t+1} than it is in period t. The next example illustrates essentially the opposite situation in which new constraints emerge in the course of

---

[2] Analogously to example 5.7, we can show that theorem 5.4 applies in this linear-quadratic optimization problem. Hence, the feasibility and first-order condition (6.8) plus the transversality condition are sufficient for optimality.

time. A decision maker who would want to reconsider his or her choice in period $t + 1$ would be more restricted than he or she is in period t.

Example 6.2   Suppose that a society has access to a non-renewable resource and that it derives utility solely from the consumption of this resource. Denoting the resource stock at the start of period s by x_s and the rate of consumption in period s by c_s, it follows that

$$x_{s+1} = x_s - c_s \tag{6.10}$$

and that the constraints

$$0 \leq c_s \leq x_s \tag{6.11}$$

must be satisfied for all $s \in \mathbb{N}_0$. We assume that, in every period $t \in \mathbb{N}_0$, the society has the objective of maximizing

$$\sum_{s=t}^{+\infty} \beta^{(s-t)} c_s^\alpha \tag{6.12}$$

subject to the constraints (6.10)–(6.11) and the initial resource stock $x_t > 0$, where $\alpha \in (0, 1)$ and $\beta \in (0, 1)$ are fixed parameters.

So far, the problem is just a special case of example 5.6 that occurs for $R = 1$.[3] Now assume, however, that the society in period t wants to demonstrate its concern for future generations and therefore it promises to provide at least as much consumption to the people living in period $t + 1$ as to those living in period t.[4] Formally, the society in period t imposes the additional constraint

$$c_t \leq c_{t+1}. \tag{6.13}$$

We denote the problem of maximizing the objective functional in (6.12) for a given initial resource stock x_t and subject to the constraints (6.10)–(6.11) and (6.13) by $\mathbf{P}(x_t, t)$. Note that this problem includes the constraint (6.13) but that it does not include the constraint $c_s \leq c_{s+1}$ for any $s > t$. In what follows, we prove that the optimal solution $(x_t)_{t=0}^{+\infty}$ of problem $\mathbf{P}(x, 0)$ is not dynamically consistent relative to the sequence $(\mathbf{P}_t)_{t=0}^{+\infty}$ defined by $\mathbf{P}_t = \mathbf{P}(x_t, t)$ for all $t \in \mathbb{N}_0$.

To solve problem $\mathbf{P}_0$, we first note that the constraint (6.13) of that problem involves only the variables c_0 and c_1. No system variable dated $s \geq 2$ occurs in this constraint.

---

[3] The main point of this example can also be made in the general case where R is an arbitrary number satisfying $0 < R < \beta^{-1/\alpha}$, but for the sake of simplicity we consider only the special case $R = 1$.

[4] An alternative interpretation is that the political process in period t is dominated by those individuals alive in periods t and $t + 1$ and that condition (6.13) below is a result of this process.

The objective functional (6.12) for $t = 0$ can therefore be rewritten in the form

$$c_0^\alpha + \beta c_1^\alpha + \beta^2 V(x_0 - c_0 - c_1), \tag{6.14}$$

where $V : \mathbb{R}_+ \mapsto \mathbb{R}_+$ is the current value optimal value function of the problem without the constraint (6.13). You were asked to prove in exercise 5.8 that this function is given by

$$V(x) = \frac{x^\alpha}{[1 - \beta^{1/(1-\alpha)}]^{1-\alpha}}.$$

The government in period 0 maximizes the objective functional in (6.14) subject to $0 \le c_0 \le c_1$ and $c_0 + c_1 \le x_0$. It is clear from the form of (6.14) that the constraints $c_0 \ge 0$ and $c_0 + c_1 \le x_0$ cannot be binding in the optimal solution. Hence, we need to consider only the constraint $c_0 \le c_1$. The Lagrangian function of the problem is therefore

$$L = c_0^\alpha + \beta c_1^\alpha + \frac{\beta^2 (x_0 - c_0 - c_1)^\alpha}{[1 - \beta^{1/(1-\alpha)}]^{1-\alpha}} + \lambda(c_1 - c_0)$$

and the first-order conditions are

$$\alpha c_0^{\alpha-1} - \frac{\alpha \beta^2 (x_0 - c_0 - c_1)^{\alpha-1}}{[1 - \beta^{1/(1-\alpha)}]^{1-\alpha}} - \lambda = 0,$$

$$\alpha \beta c_1^{\alpha-1} - \frac{\alpha \beta^2 (x_0 - c_0 - c_1)^{\alpha-1}}{[1 - \beta^{1/(1-\alpha)}]^{1-\alpha}} + \lambda = 0,$$

$$\lambda \ge 0,$$

$$\lambda(c_1 - c_0) = 0.$$

We first show that the constraint $c_0 \le c_1$ must be binding. If this is not the case, the last condition in the above list (complementary slackness condition) implies that the Lagrange multiplier λ is equal to 0 and the first two conditions therefore yield

$$\alpha c_0^{\alpha-1} - \frac{\alpha \beta^2 (x_0 - c_0 - c_1)^{\alpha-1}}{[1 - \beta^{1/(1-\alpha)}]^{1-\alpha}} = \alpha \beta c_1^{\alpha-1} - \frac{\alpha \beta^2 (x_0 - c_0 - c_1)^{\alpha-1}}{[1 - \beta^{1/(1-\alpha)}]^{1-\alpha}} = 0.$$

Obviously, this implies $c_1^{1-\alpha} = \beta c_0^{1-\alpha}$ which contradicts $c_1 \ge c_0$. Consequently, the constraint $c_0 \le c_1$ must be binding, that is, $c_0 = c_1$ must hold. Denoting the common value of c_0 and c_1 by c and substituting into the first two first-order conditions, we obtain the equations

$$\alpha c^{\alpha-1} - \frac{\alpha \beta^2 (x_0 - 2c)^{\alpha-1}}{[1 - \beta^{1/(1-\alpha)}]^{1-\alpha}} - \lambda = \alpha \beta c^{\alpha-1} - \frac{\alpha \beta^2 (x_0 - 2c)^{\alpha-1}}{[1 - \beta^{1/(1-\alpha)}]^{1-\alpha}} + \lambda = 0,$$

which can be solved for c and λ. This yields in particular

$$c_0 = c_1 = c = \frac{x_0 (1 + \beta)^{1/(1-\alpha)} [1 - \beta^{1/(1-\alpha)}]}{2(1 + \beta)^{1/(1-\alpha)} [1 - \beta^{1/(1-\alpha)}] + (2\beta^2)^{1/(1-\alpha)}}.$$

The remaining consumption rates $(c_s)_{s=2}^{+\infty}$ can easily be found from example 5.6, because from period $s = 2$ onwards the problem $\mathbf{P}_0$ is identical to the model discussed in that example. More specifically, it must hold that

$$c_s = (x_0 - 2c)[1 - \beta^{1/(1-\alpha)}]\beta^{(s-2)/(1-\alpha)}.$$

Because of $\beta \in (0, 1)$, it follows that the sequence $(c_s)_{s=2}^{+\infty}$ is strictly decreasing. Noting that problem $\mathbf{P}_t$ includes the constraint $c_t \le c_{t+1}$, this demonstrates that the optimal solution to $\mathbf{P}_0$ is dynamically inconsistent relative to the sequence $(\mathbf{P}_t)_{t=0}^{+\infty}$.

In the last two examples, the sequences of optimization problems $(\mathbf{P}_t)_{t=0}^{+\infty}$ had the property that there exist pairs of different time periods t and s such that the corresponding problems $\mathbf{P}_t$ and $\mathbf{P}_s$ contain common choice variables, but differ from each other with respect to the constraints restricting the choice of these variables. This feature was the source of the incentives to deviate from an optimal solution in the course of time. The last example of this section presents a model in which the optimal solution is dynamically inconsistent because there exist pairs of different time periods t and s such that the corresponding decision problems $\mathbf{P}_t$ and $\mathbf{P}_s$ contain common choice variables but differ from each other with respect to their objective functionals.

Example 6.3 This example of a dynamically inconsistent solution to a dynamic optimization problem involves non-geometric discounting. Formally, this means that the decision maker in period t evaluates a consumption stream $(c_s)_{s=t}^{+\infty}$ according to the utility functional

$$\sum_{s=t}^{+\infty} B(s, t)u(c_s),$$

where the time-preference factor $B(s, t)$ is not of the geometric form $B(s, t) = \text{const.} \times \delta^{s-t}$ for some positive constant δ. For simplicity, let us focus on one of the most popular non-geometric discounting functions, the so-called β-δ model. This model is defined by

$$B(s, t) = \begin{cases} 1 & \text{if } s = t, \\ \beta\delta^{s-t-1} & \text{if } s > t, \end{cases}$$

where β and δ are parameters in the interval $(0, 1)$. If $\beta = \delta$, then $B(s, t)$ is the usual geometric time-preference factor. However, when $\beta \ne \delta$, it is a non-geometric discounting function. The parameter β is the time-preference factor that is applied between the current period and the next one, whereas the parameter δ is the time-preference factor that is applied between any two other adjacent periods in the future.

Now suppose that the decision maker seeks to solve the simple saving problem introduced in example 5.1 under the assumption of β-δ preferences. As in example 5.6, we assume that the utility function takes the form $u(c) = c^\alpha$ with $\alpha \in (0, 1)$ and that the gross rate of return is a constant $R \in (0, \delta^{-1/\alpha})$. Furthermore, we impose the natural borrowing constraint. Formally, the decision maker in period 0 maximizes

$$c_0^\alpha + \beta \sum_{t=1}^{+\infty} \delta^{t-1} c_t^\alpha$$

subject to

$$x_{t+1} = R(x_t - c_t), \quad x_t \geq 0, \quad c_t \geq 0,$$

and the given initial wealth x_0. Analogously to example 5.6, we can show that the unique optimal solution to this problem is given by

$$c_t = \begin{cases} \theta x_0 & \text{if } t = 0, \\ \theta x_0 (\beta R)^{1/(1-\alpha)} (\delta R)^{(t-1)/(1-\alpha)} & \text{if } t \geq 1, \end{cases}$$

where

$$\theta = \frac{1 - (\delta R^\alpha)^{1/(1-\alpha)}}{1 + (\beta R^\alpha)^{1/(1-\alpha)} - (\delta R^\alpha)^{1/(1-\alpha)}}. \tag{6.15}$$

In particular, the optimal consumption rate in period 1 is

$$c_1 = \theta x_0 (\beta R)^{1/(1-\alpha)}.$$

If the decision maker implements the optimal consumption rate for period 0, that is, if he or she consumes $c_0 = \theta x_0$ units in period 0, his or her wealth changes from x_0 to $x_1 = R(x_0 - c_0) = (1 - \theta) R x_0$. If the decision maker would re-optimize the consumption profile in period 1, he or she would choose first-period consumption according to

$$\hat{c}_1 = \theta x_1 = \theta (1 - \theta) R x_0.$$

Because of

$$(1 - \theta)R = \frac{(\beta R)^{1/(1-\alpha)}}{1 + (\beta R^\alpha)^{1/(1-\alpha)} - (\delta R^\alpha)^{1/(1-\alpha)}},$$

it follows that $\hat{c}_1 = c_1$ if and only if $\beta = \delta$. This shows that whenever $\beta \neq \delta$, the optimal solution is dynamically inconsistent.

6.2 Optimization without commitment

Consider an optimization problem that has a dynamically inconsistent solution. So far, we have assumed that the problem is solved in period 0 and that the solution for the entire planning horizon is also implemented in period 0. We have seen in the previous section that the decision maker would deviate from this solution if he or she had a chance to do that. This shows that the solution concept we have applied so far requires that the decision maker does not have any opportunities to revise his or her choice or that he or she has the power to commit in period 0 to carry out all the actions and choices described in the optimal solution. Hence, we call this solution the *commitment solution*.

Alternatively, we may assume that there is no technology available to the decision maker to bind himself or herself to the solution derived in period 0. Such a scenario is called decision making under *discretion*. In that case, the decision maker will give in to the incentives to deviate from the initially derived solution in the course of time. In the present section, we discuss how to define and how to solve for optimal solutions under discretion. We introduce the basic ideas in a general setting and illustrate them afterwards by means of the specific examples that have already been used in section 6.1.

As in the previous section, we assume that a decision maker is facing the dynamic optimization problem $\mathbf{P}_t$ in period t and we suppose that problem $\mathbf{P}_t$ has the commitment solution $(c_{s,t})_{s=t}^{+\infty}$. That is, if the decision maker can choose a sequence of control variables in period t and believes that he or she will be able to stick to that sequence from period t onwards, then he or she would choose $(c_{s,t})_{s=t}^{+\infty}$. A naive approach to model the behaviour of such a discretionary decision maker would be to assume that for every $t \in \mathbb{N}_0$ he or she implements $c_{t,t}$ in period t. Formally, the *naive solution* is the sequence $(c_{t,t})_{t=0}^{+\infty}$. This is not a very appealing solution concept, though, because it assumes that the decision maker believes in every period that he or she has commitment over the rest of the planning horizon, whereas this belief turns out to be wrong in every period s for which dynamic inconsistency leads to $c_{s,s} \neq c_{t,s}$ for some $t < s$. Such behaviour is not consistent with the hypothesis of rationality because a rational agent would anticipate to deviate from a previously derived solution if incentives to do so appear.

Anticipating future deviations is tantamount to saying that the decision maker in period t believes that decisions at any later period $s > t$ are taken on the basis of the optimization problem $\mathbf{P}_s$ and, hence, that the control variables $(c_s)_{s=t+1}^{+\infty}$ are not under the control of the decision maker of period t. To derive a rational solution to optimization problems under lack of commitment, we therefore apply the so-called *multiple-selves model*. According to that model, the decision maker consists of an infinite sequence of separate selves, one for each period. Each self is supposed to be an independent decision maker for his or her period and every self takes the decisions made by the other selves as given. Formally, we define the *sophisticated solution* to a dynamic optimization problem under discretion as a Nash equilibrium of a game among the different selves of which the decision maker consists. In what follows, we illustrate these concepts by the three examples from the previous section.

Example 6.4 Let us reconsider the problem of a central bank that has been described in example 6.1. We have seen that in the commitment solution the central bank in period 0 chooses the inflation rate

$$\pi_0 = \frac{\alpha \kappa \bar{y}}{\alpha^2 + \kappa(1 - \beta \sigma_1)},$$ (6.16)

where $\sigma_1 \in (0, 1)$ is the smaller eigenvalue of the system matrix in equation (6.8). The other inflation rates in the commitment solution are given by $\pi_t = \pi_0 \sigma_1^t$. Let us now assume that the central bank does not have the ability to make a binding commitment for future inflation rates. In the naive solution, the central bank believes in every period that it has commitment power. Because every self of the central bank faces the same problem, it follows that the naive solution is given by the constant sequence of inflation rates $(\pi_0, \pi_0, \ldots)$ with π_0 specified in (6.16) and the corresponding output values $(y_0, y_0, \ldots)$, where y_0 is given by (6.9). This shows that in the naive solution the rate of inflation is at least as high as in the commitment solution. In period 0, the two values coincide but in all other periods the rate of inflation under commitment is strictly smaller than under naive discretionary behaviour: lack of commitment results in a positive inflation bias.

We now turn to the sophisticated solution. The central bank in period t decides upon period-t output y_t and period-t inflation π_t, but it takes the variables y_s and π_s for all $s > t$ as given. The period-t self of the central bank faces the Phillips curve constraint

$$\pi_t = \beta \pi_{t+1} + \alpha y_t$$

and seeks to maximize the objective functional

$$\sum_{s=t}^{+\infty} \beta^{s-t} \left[-\pi_s^2 - \kappa(y_s - \bar{y})^2 \right].$$

The only term in the infinite sum constituting the objective functional that involves the decision variables of the central bank in period t is the first one. Obviously, this implies that the problem of the central bank in period t is equivalent to the maximization of

$$-\pi_t^2 - \kappa(y_t - \bar{y})^2$$

subject to the Phillips curve constraint, where π_{t+1} is treated as fixed. The unique solution to this problem is given by

$$y_t = \frac{\kappa \bar{y} - \alpha \beta \pi_{t+1}}{\alpha^2 + \kappa}$$

and

$$\pi_t = \frac{\beta \kappa \pi_{t+1} + \alpha \kappa \bar{y}}{\alpha^2 + \kappa}.$$ (6.17)

These equations determine the behaviour of the period-t central bank as a function of π_{t+1}. Since all the selves of the central bank are facing exactly the same problem, equation (6.17) has to hold for all periods $t \in \mathbb{N}_0$. If we write (6.17) in explicit form, we obtain the linear difference equation

$$\pi_{t+1} = \frac{\alpha^2 + \kappa}{\beta\kappa}\pi_t - \frac{\alpha\bar{y}}{\beta}. \qquad (6.18)$$

Note that this difference equation has a unique fixed point given by

$$\hat{\pi} = \frac{\alpha\kappa\bar{y}}{\alpha^2 + \kappa(1 - \beta)}.$$

The parameter assumptions $\beta \in (0, 1)$ and $\kappa > 0$ imply that the coefficient in front of π_t on the right-hand side of (6.18) is strictly larger than 1. This shows that the fixed point is unstable and that all trajectories of this difference equation, except for the one that corresponds to the fixed point, diverge to $+\infty$ or $-\infty$. The explosive solutions can be interpreted as bubble solutions, the fixed point as a fundamental solution. We shall focus on the latter.[5] The fact that the eigenvalue σ_1 is smaller than 1 (see the discussion in example 6.1) implies that $\hat{\pi} > \pi_0$, where π_0 is the rate of inflation in period 0 under commitment, given in (6.16). This shows that the rate of inflation in the sophisticated solution without commitment is strictly larger than what it would be in the naive solution, which, in turn, is at least as large as it would be in the commitment solution. The inflation bias due to the lack of commitment is stronger if the decision maker is sophisticated than if he or she is behaving in a naive way.

Solving the above example for the sophisticated solution under lack of commitment was quite simple, actually simpler than solving it for the commitment solution. This is the case because the decision problem of every self is a simple static optimization problem parameterized by next period's inflation rate. As a consequence, the only connection between the decision problems of two consecutive selves is that the inflation rate chosen by the later self affects the Phillips curve constraint that is relevant for the earlier self. The reason for this simple structure is that the underlying optimization problem contains no state variables but only control variables. The next two examples involve both control and state variables, and we will see that there is a two-way interrelation between the optimization problems of any two consecutive selves. As before, the decisions made in period $t + 1$ affect the period-t decision problem, but the self deciding in period t can also affect the decisions of its successors via the state variable.

---

[5] Note that every self of the central bank solves a static optimization problem for which the first-order condition is necessary and sufficient for optimality. There is no transversality condition that would rule out explosive solutions.

Example 6.5 Here we reconsider the problem of the society living off a non-renewable resource, which was introduced in example 6.2. Recall that this society wants to demonstrate concern for the future generation by promising at least as much consumption in the next period as there is in the current period. We shall now derive the naive solution as well as the sophisticated one for this problem in the absence of commitment.

Let us start by deriving the naive solution. In our discussion in example 6.2, we have proved that the government in period 0 chooses to consume $c_0 = Bx_0$, where

$$B = \frac{(1+\beta)^{1/(1-\alpha)}[1 - \beta^{1/(1-\alpha)}]}{2(1+\beta)^{1/(1-\alpha)}[1 - \beta^{1/(1-\alpha)}] + (2\beta^2)^{1/(1-\alpha)}}.$$

The resource stock at the start of period 1 is therefore equal to $x_1 = (1 - B)x_0$. The government in period 1 then faces the very same optimization problem as the government from period 0, except for the fact that the resource stock is given by x_1 rather than by x_0. Hence, the naive government in period 1 chooses $c_1 = Bx_1$, which yields $x_2 = (1 - B)x_1 = (1 - B)^2 x_0$. Proceeding in this way, we find that the naive solution without commitment generates the consumption rates $c_t = B(1 - B)^t x_0$ and the resource stocks $x_t = (1 - B)^t x_0$. Because of $B \in (0, 1/2)$, it follows that the resource stocks as well as the consumption rates converge monotonically towards 0, which implies in particular that each government's promise to let the succeeding generation consume at least as much as the current generation is violated along the naive solution. The speed of convergence of the resource stocks and the consumption rates is determined by the number $1 - B$, which is always strictly larger than $1/2$. This shows that, irrespective of the size of the time-preference factor β, the speed of convergence is bounded from below. Note that the model without the crucial constraint $c_t \leq c_{t+1}$ was discussed in example 5.6, where we showed that the speed of convergence is determined by the factor $\beta^{1/(1-\alpha)}$ (recall that we are presently assuming that $R = 1$), which can be arbitrarily close to 0 if the society has a very strong time-preference. Thus, even if the society is constantly breaking its promise to let the future generation consume as much as the present one, the attempt to do so at least slows down the resource exploitation.

Let us now analyze the sophisticated solution, which turns out to have quite a simple structure. As a matter of fact, if the government in period t understands that consumption in period $t + 1$ will be chosen by another government and therefore takes c_{t+1} as given, and if the government in period t chooses c_t subject to the constraint $c_t \leq c_{t+1}$, then it follows that in the sophisticated solution this inequality must hold for all $t \in \mathbb{N}_0$. In other words, the consumption sequence generated by the sophisticated solution must be non-decreasing. However, the only non-decreasing consumption sequence that is feasible, given the finite resource stock that is available at time 0, is the sequence $c_t = 0$ for all $t \in \mathbb{N}_0$. We therefore conclude that in the sophisticated solution, the society consumes nothing and the resource stock remains constant throughout time.

Example 6.6 Finally, let us reconsider the simple saving problem with non-geometric discounting that we solved for the commitment solution in example 6.3. As before, we assume that the time-preference of the agent is described by the β-δ model, that the agent is subject to the natural borrowing constraint, and that the gross rate of return on asset holdings is a constant $R \in (0, \delta^{-1/\alpha})$. From the results derived in example 6.3, we know that the naive solution under discretion consists in consuming the fraction θ of total wealth in every period, that is, $c_t = \theta x_t$ for all $t \in \mathbb{N}_0$, where θ is given in (6.15).

The simplest way to derive the sophisticated solution to this problem is via a recursive approach. Self t takes the total wealth level x_t as given and seeks to determine period-t consumption c_t optimally. In doing so, it takes the behaviour of all future selves as given. Even if self t can make its choice of c_t dependent on all past events, we focus here on the case where it conditions the choice of c_t on the current state x_t only.[6] Formally, we assume that self t chooses a function $\varphi_t : \mathbb{R}_+ \mapsto \mathbb{R}_+$ and determines c_t according to $c_t = \varphi_t(x_t)$. Furthermore, because the model has a stationary discounted structure, we will focus attention on symmetric equilibria in which all selves use the same strategy so that we can drop the time subscript from the strategy φ_t. Together with the state equation of the model, this implies that $x_{t+s+1} = \psi^{(s)}(x_{t+1})$ holds for all $s \in \mathbb{N}_0$, where

$$\psi(x) = R[x - \varphi(x)] \tag{6.19}$$

and where $\psi^{(s)}$ denotes the sth iteration of ψ. This allows us to express the objective function of self t as

$$u(c_t) + \beta \sum_{s=0}^{+\infty} \delta^s u(c_{t+s+1}) = u(c_t) + \beta \sum_{s=0}^{+\infty} \delta^s u(\varphi(\psi^{(s)}(x_{t+1}))) = u(c_t) + \beta V(x_{t+1}),$$

where

$$V(x) = \sum_{s=0}^{+\infty} \delta^s u(\varphi(\psi^{(s)}(x))).$$

---

[6] In the next chapter on dynamic games, we will call such a strategy a closed-loop strategy.

We notice that the above definition of the function V implies the recursive relation

$$V(x) = u(\varphi(x)) + \delta V(\psi(x)). \tag{6.20}$$

A symmetric (or stationary) Nash equilibrium of the model is a function φ such that there exists a pair of functions (ψ, V) with the following properties: conditions (6.19) and (6.20) hold and the pair $(c, y) = (\varphi(x), \psi(x))$ solves the problem of maximizing $u(c) + \beta V(y)$ subject to the constraint $y = R(x - c)$.

To derive a stationary Nash equilibrium, we use a guess-and-verify approach. Recall that the utility function is assumed to be $u(c) = c^\alpha$ with $\alpha \in (0, 1)$. Based on the results that we have derived earlier for the commitment solution, we conjecture that $\varphi(x) = \bar{\theta}x$ and $V(x) = Ax^\alpha$ for some positive coefficients $\bar{\theta}$ and A. Substituting this into (6.19) and (6.20), we obtain $\psi(x) = R(1 - \bar{\theta})x$ and

$$Ax^\alpha = \bar{\theta}^\alpha x^\alpha + \delta A R^\alpha (1 - \bar{\theta})^\alpha x^\alpha.$$

The last equation can only hold for all $x \in \mathbb{R}_+$ if

$$A = \frac{\bar{\theta}^\alpha}{1 - \delta R^\alpha (1 - \bar{\theta})^\alpha}. \tag{6.21}$$

The optimization problem to be solved by a self with total wealth x consists of the maximization of $c^\alpha + \beta A y^\alpha$ subject to $y = R(x - c)$. Substituting the constraint into the objective function, we can write the latter as

$$c^\alpha + \beta A R^\alpha (x - c)^\alpha.$$

This objective function is strictly concave such that the first-order optimality condition is sufficient for optimality. Solving the first-order condition for c, it is straightforward to obtain

$$c = \frac{x}{1 + (\beta A R^\alpha)^{1/(1-\alpha)}}.$$

This shows that our conjecture is correct if and only if $\bar{\theta} = [1 + (\beta A R^\alpha)^{1/(1-\alpha)}]^{-1}$, which is equivalent to

$$A = (\beta R^\alpha)^{-1} \left(\frac{1 - \bar{\theta}}{\bar{\theta}} \right)^{1-\alpha}.$$

Combining this result with equation (6.21), we obtain after simple rearrangements that

$$\bar{\theta}\beta R^\alpha + (1 - \bar{\theta})\delta R^\alpha = (1 - \bar{\theta})^{1-\alpha}. \tag{6.22}$$

The term on the left-hand side of this equation is a non-negative and linear function of $\bar{\theta}$ which attains the value $\delta R^\alpha < 1$ when $\bar{\theta} = 0$ and the value $\beta R^\alpha > 0$ when $\bar{\theta} = 1$. The right-hand side is a strictly concave, strictly decreasing, and continuous function of $\bar{\theta}$ that takes the value 1 when $\bar{\theta} = 0$ and the value 0 when $\bar{\theta} = 1$. It is obvious that these properties ensure that there exists a unique value $\bar{\theta} \in (0, 1)$ satisfying equation (6.22).

Let us compare the consumption rate $\bar{\theta}$ determined by equation (6.22) to the corresponding value in the commitment solution and the naive solution. The latter is given by θ as defined in equation (6.15), which can also be written as

$$[\theta(\beta R^\alpha)^{1/(1-\alpha)} + (1 - \theta)(\delta R^\alpha)^{1/(1-\alpha)}]^{1-\alpha} = (1 - \theta)^{1-\alpha}. \tag{6.23}$$

The right-hand sides of (6.22) and (6.23) are the same function evaluated at $\bar{\theta}$ and θ, respectively. Let us denote the left-hand side of (6.22) by $\bar{g}(\bar{\theta})$ and note that $\bar{g}$ is a linear function. The left-hand side of (6.23), on the other hand, is a strictly concave function of θ provided that $\beta \neq \delta$. Let us call this function $g(\theta)$. Because of these properties and $g(0) = \bar{g}(0) = \delta R^\alpha$ and $g(1) = \bar{g}(1) = \beta R^\alpha$, it follows that the graph of the function g is strictly above the graph of $\bar{g}$ on the interval $(0, 1)$ when $\beta \neq \delta$. Obviously, this implies that the solution to (6.23) must be strictly smaller than the solution to (6.22) whenever $\beta \neq \delta$ (the two solutions coincide in the case $\beta = \delta$). Hence, we conclude that the first-period consumption rate under commitment, θ, is smaller than the constant consumption rate $\bar{\theta}$ in the sophisticated solution without commitment. A surprising aspect of this finding is that it is independent of whether $\beta > \delta$ or $\beta < \delta$ holds.

6.3 Optimization with partial commitment

In the previous section, we have studied how a dynamic optimization problem with a dynamically inconsistent commitment solution can be solved in the absence of a commitment technology. More specifically, we have assumed that the decision maker has no commitment power whatsoever, which is equivalent to saying that a separate self is in charge in every period. In the present section, we discuss a model in which the decision maker has partial commitment in the sense that a new self takes over with a certain probability $q \in [0, 1]$ in each period. We explain this approach only in the context of the New Keynesian model already discussed in the preceding sections.

Example 6.7 Consider the optimization problem of the central bank as discussed in examples 6.1 and 6.4. Suppose, however, that a governor of the central bank has to be elected in every period and that an office holder can make a binding commitment for policy decisions during his or her own term of office but not for those decisions made by his or her successors. For simplicity, we assume that the probability of remaining in office in period $t + 1$ conditional on being in office in period t is given by $q \in [0, 1]$.

If $q = 0$, no governor is ever re-elected and we are in the discretionary case. If $q = 1$, there is only a single office holder throughout the entire infinite planning period and we have the same situation as in the model with full commitment. Partial commitment corresponds to values of q strictly between 0 and 1.

We first observe that all newly appointed governors face exactly the same optimization problem.[7] In particular, since they are not bound by any promises made by their predecessors, the private-sector forecasts for inflation rates during their own terms of office are independent of which policy choices were made by their predecessors during their terms of office. It is therefore sufficient to consider one particular office holder and to study how he or she sets the instruments during his or her term of office. Let us therefore interpret the variable t as the tenure (or age) of the office holder under consideration.[8] By π_t, we therefore mean the inflation rate set by a central banker that has been in office for t periods already. Analogously, y_t is the output gap implemented by a central banker after having been in office for t periods. In period t, the office holder chooses π_t and y_t subject to the Phillips curve constraint

$$\pi_t = \beta \pi_{t+1}^e + \alpha y_t, \tag{6.24}$$

where π_{t+1}^e denotes the one-period ahead inflation forecast of the private sector. Since the private sector has rational expectations, it anticipates in period t that next period's inflation rate is set by the current office holder with probability q and by a newly appointed governor with probability $1 - q$. The rational expectation of next period's rate of inflation is therefore

$$\pi_{t+1}^e = q \pi_{t+1} + (1 - q)\tilde{\pi}_0, \tag{6.25}$$

where π_{t+1} is the rate of inflation that has been announced by the current office holder for his or her period $t + 1$ of office and where $\tilde{\pi}_0$ denotes the inflation rate set by a newly appointed governor in his or her period 0 of office. The tilde in the notation $\tilde{\pi}_0$ indicates that this variable is not under the control of the current office holder and, hence, must be considered as an exogenous variable of the latter's optimization problem. We use an analogous notation also for other variables, in particular, $\tilde{\pi}_s$ and $\tilde{y}_s$ denote the rate of inflation and the output gap, respectively, implemented by another office holder in his or her period s. The above formula shows that in the case of partial commitment the central bank has control over private-sector expectations, but only to a limited extent.

---

[7] This is the case because the model does not contain any pre-determined variables.

[8] We shall not need any variable to denote calendar time as the latter will turn out to be irrelevant for the present solution.

The office holder under consideration chooses sequences $(\pi_t)_{t=0}^{+\infty}$ and $(y_t)_{t=0}^{+\infty}$ satisfying the constraints (6.24) and (6.25) so as to maximize the objective functional

$$\sum_{t=0}^{+\infty} \beta^t \left\{ q^t \left[-\pi_t^2 - \kappa(y_t - \bar{y})^2 \right] + (1-q) \sum_{s=0}^{t-1} q^s \left[-\tilde{\pi}_s^2 - \kappa(\tilde{y}_s - \bar{y})^2 \right] \right\}.$$

The term inside the curly brackets in this formula is the expected value of utility in period t taking into account that the office holder under consideration may have been replaced by that time. The probability that he or she is still in office in period t is equal to q^t. The probability that an office holder of tenure s is in charge during period t, on the other hand, is equal to $(1-q)q^s$. This is the case because for the tenure of an office holder to be s, this office holder must have been re-elected exactly s times (probability q^s) and his or her predecessor must have stepped down (probability $1-q$). Because the second term inside the curly brackets of the above formula is independent of the decisions of the office holder under consideration, it is irrelevant for the maximization problem and can therefore be dropped. This shows that the central bank maximizes

$$\sum_{t=0}^{+\infty} (\beta q)^t \left[-\pi_t^2 - \kappa(y_t - \bar{y})^2 \right]$$

subject to (6.24) and (6.25). The two constraints can be combined to

$$\pi_t = \beta q \pi_{t+1} + (1-q)\beta \tilde{\pi}_0 + \alpha y_t \tag{6.26}$$

such that the Lagrangian of the central bank's optimization problem is given by

$$L = \sum_{t=0}^{+\infty} (\beta q)^t \left\{ -\pi_t^2 - \kappa(y_t - \bar{y})^2 + \lambda_t \left[\beta q \pi_{t+1} + (1-q)\beta \tilde{\pi}_0 + \alpha y_t - \pi_t \right] \right\}. \tag{6.27}$$

The Lagrangian function can be rewritten as

$$L = -\pi_0^2 - \kappa(y_0 - \bar{y})^2 + \lambda_0(\alpha y_0 - \pi_0)$$
$$+ \sum_{t=1}^{+\infty} (\beta q)^t \left[-\pi_t^2 - \kappa(y_t - \bar{y})^2 + \lambda_t(\alpha y_t - \pi_t) + \lambda_{t-1}\pi_t \right] + K,$$

where K does not depend on any decision variables of the office holder under consideration. As in the case of the commitment solution, we can use the first-order optimality conditions to derive equations (6.6) and (6.7), which are reproduced here for convenience:

$$\pi_0 = (\kappa/\alpha)(\bar{y} - y_0), \tag{6.28}$$

$$\pi_t = (\kappa/\alpha)(y_{t-1} - y_t). \tag{6.29}$$

Equations (6.26) and (6.29) can be rewritten in matrix form as

$$\begin{pmatrix} \pi_{t+1} \\ y_{t+1} \end{pmatrix} = \begin{pmatrix} 1/(\beta q) & -\alpha/(\beta q) \\ -\alpha/(\beta \kappa q) & 1+\alpha^2/(\beta \kappa q) \end{pmatrix} \begin{pmatrix} \pi_t \\ y_t \end{pmatrix} + \begin{pmatrix} -(1-q)\tilde{\pi}_0/q \\ \alpha(1-q)\tilde{\pi}_0/(q\kappa) \end{pmatrix}. \quad (6.30)$$

The system matrix has the same structure as in the commitment solution and it is straightforward to verify that it has one eigenvalue larger than $1/(\beta q)$ and one eigenvalue between 0 and 1. We denote the latter by $\sigma_q.$[9] The bounded solutions of the non-autonomous linear difference equation (6.30) are therefore of the form

$$\pi_t = \pi^* + (\pi_0 - \pi^*)\sigma_q^t \text{ and } y_t = y^* + (y_0 - y^*)\sigma_q^t,$$

where π^* and y^* are the asymptotic values of π_t and y_t as t approaches infinity, and where

$$y_0 - y^* = \frac{(1 - \beta q \sigma_q)(\pi_0 - \pi^*)}{\alpha}. \quad (6.31)$$

Condition (6.31) can be proved in the same way as we derived equation (6.9) in example 6.1. In particular, the result $\lim_{t \to +\infty} y_t = y^*$ together with (6.29) shows that $\lim_{t \to +\infty} \pi_t = 0$. Hence, we must have $\pi^* = 0$. Using this observation in (6.26), we find that $\lim_{t \to +\infty} y_t = y^* = -(1 - q)(\beta/\alpha)\tilde{\pi}_0$. Substituting these values for π^* and y^* into (6.31), it follows that

$$y_0 = \frac{(1 - \beta q \sigma_q)\pi_0 - (1 - q)\beta \tilde{\pi}_0}{\alpha}.$$

Now note that all office holders are identical and operate in identical environments. Therefore, all of them will choose the same sequences $(\pi_t)_{t=0}^{+\infty}$ and $(y_t)_{t=0}^{+\infty}$. Consequently, we can set $\tilde{\pi}_0 = \pi_0$ in the last displayed equation and it follows that

$$y_0 = \frac{[1 - \beta + \beta q(1 - \sigma_q)]\pi_0}{\alpha}.$$

Solving this equation along with (6.28), we finally get

$$\pi_0 = \frac{\alpha \kappa \bar{y}}{\alpha^2 + \kappa[1 - \beta + \beta q(1 - \sigma_q)]} \quad \text{and} \quad y_0 = \frac{\kappa[1 - \beta + \beta q(1 - \sigma_q)]\bar{y}}{\alpha^2 + \kappa[1 - \beta + \beta q(1 - \sigma_q)]}.$$

In an exercise, the reader will be asked to prove that $\lim_{q \to 1} \sigma_q = \sigma_1$, where σ_1 is defined in example 6.1, and that

$$\lim_{q \to 0} \sigma_q = \frac{\kappa}{\alpha^2 + \kappa}.$$

---

[9] This notation is consistent with the notation from example 6.1. Note that the parameter value $q = 1$ corresponds to the case of full commitment such that σ_1 in the present example has the same interpretation as σ_1 from example 6.1.

This implies in turn that $\lim_{q \to 0}[q(1 - \sigma_q)] = 0$. These results confirm that the solution under partial commitment approaches the solution under full commitment if q approaches 1, and that it approaches the sophisticated discretionary solution as q approaches 0.[10] Finally, we can compute the long-run output gap as[11]

$$y^* = -(1 - q)(\beta/\alpha)\pi_0 = \frac{-(1 - q)\beta\kappa\bar{y}}{\alpha^2 + [1 - \beta + \beta q(1 - \sigma_q)]\kappa}.$$

It is interesting to note that this value is negative. Every decision maker therefore targets zero inflation ($\pi^* = 0$) and is willing to accept a negative long-run output gap $y^* < 0$.

6.4   EXERCISES

EXERCISE 6.1   Consider the dynamic optimization problem $\mathbf{Q}(t)$ of maximizing

$$\sum_{s=t}^{+\infty} \beta^{s-t} \left(-c_s^2 + c_{s+1}\right)$$

where $\beta \in (0, 1)$ is the time-preference factor and $(c_s)_{s=t}^{+\infty}$ is a sequence of control variables with $c_s \in \mathbb{R}$ for all $s \in \mathbb{N}_0$. No initial value is given for this sequence.

(a) Derive the first-order optimality conditions for problem $\mathbf{Q}(0)$ clearly distinguishing between the first-order condition for the optimal choice of c_0 and those for the optimal choice of c_t for $t \geq 1$. Show that the optimal solution to problem $\mathbf{Q}(0)$ is dynamically inconsistent relative to the sequence $(\mathbf{Q}(t))_{t=0}^{+\infty}$.

(b) Apply the multiple-selves model to the above optimization problem. The self in period t decides on c_t so as to solve $\mathbf{Q}(t)$. Determine the naive as well as the sophisticated solution to the optimization problem in the absence of commitment. Are these solutions different?

EXERCISE 6.2   Consider a decision maker who in every period $t \in \mathbb{N}_0$ discounts utility derived in period $s \geq t$ by the non-geometric discount factor

$$H(s, t) = [1 + \alpha(s - t)]^{-\beta},$$

---

[10] The reader should notice that in the case of partial commitment inflation and output are stochastic processes driven by the exogenous and random re-elections of the office holders. The statements of convergence should therefore be interpreted as being conditional on the office holder under consideration remaining in charge of policy. This should be clear from the interpretation of t as the tenure of a given office holder and not calendar time.

[11] By 'long-run' we mean the limit as the tenure t of the decision maker approaches infinity.

where α and β are positive parameters. Consider the dynamic optimization problem $\mathbf{P}(x, t)$ of maximizing

$$\sum_{s=t}^{+\infty} H(s, t)U(x_s, x_{s+1}), \tag{6.32}$$

subject to the initial condition $x_t = x$. Here, $(x_s)_{s=t}^{+\infty}$ is a sequence of state variables satisfying $x_s \in \mathbb{R}$ for all $s \in \mathbb{N}_0$. Derive the Euler equation for problem $\mathbf{P}(x, 0)$ and consider any particular solution $(x_t)_{t=0}^{+\infty}$ of this equation. Assuming that $(x_t)_{t=0}^{+\infty}$ is indeed the optimal solution to $\mathbf{P}(x, 0)$ show that it is (in general) dynamically inconsistent relative to the sequence of optimization problems $(\mathbf{P}(x_t, t))_{t=0}^{+\infty}$.

EXERCISE 6.3 Consider the dynamic optimization problem $\mathbf{Q}(t)$ of maximizing

$$\sum_{s=t}^{+\infty} \beta^{s-t} u(c_s),$$

subject to the single constraint

$$\sum_{s=t}^{+\infty} \delta^{s-t} c_s \leq 1,$$

where $\beta \in (0, 1)$ and $\delta \in (0, 1)$ are given numbers, $u : \mathbb{R}_+ \mapsto \mathbb{R}$ is a strictly increasing, strictly concave, and smooth utility function, and $(c_s)_{s=t}^{+\infty}$ with $c_s \in \mathbb{R}$ is a sequence of control variables for which no initial value is given.

(a) Write down a Lagrangian function for the optimization problem $\mathbf{Q}(t)$ and derive the first-order optimality conditions.

(b) From now on, assume that marginal utility is given by $u'(c) = c^{-\sigma}$, where σ is a positive parameter. Furthermore, assume that $\beta \delta^{\sigma-1} < 1$. Use the first-order conditions and the constraint of $\mathbf{Q}(t)$ to verify that the optimal solution to $\mathbf{Q}(t)$ must satisfy

$$c_s = \left[1 - (\beta \delta^{\sigma-1})^{1/\sigma}\right] (\beta/\delta)^{(s-t)/\sigma}.$$

(c) Is the solution to problem $\mathbf{Q}(0)$ derived in part (b) dynamically consistent relative to $(\mathbf{Q}(t))_{t=0}^{+\infty}$ or not?

EXERCISE 6.4 Consider the one-sector optimal growth model that was discussed in examples 5.2 and 5.8 as well as in exercise 5.7 and assume that there is no technological progress, that the decision maker has a logarithmic utility function, and that the technology is described by a Cobb–Douglas production function. Instead of the usual geometric discounting function, however, assume that the time-preference of the decision maker is described by the β-δ model introduced in example 6.3. Formally, the decision maker in period t solves problem $\mathbf{P}(k_t, t)$, which consists of maximizing

$$\ln c_t + \beta \sum_{s=t+1}^{+\infty} \delta^{s-t-1} \ln c_s$$

subject to

$$k_{s+1} = Ak_s^\alpha - c_s, \ k_{s+1} \geq 0, \ c_s \geq 0,$$

and the given initial capital stock k_t. Determine an optimal pair $((k_{t+1})_{t=0}^{+\infty}, (c_t)_{t=0}^{+\infty})$ of problem $\mathbf{P}(k_0, 0)$ and show that it is dynamically inconsistent relative to $(\mathbf{P}(k_t, t))_{t=0}^{+\infty}$ whenever $\beta \neq \delta$.

EXERCISE 6.5 Reconsider problem $\mathbf{P}(x, 0)$ from exercise 6.2 and assume that $U(x, y) = -x^2 + y$.
(a) Solve the model for the commitment solution, that is, derive the unique solution $(x_t)_{t=0}^{+\infty}$ of the Euler equation for problem $\mathbf{P}(x, 0)$. Show that this solution satisfies the condition $\lim_{t \to +\infty} x_t = 1/2$.
(b) Derive the sophisticated no-commitment solution to this problem by applying the multiple-selves model. That is, assume that self t takes the initial value x_t as well as the future states $(x_s)_{s=t+2}^{+\infty}$ as given and chooses x_{t+1} so as to maximize the objective functional in (6.32). Show that there exists a constant $\bar{x} \neq 1/2$ such that $x_t = \bar{x}$ holds for all $t \geq 1$.
(c) Is the solution derived in part (b) different from the naive solution under discretion?

EXERCISE 6.6 Reconsider the one-sector growth model with non-geometric discounting from exercise 6.4. Determine both the naive and the sophisticated solution under lack of commitment. Show that these two solutions coincide in this problem.

EXERCISE 6.7 Derive the eigenvalues of the system matrix in equation (6.30) and show that one of them (called σ_q in example 6.7) is in the interval $(0, 1)$, whereas the other one is larger than $1/(\beta q)$. Prove that $\lim_{q \to 1} \sigma_q = \sigma_1$, where σ_1 is defined in example 6.1 and that $\lim_{q \to 0} \sigma_q = \kappa/(\alpha^2 + \kappa)$.

EXERCISE 6.8 Apply the multiple-selves model with partial commitment (as outlined in section 6.3) to the optimization problem from exercise 6.1. More specifically, assume that the probability that a self remains in charge is equal to $q \in [0, 1]$ and that it is replaced by a new self with probability $1 - q$. Every self makes a binding commitment for decisions during its entire own tenure but it takes decisions made by later selves as given.

(a) Convince yourself that the optimization problem of every given self can be written as the maximization of

$$\sum_{t=0}^{+\infty} (\beta q)^t \left[-c_t^2 + q c_{t+1} + (1-q)\tilde{c}_0 \right],$$

where t denotes the tenure of the self under consideration and where $\tilde{c}_0$ is the control value set by another self in the first period of its term of office.

(b) Determine the optimal solution under the assumption of partial commitment. How does this solution differ from the commitment solution and from the solution without any commitment power?

6.5 COMMENTS AND REFERENCES

The fact that the solutions of dynamic optimization problems can be dynamically inconsistent has first been pointed out by Strotz [87]. Further work on solving such models in the absence of commitment was carried out by Pollak [74] and Phelps and Pollak [73].

The basic idea underlying the model of examples 6.1 and 6.4 is due to Kydland and Prescott [52]. It was further developed by Barro and Gordon [7, 8]. For a more recent discussion of these ideas in a stochastic setting, we refer to Clarida et al. [21] and to Galí [34]. The effects of non-geometric discounting were already analyzed by Strotz [87], but have been made popular more recently by Laibson [53]. An excellent survey of modelling time-preference, including a discussion of non-geometric discounting, can be found in Frederick et al. [33]. Optimization under partial commitment as discussed in section 6.3 is treated in Roberds [78]. Example 6.7, in which the New Keynesian model of monetary policy is solved under the assumption of partial commitment, is based on Schaumburg and Tambalotti [82]. The discounting function H used in exercise 6.2 is called the hyperbolic discounting function.

Further models in which the issue of dynamic inconsistency arises and in which the solutions under commitment differ from those under discretion will be discussed in chapters 7 and 8.

7 Dynamic games

The present chapter discusses models with more than one decision maker, each one solving a dynamic optimization problem. The individual optimization problems are linked in various ways: there exist state variables that can be influenced by the actions of all decision makers, and the control variables of any one decision maker may also affect the other decision makers' objective functionals. The decision makers are well aware of these interrelations and take them into account when choosing their own actions. In other words, they act strategically. Such models are called dynamic games.

Due to the possibility of strategic interactions between the decision makers, dynamic games allow for a rich set of solutions and the present chapter can only provide a very limited survey of some solution concepts as well as of certain technical complications that can arise. We start by outlining a rather general framework in section 7.1. Thereafter, we discuss Nash equilibria under the assumptions that the players move simultaneously and condition their actions on calendar time as well as on the current state of the system. We show that even this restricted setting allows typically for uncountably many equilibria. We then introduce in section 7.3 the most popular equilibrium refinement in this kind of model, namely Markov perfection. Finally, in section 7.4 we briefly discuss situations in which some of the decision makers choose before their opponents such that the decision process is a hierarchical one.

7.1 A general framework

Suppose that there exists a finite set $\mathbf{M} = \{1, 2, \ldots, m\}$ of players, each one solving a dynamic optimization problem such as the standard problem introduced in section 5.1. These m optimization problems, however, are interconnected in the sense that (i) the state variable $x_t \in \mathbb{R}^n$ is the same for the problems of all m players and (ii) the control variable of player i at time t, $c_t^i \in \mathbb{R}^{k^i}$, does not only affect player i's objective functional, but potentially those of all other players as well. More specifically, the objective functional of player i's problem is assumed to be of the form

$$\sum_{t=0}^{+\infty} F^i(x_t, c_t, t), \tag{7.1}$$

where $x_t \in X \subseteq \mathbb{R}^n$ is the state of the system at time t, $c_t = (c_t^1, c_t^2, \ldots, c_t^m)$ is the vector of control variables applied by all m players at time t, and $F^i : \bar{\Omega} \mapsto \mathbb{R}$ is the instantaneous utility function of player i. The set of feasible controls for player i at time t when the state of the system is x is given by $\bar{G}^i(x, t) \subseteq \mathbb{R}^{k^i}$. The common domain of the functions F^i, $i \in \mathbf{M}$, is

$$\bar{\Omega} = \{(x, c, t) \mid x \in X, t \in \mathbb{N}_0, c \in \bar{G}^1(x, t) \times \bar{G}^2(x, t) \times \ldots \times \bar{G}^m(x, t)\}.$$

The initial state $x_0 \in X$ is given and the system evolves according to the difference equation

$$x_{t+1} = f(x_t, c_t, t), \tag{7.2}$$

where $f : \bar{\Omega} \mapsto X$ is the system dynamics of the game.

Before we can discuss how the m players interact, we need to specify what they know at each point in time. To this end, we define the *history* of the game at time t, denoted by h_t, as the collection of all players' actions from the past, plus the sequence of states generated by these actions. Formally, the history of the game at time t is $h_0 = (x_0)$ if $t = 0$ and $h_t = (c_0, c_1, \ldots, c_{t-1}, x_0, x_1, \ldots, x_t)$ if $t \geq 1$.[1] The set of all possible histories at time t is denoted by H_t. A *time-t strategy* for player i is defined as a function $\sigma_t^i : H_t \mapsto \mathbb{R}^{k^i}$ satisfying

$$\sigma_t^i(c_0, c_1, \ldots, c_{t-1}, x_0, x_1, \ldots, x_t) \in \bar{G}^i(x_t, t).$$

According to this strategy, player i chooses the control variable $c_t^i = \sigma_t^i(h_t)$ whenever the history of the game at time t is equal to $h_t = (c_0, c_1, \ldots, c_{t-1}, x_0, x_1, \ldots, x_t)$. A *strategy* for player i is a sequence of time-t strategies, one for each period $t \in \mathbb{N}_0$. We use the notation $\sigma^i = (\sigma_t^i)_{t=0}^{+\infty}$ to denote a strategy of player $i \in \mathbf{M}$. Finally, a *strategy profile* $(\sigma^1, \sigma^2, \ldots, \sigma^m)$ is a collection of strategies, one for each player of the game.

Consider any fixed strategy profile $(\sigma^1, \sigma^2, \ldots, \sigma^m)$. In period $t = 0$, the history of the game consists only of the current state x_0. Hence, the strategy profile $(\sigma^1, \sigma^2, \ldots, \sigma^m)$ determines the players' controls in period 0 by $c_0^i = \sigma_0^i(x_0)$ for all $i \in \mathbf{M}$. Substituting these controls into the state equation (7.2), we can compute the state in period 1 as $x_1 = f(x_0, c_0, 0)$. The history of the game in period 1 is then

---

[1] The reader may wonder why the initial state x_0 forms part of the history of the game despite the fact that x_0 is an exogenously given initial value. This is the case because we want the current state x_t to be included in the history of the game at time t and because at $t = 0$ the current state is the initial state x_0.

given by $h_1 = (c_0^1, c_0^2, \ldots, c_0^m, x_1)$ and the strategy profile determines the controls $c_1 = (c_1^1, c_1^2, \ldots, c_1^m)$ as functions of h_1. Again, we can substitute these values into (7.2) which yields the state in period 2, namely $x_2 = f(x_1, c_1, 1)$. Continuing in this way, it is possible to determine the entire state trajectory $(x_t)_{t=0}^{+\infty}$ that is generated by the strategy profile $(\sigma^1, \sigma^2, \ldots, \sigma^m)$. Since the strategy profile uniquely determines a state trajectory as well as all controls in all periods, it is possible to evaluate the objective functional (7.1) for all $i \in \mathbf{M}$.[2] Let us denote this value of the objective functional by $J^i(\sigma^1, \sigma^2, \ldots, \sigma^m)$ in order to emphasize that it is uniquely determined by the strategy profile $(\sigma^1, \sigma^2, \ldots, \sigma^m)$.

We are now ready to define the most important equilibrium concept for the dynamic game under consideration, namely the Nash equilibrium. Intuitively, a Nash equilibrium is a strategy profile such that no player has an incentive to unilaterally deviate from his or her strategy. In order to formalize this concept, we have to specify which deviations are allowed. This is done by fixing a *strategy space* $\mathbf{S}$, that is, a certain set of strategy profiles. Typically, the specification of the strategy space includes restrictions of the sets of variables on which time-t strategies may depend (for example, only on the current state variable, or only on actions and states from the last ℓ periods). Sometimes, only strategies that have convenient properties such as continuity or differentiability are allowed or even the functional forms are restricted (for example, only linear strategies). In what follows, we take an arbitrary strategy space $\mathbf{S}$ as given. A *Nash equilibrium* with strategy space $\mathbf{S}$ is a strategy profile $(\sigma^1, \sigma^2, \ldots, \sigma^m) \in \mathbf{S}$ such that

$$J^i(\sigma^1, \sigma^2, \ldots, \sigma^i, \ldots, \sigma^m) \geq J^i(\sigma^1, \sigma^2, \ldots, \bar{\sigma}^i, \ldots, \sigma^m)$$

holds for all $i \in \mathbf{M}$ and for all strategies $\bar{\sigma}^i$ for which the profile $(\sigma^1, \sigma^2, \ldots, \bar{\sigma}^i, \ldots, \sigma^m)$ is contained in $\mathbf{S}$. Note that the strategy space $\mathbf{S}$ enters this definition in two ways: the Nash equilibrium itself has to be an element of $\mathbf{S}$, and only those deviations are admitted that lead to strategy profiles in $\mathbf{S}$.

Before we proceed to explain other equilibrium definitions, let us make an important remark. Although we are dealing with dynamic games, the equilibrium definition given above is exactly the same as in static games. More specifically, we interpret the dynamic game as a normal form game in which every player chooses a strategy once and for all, and the dynamics of the model unfold only as these strategies are applied and generate dynamic paths of state and control variables. Since a strategy specifies what a player does at each instant $t \in \mathbb{N}_0$ after every possible history $h_t \in H_t$, the dynamic evolution of the game is completely determined once the strategies have been chosen.

---

[2] As before, we assume that the infinite sum in (7.1) has a finite limit.

Now note that a Nash equilibrium as defined above does not involve any hierarchy among the players. More specifically, it is not the case that one player's strategy choice can affect any other player's choice. We say that the Nash equilibrium involves simultaneous moves. In some situations, however, there exists a hierarchy among the decision makers in the sense that one player has to determine his or her strategy before another player. In this case, we call the former player a *leader* and the latter one a *follower*. Dynamic games in which there exist leaders and followers are called *hierarchical dynamic games*. In a general game with m players, we can think of many different hierarchical structures involving two levels (leaders and followers) or even more levels. Instead of stating a general definition of equilibria of hierarchical dynamic games, we simply explain one possible case and leave it to the reader to develop the equilibrium definitions in other situations of interest.

Suppose that the set of players $\mathbf{M} = \{1, 2, \ldots, m\}$ can be partitioned into the set of leaders $\mathbf{M}_L = \{1, 2, \ldots, m_L\}$ and the set of followers $\mathbf{M}_F = \{m_L + 1, m_L + 2, \ldots, m\}$, where $m_L \in \{1, 2, \ldots, m - 1\}$. Since the leaders choose their strategies first, the followers' strategies may depend on those of the leaders. Let $(\sigma^1, \sigma^2, \ldots, \sigma^{m_L})$ be an arbitrary strategy profile containing one strategy for each leader $i \in \mathbf{M}_L$. Given this strategy profile, the state equation in (7.2) and the objective functionals in (7.1) define a dynamic game $\Gamma_F(\sigma^1, \sigma^2, \ldots, \sigma^{m_L})$ among the remaining players $i \in \mathbf{M}_F$. Suppose that these players, that is, the followers, determine their strategies according to the definition of a Nash equilibrium for the game $\Gamma_F(\sigma^1, \sigma^2, \ldots, \sigma^{m_L})$. Suppose furthermore that there exists a unique Nash equilibrium in $\Gamma_F(\sigma^1, \sigma^2, \ldots, \sigma^{m_L})$ for all strategy profiles of the leaders.[3] This means that there exists a mapping $\mathcal{B}$, called the *best response function*, that assigns to every strategy profile of the leaders, $(\sigma^1, \sigma^2, \ldots, \sigma^{m_L})$, the unique Nash equilibrium $\mathcal{B}(\sigma^1, \sigma^2, \ldots, \sigma^{m_L})$ of the game $\Gamma_F(\sigma^1, \sigma^2, \ldots, \sigma^{m_L})$ played by the followers. The *hierarchical Nash equilibrium* of the original game with leaders $\mathbf{M}_L$ and followers $\mathbf{M}_F$ is the usual Nash equilibrium in the game Γ_L among the leaders $i \in \mathbf{M}_L$ that is defined by the state equation (7.2) and the objective functionals (7.1) for all $i \in \mathbf{M}_L$, where the control variables c_t^i of all followers $i \in \mathbf{M}_F$ are replaced by $\sigma_t^i(h_t)$ and where $(\sigma^{m_L+1}, \sigma^{m_L+2}, \ldots, \sigma^m) = \mathcal{B}(\sigma^1, \sigma^2, \ldots, \sigma^{m_L})$.

It cannot be overemphasized that solving a dynamic game for a hierarchical Nash equilibrium defined in that way is a rather complicated matter. One reason for this is that the strategies of the leaders appear in the dynamic optimization problems of the leaders via the best response function of the followers. The choice sets of these optimization problems are therefore high-dimensional function spaces. To see this more clearly, note for example that the state equation in the leaders' game Γ_L is

---

[3] As we will see below, this is a very strong assumption which holds only in very special circumstances.

given by

$$x_{t+1} = f\left(x_t, c_t^1, c_t^2, \ldots, c_t^{m_L}, \sigma_t^{m_L+1}(h_t), \sigma_t^{m_L+2}(h_t), \ldots, \sigma_t^m(h_t), t\right)$$
$$= f\left(x_t, c_t^1, c_t^2, \ldots, c_t^{m_L}, \mathcal{B}(\sigma^1, \sigma^2, \ldots, \sigma^{m_L})(h_t), t\right).$$

This shows that next period's state, x_{t+1}, depends not only on the current state x_t and the current controls of the leaders $(c_t^1, c_t^2, \ldots, c_t^{m_L})$, but also on their strategies $(\sigma^1, \sigma^2, \ldots, \sigma^{m_L})$. Hence, the dynamic optimization problem of each leader $i \in \mathbf{M}_L$ is not of the standard form discussed in section 5.1. We shall return to this issue in section 7.4 below.

7.2 Nash equilibria with closed-loop strategies

So far, we have proceeded under the assumption that before taking their actions at time t the players know the entire history of the game at time t, which contains information about the values of all control and state variables up to time $t - 1$ as well as about the current state x_t. This means that the players can condition their actions in period t on a huge amount of information. It will not come as a surprise that in general a game with this kind of information structure has a plethora of equilibria such that the predictive power of the model is rather limited. For this reason, it has become common to either restrict the strategy space from which the players can choose their strategies or to impose additional properties on the Nash equilibria – so-called equilibrium refinements. In the rest of the present section, we follow the former approach, whereas section 7.3 is devoted to one particular equilibrium refinement, namely Markov-perfection. Throughout the discussion in these two sections, we consider games in which the players move simultaneously.

Let us suppose that the players can condition their actions in period t only on the date t and on the current state x_t. Formally, this means that the time-t strategies can be considered as functions defined on the state space X rather than on the set of possible histories H_t. For this reason, we adopt a notational simplification and henceforth write $c_t^i = \sigma_t^i(x_t)$. Strategies of this form are called *closed-loop* strategies.[4] We denote the set of closed-loop strategy profiles by $\mathbf{S}_{CL}$.

Let us start the discussion of dynamic games with closed-loop strategies by formulating the optimization problem that an arbitrary but fixed player $i \in \mathbf{M}$ has to solve. To this end, we consider a given strategy profile $(\sigma^1, \sigma^2, \ldots, \sigma^m) \in \mathbf{S}_{CL}$ and define the functions $\hat{F}^i$ and $\hat{f}^i$ on the domain $\hat{\Omega}^i = \{(x, c^i, t) \mid x \in X, t \in \mathbb{N}_0, c^i \in \bar{G}^i(x, t)\}$

---

[4] Unfortunately, the terminology used in the literature is ambiguous and inconsistent. Some authors refer to these strategies also as Markovian strategies, memoryless perfect state strategies, or as feedback strategies.

by

$$\hat{F}^i(x, c^i, t) = F^i\left(x, \sigma_t^1(x), \sigma_t^2(x), \ldots, c^i, \ldots, \sigma_t^m(x), t\right)$$

and

$$\hat{f}^i(x, c^i, t) = f\left(x, \sigma_t^1(x), \sigma_t^2(x), \ldots, c^i, \ldots, \sigma_t^m(x), t\right),$$

respectively, where c^i appears on the right-hand sides of these equations as the $(i+1)$-st argument of the functions $\hat{F}^i$ and $\hat{f}^i$. Since player i takes the equilibrium strategies of his or her opponents as given, he or she must solve the dynamic optimization problem of maximizing

$$\sum_{t=0}^{+\infty} \hat{F}^i\left(x_t, c_t^i, t\right)$$

subject to a given initial state x_0 and the constraints $x_{t+1} = \hat{f}^i(x_t, c_t^i, t)$ and $c_t^i \in \bar{G}^i(x_t, t)$. The given strategy profile $(\sigma^1, \sigma^2, \ldots, \sigma^m)$ qualifies as a closed-loop Nash equilibrium if the optimal pair $((x_t)_{t=0}^{+\infty}, (c_t)_{t=0}^{+\infty})$ of this optimization problem satisfies the condition $c_t^i = \sigma_t^i(x_t)$ for all $t \in \mathbb{N}_0$ and all $i \in \mathbf{M}$, that is, if the optimal control path of every player $i \in \mathbf{M}$ can be synthesized by the equilibrium strategy σ^i.

Given the other players' strategies σ^j, $j \neq i$, the above dynamic optimization problem has the standard form introduced in section 5.1, and it follows that all methods introduced in chapter 5 can be applied. Note, however, that the dynamic optimization problem to be solved by player i depends on the strategies of all other players because the functions $\hat{F}^i$ and $\hat{f}^i$ are defined in terms of these strategies. This has a couple of important consequences. First of all, it is rather unlikely that we can find all closed-loop Nash equilibria of a game, because most optimality conditions for dynamic optimization problems require non-trivial assumptions (for example, smoothness of concavity of utility functions). Since the individual utility functions $\hat{F}^i$ depend on the unknown strategies of the opponents, such assumptions are virtually impossible to verify. For this reason, we usually restrict the analysis to the verification of the Nash equilibrium property for a candidate strategy profile $(\sigma^1, \sigma^2, \ldots, \sigma^m)$. In that case, the assumptions on the individual optimization problems can be verified. A second consequence of the fact that the individual optimization problems depend on the strategies of the opponents is that we have to solve the dynamic optimization problems of all m players along with a fixed point problem. That is, we start from the candidate strategy profile $(\sigma^1, \sigma^2, \ldots, \sigma^m)$, solve the individual players' optimization problems (which depend on the given strategy profile), and, finally, have to verify that the state and control paths found in the second step are generated by the candidate strategy profile which we started with in the first step. Let us illustrate this approach by means of the following example of a duopoly with sticky-prices.

Example 7.1   Consider a duopoly, that is, an industry consisting of two firms producing a homogeneous good. The quantity produced by firm $i \in \{1, 2\}$ at time t is denoted by q_t^i and is restricted to be non-negative. The price of the good at time t is denoted by p_t. We assume that the market price evolves according to the equation[5]

$$p_t = \gamma \tilde{D}\left(q_t^1 + q_t^2\right) + (1 - \gamma)p_{t-1},$$

where $\tilde{D} : \mathbb{R}_+ \mapsto \mathbb{R}_+$ is a downward-sloping inverse demand function and where $\gamma \in [0, 1]$ measures how sensitively the market price p_t reacts to the market forces. The initial price p_{-1} is exogenously given. If $\gamma = 0$, then the price does not respond at all to market demand and is exogenously fixed at the initial value p_{-1}. If $\gamma = 1$, then there is no price rigidity and the market price in period t depends solely on the total quantity produced by the two firms in period t. Intermediate values of γ correspond to prices that are somewhat rigid.

Each firm i seeks to maximize its discounted profit flow over the infinite time-horizon, which is given by

$$\sum_{t=0}^{+\infty} \beta^t \left[p_t q_t^i - (c/2)(q_t^i)^2 \right],$$

where $\beta \in (0, 1)$ is the time-preference factor and where $c > 0$ is a cost parameter.

Before we solve the model for the most interesting case in which $\gamma \in (0, 1)$, let us briefly discuss the boundary cases $\gamma = 0$ and $\gamma = 1$. In the former case, the state equation implies that $p_t = p_{-1}$ holds for all $t \in \mathbb{N}_0$. In words, the market price is constant and independent of the quantities produced. This deprives the model of its dynamic nature and has the consequence that the firms maximize their profits in each period separately. They can achieve this by choosing q_t^i such that the marginal production cost cq_t^i equals the price p_{-1}. The boundary case $\gamma = 0$ can therefore be considered as the competitive limit of the model. In the other boundary case $\gamma = 1$, it holds that $p_t = \tilde{D}(q_t^1 + q_t^2)$, which means that the firms face the inverse demand function $\tilde{D}$ in every period. Again, this eliminates the dynamic character of the competition because the price p_t depends only on the current production levels q_t^1 and q_t^2. It follows therefore that the two firms play a standard static Cournot–Nash equilibrium in every period.

---

[5] The reader may notice that we formulate the state equation in a slightly different format than in the presentation of the general modelling framework in section 7.1. More specifically, this state equation expresses the current price p_t as a function of current quantities and last period's price. In the general framework from above, the state equation expresses the next period's state variable as a function of the current state and the current controls. This difference, however, is merely a matter of notation and interpretation. Indeed, if we introduce the new variable $x_t = p_{t-1}$, we are back in the general framework. We have chosen not to do so because otherwise the price in period t would have been denoted by x_{t+1}, which might be confusing.

Now let us try to solve the game in the case where $\gamma \in (0, 1)$. In order to avoid cumbersome technicalities, we modify the game in such a way that it has a linear-quadratic structure. More specifically, we ignore the non-negativity constraint on q_t^i and we assume a linear inverse demand function of the form $\tilde{D}(\tilde{Q}) = 1 - b\tilde{Q}$, even if this function can become negative for large $\tilde{Q}$. Thus, the state equation becomes

$$p_t = \gamma\left[1 - b\left(q_t^1 + q_t^2\right)\right] + (1 - \gamma)p_{t-1},$$

where b is a positive parameter.

Because the two firms are identical, we try to find a symmetric closed-loop Nash equilibrium of the dynamic game, that is, a strategy profile $(\sigma^1, \sigma^2) \in \mathbf{S}_{CL}$ satisfying $\sigma^1 = \sigma^2$. To ease the notation we simply write σ for the strategy used by both players. Recall that $\sigma = (\sigma_t)_{t=0}^{+\infty}$, where σ_t denotes the time-t strategy of the two players that, according to the notational convention explained in footnote 5, maps last period's price p_{t-1} to the production quantities of the two players in period t. Finally, we assume that the time-t strategies σ_t are differentiable functions of the price p_{t-1}. This allows us to apply the variational approaches explained in sections 5.2 and 5.3 to the individual players' optimization problems.

We solve player i's problem using the Lagrangian approach. As a first step, we note that the functions $\hat{F}^i$ and $\hat{f}^i$ are given by

$$\hat{F}^i(p, q, t) = \beta^t\{\gamma q[1 - b(q + \sigma_t(p))] + (1 - \gamma)pq - (c/2)q^2\}$$

and

$$\hat{f}^i(p, q, t) = \gamma[1 - b(q + \sigma_t(p))] + (1 - \gamma)p,$$

respectively, where we have dropped the player-superscript i from the production quantity q^i. Note that the constraint qualification from theorem 5.5 is satisfied because $\hat{f}_2^i(p, q, t) = -b\gamma \neq 0$. The necessary optimality conditions of the Lagrangian approach stated in that theorem are therefore

$$\beta^t\{\gamma[1 - 2bq_t - b\sigma_t(p_{t-1})] + (1 - \gamma)p_{t-1} - cq_t\} - b\gamma\lambda_t = 0,$$
$$(\beta^{t+1}q_{t+1} + \lambda_{t+1})[1 - \gamma - b\gamma\sigma_{t+1}'(p_t)] - \lambda_t = 0,$$

where $(\lambda_t)_{t=0}^{+\infty}$ is the sequence of Lagrange multipliers. In the next step, we eliminate the Lagrange multipliers from these equations and substitute $\sigma_t(p_{t-1})$ and $\sigma_{t+1}(p_t)$ for q_t and q_{t+1}, respectively. After some algebra, this yields the equation

$$\gamma[1 - 3b\sigma_t(p_{t-1})] + (1 - \gamma)p_{t-1} - c\sigma_t(p_{t-1})$$
$$= \beta[1 - \gamma - b\gamma\sigma_{t+1}'(p_t)]\{\gamma[1 - 2b\sigma_{t+1}(p_t)] + (1 - \gamma)p_t - c\sigma_{t+1}(p_t)\}. \quad (7.3)$$

Note furthermore that in equilibrium the state equation can be written as

$$p_t = \gamma[1 - 2b\sigma_t(p_{t-1})] + (1 - \gamma)p_{t-1}. \tag{7.4}$$

It should be apparent that system (7.3)–(7.4) is hard to solve because it is a functional-difference equation involving the unknown time-t strategies $(\sigma_t)_{t=0}^{+\infty}$ as well as their derivatives. This is a consequence of the fact that the dynamic optimization problem of player i must be solved simultaneously with a fixed point problem for the strategies. Since there are no systematic analytical methods available to handle this kind of dynamic equation, we can only resort to numerical approximations or to a guess-and-verify approach. In what follows, we outline some results that can be obtained by the latter method.

The dynamic game under consideration has a linear-quadratic structure, because the state equation is a linear function of the state and control variables and because the objective functionals of the two players are quadratic with respect to the state and the controls. It is therefore not unreasonable to assume that there exist Nash equilibria consisting of time-t strategies that are linear with respect to the state variable. The most general form of such a function would be $\sigma_t(p) = A_t + B_t p$. For the purpose of the present discussion, however, it is sufficient to restrict attention to those time-t strategies in which the coefficient of the state variable p is constant, that is, we consider strategies of the form

$$\sigma_t(p) = A_t + Bp.$$

Substituting the conjectured form of the strategies into (7.3)–(7.4), we obtain

$$\begin{pmatrix} A_{t+1} \\ p_t \end{pmatrix} = \begin{pmatrix} -Q/\Delta & -R/\Delta \\ -2b\gamma & 1 - \gamma - 2bB\gamma \end{pmatrix} \begin{pmatrix} A_t \\ p_{t-1} \end{pmatrix} + \gamma \begin{pmatrix} -Z/\Delta \\ 1 \end{pmatrix}, \tag{7.5}$$

where

$\Delta = \beta(c + 2b\gamma)(1 - \gamma - bB\gamma),$

$Q = 2b\beta\gamma(1 - \gamma - bB\gamma)[1 - \gamma - B(2b\gamma + c)] - 3b\gamma - c,$

$R = 1 - \gamma - B(3b\gamma + c) - \beta(1 - \gamma - bB\gamma)(1 - \gamma - 2bB\gamma)[1 - \gamma - B(2b\gamma + c)],$

$Z = 1 - \beta(1 - \gamma - bB\gamma)[2 - \gamma - B(2b\gamma + c)].$

For the above formulas to make sense, we have to ensure that $\Delta \neq 0$. We do this by restricting ourselves to values of B that satisfy $B < B_1$, where $B_1 = (1 - \gamma)/(b\gamma) > 0$. The assumption $B < B_1$ implies that $\Delta > 0$. We also assume that $B > B_2$, where

$$B_2 = -\frac{(2b + c)[1 - \beta(1 - \gamma)] + b\gamma}{b\beta\gamma(2b + c)} < 0.$$

For all values $B \in (B_2, B_1)$, there exists a unique fixed point of equation (7.5), which is given by

$$A^*(B) = \frac{1 - B(b\gamma + c) - \beta(1 - Bc)(1 - \gamma - bB\gamma)}{(2b + c)[1 - \beta(1 - \gamma)] + b\gamma[1 + B\beta(2b + c)]},$$

$$p^*(B) = \frac{b\gamma + c[1 - \beta(1 - \gamma - bB\gamma)]}{(2b + c)[1 - \beta(1 - \gamma)] + b\gamma[1 + B\beta(2b + c)]}.$$

The trace and determinant of the system matrix in (7.5) are given by

$$T = \frac{3b\gamma + c}{\beta(2b\gamma + c)(1 - \gamma - bB\gamma)} + \frac{c(1 - \gamma)}{2b\gamma + c}$$

and

$$D = \frac{(1 - \gamma)(b\gamma + c)}{\beta(2b\gamma + c)(1 - \gamma - bB\gamma)},$$

and it holds that

$$D - T + 1 = -\frac{\gamma\{(2b + c)[1 - \beta(1 - \gamma)] + b\gamma + bB\beta\gamma(2b + c)\}}{\beta(2b\gamma + c)(1 - \gamma - bB\gamma)}.$$

This demonstrates that the inequality $D < T - 1$ is satisfied for all $B \in (B_2, B_1)$. Finally, both T and D are obviously positive whenever $B \in (B_2, B_1)$. Taking all these properties into account and using the results from section 2.3 it follows that, whenever $B \in (B_2, B_1)$, the system matrix in (7.5) has two positive eigenvalues, one of which is stable whereas the other one is unstable.

Now suppose that the vector $(1, 0)^{\top}$ is an eigenvector of the system matrix in (7.5). Obviously, this would imply that $-2b\gamma = 0$, which is a contradiction. It follows therefore that the stable manifold of the fixed point, which has the direction of the eigenvector corresponding to the stable eigenvalue, is not parallel to the A-axis (which is the locus of points satisfying $p = 0$). This, in turn, ensures that for every given initial value p_{-1} we can find a unique initial value A_0 such that the point $(A_0, p_{-1})^{\top}$ is located on the stable manifold of the fixed point. Thus, for every $B \in (B_2, B_1)$, there exists a unique trajectory of equation (7.5) that starts at the given initial state p_{-1} and converges to the fixed point $(A^*(B), p^*(B))^{\top}$. All of these trajectories correspond to closed-loop Nash equilibria of the linear-quadratic dynamic game under consideration.[6] To summarize, for every fixed initial value p_{-1} there exists a continuum (indexed by

---

[6] The details of the proof of this claim are omitted. Since the underlying model has a linear-quadratic structure and since the proposed time-t strategies are linear with respect to the state variable, each player's optimization problem is a linear-quadratic dynamic optimization problem. The optimality of the proposed solution can therefore be verified using theorem 5.4 (see also example 5.7). We would like to point out, however, that in the present example there is an additional complication, namely that the utility function $\hat{F}^i(p, q, t)$ is not jointly concave with respect to (p, q).

$B \in (B_2, B_1))$ of different Nash equilibria with a closed-loop strategy space. This is the main point we wanted to make by the present example.

Let us add a few comments on the fixed point $(A^*(B), p^*(B))^\top$. The assumption $B > B_2$ ensures that both the numerator and the denominator of the expression for $p^*(B)$ are positive. A slight strengthening of this assumption, namely $B > B_3 := -[1 - \beta(1 - \gamma)]/(b\beta\gamma)$, implies furthermore that $p^*(B) < 1$. Consequently, it holds in all the closed-loop Nash equilibria corresponding to values $B \in (B_3, B_1)$ that the long-run price $p^*(B)$ is contained in $(0, 1)$. Furthermore, from the state equation (7.4) we obtain that $q^*(B) := \lim_{t \to +\infty} q_t^i = \lim_{t \to +\infty} \sigma_t(p_{t-1})$ exists and satisfies

$$p^*(B) = \gamma[1 - 2bq^*(B)] + (1 - \gamma)p^*(B),$$

which, together with $p^*(B) \in (0, 1)$, implies that the conditions $q^*(B) > 0$ and $\tilde{D}(2q^*(B)) = 1 - 2bq^*(B) > 0$ hold. This shows that whenever B is chosen from the interval (B_3, B_1) the neglected non-negativity constraints on the price and the production quantities are satisfied at least asymptotically.

The above example illustrates how the guess-and-verify approach can be used to identify Nash equilibria of dynamic games. It also clearly demonstrates that such games can have (and typically do have) many Nash equilibria, even if we impose the closed-loop information structure. This phenomenon is called *informational non-uniqueness*. The root of informational non-uniqueness is that an optimal control path of any player's dynamic optimization problem can be synthesized by uncountably many closed-loop strategies. Suppose, for example, that the optimal pair of player i's optimization problem is given by $((\bar{c}_t^i)_{t=0}^{+\infty}, (\bar{x}_t)_{t=0}^{+\infty})$. The optimal control $\bar{c}_t^i$ can be represented as the value at $x = \bar{x}_t$ of any closed-loop strategy of the form $\sigma_t^i(x) = \bar{c}_t^i + \zeta(x - \bar{x}_t)$, where $\zeta : \mathbb{R}^n \mapsto \mathbb{R}^{k^i}$ is an arbitrary function satisfying $\zeta(0) = 0$. This is obvious because $\sigma_t^i(\bar{x}_t) = \bar{c}_t^i$ holds for all these time-t strategies. By choosing different representations of its optimal control path, that is, different functions ζ, player i can typically affect the decision problems of its opponents.

Because of the problem of equilibrium multiplicity, it is common to impose further restrictions on the strategy space or additional requirements on the equilibria. For example, we could assume that the strategies are independent of the current state variable x_t, that is, that every time-t strategy is a constant function of the state. In this case, it holds for all $x \in X$ that $\sigma_t^i(x) = c_t^i$, where c_t^i is a fixed element in $\mathbb{R}^{k^i}$. Strategies of that form are called *open-loop* strategies and the corresponding strategy space will be denoted by $\mathbf{S}_{OL}$. Nash equilibria with strategy space $\mathbf{S}_{OL}$ are known as *open-loop* Nash equilibria. In the sticky-price duopoly model from above, there exists a unique symmetric open-loop Nash equilibrium, as will be demonstrated in the following example.

Example 7.2 Consider the sticky-price model from example 7.1. An open-loop strategy $\sigma = (\sigma_t)_{t=0}^{+\infty}$ is obviously of the form $\sigma_t(p) = A_t + Bp$ with $B = 0$. Hence, the analysis from example 7.1 applies. Moreover, the particular value $B = 0$ is contained in the parameter interval (B_2, B_1) for which we constructed Nash equilibria. It follows therefore that for $B = 0$ there exists a unique solution to system (7.5) that converges to the fixed point $(A^*(0), p^*(0))^\top$. This solution must therefore correspond to the unique symmetric open-loop Nash equilibrium of the game.

Every open-loop strategy is obviously a (degenerate) closed-loop strategy. We say that a closed-loop strategy is *non-degenerate* if it is not an open-loop strategy. Recall that a profile consisting of open-loop strategies qualifies as an open-loop Nash equilibrium if no player can benefit by deviating within $\mathbf{S}_{OL}$ from its equilibrium strategy. In general, an enlargement of the strategy space could destroy the Nash equilibrium property of a strategy profile, because in a larger strategy space players have more possibilities to deviate than in a smaller strategy space. The following theorem, however, proves that by changing the strategy space from $\mathbf{S}_{OL}$ to $\mathbf{S}_{CL}$ this does not happen.

Theorem 7.1 Consider a dynamic game as defined in section 7.1 and let $(\sigma^1, \sigma^2, \ldots, \sigma^m) \in \mathbf{S}_{OL}$ be a given strategy profile consisting of open-loop strategies. If $(\sigma^1, \sigma^2, \ldots, \sigma^m)$ is an open-loop Nash equilibrium, then it is also a closed-loop Nash equilibrium

PROOF: Let $(\sigma^1, \sigma^2, \ldots, \sigma^m) \in \mathbf{S}_{OL}$ be an open-loop Nash equilibrium and suppose that it is not a closed-loop Nash equilibrium. Then there exists a player $i \in \mathbf{M}$ and a closed-loop strategy $\bar{\sigma}^i$ such that

$$J^i(\sigma^1, \sigma^2, \ldots, \sigma^i, \ldots, \sigma^m) < J^i(\sigma^1, \sigma^2, \ldots, \bar{\sigma}^i, \ldots, \sigma^m).$$

Let $(\bar{x}_t)_{t=0}^{+\infty}$ be the state trajectory generated by the strategy profile $(\sigma^1, \sigma^2, \ldots, \bar{\sigma}^i, \ldots, \sigma^m)$ and define the open-loop strategy $\hat{\sigma}^i$ by $\hat{\sigma}_t^i(x) = \bar{\sigma}_t^i(\bar{x}_t)$ for all $x \in X$. It is clear that the strategy profile $(\sigma^1, \sigma^2, \ldots, \hat{\sigma}^i, \ldots, \sigma^m)$ generates the same state trajectory and the same control paths as the strategy profile $(\sigma^1, \sigma^2, \ldots, \bar{\sigma}^i, \ldots, \sigma^m)$. Consequently, it must hold that

$$J^i(\sigma^1, \sigma^2, \ldots, \sigma^i, \ldots, \sigma^m) < J^i(\sigma^1, \sigma^2, \ldots, \bar{\sigma}^i, \ldots, \sigma^m)$$
$$= J^i(\sigma^1, \sigma^2, \ldots, \hat{\sigma}^i, \ldots, \sigma^m).$$

Because of $(\sigma^1, \sigma^2, \ldots, \hat{\sigma}^i, \ldots, \sigma^m) \in \mathbf{S}_{OL}$, this is a contradiction to the assumption that the original strategy profile $(\sigma^1, \sigma^2, \ldots, \sigma^m)$ is an open-loop Nash equilibrium, which completes the proof of the theorem.

Let us try to understand in which way open-loop Nash equilibria differ from non-degenerate closed-loop Nash equilibria. There are two issues that we want to comment on. The first one is that it is sometimes claimed in the literature that an open-loop strategy reflects a higher level of commitment than other closed-loop strategies. Commitment, however, is not an issue here, because we have assumed that a player decides at time 0 which strategy $\sigma^i = (\sigma_t^i)_{t=0}^{+\infty}$ he or she wants to play and then sticks to that strategy forever. That is, we have assumed perfect commitment anyway. Moreover, neither in a closed-loop Nash equilibrium of a game as described in section 7.1 nor in an open-loop Nash equilibrium does any player have an incentive to deviate from his or her strategy at any point in time. To prove this formally, we introduce a whole family of games $\Gamma(x, s)$, where $x \in X$ denotes the initial state and $s \in \mathbb{N}_0$ the initial time of the game. More specifically, let the game $\Gamma(x, s)$ be defined by the set of players $\mathbf{M} = \{1, 2, \ldots, m\}$, the objective functionals

$$\sum_{t=s}^{+\infty} F^i(x_t, c_t, t),$$

the constraints

$$c_t^i \in \bar{G}^i(x_t, t) \quad \text{and} \quad x_{t+1} = f(x_t, c_t, t)$$

for all $t \geq s$, and the initial condition $x_s = x$. The games $\Gamma(x, s)$ will be referred to as the *subgames* of the original game $\Gamma(x_0, 0)$.

Now suppose that the original game $\Gamma(x_0, 0)$ admits a simultaneous move Nash equilibrium $(\sigma^1, \sigma^2, \ldots, \sigma^m)$ and that this equilibrium generates the state trajectory $(x_t)_{t=0}^{+\infty}$. We say that the Nash equilibrium is *dynamically consistent* if it holds for all $t \subset \mathbb{N}_0$ that the strategy profile $(\sigma^1, \sigma^2, \ldots, \sigma^m)$ is a Nash equilibrium of the subgame $\Gamma(x_t, t)$. In other words, in a dynamically consistent Nash equilibrium there do not exist any incentives for the players to deviate during the dynamic evolution of the game from the strategies which they have chosen at time 0. If the system arrives after t periods at state x_t and if the players evaluate their decisions according to the continuation game $\Gamma(x_t, t)$, then their original strategies for the game $\Gamma(x_0, 0)$ still form an equilibrium, that is, each player's strategy is a best response to all the other players' strategies. The following theorem proves that every simultaneous-move Nash equilibrium with strategy space $\mathbf{S}_{CL}$ or $\mathbf{S}_{OL}$ is dynamically consistent.

Theorem 7.2 Let $\Gamma(x_0, 0)$ be a dynamic game as defined in section 7.1 and let $(\sigma^1, \sigma^2, \ldots, \sigma^m)$ be either a closed-loop Nash equilibrium or an open-loop Nash equilibrium. Then it follows that $(\sigma^1, \sigma^2, \ldots, \sigma^m)$ is dynamically consistent.

PROOF: We have seen above that every player $i \in \mathbf{M}$ of the game solves a dynamic optimization problem which has the standard form introduced in section 5.1. Hence, the principle of optimality from lemma 5.1 applies to all of these problems. It follows that the controls and states generated by the equilibrium strategy chosen at time 0 must constitute an optimal solution to the dynamic optimization problem that player i solves in game $\Gamma(x_t, t)$, provided that all opponents $j \neq i$ stick to their equilibrium strategies σ^j. Because the equilibrium strategy of player i, σ^i, generates exactly those controls and states, it is an optimal strategy for player i. Hence, σ^i is a best response to the opponents' strategies also in the subgame $\Gamma(x_t, t)$.

In the proof of the above theorem, we have applied the principle of optimality from lemma 5.1. This result has been derived for dynamic optimization problems in standard form and we know from chapter 6 that there are modifications of the standard framework (for example, non-geometric discounting) under which the principle of optimality fails. It is obvious that in such situations the result stated in theorem 7.2 would also cease to hold.

The above discussion shows that open-loop strategies neither reflect nor require a different level of commitment than non-degenerate closed-loop strategies. The real difference between open-loop strategies and non-degenerate closed-loop strategies is that the former prevent strategic interactions that are possible under the latter. For example, if player i uses an open-loop strategy, then this implies that the other players have no possibility to affect player i's actions, because these actions depend only on the exogenous time variable. If player i, however, uses a non-degenerate closed-loop strategy, then the opponents can influence player i's actions indirectly via the state variable, which they can control (at least to a certain extent) through their own actions. Another form of strategic interaction which is ruled out by open-loop strategies but which can occur in a game with closed-loop strategies is that the incentives of one player can depend on the strategies chosen by the opponents. This is illustrated by the following example.

Example 7.3 Consider a dynamic game with two players $i \in \{1, 2\}$. Player 1 has control over the variables $(c_t^1)_{t=0}^{+\infty}$ and maximizes

$$\sum_{t=0}^{+\infty} \left[F^1(x_t, c_t^1, t) + g^1(c_t^2, t) \right].$$

Player 2 has control over the variables $(c_t^2)_{t=0}^{+\infty}$ and maximizes

$$\sum_{t=0}^{+\infty} F^2(x_t, c_t^2, t).$$

The state equation of the game is

$$x_{t+1} = f\left(x_t, c_t^1, t\right)$$

and an initial value x_0 is given. The important features of this game are that only player 1 can influence the evolution of the state, that player 2's objective functional is independent of the controls of player 1, and that the control variables of player 2 enter the utility function of player 1 in an additively separable form.

Suppose first that both players use open-loop strategies. In this case, the term $g^1(c_t^2, t)$ in the utility functional of player 1 is exogenous for player 1's optimization problem. Since this term is additively separated, it is actually irrelevant for the solution to that problem. Thus, player 1 only needs to maximize

$$\sum_{t=0}^{+\infty} F^1\left(x_t, c_t^1, t\right)$$

subject to

$$x_{t+1} = f\left(x_t, c_t^1, t\right).$$

Suppose that this dynamic optimization problem has a unique solution consisting of the control path $(\tilde{c}_t^1)_{t=0}^{+\infty}$ and a corresponding state trajectory $(\tilde{x}_t)_{t=0}^{+\infty}$. Note that this solution is completely independent of player 2's actions. Together with the fact that player 2 cannot influence the evolution of the state, it follows that, for player 2's optimization problem, the state trajectory $(\tilde{x}_t)_{t=0}^{+\infty}$ is exogenous. Consequently, player 2 need not solve a dynamic optimization problem but he or she maximizes $F^2(\tilde{x}_t, c_t^2, t)$ for each $t \in \mathbb{N}_0$ separately. Assuming that the static optimization problem of maximizing $F^2(x, c, t)$ with respect to c has a unique solution given by $c = \phi_t(x)$, it follows that an open-loop Nash equilibrium is given by the strategies $\sigma^i = (\sigma_t^i)_{t=0}^{+\infty}$ for $i \in \{1, 2\}$, where $\sigma_t^1(x) = \tilde{c}_t^1$ and $\sigma_t^2(x) = \phi_t(\tilde{x}_t)$. Note furthermore that while player 1 can affect player 2's actions via the state variable, player 2 has no influence on the behaviour of player 1 whatsoever. There exists only a very limited scope for strategic interactions.

Now let us turn to the case in which the players can use closed-loop strategies. No matter which closed-loop strategy σ^1 player 1 uses, it holds that the equilibrium state trajectory is determined by the equation

$$x_{t+1} = f\left(x_t, \sigma_t^1(x_t), t\right),$$

such that player 2 cannot affect the evolution of the state.[7] Let us again denote the equilibrium state trajectory by $(\tilde{x}_t)_{t=0}^{+\infty}$. As in the open-loop case discussed above,

---

[7] This would not be the case if player 1 were allowed to use general history-dependent strategies that can depend on player 2's past controls.

the solution to player 2's optimization problem must satisfy $c_t^2 = \phi_t(\tilde{x}_t)$. However, this relation can be generated by infinitely many closed-loop strategies. Examples are $\sigma_t^2(x) = \phi_t(\tilde{x}_t), \sigma_t^2(x) = \phi_t(x), \sigma_t^2(x) = \phi_t(\gamma x + (1 - \gamma)\tilde{x}_t)$, or $\sigma_t^2(x) = \gamma\phi_t(x) + (1 - \gamma)\phi_t(\tilde{x}_t)$, where γ is an arbitrary real number. Substituting these different forms back into the objective functional of player 1, it is clear that player 2's strategy choice affects the solution to player 1's optimization problem, because except for the open-loop strategy $\sigma_t^2(x) = \phi_t(\tilde{x}_t)$, the term $g^1(c_t^2, t) = g^1(\sigma_t^2(x_t), t)$ now depends in a non-trivial way on the state variable x_t. Hence, depending on which strategy player 2 chooses in order to represent his or her optimal choice c_t^2, player 1 faces different incentives to steer the state variable. This will typically result in a continuum of different closed-loop Nash equilibria, yet another instance of informationally non-unique closed-loop Nash equilibria.

We conclude the section by pointing out that apparently innocuous transformations of variables may affect the distinction between open-loop Nash equilibria and non-degenerate closed-loop Nash equilibria. This observation is closely related to the property of informational non-uniqueness. For the purpose of illustration, let us return once more to the sticky-price duopoly model from example 7.1.

Example 7.4 The state equation of the sticky-price model is given by

$$p_t = \gamma\left[1 - b\left(q_t^1 + q_t^2\right)\right] + (1 - \gamma)p_{t-1}.$$

Defining

$$z_t^i = \frac{\gamma + (1 - \gamma)p_{t-1}}{2} - b\gamma q_t^i \tag{7.6}$$

we can rewrite the state equation as

$$p_t = z_t^1 + z_t^2. \tag{7.7}$$

In what follows, we shall treat the variables z_t^i (instead of q_t^i) as the control variables of player i. Up to a positive multiplicative constant which is irrelevant for the maximization, the objective functional of player i can be expressed in terms of the new variables as

$$\sum_{t=0}^{+\infty} \beta^t \left[\frac{\gamma + (1 - \gamma)p_{t-1}}{2} - z_t^i\right] \left\{\left(1 + \frac{c}{2b\gamma}\right)z_t^i + z_t^j - \frac{c[\gamma + (1 - \gamma)p_{t-1}]}{4b\gamma}\right\},$$

$$\tag{7.8}$$

where $j \in \{1, 2\} \setminus \{i\}$ denotes the opponent of player i. A symmetric open-loop Nash equilibrium for the game in which player $i \in \{1, 2\}$ chooses the control path $(z_t^i)_{t=0}^{+\infty}$ so as to maximize the objective functional in (7.8) subject to the state constraint (7.7) exists and is unique. However, this open-loop Nash equilibrium does not coincide with the one from example 7.2. As a matter of fact, it is straightforward to verify that it generates a different state trajectory and leads to a different long-run equilibrium price p^* than the open-loop Nash equilibrium from example 7.2. Moreover, it can be shown that the unique symmetric open-loop Nash equilibrium of the present game corresponds to the closed-loop Nash equilibrium of the original game from example 7.1 with parameter $B = (1 - \gamma)/(2b\gamma)$. This should not be unexpected because of equation (7.6), which can be solved for q_t^i as

$$q_t^i = \frac{\gamma - 2z_t^i}{2b\gamma} + \frac{(1 - \gamma)p_{t-1}}{2b\gamma}.$$

The reader will be asked to verify some of the claims made above in exercise 7.3.

7.3 Markov-perfect Nash equilibria

In the previous section, we have demonstrated that all simultaneous-move Nash equilibria with a closed-loop strategy space are dynamically consistent if the game has the standard features as outlined in section 7.1. In the present section, we study the equilibrium refinement of Markov-perfection which strengthens dynamic consistency. We continue to use the notation introduced in section 7.2 regarding the subgames of the original game. A Nash equilibrium $(\sigma^1, \sigma^2, \ldots, \sigma^m)$ of $\Gamma(x_0, 0)$ is called *Markov-perfect* if the strategy profile $(\sigma^1, \sigma^2, \ldots, \sigma^m)$ constitutes a Nash equilibrium of all subgames $\Gamma(x, s)$, where $x \in X$ and $s \in \mathbb{N}_0$. Recall that for dynamic consistency we have only required that a strategy profile is a Nash equilibrium for all subgames $\Gamma(x_t, t)$, where $(x_t)_{t=0}^{+\infty}$ is the state trajectory generated by the strategy profile. The following simple example demonstrates that not all closed-loop Nash equilibria are Markov-perfect.

Example 7.5 Let there be $m = 2$ players and consider the game defined by the objective functionals

$$-\sum_{t=0}^{+\infty} \beta^t x_t^2 \left(c_t^i \right)^2$$

and the system dynamics

$$x_{t+1} = x_t c_t^1 c_t^2.$$

The state space is assumed to be $X = \mathbb{R}$ and the feasible control sets are also given by $\bar{G}^i(x, t) = \mathbb{R}$. The initial state is an arbitrary element $x_0 \in X$.

It is obvious from the objective functionals that the maximal utility that any player can possibly obtain is equal to 0. Hence, any strategy profile (σ^1, σ^2) which ensures that both players obtain $J^i(\sigma^1, \sigma^2) = 0$ trivially qualifies as a Nash equilibrium. Now consider the symmetric strategy profile (σ^1, σ^2) defined by

$$\sigma_t^1(x) = \sigma_t^2(x) = \begin{cases} 0 & \text{if } t = 0, \\ x & \text{if } t > 0. \end{cases}$$

Because of $c_0^i = \sigma_0^i(x) = 0$ for $i \in \{1, 2\}$, it follows from the state equation that $x_t = 0$ holds for all $t \geq 1$. Obviously, this implies $J^i(\sigma^1, \sigma^2) = 0$, which proves that (σ^1, σ^2) is a closed-loop Nash equilibrium.

The closed-loop Nash equilibrium (σ^1, σ^2) is not Markov-perfect, though. To see this, consider for example the subgame $\Gamma(1, 1)$. Since for all $t \geq 1$ both players choose $c_t^i = \sigma_t^i(x_t) = x_t$, it follows from the state equation and from $x_1 = 1$ that $x_t = 1$ holds for all $t \geq 1$. Substituting this into the objective functional, we obtain for both players the value

$$-\sum_{t=1}^{+\infty} \beta^t x_t^2 (c_t^i)^2 = -\frac{\beta}{1 - \beta} < 0.$$

Each of the two players could benefit from a unilateral deviation from σ^i, for example, by using the strategy defined by $\hat{\sigma}_t^i(x) = 0$ for all $t \in \mathbb{N}_0$ and all $x \in X$. This strategy would yield the overall utility 0 in the subgame $\Gamma(1, 1)$. We conclude that the closed-loop Nash equilibrium (σ^1, σ^2) is not Markov-perfect.

The reason for the failure of Markov-perfection of the closed-loop Nash equilibrium in the above example is the commitment of the players to choose $c_t^i = x_t$ in all subgames that start at some time $t \geq 1$. We have seen that this commitment is not credible because both players find it optimal to deviate from this strategy in the subgame $\Gamma(1, 1)$. Markov-perfection requires that Nash equilibria do not contain any promises or commitments that lack credibility. All players must have incentives to stick to the announced strategies, not only in those subgames that they reach along the equilibrium path (that would be the property of dynamic consistency), but also in subgames off the equilibrium path.

Let us continue by discussing a Markov-perfect Nash equilibrium in an example with economic content.

Example 7.6 Consider a game with m identical players $i \in \mathbf{M} = \{1, 2, \ldots, m\}$ who want to maximize the objective functional

$$\sum_{t=0}^{+\infty} \beta^t \ln c_t^i \tag{7.9}$$

subject to the state equation

$$x_{t+1} = A_t x_t^\alpha - \sum_{i=1}^{m} c_t^i$$

and the constraints $x_{t+1} \geq 0$ and $c_t^i \geq 0$ for all $t \in \mathbb{N}_0$ and all $i \in \mathbf{M}$. Here, α and β are parameters in the open unit interval $(0, 1)$ and $(A_t)_{t=0}^{+\infty}$ is an exogenously given sequence of positive real numbers. The game describes the joint exploitation of a common property resource by m non-cooperating agents. The natural growth of the resource in the absence of exploitation is given by the difference equation $x_{t+1} = A_t x_t^\alpha$, the consumption rate of agent i at time t is c_t^i, and the instantaneous utility functions of the agents are logarithmic with respect to their consumption rates.

Because the players are identical, we try to find a symmetric Markov-perfect Nash equilibrium $(\sigma^1, \sigma^2, \ldots, \sigma^m)$ where $\sigma^i = \sigma$ holds for all $i \in \mathbf{M}$. Moreover, we conjecture that $\sigma_t(x) = \gamma A_t x^\alpha$ holds for a suitably chosen positive coefficient γ. If this conjecture is correct, then player i maximizes (7.9) subject to

$$x_{t+1} = [1 - (m-1)\gamma] A_t x_t^\alpha - c_t^i$$

and the constraints $x_{t+1} \geq 0$ and $c_t^i \geq 0$. Provided that $\gamma < 1/(m-1)$ holds, this problem is formally equivalent to the one-sector optimal growth model from example 5.8 and exercise 5.7. We know therefore that the optimal solution satisfies $c_t^i = (1 - \alpha\beta)[1 - (m-1)\gamma] A_t x_t^\alpha$. Hence, our conjecture about the form of the time-t strategies is correct if and only if the parameter γ satisfies $\gamma = (1 - \alpha\beta)[1 - (m-1)\gamma]$, which is the case if and only if

$$\gamma = \frac{1 - \alpha\beta}{1 + (m-1)(1 - \alpha\beta)}. \tag{7.10}$$

To see that the closed-loop Nash equilibrium $(\sigma, \sigma, \ldots, \sigma)$ is Markov-perfect just note that the above arguments are completely independent of the initial time and the initial state of the model. Hence, the proposed strategy profile qualifies as a closed-loop Nash equilibrium for any subgame $\Gamma(x, t)$ with $x \geq 0$ and $t \in \mathbb{N}_0$.

Probably the most popular way to verify Markov-perfection is by applying the recursive approach. This is the case because the recursive approach automatically takes care of all possible subgames. The following theorem states sufficient conditions for a Markov-perfect closed-loop Nash equilibrium.

Theorem 7.3 Consider the game $\Gamma(x_0, 0)$ defined in section 7.1 and let $(\sigma^1, \sigma^2, \ldots, \sigma^m)$ be a given profile of closed-loop strategies. Suppose that there exist functions $V^i : X \times \mathbb{N}_0 \mapsto \mathbb{R}$ such that the following properties hold for all $i \in \mathbf{M}$, all $x \in X$, and all $t \in \mathbb{N}_0$

$$V^i(x, t) = \sup \left\{ F^i\left(x, \Sigma_t^i(x, c^i), t\right) + V^i\left(f\left(x, \Sigma_t^i(x, c^i), t\right), t + 1\right) \mid c^i \in \bar{G}^i(x, t) \right\},$$
(7.11)

$$V^i(x, t) = F^i(x, \Sigma_t(x), t) + V^i(f(x, \Sigma_t(x), t), t + 1).$$
(7.12)

Here

$$\Sigma_t^i(x, c^i) = \left(\sigma_t^1(x), \sigma_t^2(x), \ldots, c^i, \ldots, \sigma_t^m(x)\right)$$

and

$$\Sigma_t(x) = \left(\sigma_t^1(x), \sigma_t^2(x), \ldots, \sigma_t^m(x)\right).$$

Moreover, suppose that for all $i \in \mathbf{M}$ and all feasible state trajectories it holds that

$$\lim_{t \to +\infty} V^i(x_t, t) = 0.$$
(7.13)

Then it follows that the strategy profile $(\sigma^1, \sigma^2, \ldots, \sigma^m)$ is a Markov-perfect Nash equilibrium of the game.

PROOF: The proof follows by applying theorems 5.8 and 5.10 to the individual dynamic optimization problem that an arbitrary player $i \in \mathbf{M}$ has to solve given the strategies of his or her opponents.[8]

Example 7.7 Let us use the above theorem to verify that the strategy profile $(\hat{\sigma}, \hat{\sigma}, \ldots, \hat{\sigma})$ defined by $\hat{\sigma}_t(x) = 0$ is a Markov-perfect Nash equilibrium of the game considered in example 7.5. Obviously, this strategy profile ensures that $J^i(\hat{\sigma}, \hat{\sigma}, \ldots, \hat{\sigma}) = 0$ holds for all $i \in \mathbf{M}$. This suggests to use the constant value functions defined by $V^i(x, t) = 0$ for all $t \in \mathbb{N}_0$ and all $i \in \mathbf{M}$. Condition (7.11) becomes

$$0 = \sup\{-\beta^t x^2 (c^i)^2 \mid c^i \in \mathbb{R}\},$$

which is obviously true. Because the right-hand side of this equation is maximized at $c^i = \hat{\sigma}_t(x) = 0$, equation (7.12) holds as well. Finally, condition (7.13) holds trivially.

---

[8] Strictly speaking, we must apply versions of theorems 5.8 and 5.10 that are appropriately modified for the primitive form that we have been using in section 7.1.

In many applications in economics, the dynamic game has the special feature of stationarity. This is the case if the objective functional of each player $i \in \mathbf{M}$ has the form

$$\sum_{t=0}^{+\infty} (\beta^i)^t F^i(x_t, c_t),$$

if the state equation can be written as

$$x_{t+1} = f(x_t, c_t),$$

and if the control constraints are of the form $c_t^i \in G^i(x_t)$. We call such a dynamic game a *stationary discounted dynamic game*. Note that different players may have different time-preference factors $\beta^i \in (0, 1)$.

Consider a strategy profile $(\sigma^1, \sigma^2, \ldots, \sigma^m)$ consisting of *stationary* closed-loop strategies. Such a strategy σ^i is a constant sequence of time-t strategies $(\sigma_t^i)_{t=0}^{+\infty}$ where $\sigma_t^i = \sigma_s^i$ for all $t \in \mathbb{N}_0$ and all $s \in \mathbb{N}_0$. It is easy to see that in the case where all players $j \neq i$ use a stationary closed-loop strategy, player i's optimization problem is a stationary discounted dynamic optimization problem as discussed in section 5.5. It is also straightforward to verify that every subgame $\Gamma(x, t)$ is identical to the subgame $\Gamma(x, s)$ for all $s \in \mathbb{N}_0$. This implies the following simple lemma.

Lemma 7.1 Let $\Gamma(x_0, 0)$ be a stationary discounted dynamic game and let $(\sigma^1, \sigma^2, \ldots, \sigma^m)$ be a profile of stationary closed-loop strategies. If $(\sigma^1, \sigma^2, \ldots, \sigma^m)$ is a closed-loop Nash equilibrium of every game of the form $\Gamma(x, 0)$, where $x \in X$, then it is Markov-perfect.

PROOF: The result follows simply from the facts that $\Gamma(x, t)$ is identical to $\Gamma(x, 0)$ for all $t \in \mathbb{N}_0$ and that the strategy profile is stationary.

We illustrate the application of this lemma by revisiting the sticky-price duopoly model from examples 7.1 and 7.2.

Example 7.8 Consider once more the sticky-price duopoly game from examples 7.1 and 7.2. We have proved that the system matrix in (7.5) has a unique stable eigenvalue λ in the interval $(0, 1)$ provided that $B \in (B_2, B_1)$ holds. Moreover, from the construction that has been applied in example 7.1 it is clear that the stable manifold of the fixed point $(A^*(B), p^*(B))^\top$ (which is a linear manifold in this example) is parallel to the p-axis if and only if an eigenvector corresponding to the stable eigenvalue λ is given by $(0, 1)^\top$. It is straightforward to see that this is the case if and only if $R = 0$ and $1 - \gamma - 2bB\gamma = \lambda$. The latter condition together with the fact that the stable eigenvalue satisfies $\lambda \in (0, 1)$ implies that

$$B_2 < -\frac{1}{2b} < B < \frac{1 - \gamma}{2b\gamma} < B_1. \tag{7.14}$$

Furthermore, we observe that R is a third-degree polynomial in B with a positive coefficient in front of the cubic term B^3, and that

$$R|_{B=-1/(2b)} = \frac{2(2b + c)(1 - \beta) + 2b\gamma(1 + \beta) + \beta\gamma c}{4b} > 0,$$

$$R|_{B=(1-\gamma)/(2b\gamma)} = -\frac{(1 - \gamma)(c + b\gamma)}{2b\gamma} < 0.$$

These properties imply that there exists a unique value $B^* \in (B_2, B_1)$ that satisfies (7.14) and $R = 0$. For this value B^*, the stable manifold of the fixed point is parallel to the p-axis, and this manifold is given by the equation $A = A^*(B^*)$. The strategy defined by $\sigma_t(p) = A^*(B^*) + B^* p$ therefore qualifies as a closed-loop Nash equilibrium of the game irrespective of the particular initial price p_{-1}. According to lemma 7.1, this closed-loop Nash equilibrium is Markov-perfect.

Now consider the closed-loop Nash equilibria for $B \neq B^*$. Whenever $B \neq B^*$, the stable manifold of the difference equation (7.5) is still linear but not parallel to the p-axis. Formally, the stable manifold can be expressed as $A - A^*(B) = \delta[p - p^*(B)]$, where $\delta \neq 0$. Since the point $(A_0, p_{-1})^\top$ must be located on the stable manifold, it follows that the point $(A_0, \hat{p}_{-1})^\top$ is not located on the stable manifold whenever $\hat{p}_{-1} \neq p_{-1}$. The trajectory of system (7.5) that starts in $(A_0, \hat{p}_{-1})^\top$ must therefore diverge. Moreover, it can be shown that the value of the objective functional along this trajectory is $-\infty$. Hence, the solution generated by a closed-loop strategy $\sigma_t(p) = A_t + Bp$ with $B \neq B^*$ does not qualify as a Nash equilibrium for any subgame $\Gamma(\hat{p}_{-1}, 0)$ with $\hat{p}_{-1} \neq p_{-1}$. This implies that the closed-loop Nash equilibria corresponding to $B \neq B^*$ do not qualify as Markov-perfect Nash equilibria of the original game $\Gamma(p_{-1}, 0)$. Note in particular that the open-loop Nash equilibrium, which is the equilibrium corresponding to $B = 0$, is not Markov-perfect because $B^* \neq 0$.

7.4 Hierarchical dynamic games

In the present section, we discuss some issues that arise in connection with hierarchical equilibria. We have already briefly indicated in section 7.1 how such equilibria can be defined. Now we illustrate this general approach by a number of examples, restricting

Dynamic optimization

the attention to the most common situation in which there is a single leader L and a single follower F, that is, the set of players is $\mathbf{M} = \{L, F\}$. Such a game is usually called a *Stackelberg game*. The leader maximizes

$$\sum_{t=0}^{+\infty} F^L\left(x_t, c_t^L, c_t^F, t\right),$$

whereas the follower maximizes

$$\sum_{t=0}^{+\infty} F^F\left(x_t, c_t^L, c_t^F, t\right).$$

The state equation is given by

$$x_{t+1} = f\left(x_t, c_t^L, c_t^F, t\right) \tag{7.15}$$

and the initial state x_0 is given.

Let us start with the case where both players use open-loop strategies. Since an open-loop strategy is a sequence of controls, we simplify the presentation by saying that player $i \in \{L, F\}$ chooses the control path $(c_t^i)_{t=0}^{+\infty}$ instead of the strategy $\sigma^i = (\sigma_t^i)_{t=0}^{+\infty}$. Consider an arbitrary control path of the leader $(c_t^L)_{t=0}^{+\infty}$. Given this path and assuming that $f_3(x_t, c_t^L, c_t^F, t)$ has full rank, theorem 5.5 states that for an interior optimal solution to the follower's problem there exists a sequence of Lagrange multipliers $(\lambda_t)_{t=0}^{+\infty}$ such that the conditions

$$F_3^F\left(x_t, c_t^L, c_t^F, t\right) + \lambda_t f_3\left(x_t, c_t^L, c_t^F, t\right) = 0 \tag{7.16}$$

and

$$F_1^F\left(x_{t+1}, c_{t+1}^L, c_{t+1}^F, t+1\right) + \lambda_{t+1} f_1\left(x_{t+1}, c_{t+1}^L, c_{t+1}^F, t+1\right) - \lambda_t = 0 \tag{7.17}$$

hold for all $t \in \mathbb{N}_0$. Let us furthermore assume that the model satisfies the assumptions under which the transversality condition

$$\lim_{t \to +\infty} \lambda_t x_{t+1} = 0 \tag{7.18}$$

holds necessarily. In many cases, the difference equations (7.15)–(7.17) together with the transversality condition (7.18) and the initial value x_0 are sufficient to uniquely determine the follower's optimal control path $(c_t^F)_{t=0}^{+\infty}$. In terms of the notation introduced in section 7.1, the best response function $\mathcal{B}$ of the follower is implicitly determined by these four conditions. When we solve the leader's problem, we need to take the best response of the follower into account. In order to do this, we augment the leader's problem by the conditions that describe the follower's best response. Hence, the leader's problem consists of the maximization of

$$\sum_{t=0}^{+\infty} F^L\left(x_t, c_t^L, c_t^F, t\right)$$

subject to (7.15)–(7.18) as well as the given initial state x_0. The optimal solution to this problem along with the follower's best response is an open-loop Stackelberg equilibrium of the game.

Condition (7.16) can typically be used to eliminate the follower's control variables $(c_t^F)_{t=0}^{+\infty}$ from the leader's problem.[9] The remaining variables of this optimization problem are $(x_t)_{t=0}^{+\infty}$, $(c_t^L)_{t=0}^{+\infty}$, and $(\lambda_t)_{t=0}^{+\infty}$. Since there does not exist an initial value λ_0, the variable λ_t is not pre-determined and plays the role of a control variable for the leader's problem. Hence, the leader's problem is a dynamic optimization problem with the state variable x_t and the control variables (c_t^L, λ_t). The system dynamics are given by (7.15), there is an initial value for the state, x_0, and a terminal condition (7.18). In addition, there exists the constraint (7.17), which forms an intertemporal link of the leader's control variables c_t^L and λ_t very much like equation (6.1) in section 6.1. It will therefore not come as a surprise that an open-loop Stackelberg equilibrium can be dynamically inconsistent. The following example illustrates the general procedure for finding an open-loop Stackelberg equilibrium in a simple economic context.

Example 7.9 Consider a dynamic principal-agent problem in which the principal employs an agent to accumulate an asset. The stock of the asset at the beginning of period t is denoted by x_t and the agent can spend effort $e_t \geq 0$ in order to increase the asset stock. The principal has no direct influence on asset accumulation. The dynamics of the asset stock are therefore described by the state equation

$$x_{t+1} = \alpha x_t + e_t, \tag{7.19}$$

where $\alpha > 0$ is an intrinsic growth factor of the asset stock. The initial asset stock $x_0 > 0$ is given.

The investment activity is costly for the agent, and we assume these costs to be quadratic in effort e_t. The asset, however, belongs to the principal and it creates utility that is proportional to the size of the asset stock. In order to induce the agent to spend effort, the principal promises to transfer to the agent the fraction $\tau_t \in [0, 1]$ of (the utility derived from) the asset in period $t + 1$. Both players discount future utilities

---

[9] Note that (7.16) consists of k^F equations, where k^F denotes the number of control variables of the follower. Instead of eliminating the k^F components of c_t^F, we could alternatively eliminate any k^F components of the vector (λ_t, c_t^F).

with the factor $\beta \in (0, 1)$. These assumptions are captured by the objective functionals

$$\sum_{t=0}^{+\infty} \beta^t (1 - \tau_t) x_{t+1}$$

for the principal and

$$\sum_{t=0}^{+\infty} \beta^t \left[\tau_t x_{t+1} - e_t^2 / 2 \right]$$

for the agent. The principal is the leader and the agent is the follower, and we assume that $\alpha\beta < 1$ holds.

In order to transform the game into the form that we have described in the general discussion above, we use the state equation (7.19) to eliminate x_{t+1} from the period-t utilities in the objective functionals. In this way, we obtain the utility functions $F^L(x_t, \tau_t, e_t, t) = \beta^t (1 - \tau_t)(\alpha x_t + e_t)$ for the leader and $F^F(x_t, \tau_t, e_t, t) = \beta^t [\tau_t (\alpha x_t + e_t) - e_t^2 / 2]$ for the follower. Equations (7.16) and (7.17) become $\beta^t (\tau_t - e_t) + \lambda_t = 0$ and $\alpha(\beta^{t+1} \tau_{t+1} + \lambda_{t+1}) - \lambda_t = 0$. Introducing the notation $\tilde{\lambda}_t = \lambda_t \beta^{-t}$, we can write these equations as

$$e_t = \tilde{\lambda}_t + \tau_t \tag{7.20}$$

and

$$\tilde{\lambda}_{t+1} = \tilde{\lambda}_t / (\alpha\beta) - \tau_{t+1}. \tag{7.21}$$

For any given strategy $(\tau_t)_{t=0}^{+\infty}$ of the leader, condition (7.21) is a one-dimensional non-homogeneous linear difference equation in $\tilde{\lambda}_t$. Applying the results from section 2.4, we obtain the general solution

$$\tilde{\lambda}_t = A(\alpha\beta)^{-t} + \sum_{s=1}^{+\infty} (\alpha\beta)^s \tau_{t+s}$$

where A is an undetermined coefficient. Combining this result with (7.20), it follows that

$$e_t = A(\alpha\beta)^{-t} + \sum_{s=0}^{+\infty} (\alpha\beta)^s \tau_{t+s}.$$

The assumptions $\tau_t \in [0, 1]$ and $0 < \alpha\beta < 1$ imply that the infinite sum $\sum_{s=0}^{+\infty} (\alpha\beta)^s \tau_{t+s}$ has a finite value. If the coefficient A was different from 0, then it would follow from $0 < \alpha\beta < 1$ that e_t becomes unbounded. More specifically, as e_t must be non-negative, it follows that $e_t \approx A(\alpha\beta)^{-t}$.[10] Together with the state equation (7.19) and the

---

[10] The notation $p_t \approx q_t$ means that the two terms p_t and q_t grow asymptotically at the same rate, that is, there exists a constant $d \in (0, +\infty)$ such that $\lim_{t \to +\infty} p_t / q_t = d$.

definition of $\tilde{\lambda}_t$, we obtain $x_{t+1} \geq e_t \approx A(\alpha\beta)^{-t}$ and $\lambda_t = \beta^t \tilde{\lambda}_t \approx A\alpha^{-t}$. Obviously, this contradicts the transversality condition (7.18), and we can therefore conclude that $A = 0$ must hold and, hence, that

$$e_t = \sum_{s=0}^{+\infty} (\alpha\beta)^s \tau_{t+s}. \tag{7.22}$$

To summarize the discussion so far, we have shown that for every open-loop strategy of the leader – here represented by the sequence of transfer rates $(\tau_t)_{t=0}^{+\infty}$ – there exists a unique best response open-loop strategy of the follower $(e_t)_{t=0}^{+\infty} = \mathcal{B}((\tau_t)_{t=0}^{+\infty})$, which is defined by equation (7.22). The interpretation of condition (7.22) is that the agent's marginal cost of effort, e_t, coincides with the marginal utility, where the latter consists of the sum of the appropriately discounted utilities that the effort spent in period t has throughout the entire future.

Equation (7.22) is a compact description of the solution to the first-order conditions (7.20)–(7.21) and the transversality condition (7.18). The principal seeks to maximize his or her objective functional subject to the state equation (7.19) and the best response function (7.22). Typically, however, it is more convenient to work directly with the first-order conditions of the agent's optimization problem. Hence, we formulate the leader's problem as the maximization of

$$\sum_{t=0}^{+\infty} \beta^t (1 - \tau_t)(\alpha x_t + e_t) \tag{7.23}$$

subject to (7.18)–(7.21). We use (7.20) to eliminate the variable $\tilde{\lambda}_t$. Hence, the leader's problem turns into the maximization of (7.23) subject to (7.19), equation $e_{t+1} = (e_t - \tau_t)/(\alpha\beta)$, the initial value x_0, and the transversality condition $\lim_{t \to +\infty} \beta^t (e_t - \tau_t) x_{t+1} = 0$. The Lagrangian for this problem is

$$L = \sum_{t=0}^{+\infty} \beta^t \{(1 - \tau_t)(\alpha x_t + e_t) + \mu_t(\alpha x_t + e_t - x_{t+1}) + v_t[(e_t - \tau_t)/(\alpha\beta) - e_{t+1}]\},$$

where $(\mu_t)_{t=0}^{+\infty}$ and $(v_t)_{t=0}^{+\infty}$ are sequences of Lagrange multipliers. Taking derivatives with respect to the decision variables e_t, x_{t+1}, and τ_t, we obtain the first-order conditions. More specifically, for the optimal choice of e_t we obtain the condition

$$1 - \tau_t + \mu_t + v_t/(\alpha\beta) = \begin{cases} 0 & \text{if } t = 0, \\ v_{t-1}/\beta & \text{if } t \geq 1, \end{cases}$$

for the optimal choice of x_{t+1} we obtain

$$-\mu_t + \alpha\beta(1 - \tau_{t+1} + \mu_{t+1}) = 0,$$

and for the optimal choice of τ_t we get

$$\tau_t = 0 \quad \Rightarrow \quad \alpha x_t + e_t + \nu_t/(\alpha\beta) \geq 0,$$

$$\tau_t \in (0, 1) \quad \Rightarrow \quad \alpha x_t + e_t + \nu_t/(\alpha\beta) = 0,$$

$$\tau_t = 1 \quad \Rightarrow \quad \alpha x_t + e_t + \nu_t/(\alpha\beta) \leq 0.$$

The latter set of conditions for τ_t follows from the linearity of the Lagrangian with respect to τ_t and from the fact that $\tau_t \in [0, 1]$ must hold. It is not easy to verify that the above conditions have a unique solution that satisfies the feasibility and transversality conditions. The structure of the problem, however, suggests that the principal should apply the same transfer rate τ_t in all periods $t \geq 1$ but possibly a different transfer rate τ_0 in period 0. It is indeed the case that there exists a unique set of system variables and multipliers which have this property and which satisfy the necessary optimality conditions. This set of variables is given by[11]

$$\tau_t = \begin{cases} \max\{1 - \alpha x_0, 0\}/2 & \text{if } t = 0, \\ 1/2 & \text{if } t \geq 1, \end{cases}$$

$$e_t = \begin{cases} \max\{1 - \alpha x_0, 0\}/2 + \alpha\beta/[2(1 - \alpha\beta)] & \text{if } t = 0, \\ 1/[2(1 - \alpha\beta)] & \text{if } t \geq 1, \end{cases}$$

$$x_t = \begin{cases} \dfrac{\max\{1 + \alpha x_0, 2\alpha x_0\}}{2} + \dfrac{\alpha\beta}{2(1 - \alpha\beta)} & \text{if } t = 1, \\ \left[x_1 - \dfrac{1}{2(1 - \alpha)(1 - \alpha\beta)} \right]\alpha^{t-1} + \dfrac{1}{2(1 - \alpha)(1 - \alpha\beta)} & \text{if } t \geq 2, \end{cases}$$

$$\mu_t = \frac{\alpha\beta}{2(1 - \alpha\beta)},$$

$$\nu_t = \beta\left[\frac{1}{2(1 - \alpha)(1 - \alpha\beta)} - x_1 \right]\alpha^{t+1} - \frac{\alpha\beta}{2(1 - \alpha)(1 - \alpha\beta)}.$$

We can therefore be quite confident that this solution qualifies as the open-loop Stackelberg equilibrium of the game even if none of our sufficiency theorems applies, because the required convexity properties do not hold.

The open-loop Stackelberg equilibrium in the present example is dynamically inconsistent in the following sense. If the leader had the opportunity to choose a new strategy in period $t > 0$ (when the state has evolved to x_t), he or she would not choose $\tau_t = 1/2$ as announced in period 0, but would choose the smaller control

---

[11] For simplicity, we assume that $\alpha \neq 1$. The case $\alpha = 1$ can also be dealt with, but the formulas take slightly different forms.

$\tau_t = \max\{1 - \alpha x_t, 0\}/2 < 1/2$ instead. This is the case because the problem is stationary such that the open-loop Stackelberg equilibrium in the game $\Gamma(x_t, t)$ must have the very same structure as the open-loop Stackelberg equilibrium of the game $\Gamma(x_0, 0)$. On an intuitive level, the stock x_t is pre-determined in period t and therefore the principal has an incentive to select a small transfer τ_t in order to reap a higher immediate payoff $(1 - \tau_t)(\alpha x_t + e_t)$. The values x_{t+s} for $s > 0$, however, are not fixed in period t and the principal therefore promises higher transfer rates in order to induce the agent to exert effort. On a more formal level, we see that the principal's optimization problem contains the difference equation $e_{t+1} = (e_t - \tau_t)/(\alpha\beta)$, where e_t is a control variable, that is, a jump variable. Hence, we are in exactly the same situation that we discussed at the outset of section 6.1.

The root of the dynamic inconsistency of the open-loop Stackelberg equilibrium in the above example 7.9 is the fact that the follower's control variable e_t is not pre-determined in the leader's optimization problem, but that it can be influenced by the leader. In other Stackelberg games, however, it may be the case that the follower's control variable cannot be affected by the leader. In such a game, an open-loop Stackelberg equilibrium may well be dynamically consistent. The following example of a saving problem with two players illustrates this possibility.[12]

Example 7.10 We consider a dynamic game in which two players can influence the evolution of a productive asset stock. The asset stock at the beginning of period t is denoted by $x_t \geq 0$ and is used to produce output y_t according to the Cobb–Douglas production technology $y_t = Ax_t^\alpha$, where $A > 0$ and $\alpha \in (0, 1)$ are model parameters. The leader sets aside the fraction $1 - s_t^L$ of the available output for his or her own consumption, which is therefore given by $c_t^L = (1 - s_t^L)Ax_t^\alpha$. The rest of output, $s_t^L Ax_t^\alpha$, is left for the follower who consumes $c_t^F = (1 - s_t^F)s_t^L Ax_t^\alpha$ and saves $s_t^F s_t^L Ax_t^\alpha$ for the next period. Both players seek to maximize the discounted utility of consumption, where we assume the same logarithmic utility function for both players. It follows that the state equation is given by

$$x_{t+1} = s_t^F s_t^L Ax_t^\alpha$$

and that the objective functionals of the leader and the follower are

$$\sum_{t=0}^{+\infty} \beta^t \ln\left[\left(1 - s_t^L\right)Ax_t^\alpha\right] \tag{7.24}$$

---

[12] Another example is provided in exercise 7.7.

and

$$\sum_{t=0}^{+\infty} \beta^t \ln\left[(1 - s_t^F)s_t^L A x_t^\alpha\right],$$

respectively.

Noting that the follower's optimization problem can be rewritten as the maximization of

$$\sum_{t=0}^{+\infty} \beta^t \ln\left(c_t^F\right)$$

subject to the constraints $c_t^F \geq 0$, $x_{t+1} \geq 0$, and $x_{t+1} = s_t^L A x_t^\alpha - c_t^F$, we can see that this is just the one-sector optimal growth model with logarithmic utility function and Cobb–Douglas technology. We have proved in example 5.8 that the optimal solution is given by $s_t^F = \alpha\beta$ for all $t \in \mathbb{N}_0$. Hence, the leader's optimization problem reduces to the maximization of (7.24) subject to $s_t^L \in [0, 1]$ and the state equation

$$x_{t+1} = s_t^L \alpha\beta A x_t^\alpha.$$

Because of the logarithmic utility function, the maximization of (7.24) is equivalent to the maximization of

$$\sum_{t=0}^{+\infty} \beta^t \ln\left[(1 - s_t^L)\alpha\beta A x_t^\alpha\right].$$

This shows that the leader's optimization problem is also equivalent to the one-sector optimal growth model with logarithmic utility function and Cobb–Douglas technology. Hence, the leader's optimal saving rate is equal to $s_t^L = \alpha\beta$, too. The open-loop Stackelberg equilibrium therefore features constant saving rates for both players. These saving rates are moreover independent of the initial state of the game, x_0. It follows that these strategies not only qualify as an open-loop Stackelberg equilibrium of the game $\Gamma(x_0, 0)$, but of all games $\Gamma(x, t)$ where $x \geq 0$ and $t \in \mathbb{N}_0$. Consequently, the open-loop Stackelberg equilibrium in this example is not only dynamically consistent, it is actually Markov-perfect.

Let us now turn to Stackelberg equilibria in games where the players use closed-loop strategies. As we will see, this equilibrium concept raises a number of problematic technical and conceptual issues. To get a first impression of these problems, recall that the leader takes the best response $\mathcal{B}(\sigma^L)$ of the follower into account when he or she chooses his or her strategy σ^L. This requires that the best response function $\mathcal{B}$ exists, that it is unique, and that its value $\mathcal{B}(\sigma^L)$ can be characterized for all possible strategies σ^L of the leader. All three properties may fail to hold. To illustrate this problem, we consider the following example.

Example 7.11 There exists one productive asset with constant return $R > 0$. The stock of the asset x_t evolves according to the difference equation

$$x_{t+1} = R\left(x_t - c_t^L - c_t^F\right),$$

where c_t^L and c_t^F are the non-negative consumption rates of the leader and the follower, respectively. It is required that the asset stock is non-negative in all periods. The leader and the follower seek to maximize the objective functionals

$$\sum_{t=0}^{+\infty} \beta^t \left(c_t^L\right)^\alpha$$

and

$$\sum_{t=0}^{+\infty} \beta^t \left(c_t^F\right)^\alpha, \tag{7.25}$$

respectively, where $\alpha \in (0, 1)$, $\beta \in (0, 1)$, and $0 < R < \beta^{-1/\alpha}$. Now suppose that the leader plays the closed-loop strategy $\sigma^L = (\sigma_t^L)_{t=0}^{+\infty}$, where $\sigma_t^L : \mathbb{R}_+ \mapsto \mathbb{R}_+$ is a time-t strategy that maps the state space into the control set. To derive the follower's best response $\mathcal{B}(\sigma^L)$, we have to solve the dynamic optimization problem of maximizing (7.25) subject to the constraints

$$x_{t+1} = R\left[x_t - \sigma_t^L(x_t) - c_t^F\right]$$

and

$$0 \le c_t^F \le x_t - \sigma_t^L(x_t)$$

for all $t \in \mathbb{N}_0$. In order to solve the overall game, we need to know $\mathcal{B}(\sigma^L)$ for all feasible strategies σ^L of the leader. An analytical expression for $\mathcal{B}(\sigma^L)$ can be derived in the case where the strategy of the leader has the form $\sigma_t^L(x) = \gamma x$ (see example 7.13 below), but such a solution is not known for other functional forms of σ_t^L. Moreover, it is highly unlikely that an optimal solution to the leaders problem exists for all feasible strategies σ^L of the leader because the follower's problem lacks sufficient convexity properties if the time-t strategies σ_t^L are arbitrary non-linear functions. Last but not least, even if it is possible to compute an optimal control path for the follower, this control path can be synthesized by many different closed-loop strategies. It is therefore not clear which optimization problem the leader should try to solve.

A second technical difficulty is that the leader's optimization problem has non-standard features and that no off-the-shelf optimization techniques are known that can be used to solve it. To illustrate this issue, we return to example 7.9, but this time we allow the leader to play an arbitrary closed-loop strategy.

Example 7.12 Suppose that the leader in example 7.9 chooses the closed-loop strategy $\sigma_t(x)$. In that case, the follower wants to maximize

$$\sum_{t=0}^{+\infty} \beta^t \left[\sigma_t(x_t)(\alpha x_t + e_t) - e_t^2/2 \right]$$

subject to

$$x_{t+1} = \alpha x_t + e_t.$$

Let us rewrite this problem in reduced form by using the state equation to eliminate the follower's control variable e_t. This yields the problem of maximizing

$$\sum_{t=0}^{+\infty} \beta^t \left[\sigma_t(x_t)x_{t+1} - (1/2)(x_{t+1} - \alpha x_t)^2 \right].$$

As has been pointed out in the discussion of example 7.11, it is unlikely that this optimization problem has a solution if the time-t strategies σ_t are arbitrary non-linear functions. But let us assume that a solution does indeed exist and that it is an interior solution. Then it follows that the Euler equation

$$\sigma_t(x_t) - x_{t+1} + \alpha x_t + \beta[\sigma'_{t+1}(x_{t+1})x_{t+2} + \alpha(x_{t+2} - \alpha x_{t+1})] = 0 \qquad (7.26)$$

holds. This condition is sometimes referred to as the *implementability constraint*. The leader's problem can be formulated as the maximization of

$$\sum_{t=0}^{+\infty} \beta^t [1 - \sigma_t(x_t)]x_{t+1} \qquad (7.27)$$

subject to (7.26) and the initial value x_0. Note that it is not sufficient to find a sequence of values $(\sigma_t(x_t))_{t=0}^{+\infty}$ but we need to determine an optimal strategy $\sigma = (\sigma_t)_{t=0}^{+\infty}$, that is, a sequence of functions. The values of these functions appear both in the objective functional (7.27) and in the implementability constraint (7.26), and the derivatives of the time-t strategies appear in the implementability constraint (7.26). Due to this feature, the leader's optimization problem is a non-standard problem for which no general optimization techniques are available.

So far, we have identified the following technical problems that can occur in hierarchical games when players use closed-loop strategies: (i) the possible non-existence of a best response for the follower, (ii) the generic (informational) non-uniqueness of the best response of the follower, (iii) the difficulty of determining the best response of the follower to all feasible strategies of the leader, and (iv) the non-standard features of the dynamic optimization problem of the leader. These difficulties arise under almost all conceivable circumstances such that the derivation of closed-loop Stackelberg equilibria seems to be possible only in degenerate cases.[13] It is often suggested in the literature to circumvent the above mentioned problems by restricting the strategy space of the leader to a finite-dimensional subspace of the set of closed-loop strategies. For example, we could consider all closed-loop strategies that can be expressed as poly-nomials of degree smaller than or equal to some given finite number. The following example demonstrates the application of this approach to the game from example 7.11.

Example 7.13 Suppose that the leader in the game from example 7.11 can only use strategies of the form $\sigma_t^L(x) = \gamma x$, where $\gamma \in [0, 1]$. Thus, the strategy space for the leader is a one-dimensional subset of the set of all closed-loop strategies which can be parametrized by γ. As has been shown in example 7.11, the follower's optimization problem in this case boils down to maximizing

$$\sum_{t=0}^{+\infty} \beta^t \left(c_t^F\right)^\alpha$$

subject to $x_{t+1} = R[(1 - \gamma)x_t - c_t^F]$, $c_t^F \geq 0$, and $x_{t+1} \geq 0$. If $\gamma = 1$, then it is obvious that the only feasible control path for the follower is given by $c_t^F = 0$ for all $t \in \mathbb{N}_0$. The best response to the leader's strategy corresponding to $\gamma = 1$ can therefore be written in the form $c_t^F = \delta x_t$ with $\delta = 0$. In a slight abuse of notation, we express this as $\mathcal{B}(1) = 0$, where the argument of the best response function $\mathcal{B}$ is the parameter value of γ that characterizes the leader's strategy and the value of $\mathcal{B}$ is the parameter δ appearing in the follower's response. Note that in the case where the leader chooses $\gamma = 1$, the asset stock is depleted within the first period and the leader therefore receives the payoff $J(1) = x_0^\alpha$.

Let us now turn to the case where $\gamma \in [0, 1)$. If we define the new control variable $d_t^F = c_t^F/(1 - \gamma)$, we can rewrite the follower's problem as the maximization of

$$(1 - \gamma)^\alpha \sum_{t=0}^{+\infty} \beta^t \left(d_t^F\right)^\alpha$$

subject to the constraints

$$x_{t+1} = \tilde{R}\left(x_t - d_t^F\right),$$

$d_t^F \geq 0$, and $x_{t+1} \geq 0$, where $\tilde{R} = (1 - \gamma)R$. The term $(1 - \gamma)^\alpha$ in the objective func-tional is a positive constant that the follower takes as given, and which is therefore irrelevant for the solution to this problem. Hence, the follower's problem is identi-cal to the simple saving problem that we have already solved in example 5.6. Since

---

[13] See exercise 7.7 for an example.

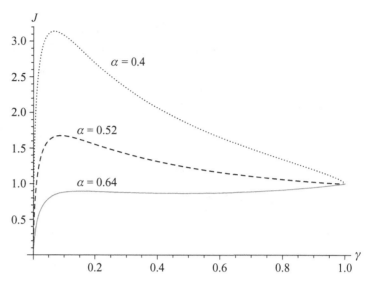

Figure 7.1 $J(\gamma)$ for $x_0 = R = 1$, $\beta = 0.96$, and $\alpha \in \{0.4, 0.52, 0.64\}$

$R \in (0, \beta^{-1/\alpha})$ has been assumed, it follows also that $\tilde{R} \in (0, \beta^{-1/\alpha})$. Consequently, we may conclude from our discussion in example 5.6 that the optimal solution satisfies the condition $d_t^F = [1 - (\beta \tilde{R}^\alpha)^{1/(1-\alpha)}]x_t$. Using the definition of $\tilde{R}$, we therefore see that the follower's best response is given by the closed-loop strategy $c_t^F = \sigma_t^F(x_t)$ with $\sigma_t^F(x) = \mathcal{B}(\gamma)x$ and[14]

$$\mathcal{B}(\gamma) = (1 - \gamma)\left\{1 - [\beta R^\alpha(1 - \gamma)^\alpha]^{1/(1-\alpha)}\right\}.$$

We can now evaluate the leader's objective functional for the case where the leader chooses the strategy $\sigma_t^L(x) = \gamma x$ and the follower plays the best response $\sigma_t^F(x) = \mathcal{B}(\gamma)x$. The state equation in this case becomes

$$x_{t+1} = R[x_t - \gamma x_t - \mathcal{B}(\gamma)x_t] = [\beta(1 - \gamma)R]^{1/(1-\alpha)}x_t.$$

The solution to this homogeneous linear difference equation is $x_t = [\beta(1 - \gamma)R]^{t/(1-\alpha)}x_0$. Substituting this result into the objective functional of the leader, we obtain

$$\sum_{t=0}^{+\infty} \beta^t \left(c_t^L\right)^\alpha = \sum_{t=0}^{+\infty} \beta^t (\gamma x_t)^\alpha = x_0^\alpha \gamma^\alpha \sum_{t=0}^{+\infty} \beta^t [\beta(1 - \gamma)R]^{\alpha t/(1-\alpha)}$$

$$= \frac{x_0^\alpha \gamma^\alpha}{1 - [\beta(1 - \gamma)^\alpha R^\alpha]^{1/(1-\alpha)}}.$$

We denote this expression by $J(\gamma)$ and note that $\lim_{\gamma \to 1} J(\gamma) = J(1) = x_0^\alpha$.

---

[14] Note that the closed-loop representation $c_t^F = \mathcal{B}(\gamma)x_t$ is not the only way in which we can write the best response of the follower. We could as well use an open-loop representation of the follower's optimal solution or many other forms.

The leader's optimal strategy of the proposed form $\sigma_t^L(x) = \gamma x$ can be determined by maximizing $J(\gamma)$ with respect to $\gamma \in [0, 1]$. The function J is continuous on the compact interval $[0, 1]$ and continuously differentiable on $(0, 1)$. This implies that a maximum exists. Furthermore, it holds that $J(0) = 0 < J(1) = x_0^\alpha$, which rules out a boundary optimum at $\gamma = 0$. If $\alpha < 1/2$, then we have $\lim_{\gamma \to 1} J'(\gamma) = -\infty$, which rules out a boundary optimum at $\gamma = 1$. For $\alpha \geq 1/2$, the derivative $J'(1)$ is finite and a boundary optimum could in principle occur. Figure 7.1 shows the graph of the function J for the parameter values $x_0 = R = 1$, $\beta = 0.96$, and $\alpha \in \{0.4, 0.52, 0.64\}$. In the case $\alpha = 0.4$, we can clearly see an interior maximum at $\gamma \approx 0.068$. For $\alpha = 0.52$, there still exists an interior maximum at $\gamma \approx 0.09$. But for $\alpha = 0.64$ a corner solution occurs at $\gamma = 1$.

It must be emphasized that the practice of restricting the leader's strategy space to a finite-dimensional subset typically does not yield the true closed-loop Stackelberg equilibrium of the original game. Moreover, even in such a restricted strategy space, there may not exist a solution to the leader's optimization problem at all.[15] Hence, unless there are good economic reasons to assume that the leader does not have access to all closed-loop strategies, this practice can only be considered as a questionable device for finding some solution.

7.5 EXERCISES

EXERCISE 7.1 Consider a dynamic game with two players $i \in \{1, 2\}$ who maximize

$$\sum_{t=0}^{+\infty} \beta^t \left[x_t - (1/2)\left(c_t^i\right)^2 \right]$$

subject to the state equation

$$x_{t+1} = \alpha x_t + c_t^1 + c_t^2$$

and the non-negativity constraints $c_t^1 \geq 0$, $c_t^2 \geq 0$, and $x_{t+1} \geq 0$ for all $t \in \mathbb{N}_0$. Here, α and β are positive parameters satisfying $\beta < 1$ and $\alpha\beta < 1$. Derive an open-loop Nash equilibrium under the assumption that the players move simultaneously and show that this equilibrium is Markov-perfect.

EXERCISE 7.2 Consider the model from exercise 7.1, but assume that instead of c_t^i player i controls $d_t^i = c_t^i + (\alpha/2)x_t$.

---

[15] An example where this happens is provided in exercise 7.6 below.

Dynamic optimization

(a) Rewrite the game in terms of the new variables.
(b) Derive an open-loop Nash equilibrium under simultaneous play and show that it differs from the open-loop Nash equilibrium derived in exercise 7.1 and that it is not Markov-perfect.

EXERCISE 7.3 Consider the variation of the sticky-price duopoly game described in example 7.4. The players maximize the objective functionals in (7.8) subject to the state equation (7.7). Derive the first-order conditions for a symmetric open-loop Nash equilibrium of the game and determine the fixed point of these equations. Verify that this fixed point coincides with $p^*(B)$ from example 7.1 provided that $B = (1 - \gamma)/(2b\gamma)$.

EXERCISE 7.4 Consider the model from examples 7.11 and 7.13, but assume that the two players move simultaneously. Prove that there exists a unique symmetric Nash equilibrium in which both players use closed-loop strategies of the form $\sigma_t(x) = \gamma x$. Is this Nash equilibrium Markov-perfect?

EXERCISE 7.5 Consider a dynamic game with two players $i \in \{1, 2\}$. Player 1 has control over the variables $(u_t)_{t=0}^{+\infty}$ and maximizes

$$\sum_{t=0}^{+\infty} \beta^t \left[x_t u_t - (1/2)u_t^2 \right].$$

Player 2 has control over the variables $(v_t)_{t=0}^{+\infty}$ and maximizes

$$\sum_{t=0}^{+\infty} \beta^t \left[x_t + u_t - (1/2)v_t^2 \right].$$

The state equation of the game is given by

$$x_{t+1} = v_t$$

and there are no further constraints on any of the control or state variables. An initial value $x_0 \in \mathbb{R}$ is given. The players move simultaneously.

(a) Suppose that player 1 chooses a time-t strategy of the closed-loop form $\sigma_t(x) = z_t + \gamma x$, where γ is a real number and where $(z_t)_{t=0}^{+\infty}$ is a sequence of real numbers. What is player 2's best response to such a strategy?
(b) Show that for every $\gamma \in \mathbb{R}$, there exists a sequence $(z_t)_{t=0}^{+\infty}$ such that player 1's strategy $\sigma = (\sigma_t)_{t=0}^{+\infty}$ defined in part (a) together with player 2's corresponding best response forms a closed-loop Nash equilibrium. Which of these Nash equilibria is an open-loop Nash equilibrium? Which one is Markov-perfect?

EXERCISE 7.6 Reconsider the model from exercise 7.5, but this time assume that player 1 is the leader and that player 2 is the follower. Assume furthermore that the initial state is given by $x_0 = 0$.

(a) Assume that player 1 chooses the strategy $\sigma_t(x) = \gamma x^2$. Prove that for all sufficiently large values of γ, there does not exist a best response of player 2.

(b) Suppose that player 1 uses the strategy $\sigma_t(x) = z_t + \gamma x$, where γ is a real number and where $(z_t)_{t=0}^{+\infty}$ is a sequence of real numbers. Assuming that player 2 chooses the best response to this strategy, express player 1's objective functional in terms of γ and $(z_t)_{t=0}^{+\infty}$. Show that there does not exist an optimal strategy for player 1 of the postulated form. [Hint: Evaluate the objective functional of player 1 in the case where $z_0 = 0$ and $z_t = -\beta\gamma^2$ holds for all $t \geq 1$. Then try to find an optimal value for γ.]

EXERCISE 7.7 Consider the model from exercise 7.5 once more, but this time assume that player 2 is the leader and that player 1 is the follower. Assume that the initial state x_0 is an arbitrary real number.

(a) Assume that player 2 uses an arbitrary closed-loop strategy. Convince yourself that the state trajectory is exogenous to player 1's optimization problem and that player 1's best response must imply that $u_t = x_t$ holds for all $t \in \mathbb{N}_0$.

(b) Compute the unique open-loop Stackelberg equilibrium of this game and show that it is dynamically consistent.

(c) Prove that there exists a closed-loop Stackelberg equilibrium of this game.

EXERCISE 7.8 Consider the model from example 7.9, but assume that the two players move simultaneously. Prove that there exists a unique closed-loop Nash equilibrium and that $e_t = \tau_t = 0$ holds in this equilibrium for all $t \in \mathbb{N}_0$.

7.6 COMMENTS AND REFERENCES

Dynamic games are popular in several fields in economics, most notably in environmental and resource economics and in industrial organization. An excellent reference book for applications of dynamic game theory in economics is Van Long [92], another one that presents dynamic games in continuous-time formulation is Dockner *et al.* [28]. Not primarily written for economists but nevertheless very useful is the text book by Başar and Olsder [10], which stresses especially the different informational assumptions in dynamic games.

The sticky-price duopoly model discussed in examples 7.1, 7.2, and 7.8 was developed by Fershtman and Kamien [32]. The observation that games in which players use closed-loop strategies typically have a continuum of simultaneous-move Nash equilibria (informational non-uniqueness) was first made by Başar [9]. Theorem 7.1 is a special case of a much more general result that can be found in Başar and Olsder [10]. Example 7.6 is based on Levhari and Mirman [59]. A generalization of this example can be found in Mitra and Sorger [68].

The observation that open-loop Stackelberg equilibria are often dynamically inconsistent has been made by many authors. Xie [97] pointed out that the occurrence of dynamic inconsistency depends on whether or not the Lagrange multiplier (or the control variable) of the follower forms a pre-determined variable in the leader's optimization problem. The technical and conceptual difficulties regarding Stackelberg equilibria with closed-loop strategies have already been mentioned by Başar and Olsder [10] and Dockner *et al.* [28]; see also Shimomura and Xie [83] or Van Long and Sorger [93].

8 Dynamic competitive equilibrium

In the previous chapter, we have analyzed models in which several decision makers interact strategically. They solve interconnected dynamic optimization problems and the strategic nature of the interaction arises because of the assumption that each decision maker (player) is aware of and takes into account the influence of his or her own strategy choice on the decision problems of the other agents. The present chapter deals with interconnected dynamic optimization problems as well, but now we assume that there is no strategic interaction. Every agent's optimization problem depends on an aggregate system variable, which itself is influenced by the actions of all agents together. Nevertheless, every agent takes the dynamic evolution of the aggregate system variable as given: we say that the agents act competitively. These assumptions are usually justified by the fact that there exists a very large number of decision makers (often infinitely many of them), all of which are 'small' relative to the size of the entire economy. In such a situation, every individual decision maker can safely neglect his or her own influence on the aggregate system and on the other decision makers' optimization problems.

In the first two sections of this chapter, we present two different definitions of dynamic competitive equilibrium. In section 8.1, the decision makers take the trajectory of the aggregate system variable as given, whereas in section 8.2 they take the law of motion of this variable as given. In sections 8.3 and 8.4, we assume that in addition to the many competitively behaving agents there exists an additional 'big' player (typically a policy maker) who is aware of his or her influence on the evolution of the aggregate system and who can also affect the decision problems of the competitive agents. This player is assumed to act like a Stackelberg leader, that is, he or she chooses a strategy before the competitive agents do so. We distinguish between the case where there exists a commitment technology for the policy maker (section 8.3) and the case of discretionary policy where no such device is available (section 8.4).

8.1 The sequence formulation

In what follows, we describe a general framework in which we can define the concept of dynamic competitive equilibrium. We continue to denote the set of decision makers (or agents) by $\mathbf{M}$ but we do not restrict this set to be finite. Indeed, in many applications it is assumed that the set $\mathbf{M}$ is a continuum (for example, the unit interval $[0, 1]$). Let $(x_t^i)_{t=0}^{+\infty}$ be a sequence of system variables under the control of agent $i \in \mathbf{M}$. We assume that $x_t^i \in X^i$ holds for all $i \in \mathbf{M}$, where X^i is called agent i's system domain. Furthermore, we denote by $\mathbf{x}_t = (x_t^i \mid i \in \mathbf{M})$ the profile of the system variables of all agents at time t, and by $\mathbf{X} = \prod_{i \in \mathbf{M}} X^i$ the set of all possible profiles.

In addition to the *individual* system variables x_t^i, there exists also an *aggregate* system variable $z_t \in Z$, where Z is the aggregate system domain of the model. Formally, the aggregate system variable at time t, z_t, is simply the value of a given mapping $\mathbf{A} : \mathbf{X} \times \mathbb{N}_0 \mapsto Z$ applied to the profile of individual system variables at time t, that is,

$$z_t = \mathbf{A}(\mathbf{x}_t, t). \tag{8.1}$$

We shall refer to equation (8.1) as the *aggregation condition*. In many applications, z_t is some average or index of the individual system variables. Another frequently occurring example is that z_t is a vector of market prices that result from the actions x_t^i chosen by the individual market participants $i \in \mathbf{M}$.

Agent $i \in \mathbf{M}$ chooses the sequence $(x_t^i)_{t=0}^{+\infty}$ so as to maximize

$$\sum_{t=0}^{+\infty} U^i\left(x_t^i, x_{t+1}^i, z_t, t\right) \tag{8.2}$$

subject to the constraints

$$x_{t+1}^i \in G^i\left(x_t^i, z_t, t\right) \tag{8.3}$$

for all $t \in \mathbb{N}_0$. Here, $U^i : X^i \times X^i \times Z \times \mathbb{N}_0 \mapsto \mathbb{R}$ is agent i's utility function and $G^i(x^i, z, t) \subseteq X^i$ is a non-empty transition possibility set for all $(x^i, z, t) \in X^i \times Z \times \mathbb{N}_0$. Depending on whether the individual system variable x_t^i is pre-determined or not the optimization problem of agent i can also include an initial condition for x_t^i.

Note that agent i's optimization problem does not directly depend on the system variables of the other agents, but only indirectly so via the sequence of aggregate system variables $(z_t)_{t=0}^{+\infty}$. The latter variables are jointly determined by all agents' actions as captured by the aggregation condition (8.1). The crucial assumption which distinguishes the competitive model from the dynamic games discussed in the previous chapter is that the agents in the competitive model take the aggregate system variables as given and do not realize that the latter depend on their own actions. Consequently, they also do not realize that their own actions can influence their competitors' decision problems. We refer to the agents in this model as *competitive agents*.

A *dynamic competitive equilibrium* in *sequence formulation* for the above model is a family of trajectories of individual system variables $\{(x_t^i)_{t=0}^{+\infty} \mid i \in \mathbf{M}\}$ together with a trajectory of aggregate system variables $(z_t)_{t=0}^{+\infty}$ such that: (i) given $i \in \mathbf{M}$ and $(z_t)_{t=0}^{+\infty}$, the trajectory $(x_t^i)_{t=0}^{+\infty}$ solves agent i's optimization problem defined by (8.2)–(8.3) and (ii) condition (8.1) holds for all $t \in \mathbb{N}_0$.

Because in a dynamic competitive equilibrium all agents solve standard dynamic optimization problems, we can apply the methods discussed in chapter 5. Suppose, for example, that the assumptions of theorem 5.1 are satisfied for all individual optimization problems and that the solutions of these problems are interior ones. Then it follows for all $i \in \mathbf{M}$ and for all $t \in \mathbb{N}_0$ that the Euler equation

$$U_2^i\left(x_t^i, x_{t+1}^i, z_t, t\right) + U_1^i\left(x_{t+1}^i, x_{t+2}^i, z_{t+1}, t+1\right) = 0$$

holds. We can eliminate the aggregate system variables from these equations using the aggregation condition (8.1). This results in a system of implicit second-order difference equations, one for each competitive agent $i \in \mathbf{M}$. These equations together with the corresponding initial conditions and transversality conditions can be used to characterize the equilibrium. In models with many different agents, however, this is a challenging problem, because there exist as many equations as there are agents. Analytical solutions are typically only possible under special circumstances (for example, if the model has a linear-quadratic structure) or under additional simplifying assumptions like homogeneity. By the latter property, we mean that the utility functions and the initial conditions of the individual optimization problems are identical and that the aggregation operator $\mathbf{A}$ treats all agents symmetrically. In a model with homogeneous agents, it is often possible to characterize a *symmetric* dynamic competitive equilibrium, that is, an equilibrium for which $x_t^i = x_t^j$ holds for all $(i, j) \in \mathbf{M}^2$ and all t.[1] We illustrate these possibilities by the following two examples.

Example 8.1 Suppose that there exists a large number n of identical firms which produce a homogeneous good and sell it on a competitive market. The output level of firm i at time $t \geq 1$ is denoted by x_t^i and the market price for the good at time t is denoted by p_t. Market demand is described by a piecewise linear (inverse) demand function of the form $p_t = \max\{0, a - bq_t\}$, where a and b are positive parameters and where $q_t = \sum_{i=1}^{n} x_t^i$ is the aggregate supply by all firms. The firms act as price takers,

---

[1] Note, however, that the assumption of homogeneity does not rule out the existence of asymmetric competitive equilibria.

that is, they take the sequence $(p_t)_{t=1}^{+\infty}$ as given. Firm i seeks to choose a production plan $(x_t^i)_{t=1}^{+\infty}$ that maximizes

$$\sum_{t=0}^{+\infty}(\beta^i)^t\big[(p_{t+1}-\gamma^i)x_{t+1}^i-(\alpha^i/2)(x_{t+1}^i-x_t^i)^2\big], \tag{8.4}$$

where $\alpha^i>0$ is a parameter measuring the cost of adjusting the rate of output, $\beta^i\in(0,1)$ is the time-preference factor, and $\gamma^i\in(0,a)$ is the unit cost of production. There do not exist any capacity constraints for the firms, that is, every production level $x_t^i\geq 0$ is feasible. Furthermore, we assume that an initial value $x_0^i>0$ is given for every firm i.

In this example, the set of agents is $\mathbf{M}=\{1,2,\ldots,n\}$, the individual system variables are x_t^i, and the aggregate system variable is the market price p_t. In what follows, we neglect the non-negativity constraints on production levels and market prices, that is, we assume that $x_t^i\in\mathbb{R}$ and $p_t\in\mathbb{R}$.[2] Thus, individual and aggregate system variables are connected via the relation

$$p_t=a-b\sum_{i=1}^{n}x_t^i, \tag{8.5}$$

which serves as the aggregation condition. A competitive equilibrium is a family of production plans $\{(x_t^i)_{t=1}^{+\infty}\mid i\in\mathbf{M}\}$ together with a price sequence $(p_t)_{t=1}^{+\infty}$ such that for all $i\in\mathbf{M}$ and given $(p_t)_{t=1}^{+\infty}$ and x_0^i the sequence $(x_t^i)_{t=1}^{+\infty}$ maximizes the objective functional in (8.4) and such that condition (8.5) holds for all $t\geq 1$.

The Euler equation for firm i's dynamic optimization problem is given by

$$p_{t+1}-\gamma^i-\alpha^i\big(x_{t+1}^i-x_t^i\big)+\alpha^i\beta^i\big(x_{t+2}^i-x_{t+1}^i\big)=0.$$

Substituting from equation (8.5), we obtain the following system of n second-order linear difference equations for the variables $(x_t^i)_{t=0}^{+\infty}$, $i\in\mathbf{M}$

$$a-b\sum_{j=1}^{n}x_{t+1}^j-\gamma^i-\alpha^i\big(x_{t+1}^i-x_t^i\big)+\alpha^i\beta^i\big(x_{t+2}^i-x_{t+1}^i\big)=0.$$

There are n initial values x_0^i as well as n transversality conditions. Since the system is linear, which is a consequence of the linear-quadratic structure of the model, it is in principle analytically solvable. For large values of n, however, it is probably more helpful to apply numerical solution methods for linear difference equations.

In order to obtain some qualitative insights, we impose homogeneity and seek to characterize a symmetric solution to the equilibrium conditions. Let us therefore

---

[2] It will be shown that these non-negativity constraints hold automatically in equilibrium.

assume that the agents face identical decision problems, that is, that there exist param-
eters α, β, γ, and x_0 such that $\alpha^i = \alpha$, $\beta^i = \beta$, $\gamma^i = \gamma$, and $x_0^i = x_0$ hold for all
$i \in \mathbf{M}$. In a symmetric competitive equilibrium, the firms would produce the same
amounts, that is, $x_t^i = x_t$ for all $i \in \mathbf{M}$, and the demand function (8.5) would reduce to
$p_t = a - bnx_t$. Taking all of this into account, the Euler equation boils down to

$$a - bnx_{t+1} - \gamma - \alpha(x_{t+1} - x_t) + \alpha\beta(x_{t+2} - x_{t+1}) = 0,$$

which can be converted into the first-order difference equation

$$\begin{pmatrix} x_{t+2} \\ x_{t+1} \end{pmatrix} = A \begin{pmatrix} x_{t+1} \\ x_t \end{pmatrix} - \begin{pmatrix} (a - \gamma)/(\alpha\beta) \\ 0 \end{pmatrix}, \tag{8.6}$$

where the system matrix is given by

$$A = \begin{pmatrix} 1 + 1/\beta + bn/(\alpha\beta) & -1/\beta \\ 1 & 0 \end{pmatrix}.$$

Because of $\beta \in (0, 1)$, it follows that the trace $T = 1 + 1/\beta + bn/(\alpha\beta)$ and the determinant $D = 1/\beta$ satisfy $T > 2$ and $0 < D < T - 1$. Using the results from section 2.3, we can therefore see that the eigenvalues of A satisfy $0 < \lambda_1 < 1 < \lambda_2$.
Moreover, because the determinant is the product of the two eigenvalues, it follows
that $\lambda_2 > 1/\beta$. The general solution to the difference equation (8.6) is given by

$$x_t = \frac{a - \gamma}{bn} + c_1\lambda_1^t + c_2\lambda_2^t,$$

where c_1 and c_2 are undetermined coefficients. Since the optimization problem has
a linear-quadratic structure, we can use theorem 5.4 to show that every trajectory of
(8.6) which emanates from the given initial value x_0 and which satisfies the condition
$\lim_{t\to+\infty} \beta^t x_{t+1}^2 = 0$ qualifies as a solution to the firms' optimization problem. Because
$\lambda_2 > 1/\beta$, the latter condition can only hold if the coefficient c_2 is equal to 0. Hence,
by choosing $c_2 = 0$ and $c_1 = x_0 - (a - \gamma)/(bn)$, we see that a symmetric dynamic
competitive equilibrium is given by

$$x_t^i = x_t = \left[x_0 - \frac{a - \gamma}{bn} \right]\lambda_1^t + \frac{a - \gamma}{bn}$$

for all $i \in \mathbf{M}$ and all $t \in \mathbb{N}_0$, where λ_1 is the unique stable eigenvalue of the system
matrix A in (8.6). Note that this equilibrium satisfies the (hitherto neglected) non-
negativity constraints on prices and production levels because $a > \gamma$ and $x_0 > 0$ have
been assumed. It follows from the above formula that as t approaches infinity the
common output quantity x_t of all firms converges to $(a - \gamma)/(bn)$ and the market
price p_t converges to γ. Thus, in the long run, the market price approaches marginal
cost.

In the above example, we have assumed that the market demand function is exogenously given. Hence, the model describes a *partial equilibrium* framework. The following example, on the other hand, is a *general equilibrium* model. Furthermore, it does not have a linear-quadratic structure.

Example 8.2 Consider an economy populated by a unit interval $\mathbf{M} = [0, 1]$ of identical and infinitely lived households. These households jointly own a unit interval of identical firms. All firms operate in a single production sector and transform capital and labour into output using the production technology

$$Y_t^j = F\left(K_t^j, L_t^j\right),$$

where $K_t^j \geq 0$, $L_t^j \geq 0$, and $Y_t^j \geq 0$ denote capital input, labour input, and output, respectively, of firm j in period t. The function $F : \mathbb{R}_+^2 \mapsto \mathbb{R}_+$ is assumed to be a standard neoclassical production function, that is, F is smooth, non-decreasing, concave, and linear homogeneous. The firms in period t rent the factor services from the households at the prices r_t (rental rate of capital) and w_t (wage rate). All prices are stated in terms of current output such that the profit of firm j in period t is given by $F(K_t^j, L_t^j) - r_t K_t^j - w_t L_t^j$. Profit maximization implies that the factor prices satisfy the relations

$$r_t = F_1\left(K_t^j, L_t^j\right) \quad \text{and} \quad w_t = F_2\left(K_t^j, L_t^j\right) \tag{8.7}$$

for all firms j and all periods $t \in \mathbb{N}_0$. Note that these conditions together with the linear homogeneity of the production function imply that profits are equal to 0 in every period. Because the firms are identical and because there exists a unit interval of such firms, we can drop the firm superscript j from the above equations and interpret K_t, L_t, and Y_t as the aggregate capital input, labour input, and output, respectively. Output can be used either for consumption or for investment.

Household $i \in \mathbf{M}$ is endowed with an initial capital stock $k_0^i > 0$ and with one unit of labour per period. The preferences of this household are described by the utility functional

$$\sum_{t=0}^{+\infty} \beta^t u^i\left(c_t^i\right),$$

where $c_t^i \geq 0$ denotes consumption in period t, $\beta \in (0, 1)$ is the common time-preference factor of all households, and $u^i : \mathbb{R}_+ \mapsto \mathbb{R}$ is a smooth, strictly increasing, and strictly concave utility function. The household seeks to maximize its utility functional. The wealth of household $i \in \mathbf{M}$ evolves according to the flow budget constraint

$$k_{t+1}^i = (1 - \delta + r_t)k_t^i + w_t \ell_t^i - c_t^i, \tag{8.8}$$

where ℓ_t^i is the household's labour supply in period t, k_t^i its capital holdings in period t, and $\delta \in [0, 1]$ denotes the rate of capital depreciation. Finally, the household faces a *no-Ponzi game condition* of the form

$$\lim_{T \to +\infty} D_T k_{T+1}^i \geq 0,$$

where $D_t = \prod_{s=0}^{t}(1 - \delta + r_s)^{-1}$ is the discount factor for period t. Note that, given the wealth accumulation equation (8.8), the no-Ponzi game condition is equivalent to the single intertemporal budget constraint

$$\sum_{t=0}^{+\infty} D_t c_t^i \leq k_0^i + \sum_{t=0}^{+\infty} D_t w_t \ell_t^i,$$

which says that the present value of consumption expenditures must not exceed the initial endowment with capital plus the present value of lifetime labour income. This can be seen from

$$\sum_{t=0}^{+\infty} D_t \left(c_t^i - w_t \ell_t^i \right) = \lim_{T \to +\infty} \sum_{t=0}^{T} D_t \left(c_t^i - w_t \ell_t^i \right)$$

$$= \lim_{T \to +\infty} \sum_{t=0}^{T} D_t \left[(1 - \delta + r_t) k_t^i - k_{t+1}^i \right]$$

$$= k_0^i + \lim_{T \to +\infty} \left[\sum_{t=1}^{T} D_{t-1} k_t^i - \sum_{t=0}^{T} D_t k_{t+1}^i \right]$$

$$= k_0^i - \lim_{T \to +\infty} D_T k_{T+1}^i,$$

where we have used the flow budget constraint (8.8) in the second line and the definition of the discount factor D_t in the third line.

There are three markets in the economy on which output, capital, and labour are traded. Both firms and households act as price takers on these markets. Because the households do not derive utility from leisure, they supply their entire labour endowment to the firms, that is, $\ell_t^i = 1$ for all $t \in \mathbb{N}_0$ and all $i \in \mathbf{M}$. Substituting the resulting equation $L_t = 1$ as well as $K_t^j = K_t$ for all $t \in \mathbb{N}_0$ into condition (8.7) and defining the functions $f : \mathbb{R}_+ \mapsto \mathbb{R}_+$, $R : \mathbb{R}_+ \mapsto \mathbb{R}_+$, and $W : \mathbb{R}_+ \mapsto \mathbb{R}_+$ by $f(K) = F(K, 1)$, $R(K) = f'(K)$, and $W(K) = f(K) - Kf'(K)$, respectively, it follows that $r_t = R(K_t)$ and $w_t = W(K_t)$ hold for all $t \in \mathbb{N}_0$. We can therefore rewrite the households' dynamic optimization problem as follows:

$$\text{maximize} \quad \sum_{t=0}^{+\infty} \beta^t u^i \left(c_t^i \right) \tag{8.9}$$

subject to the constraints

$$k_{t+1}^i = [1 - \delta + R(K_t)]k_t^i + W(K_t) - c_t^i \tag{8.10}$$

and

$$\lim_{T \to +\infty} D_T k_{T+1}^i \geq 0. \tag{8.11}$$

Household $i \in \mathbf{M}$ chooses sequences of consumption $(c_t^i)_{t=0}^{+\infty}$ and wealth (that is, capital holdings) $(k_t^i)_{t=1}^{+\infty}$ so as to solve this optimization problem. The initial wealth k_0^i is given.

Capital market clearing requires that the households' capital supply coincides with the firms' capital demand, that is

$$\int_0^1 k_t^i \, di = K_t \tag{8.12}$$

for all $t \in \mathbb{N}_0$. Output market clearing, on the other hand, requires

$$f(K_t) = \int_0^1 \left[c_t^i + k_{t+1}^i - (1 - \delta)k_t^i \right] di. \tag{8.13}$$

One of the two market clearing conditions is redundant due to Walras' law; indeed, it follows easily from (8.10) that the two conditions (8.12) and (8.13) are equivalent.

In the present example, the set of competitive agents $\mathbf{M}$ is the unit interval of households. The individual system variables are the consumption rates c_t^i and the capital holdings k_t^i. The aggregate system variable is the aggregate capital stock K_t, which is related to the individual system variables via the capital market clearing condition (8.12). A competitive equilibrium in sequence formulation is a family of sequences $((c_t^i)_{t=0}^{+\infty}, (k_t^i)_{t=1}^{+\infty}, (K_t)_{t=0}^{+\infty} \mid i \in \mathbf{M})$ such that (i) for all $i \in \mathbf{M}$, and given k_0^i and $(K_t)_{t=0}^{+\infty}$, the sequences $(c_t^i)_{t=0}^{+\infty}$ and $(k_t^i)_{t=1}^{+\infty}$ solve the dynamic optimization problem (8.9)–(8.11) and (ii) the capital market clearing condition (8.12) holds for all $t \in \mathbb{N}_0$.

To solve the households' dynamic optimization problem, we use the Lagrangian approach. The Lagrangian function is given by

$$L = \sum_{t=0}^{+\infty} \beta^t \left\{ u^i(c_t^i) + \lambda_t^i \left[(1 - \delta)k_t^i + R(K_t)k_t^i + W(K_t) - c_t^i - k_{t+1}^i \right] \right\},$$

where λ_t^i is the Lagrange multiplier for household i in period t. The first-order conditions for c_t^i and k_{t+1}^i are $(u^i)'(c_t^i) = \lambda_t^i$ and $\lambda_t^i = \beta[1 - \delta + R(K_{t+1})]\lambda_{t+1}^i$. Eliminating the Lagrange multipliers from these two equations, we obtain the Euler equation

$$(u^i)'(c_t^i) = \beta[1 - \delta + R(K_{t+1})](u^i)'(c_{t+1}^i). \tag{8.14}$$

The transversality condition can be shown to be equivalent to the no-Ponzi game condition (8.11) holding with equality.

The conditions determining a dynamic competitive equilibrium are therefore the aggregation condition (8.12) as well as for all $i \in \mathbf{M}$ the difference equations (8.10) and (8.14), the initial value k_0^i, and the no-Ponzi game condition (8.11) with equality.

To conclude the discussion of this example, let us briefly comment on the case of homogeneous households. In this case, we have $c_t^i = c_t$ and $k_t^i = K_t$ for all $i \in \mathbf{M}$ and equations (8.10) and (8.14) simplify to

$$K_{t+1} = (1 - \delta)K_t + f(K_t) - c_t$$

and

$$u'(c_t) = \beta[1 - \delta + f'(K_{t+1})]u'(c_{t+1}).$$

Note that these are exactly the same conditions that we obtained in our discussion of the optimal growth model in example 5.8. Hence, we can conclude that the dynamic competitive equilibrium of the present model coincides with the solution to the corresponding optimal growth problem. It follows that the competitive equilibrium is Pareto efficient.

8.2 The recursive formulation

In the present section, we introduce an alternative definition of dynamic competitive equilibrium, called the recursive formulation, which is often used in the literature. The main difference between the sequence formulation and the recursive formulation is that the perfect foresight assumption of the competitive agents is captured in a different way. Under certain circumstances, the recursive formulation allows for a more compact and, hence, simpler statement of the equilibrium conditions. On the other hand, the range of models for which the recursive formulation can be applied is more restricted than that for which the sequence formulation can be used.

We continue to use the framework from the previous section. Recall that agent $i \in \mathbf{M}$ wants to find a sequence $(x_t^i)_{t=0}^{+\infty}$ so as to maximize the objective functional (8.2) subject to the constraint (8.3) and that the aggregate system variable z_t is related to the individual system variables by the aggregation condition (8.1). Recall also that the agents are not aware of the aggregation condition, but that they consider the aggregate system variables as exogenous to their own decision problem. To simplify the presentation, we assume in the present section that all components of the individual system variables x_t^i are pre-determined. In this case, it follows from the aggregation condition (8.1) that the aggregate system variable is also pre-determined.

In the sequence formulation of dynamic competitive equilibrium, we have assumed that the agents take the sequence $(z_t)_{t=0}^{+\infty}$ of aggregate system variables as given. In the recursive formulation, on the other hand, we assume that the agents take as given a law of motion according to which the aggregate state variable evolves. We refer to this law as the *perceived law of motion* and assume that it takes the form of the first-order difference equation

$$z_{t+1} = \psi(z_t, t). \tag{8.15}$$

To summarize, the agents in the model consider the initial value $z_0 \in Z$, the function $\psi : Z \times \mathbb{N}_0 \mapsto Z$, and equation (8.15) as exogenously given and, hence, as independent of their own decisions. Under these assumptions they maximize the objective functional (8.2) subject to the constraint (8.3) as well as the given initial conditions.

The assumption that the dynamics of the aggregate state variable can be described by a law of motion of the form (8.15) is of course not innocuous. It has no counterpart in the sequence formulation of competitive dynamic equilibrium. As we shall argue below, there are many applications in which a law of motion of the form (8.15) simply does not exist, such that agents' who base their choices on the existence of such a law cannot be rational. The recursive formulation of a dynamic competitive equilibrium is therefore not as generally applicable as the sequence formulation discussed in the previous section.

Because both the individual and the aggregate system variables are pre-determined, the agents can condition their own behaviour on both of these variables. At the beginning of period $s \in \mathbb{N}_0$, agent $i \in \mathbf{M}$ observes x_s^i and z_s and determines optimally next period's individual state x_{s+1}^i. Note that in line with the assumptions of competitive equilibrium, there is no strategic interaction between the agents, that is, agent i makes his or her choice of x_{s+1}^i independently of his or her opponents' individual states x_s^j for $j \neq i$. To formalize the above idea, we assume that agent i chooses the optimal (individual) successor state x_{s+1}^i according to an optimal policy function $h_\psi^i : X^i \times Z \times \mathbb{N}_0 \mapsto X^i$, that is

$$x_{s+1}^i = h_\psi^i\left(x_s^i, z_s, s\right) \tag{8.16}$$

holds for all $s \in \mathbb{N}_0$. Because the agents believe that the aggregate system dynamics are governed by the function ψ in (8.15), their optimal policy functions h_ψ^i will typically depend on ψ as indicated by the notation.

To capture perfect foresight, we require that the *actual law of motion* of the system, that is, the aggregate dynamics that result from the optimal behaviour of the individual agents as described by (8.16) coincide with the perceived law of motion in (8.15). To be able to formally state this condition, we define the mapping $\mathbf{h}_\psi : \mathbf{X} \times Z \times \mathbb{N}_0 \mapsto \mathbf{X}$

by

$$\mathbf{y} = \mathbf{h}_\psi(\mathbf{x}, z, t),$$

where $\mathbf{y} = (y^i \mid i \in \mathbf{M})$ and $y^i = h_\psi^i(x^i, z, t)$. In words, $\mathbf{h}_\psi(\mathbf{x}, z, t)$ is the profile of individual system variables in period $t + 1$ that results from the optimal behaviour of all agents if the profile in period t is $\mathbf{x}$, the aggregate state in period t is z, and all agents believe that the aggregate state evolves according to the perceived law of motion ψ.

We are now ready to state the *recursive formulation* of a dynamic competitive equilibrium. Such an equilibrium consists of a perceived law of motion $\psi : Z \times \mathbb{N}_0 \mapsto Z$ and a family of functions $h_\psi^i : X^i \times Z \times \mathbb{N}_0 \mapsto X^i$ for all $i \in \mathbf{M}$ such that (i) for all $i \in \mathbf{M}$ and given ψ, the function h_ψ^i is the optimal policy function of agent i's dynamic optimization problem (8.2)–(8.3) and (8.15) and (ii) the actual law of motion coincides with the perceived law of motion, that is, the condition

$$\psi(z, t) = \mathbf{A}(\mathbf{h}_\psi(\mathbf{x}, z, t), t) \qquad (8.17)$$

holds for all $z \in Z$, all $t \in \mathbb{N}_0$, and all profiles $\mathbf{x} \in \mathbf{X}$ that satisfy $z = \mathbf{A}(\mathbf{x}, t)$.

The very last condition in this definition, namely that equation (8.17) has to hold for all $\mathbf{x} \in \mathbf{X}$ satisfying $z = \mathbf{A}(\mathbf{x}, t)$, is the reason for the more restricted applicability of the recursive formulation of dynamic competitive equilibrium as compared to the sequence formulation. In many applications, it is not the case that the right-hand side of equation (8.17), conditional on $z = \mathbf{A}(\mathbf{x}, t)$, is independent of the profile $\mathbf{x}$. For example, if the aggregation operator $\mathbf{A}$ forms the average of all individual states x^i, $i \in \mathbf{M}$, then condition (8.17) essentially requires that the average of the values $h_\psi^i(x^i, z, s)$ depends only on z, on s, and on the average of the individual states x^i, but not on any other characteristics of the profile $(x^i \mid i \in \mathbf{M})$. This property is unlikely to hold unless the functions h_ψ^i, $i \in \mathbf{M}$, have very special forms.[3] On the other hand, the recursive formulation of dynamic competitive equilibrium is usually applicable when the agents are homogeneous and when we are interested in a symmetric equilibrium. In this case, the condition $z = \mathbf{A}(\mathbf{x}, t)$ can often be inverted such that for given z and t there exists only a single profile $\mathbf{x}$ for which condition (8.17) has to be verified.

Before we illustrate the recursive formulation of a dynamic competitive equilibrium, we need to discuss how we can obtain the individual optimal policy functions h_ψ^i. This is most easily accomplished by solving the individual dynamic optimization problems of the competitive agents via the recursive approach. The Bellman equations, however, must take into account both the dynamics of the individual system variables and those

---

[3] For example, if $X^i \subseteq \mathbb{R}^m$ holds for all $i \in \mathbf{M}$, then the said property holds if for all $i \in \mathbf{M}$ the policy function h_ψ^i is an affine linear function of x^i for which $\partial h_\psi^i(x^i, z, s)/(\partial x^i)$ is independent of i. In both of the two examples presented below, this is indeed the case. For nonlinear policy functions, however, the said property typically does not hold.

of the aggregate ones. To explain how this works, let us denote by $V_\psi^i(x^i, z, s)$ the optimal value that the agent can obtain from period $s \in \mathbb{N}_0$ onwards if the individual system variable at time s is given by $x^i \in X^i$, the aggregate one by $z \in Z$, and if the aggregate state evolves according to (8.15). Using this notation and noting that the aggregate system is perceived to evolve according to (8.15), the Bellman equation for agent i's optimization problem can be written as

$$V_\psi^i(x^i, z, s) = \sup\{U^i(x^i, y^i, z, s) + V_\psi^i(y^i, \psi(z, s), s+1) \mid y^i \in G^i(x^i, z, s)\}.$$

If for all $x^i \in X^i$, all $z \in Z$, and all $s \in \mathbb{N}_0$, the term on the right-hand side of this equation is maximized at a unique value y^i, then this defines the individual optimal policy function, that is, $y^i = h_\psi^i(x^i, z, s)$.

In the rest of this section, we reconsider the two examples from section 8.1 in order to see how they can be dealt with by using the recursive formulation of dynamic competitive equilibrium.

Example 8.3 Consider the adjustment cost model from example 8.1. The product price p_t is the aggregate state variable, which is related to the individual production levels x_t^i, $i \in \mathbf{M} = \{1, 2, \ldots, n\}$, via the inverse demand function (8.5). Because of the stationary and linear-quadratic structure of the model, we conjecture that the dynamics of the aggregate state are described by an autonomous linear difference equation. Hence, we postulate $\psi(p) = \psi_0 + \psi_1 p$, where ψ_0 and ψ_1 are undetermined real coefficients. The current value Bellman equation for firm i under the perceived law of motion is

$$V_\psi^i(x^i, p) - \sup\{[\psi(p) - \gamma^i]y^i - (\alpha^i/2)(y^i - x^i)^2 + \beta^i V_\psi^i(y^i, \psi(p)) \mid y^i \in \mathbb{R}\}.$$

The first-order condition for the maximization problem on the right-hand side of this equation is

$$\psi(p) - \gamma^i - \alpha^i(y^i - x^i) + \beta^i \frac{\partial}{\partial y^i} V_\psi^i(y^i, \psi(p)) = 0.$$

We guess that the optimal value function is a quadratic polynomial, that is, $V_\psi^i(x^i, p) = v_{01}^i + v_{02}^i p + v_{03}^i p^2/2 + (v_1^i + v_2^i p)x^i + v_3^i(x^i)^2/2$. Substituting this guess into the first-order condition, we obtain

$$\psi(p) - \gamma^i - \alpha^i(y^i - x^i) + \beta^i\left[v_1^i + v_2^i\psi(p) + v_3^i y^i\right] = 0$$

and, consequently,

$$y^i = h_\psi^i(x^i, p) = \frac{\beta^i v_1^i - \gamma^i + \left(1 + \beta^i v_2^i\right)\psi(p) + \alpha^i x^i}{\alpha^i - \beta^i v_3^i}. \tag{8.18}$$

Substituting this result as well as $\psi(p) = \psi_0 + \psi_1 p$ into the right-hand side of the Bellman equation, we obtain an expression of the form $w_{01}^i + w_{02}^i p + w_{03}^i p^2/2 + (w_1^i + w_2^i p)x^i + w_3^i(x^i)^2/2$, where w_{01}^i, w_{02}^i, w_{03}^i, w_1^i, w_2^i, and w_3^i depend on v_{01}^i, v_{02}^i, v_{03}^i, v_1^i, v_2^i, v_3^i, ψ_0, and ψ_1. For example, we have

$$w_1^i = \alpha^i \left[\psi_0(1 + \beta^i v_2^i) + \beta^i v_1^i - \gamma^i \right] / (\alpha^i - \beta^i v_3^i),$$

$$w_2^i = \alpha^i \psi_1 (1 + \beta^i v_2^i) / (\alpha^i - \beta^i v_3^i),$$

$$w_3^i = \alpha^i \beta^i v_3^i / (\alpha^i - \beta^i v_3^i).$$

In order for the Bellman equation to hold, we must have $v_{0k}^i = w_{0k}^i$, and $v_k^i = w_k^i$ for $k \in \{1, 2, 3\}$ and all $i \in \mathbf{M}$. Substituting the expressions for w_1^i, w_2^i, and w_3^i from above into the equations $v_k^i = w_k^i$ for $k \in \{1, 2, 3\}$, it follows that

$$v_1^i = \frac{\psi_0 + \beta^i \gamma^i \psi_1 - \gamma^i}{(1 - \beta^i)(1 - \beta^i \psi_1)}, \quad v_2^i = \frac{\psi_1}{1 - \beta^i \psi_1}, \quad v_3^i = 0.$$

Substituting this into (8.18), we obtain the individual optimal policy functions

$$h_\psi^i(x^i, p) = \frac{\psi_0 + \beta^i \gamma^i \psi_1 - \gamma^i}{\alpha^i(1 - \beta^i)(1 - \beta^i \psi_1)} + \frac{\psi_1}{\alpha^i(1 - \beta^i \psi_1)} p + x^i.$$

Note that $h_\psi^i(x^i, p)$ is linear with respect to x^i and that the coefficient in front of x^i is independent of i. This shows that the property mentioned in footnote 3 is satisfied. Because of $x_{t+1}^i = h_\psi^i(x_t^i, p_t)$ and (8.5), it follows that the actual law of motion of the aggregate system variable is given by

$$p_{t+1} = a - b \sum_{i=1}^n h_\psi^i(x_t^i, p_t)$$

$$= a - \sum_{i=1}^n \frac{b(\psi_0 + \beta^i \gamma^i \psi_1 - \gamma^i)}{\alpha^i(1 - \beta^i)(1 - \beta^i \psi_1)} - p_t \sum_{i=1}^n \frac{b\psi_1}{\alpha^i(1 - \beta^i \psi_1)} - b \sum_{i=1}^n x_t^i$$

$$= -\sum_{i=1}^n \frac{b(\psi_0 + \beta^i \gamma^i \psi_1 - \gamma^i)}{\alpha^i(1 - \beta^i)(1 - \beta^i \psi_1)} + p_t \left[1 - \sum_{i=1}^n \frac{b\psi_1}{\alpha^i(1 - \beta^i \psi_1)} \right]$$

Obviously, the actual law of motion coincides with the perceived law of motion $p_{t+1} = \psi(p_t)$ if and only if

$$\psi_0 = -\sum_{i=1}^n \frac{b(\psi_0 + \beta^i \gamma^i \psi_1 - \gamma^i)}{\alpha^i(1 - \beta^i)(1 - \beta^i \psi_1)}$$

and

$$\psi_1 = 1 - \sum_{i=1}^n \frac{b\psi_1}{\alpha^i(1 - \beta^i \psi_1)}. \tag{8.19}$$

These are two equations for the two unknown coefficients ψ_0 and ψ_1. In general, it is not possible to solve the equations analytically (although solving them numerically does not pose a big problem), but we can still derive some qualitative properties. For example, we can show that there exists a unique value $\psi_1 \in (0, 1)$ which satisfies equation (8.19). Indeed, the left-hand side of this equation is a strictly increasing and continuous function of $\psi_1 \in \mathbb{R}$, whereas the right-hand side is strictly decreasing and continuous for $\psi_1 \in (0, 1)$. As ψ_1 moves from 0 to 1, the left-hand side of (8.19) also moves from 0 to 1, whereas the right-hand side moves from 1 to a value that is smaller than 1. These properties prove the claim that there exists a unique value $\psi_1 \in (0, 1)$ satisfying (8.19). It is also easy to see that this equation cannot hold for any non-positive ψ_1. Indeed, if ψ_1 were non-positive, the right-hand side of (8.19) would be larger than or equal to 1, whereas the left-hand side would be smaller than or equal to 0. For all remaining values $\psi_1 > 1$, the aggregate law of motion $p_{t+1} = \psi_0 + \psi_1 p_t$ is unstable so that we conclude that there can be at most one dynamic competitive equilibrium along which the price path remains bounded.

To proceed further, let us impose homogeneity, that is, we assume that there exist real constants α, β, and γ such that $\alpha^i = \alpha$, $\beta^i = \beta$, and $\gamma^i = \gamma$ hold for all $i \in \mathbf{M}$. In that case, equation (8.19) can be rewritten as

$$\psi_1^2 - \psi_1 \left(1 + \frac{1}{\beta} + \frac{bn}{\alpha\beta} \right) + \frac{1}{\beta} = 0,$$

which coincides with the characteristic equation of the matrix A from equation (8.6). We know from our discussion in example 8.1 that there exists exactly one stable solution to this equation. Taking ψ_1 as this solution and calculating the remaining coefficients ψ_0, v_k, and v_{0k}, $k \in \{1, 2, 3\}$ from the equations stated earlier, we can verify that all the conditions for a recursively formulated dynamic competitive equilibrium are satisfied and that this equilibrium generates exactly the same production quantities and prices as the equilibrium derived via the sequence formulation. It follows therefore that the two definitions of dynamic competitive equilibrium are equivalent in the sense that they give rise to the same equilibria.

The equivalence of the equilibria derived by the two alternative formulations is no coincidence. It would also hold for the model with heterogeneous agents. Whether the agents take a perceived law of motion for the aggregate system as given or the sequence of aggregate system variables themselves does not affect their decision calculus because they do not realize the effect of their own decisions on the aggregate system. So, whenever a recursive dynamic competitive equilibrium of a model exists it must coincide with a dynamic competitive equilibrium according to the sequence formulation in the sense explained above.

Example 8.4 Now we discuss the application of the recursive formulation of a dynamic competitive equilibrium in the general equilibrium model first encountered in example 8.2. The aggregate state variable is the aggregate capital stock K_t and the individual state variables are the capital holdings k_t^i of the households $i \in \mathbf{M} = [0, 1]$. These variables are related by the aggregation condition

$$K_t = \int_0^1 k_t^i \, di.$$

The current value Bellman equation for the dynamic optimization problem of household i is

$$V_\psi^i(k^i, K) = \sup \left\{ u^i(c^i) + \beta V_\psi^i([1 - \delta + R(K)]k^i + W(K) - c^i, \psi(K)) \mid c^i \geq 0 \right\},$$

(8.20)

where the function $\psi : \mathbb{R}_+ \mapsto \mathbb{R}_+$ describes the perceived law of motion $K_{t+1} = \psi(K_t)$. As in the previous example, we can omit the time variable from the optimal value function and from the perceived law of motion because of the stationary nature of the problem.

For a given function ψ, the above Bellman equation can be solved numerically, for example, by the value iteration method. This yields the individual optimal policy functions $h_\psi^i : \mathbb{R}_+^2 \mapsto \mathbb{R}_+$, $i \in \mathbf{M}$, describing how the agents optimally choose the individual successor states $k_{t+1}^i = h_\psi^i(k_t^i, K_t)$ if the economy is in state K_t and if the agent's own capital stock is k_t^i. Consistency of perceived and actual laws of motion requires that the relation

$$\psi(K) = \int_0^1 h_\psi^i(k^i, K) \, di$$

holds for all profiles satisfying $\int_0^1 k^i \, di = K$. If the individual policy functions h_ψ^i are non-linear with respect to the respective individual states k_t^i, then this is a very unwieldy condition and it is highly unlikely that a consistent law of motion ψ exists for which it holds. In such a situation it is simply not true that the dynamics of the aggregate system can be described by the single variable K_t via a difference equation of the form $K_{t+1} = \psi(K_t)$. Not only the aggregate or average capital stock K_t matters for the aggregate dynamics, but also the distribution of this capital among the infinitely many consumers is relevant. Suppose, on the other hand, that the functions h_ψ^i are linear with respect to the individual state k^i, say $h_\psi^i(k^i, K) = \gamma_\psi(K)k^i + \bar{h}_\psi^i(K)$, and that the coefficient $\gamma_\psi(K)$ is independent of the agent index i. Then the aggregation condition can be written as

$$\psi(K) = \gamma_\psi(K) \int_0^1 k^i \, di + \int_0^1 \bar{h}_\psi^i(K) \, di.$$

For profiles which satisfy $\int_0^1 k^i \, di = K$, this boils down to

$$\psi(K) = \gamma_\psi(K)K + \int_0^1 \bar{h}_\psi^i(K) \, di,$$

which is obviously a much simpler condition as it only involves the aggregate state variable K. We can use iterative numerical procedures to find a function ψ for which it holds.

In what follows, we illustrate how a dynamic competitive equilibrium can be found in the analytically solvable case with logarithmic utility functions $u^i(c) = \ln c$, $i \in \mathbf{M}$, Cobb–Douglas production function $F(K, L) = AK^\alpha L^{1-\alpha}$, and full capital depreciation $\delta = 1$. These assumptions imply that $R(K) = \alpha AK^{\alpha-1}$ and $W(K) = (1 - \alpha)AK^\alpha$. Furthermore, based on the results for the corresponding optimal growth problem (see example 5.8), we guess that the aggregate law of motion is given by

$$K_{t+1} = \psi(K_t) := \alpha \beta A K_t^\alpha.$$

We conjecture that the optimal value function takes the form

$$V_\psi^i(k^i, K) = v_0 + v_1 \ln K + v_2 \ln(k^i + v_3 K) \tag{8.21}$$

for all $i \in \mathbf{M}$, where v_0, v_1, v_2, and v_3 are undetermined coefficients. Using all of these functional forms, the maximand on the right-hand side of the Bellman equation (8.20) becomes

$$\ln c^i + \beta\{v_0 + v_1 \ln(\alpha\beta AK^\alpha) + v_2 \ln[\alpha AK^{\alpha-1}k^i + (1 - \alpha + \alpha\beta v_3)AK^\alpha - c^i]\}.$$

Maximization with respect to c^i yields

$$c^i = \frac{AK^{\alpha-1}[\alpha k^i + (1 - \alpha + \alpha\beta v_3)K]}{1 + \beta v_2} \tag{8.22}$$

and, hence

$$h_\psi^i(k^i, K) = \alpha AK^{\alpha-1}k^i + (1 - \alpha)AK^\alpha - c^i$$

$$= AK^{\alpha-1}\frac{\alpha\beta v_2 k^i + [(1 - \alpha)\beta v_2 - \alpha\beta v_3]K}{1 + \beta v_2}. \tag{8.23}$$

Note that this policy function is indeed linear with respect to k^i and that the coefficient in front of k^i is independent of i. Using the notation introduced above, it holds that $\gamma_\psi(K) = \alpha\beta v_2 AK^{\alpha-1}/(1 + \beta v_2)$ and $\bar{h}_\psi^i(K) = [(1 - \alpha)\beta v_2 - \alpha\beta v_3]AK^\alpha/(1 + \beta v_2)$.

If we substitute the optimal value of c^i from (8.22) into the Bellman equation (8.20), we obtain an expression that has the same functional form as the conjecture (8.21). Hence, we can set the coefficients in that expression equal to the corresponding coefficients v_i, $i \in \{0, 1, 2, 3\}$, in (8.21) and solve the resulting equations. This yields the unique solution

$$v_0 = \frac{\ln(1 - \beta)}{1 - \beta} + \frac{\alpha\beta \ln \beta}{(1 - \beta)(1 - \alpha\beta)} + \frac{\ln \alpha A}{(1 - \beta)(1 - \alpha\beta)},$$

$$v_1 = -\frac{1 - \alpha}{(1 - \beta)(1 - \alpha\beta)},$$

$$v_2 = \frac{1}{1 - \beta},$$

$$v_3 = \frac{1 - \alpha}{\alpha(1 - \beta)}.$$

Substituting these values into equation (8.23), we obtain

$$h_\psi^i(k^i, K) = \alpha\beta A K^{\alpha - 1} k^i.$$

It is now easy to verify that the consistency condition holds. Indeed, for all profiles $(k^i \mid i \in \mathbf{M})$ that satisfy $\int_0^1 k^i \, di = K$, it follows that

$$\int_0^1 h_\psi^i(k^i, K) \, di = \alpha\beta A K^{\alpha - 1} \int_0^1 k^i \, di = \alpha\beta A K^\alpha = \psi(K).$$

Finally, note that in this model an unequal initial distribution of wealth does not wash out over time. This is most easily seen from the fact that

$$\frac{k_{t+1}^i}{k_{t+1}^j} = \frac{h_\psi^i(k_t^i, K_t)}{h_\psi^j(k_t^j, K_t)} = \frac{k_t^i}{k_t^j},$$

which says that the relative wealth of any two households remains constant over time.

8.3 Optimal policy under commitment

In the previous sections, we have assumed that all agents $i \in \mathbf{M}$ in the economy act competitively in the sense that they take the aggregate system variables as given. We now add another agent who chooses a sequence of variables $(g_t)_{t=0}^{+\infty}$ and who is aware of the influence of this choice on the actions of the competitive agents $i \in \mathbf{M}$ and on the aggregate state of the economy. In applications, the additional agent is usually a policy maker and the components of the *policy variable* g_t could, for instance, be tax rates, public spending variables, or monetary policy instruments. The policy maker has access to a commitment device so that he or she can choose the entire sequence $(g_t)_{t=0}^{+\infty}$ at the outset in period 0.[4] For simplicity, we assume that there exists a fixed set

---

[4] The case where no such commitment device exists will be discussed in the following section.

$\mathbf{G} \subseteq \mathbb{R}^k$ which contains all feasible values of the policy variable, that is, it holds for all $t \in \mathbb{N}_0$ that $g_t \in \mathbf{G}$.

As has been mentioned before, the policy variables have an effect on the agents' decision problems. We therefore assume that agent $i \in \mathbf{M}$ seeks to find a sequence $(x_t^i)_{t=0}^{+\infty}$ so as to maximize

$$\sum_{t=0}^{+\infty} U^i\left(x_t^i, x_{t+1}^i, z_t, g_t, t\right) \tag{8.24}$$

subject to the constraints

$$x_{t+1}^i \in G^i\left(x_t^i, z_t, g_t, t\right) \tag{8.25}$$

for all $t \in \mathbb{N}_0$. An initial value x_0^i may also be given. The aggregate system variables $(z_t)_{t=0}^{+\infty}$ are related to the individual system variables via the aggregation condition (8.1).

The policy maker has the objective functional

$$\sum_{t=0}^{+\infty} \mathbf{U}(\mathbf{x}_t, \mathbf{x}_{t+1}, g_t, t), \tag{8.26}$$

where $\mathbf{U} : \mathbf{X}^2 \times \mathbf{G} \times \mathbb{N}_0 \mapsto \mathbb{R}$ is a given function.

In many applications, the policy maker is assumed to be a social planner who seeks to maximize aggregate welfare of the society. In that case, the function $\mathbf{U}$ is simply an aggregate of the individual utility functions U^i. For example, if the set of agents is distributed on $\mathbf{M}$ according to the measure μ, then aggregate welfare of the society could be defined by (8.26) with

$$\mathbf{U}(\mathbf{x}_t, \mathbf{x}_{t+1}, g_t, t) = \int U^i\left(x_t^i, x_{t+1}^i, \mathbf{A}(\mathbf{x}_t, t), g_t, t\right) \mathrm{d}\mu(i).$$

Note that we have used the aggregation condition (8.1) to replace the aggregate system variable z_t that appears in (8.24) by $\mathbf{A}(\mathbf{x}_t, t)$. This reflects the assumption that the policy maker is aware of the mechanism which relates individual system variables to aggregate ones.

We are interested in the so-called *Ramsey problem* of finding a sequence of policy variables $(g_t)_{t=0}^{+\infty}$ which maximizes the policy maker's objective functional subject to the constraint that the economy is in a dynamic competitive equilibrium. Formally, we say that a family of individual system variables $((x_t^i)_{t=0}^{+\infty} \mid i \in \mathbf{M})$, together with sequences of aggregate system variables $(z_t)_{t=0}^{+\infty}$ and policy variables $(g_t)_{t=0}^{+\infty}$, form a *Ramsey equilibrium* if (i) given $(g_t)_{t=0}^{+\infty}$, it holds that the family $((x_t^i)_{t=0}^{+\infty} \mid i \in \mathbf{M})$ and the sequence $(z_t)_{t=0}^{+\infty}$ form a dynamic competitive equilibrium and (ii) there is no alternative sequence $(\tilde{g}_t)_{t=0}^{+\infty}$ along with a corresponding dynamic competitive equilibrium

$((\tilde{x}_t^i)_{t=0}^{+\infty} \mid i \in \mathbf{M})$ and $(\tilde{z}_t)_{t=0}^{+\infty}$ such that the inequality

$$\sum_{t=0}^{+\infty} \mathbf{U}(\tilde{\mathbf{x}}_t, \tilde{\mathbf{x}}_{t+1}, \tilde{g}_t, t) > \sum_{t=0}^{+\infty} \mathbf{U}(\mathbf{x}_t, \mathbf{x}_{t+1}, g_t, t)$$

holds.

Ramsey problems are often solved following the *primal approach*. The basic ideas of this approach are (i) to characterize those families of individual and aggregate system variables that can form dynamic competitive equilibria by an *implementability constraint*, (ii) to eliminate the policy maker's decision variables $(g_t)_{t=0}^{+\infty}$ from his or her optimization problem, and (iii) to maximize the policy maker's objective functional over individual and aggregate system variables, and subject to the implementability constraint. Rather than explaining the primal approach in the general framework outlined above, we illustrate it by means of examples. Before doing that, however, we would also like to mention that the Ramsey problem resembles in many respects a hierarchical dynamic game in which the players use open-loop strategies. The policy maker is the leader and commits to the implementation of the policy $(g_t)_{t=0}^{+\infty}$. The competitive agents $i \in \mathbf{M}$ are the followers whose joint reaction to the leader's decision is described by a dynamic competitive equilibrium. Because the structure of the model resembles a hierarchical game with open-loop strategies, it will not come as a surprise that Ramsey equilibria have properties similar to open-loop Stackelberg equilibria. In particular, Ramsey equilibria are often dynamically inconsistent, as will be shown by means of the following examples.

The first example has no economic interpretation but is merely meant to highlight the basic structure of Ramsey problems and the key steps that are necessary to solve these problems. The functional forms are chosen in order to ease the algebra. After that, we shall present two examples from the economics literature.

Example 8.5 Consider an economy populated by a unit interval $\mathbf{M} = [0, 1]$ of identical competitive agents. The representative competitive agent has the initial state x_0 and chooses the sequence $(x_t)_{t=1}^{+\infty}$ so as to maximize the objective functional

$$\sum_{t=0}^{+\infty} \beta^t [-(x_t + x_{t+1})^2 - (x_{t+1} - g_t)^2 - (x_{t+1} - z_t)^2]/2,$$

where $\beta \in (0, 1)$ is the time-preference factor, $(g_t)_{t=0}^{+\infty}$ is the sequence of variables chosen by the policy maker, and $(z_t)_{t=0}^{+\infty}$ is the sequence of aggregate state variables. The aggregate state is simply the average of the individual states which, according to the assumption of homogeneity and symmetry, implies that the aggregation condition is

$$z_t = x_t.$$

The policy maker chooses $(g_t)_{t=0}^{+\infty}$ in order to maximize the objective functional

$$\sum_{t=0}^{+\infty} \beta^t \left[-x_{t+1}^2/2 + (4 + \beta)x_{t+1} - g_t \right].$$

There are no constraints on any of the variables, in particular, the transition possibility set for the competitive agents' problem is $G(x, z, g, t) = \mathbb{R}$ and the policy variables are chosen from $\mathbf{G} = \mathbb{R}$.

The Euler equation of the competitive agents' optimization problem is

$$-(x_t + x_{t+1}) - (x_{t+1} - g_t) - (x_{t+1} - z_t) - \beta(x_{t+1} + x_{t+2}) = 0.$$

Using the aggregation condition to eliminate z_t and solving for g_t, we obtain

$$g_t = (3 + \beta)x_{t+1} + \beta x_{t+2} \tag{8.27}$$

for all $t \geq 0$. For any given sequence of policy variables $(g_t)_{t=0}^{+\infty}$, a competitive dynamic equilibrium must satisfy the non-homogeneous linear difference equation (8.27). Since only x_0 is given but not x_1, equation (8.27) has no initial value. However, the solution has to satisfy the transversality condition. Because the eigenvalue of equation (8.27) is $-(3 + \beta)/\beta$, which is strictly smaller than $-1/\beta$ for all $\beta \in (0, 1)$, there exists a unique trajectory of (8.27) for which this is the case.[5] We can therefore use (8.27) to rewrite the objective functional of the policy maker in terms of the system variables only (primal approach). This yields

$$\sum_{t=0}^{+\infty} \beta^t \left[-x_{t+1}^2/2 + x_{t+1} - \beta x_{t+2} \right].$$

To determine the optimal policy, we have to maximize this objective functional over all sequences $(x_t)_{t=1}^{+\infty}$ with $x_t \in \mathbb{R}$ for all $t \geq 1$. This is a dynamic optimization problem in reduced form in which the system variables are not pre-determined. We know from section 6.1 that this is likely to generate a dynamically inconsistent solution. As a matter of fact, the first-order optimality condition for x_1 is $-x_1 + 1 = 0$, which implies that $x_1 = 1$. The first-order condition (Euler equation) for x_{t+2} in the case where $t \geq 1$, on the other hand, is given by $-\beta + \beta[-x_{t+2} + 1] = 0$, which yields $x_{t+2} = 0$ for all $t \geq 1$. The optimal solution is therefore given by $(x_t)_{t=0}^{+\infty} = (x_0, 1, 0, 0, \ldots)$ and, using (8.27), it can be seen that the unique sequence of policy variables that implements

---

[5] This trajectory can, for example, be calculated by the variation-of-constants formula from theorem 2.5.

this solution is $(g_t)_{t=0}^{+\infty} = (3 + \beta, 0, 0, \ldots)$. If the government follows this policy, the state in period 1 becomes $x_1 = 1$ and a re-optimization from period 1 onwards yields the optimal solution $(x_t)_{t=1}^{+\infty} = (1, 1, 0, 0, \ldots)$ with the corresponding optimal policy $(g_t)_{t=1}^{+\infty} = (3 + \beta, 0, 0, \ldots)$. This clearly demonstrates dynamic inconsistency as $g_1 = 0$ is optimal from the point of view of period 0, but $g_1 = 3 + \beta$ is optimal from the point of view of period 1.

Example 8.6 In this example, we consider a modification of the general equilibrium model discussed in example 8.2. The modification has two aspects: first, we assume that the utility of the households depends not only on consumption but also on labour and, second, we introduce a government that taxes capital and labour income in order to finance an exogenously given stream of expenditures. To simplify the presentation, we assume right from the start that all firms are identical and that all households are identical as well.

The production side of the model is exactly as in example 8.2, that is, the firms choose their factor inputs in such a way that $r_t = F_1(K_t, L_t)$ and $w_t = F_2(K_t, L_t)$ hold, where K_t and L_t denote the economy-wide inputs of capital and labour, respectively, $F : \mathbb{R}_+^2 \mapsto \mathbb{R}_+$ is the production function (assumed to satisfy standard assumptions), and r_t and w_t are the rental rate of capital and the wage rate, respectively. Output produced by the firms can be used for private consumption, private investment, or public consumption. Capital depreciates at the rate $\delta \in [0, 1]$. The aggregate resource constraint of the economy, which is equivalent to the output market clearing condition, is therefore given by

$$(1 - \delta)K_t + F(K_t, L_t) = c_t + K_{t+1} + g, \tag{8.28}$$

where c_t is private consumption in period t and where $g > 0$ denotes government consumption, which is assumed to be constant over time.

The economy is populated by a unit interval $\mathbf{M} = [0, 1]$ of identical households. The representative household is endowed with $a_0 > 0$ units of wealth at the outset of period 0 and with a single unit of labour in each period $t \in \mathbb{N}_0$. Wealth can be held as capital or in the form of government bonds. Absence of arbitrage requires that both assets yield the same after-tax real return, which will be denoted by R_t for period t. Denoting by θ_t the tax rate on interest income in period t, it follows from the above assumptions that $R_t = (1 - \theta_t)(r_t - \delta)$. The household seeks to maximize the utility functional

$$\sum_{t=0}^{+\infty} \beta^t u(c_t, \ell_t), \tag{8.29}$$

where $\beta \in (0, 1)$ is a time-preference factor and where ℓ_t is the labour supply of the household in period t. The utility function $u : \mathbb{R}_+^2 \mapsto \mathbb{R}$ is assumed to satisfy standard smoothness and convexity properties and to be strictly increasing with respect to consumption and strictly decreasing with respect to labour supply. The household has to satisfy the intertemporal budget constraint

$$\sum_{t=0}^{+\infty} \tilde{D}_t c_t \leq a_0 + \sum_{t=0}^{+\infty} \tilde{D}_t (1 - \tau_t) w_t \ell_t, \tag{8.30}$$

where τ_t denotes the labour tax rate in period t and where $\tilde{D}_t = \prod_{s=0}^{t} (1 + R_t)^{-1}$ is a discount factor that takes into account that interest income in period t is taxed at the rate θ_t. The households take the prices, the tax rates, and the initial wealth a_0 as given and maximize the utility functional from (8.29) over all sequences $(c_t, \ell_t)_{t=0}^{+\infty}$ which satisfy the constraint (8.30).[6]

The aim of the government is to finance its constant per-period expenditure g in such a way that welfare as given by (8.29) is maximized. The government's budget constraint is given by

$$\sum_{t=0}^{+\infty} \tilde{D}_t g + B_0 \leq \sum_{t=0}^{+\infty} \tilde{D}_t [\theta_t (r_t - \delta) a_t + \tau_t w_t \ell_t], \tag{8.31}$$

which says that the present value of government expenditures plus the initial government debt B_0 must not exceed the present value of all tax income. The reason why the same discount factor $\tilde{D}_t$ appears both in the households' budget constraint and in that of the government is that the after-tax interest rates on both assets must coincide due to the no-arbitrage condition mentioned above. Private agents and the government can borrow and lend on the same terms.

The market clearing condition for the output market in the present model is (8.28), the labor market clearing condition is $\ell_t = L_t$, and the capital market clearing condition is $k_t = K_t$, where k_t denotes the capital holdings of the representative household. Finally, it must hold that $a_0 = K_0 + B_0$, where K_0 is the initial endowment of the economy with physical capital. The aggregate state variable of the model is the capital stock K_t and the aggregation condition coincides with the capital market clearing condition. The choice variables of the government are the tax rates $(\theta_t)_{t=0}^{+\infty}$ and $(\tau_t)_{t=0}^{+\infty}$. Since both tax instruments are distortionary, the government's optimization problem is a non-trivial one.

We are now ready to apply the primal approach to the Ramsey problem of optimal taxation. Consider first the households' optimization problem. Denoting the Lagrange

---

[6] The budget constraint of the households could equivalently be written in the form of a flow budget constraint and a no-Ponzi game condition as demonstrated in example 8.2.

multiplier of the intertemporal budget constraint of the households by λ, the Lagrangian of this optimization problem can be written as

$$L = \sum_{t=0}^{+\infty} \{\beta^t u(c_t, \ell_t) + \lambda \tilde{D}_t[(1 - \tau_t)w_t \ell_t - c_t]\} + \lambda a_0,$$

and the first-order optimality conditions are

$$\partial L / (\partial c_t) = \beta^t u_1(c_t, \ell_t) - \lambda \tilde{D}_t = 0,$$

$$\partial L / (\partial \ell_t) = \beta^t u_2(c_t, \ell_t) + \lambda \tilde{D}_t(1 - \tau_t)w_t = 0.$$

There are several implications of these conditions that we need to point out. First, by recalling the definition of $\tilde{D}_t$ it follows that $(1 + R_{t+1})\tilde{D}_{t+1} = \tilde{D}_t$. Combining this observation with the first optimality condition stated above, it follows that

$$u_1(c_t, \ell_t) - \beta(1 + R_{t+1})u_1(c_{t+1}, \ell_{t+1}) = 0, \tag{8.32}$$

which is the Euler equation for the households' optimization problem. Second, referring again to the first optimality condition stated above, we see that

$$\tilde{D}_t = \frac{\beta^t \tilde{D}_0 u_1(c_t, \ell_t)}{u_1(c_0, \ell_0)}.$$

And, third, by combining the second optimality condition with the first one, it follows that

$$\tilde{D}_t(1 - \tau_t)w_t = -\frac{\beta^t u_2(c_t, \ell_t)\tilde{D}_0}{u_1(c_0, \ell_0)}.$$

Substituting these results as well as the condition $\tilde{D}_0 = (1 + R_0)^{-1} = [1 + (1 - \theta_0)(r_0 - \delta)]^{-1}$ and the firms' first-order condition $r_0 = F_1(k_0, \ell_0)$ into the intertemporal budget constraint (8.30) of the households, it follows after some rearrangements that

$$\sum_{t=0}^{+\infty} \beta^t [u_1(c_t, \ell_t)c_t + u_2(c_t, \ell_t)\ell_t] = \{1 + (1 - \theta_0)[F_1(k_0, \ell_0) - \delta]\}u_1(c_0, \ell_0)a_0. \tag{8.33}$$

This equation is the implementability constraint. It can be shown that competitive equilibrium allocations are completely characterized by this implementability constraint and the resource constraint (8.28). To summarize, the government seeks to maximize the welfare functional (8.29) over all allocations $(\ell_t, c_t)_{t=0}^{+\infty}$ and subject to the constraints (8.28) and (8.33) in which K_t and L_t are replaced by k_t and ℓ_t, respectively. Notice that following the primal approach we have eliminated all policy variables except for θ_0 from the government's optimization problem. For the time being, we simply assume that the tax rate θ_0 is not under the control of the government. This is equivalent to treating θ_0 as an exogenous constant. We shall later return to this issue and explain how the results would change if the government could also choose θ_0.

In order to facilitate the notation, let us define the function

$$G(c, \ell, \kappa) = u(c, \ell) + \kappa[u_1(c, \ell)c + u_2(c, \ell)\ell],$$

where κ denotes the Lagrange multiplier for the implementability constraint (8.33). Using the resource constraint (8.28) to eliminate per-capita consumption c_t, the Lagrangian function for the government's optimization problem can be expressed as a function of $(\ell_t, k_{t+1})_{t=0}^{+\infty}$ as

$$L^G = \sum_{t=0}^{+\infty} \beta^t G((1-\delta)k_t + F(k_t, \ell_t) - k_{t+1} - g, \ell_t, \kappa)$$
$$- \kappa\{1 + (1-\theta_0)[F_1(k_0, \ell_0) - \delta]\}u_1((1-\delta)k_0 + F(k_0, \ell_0) - k_1 - g, \ell_0)a_0.$$

Taking derivatives with respect to the choice variables $(k_{t+1})_{t=0}^{+\infty}$, we obtain the first-order conditions

$$-G_1(c_0, \ell_0, \kappa) + \beta G_1(c_1, \ell_1, \kappa)[1 - \delta + F_1(k_1, \ell_1)] + \kappa(1 + R_0)u_{11}(c_0, \ell_0)a_0 = 0,$$
$$(8.34)$$

and for all $t \geq 1$

$$-G_1(c_t, \ell_t, \kappa) + \beta G_1(c_{t+1}, \ell_{t+1}, \kappa)[1 - \delta + F_1(k_{t+1}, \ell_{t+1})] = 0. \qquad (8.35)$$

Suppose now that the solution to the government's optimization problem converges to a fixed point. In a fixed point, it must of course be the case that

$$\frac{G_1(c_t, \ell_t, \kappa)}{u_1(c_t, \ell_t)} = \frac{G_1(c_{t+1}, \ell_{t+1}, \kappa)}{u_1(c_{t+1}, \ell_{t+1})}. \qquad (8.36)$$

Combining this observation with (8.35), we obtain

$$-u_1(c_t, \ell_t) + \beta[1 - \delta + F_1(k_{t+1}, \ell_{t+1})]u_1(c_{t+1}, \ell_{t+1}) = 0.$$

By comparing this equation to the Euler equation (8.32), it follows that $R_{t+1} = F_1(k_{t+1}, \ell_{t+1}) - \delta$ which, according to the definition of R_{t+1}, implies that $\theta_{t+1} = 0$. We therefore see that in a fixed point the capital income tax rate must be equal to 0.

Furthermore, suppose that the utility function of the households is of the form

$$u(c, \ell) = \frac{c^{1-\sigma}}{1-\sigma} + v(\ell)$$

or

$$u(c, \ell) = \frac{(c\ell^{-\gamma})^{1-\sigma}}{1 - \sigma},$$

where σ and γ are positive parameters and where $v : [0, 1] \mapsto \mathbb{R}$ is a strictly decreasing and concave function. Note that for these forms of the utility function, equation (8.36) holds for all $t \in \mathbb{N}_0$. Appealing again to the first-order condition (8.35) and the Euler equation (8.32), we find that $\theta_{t+1} = 0$ must hold for all $t \geq 1$. Hence, for the two classes of utility functions defined above, the tax rate on interest income must be equal to 0 not only in a fixed point, but even for all $t \geq 2$. Thus, the only non-zero asset tax rate can be θ_1. This form of taxation is often referred to as front loading, by which we mean that the entire intertemporal distortion caused by non-zero interest income taxation is executed at the beginning of the infinite planning horizon and shut down completely afterwards.

Front loading also shows that the tax policy is dynamically inconsistent. To prove this, we have to demonstrate that θ_1 is indeed positive. We proceed by contradiction. Assume that $\theta_1 = 0$ and suppose that the utility function takes one of the two forms specified above such that equation (8.36) holds for all $t \in \mathbb{N}_0$. If θ_1 is equal to 0, then it follows from the Euler equation (8.32) and equation (8.36) that the first two terms in equation (8.34) cancel out. Hence, (8.34) can only hold if $\kappa(1 + R_0)u_{11}(c_0, \ell_0)a_0 = 0$. Since $1 + R_0$ and $u_{11}(c_0, \ell_0)$ cannot be equal to 0, $\theta_1 = 0$ implies that either $a_0 = 0$ or that $\kappa = 0$. The first possibility is ruled out by the assumption that households have positive initial wealth. The second one says that the implementability constraint is not binding for the government, which can only be the case if government expenditure g is equal to 0 such that there is no need to collect any taxes. To summarize, we have shown that except for uninteresting borderline cases the optimal tax rate θ_1 is positive, whereas all other optimal tax rates on interest income, θ_t for $t \geq 2$, are equal to 0. The government therefore plans in period 0 to collect positive interest income tax in period 1 and to set the tax on interest income to 0 from period 2 onwards. Given the chance to reconsider its decision at any period $t \geq 1$, it would apply front loading again and therefore set a positive interest income tax rate in period $t + 1$. This proves that the optimal tax policy is dynamically inconsistent and can only be implemented if the government can commit to it.

Finally, let us briefly comment on the assumption of fixing θ_0 exogenously. In the initial period $t = 0$, assets are inelastically supplied. A tax on the interest income corresponding to the exogenously given wealth stock a_0 is therefore not distortionary. As a consequence, the government would have an incentive to tax this income at such a high rate that it can finance all government expenditure over the entire time horizon from the taxes collected in period 0 alone. That way, the government could avoid all distortions and henceforth implement a first-best solution.

The above example from the realm of fiscal policy is a prominent application of the theory of optimal policy under commitment. Our last example has a similar flavor, but it deals with monetary policy.

Example 8.7   Consider an economy in which a single, non-storable output is produced by a unit interval of identical competitive agents. The representative agent is both a household and a firm. It has access to a linear technology that transforms labour into output at a rate of one-to-one. The household's consumption demand in period t is denoted by c_t and its labour supply by ℓ_t. The government is benevolent and must provide an exogenously given constant expenditure g per period that has no effect on the competitive agents. The aggregate resource constraint of the economy (output market clearing condition) is therefore given by

$$c_t + g = \ell_t. \tag{8.37}$$

The competitive agents derive utility $u(c_t) - \alpha\ell_t$ in period t and has the time-preference factor $\beta \in (0, 1)$. This implies that the agents' utility as well as the aggregate welfare of the society are measured by

$$\sum_{t=0}^{+\infty} \beta^t [u(c_t) - \alpha\ell_t]. \tag{8.38}$$

The first-best allocation (optimal allocation) is that allocation which maximizes the objective functional in (8.38) subject to the resource constraint (8.37). It is completely characterized by the necessary and sufficient first-order optimality condition $u'(c_t) = \alpha$ and the constraint (8.37). In what follows, we denote the unique solution to these two equations by (c^*, ℓ^*). If the government can act as an omnipotent and benevolent social planner, it will implement the first-best allocation.

Now suppose that the government cannot directly choose the allocation. Instead, it only has access to a restricted set of monetary policy instruments and is subject to a budget constraint. The competitive agents take the government's policy as well as all market prices as given and maximize their utility functional in (8.38) subject to technological constraints and budget constraints. All prices adjust such that all markets clear at all dates.

There are two assets in the economy: money (cash) and one-period nominal government bonds. A bond issued in period t promises to pay one unit of money in period $t + 1$. Let us denote by q_t the price of a bond issued in period t (this is the reciprocal value of the gross nominal interest rate on bond holdings from t to $t + 1$). Furthermore, let us denote by $\bar{M}_t$ and $\bar{B}_t$ the cash in circulation and the amount of public debt outstanding at the start of period t. We assume that $\bar{M}_0 + \bar{B}_0 \geq 0$ holds, which means that the total liabilities of the government are non-negative at the start of the time horizon. The government's flow budget constraint is

$$P_t g + \bar{B}_t = \bar{M}_{t+1} - \bar{M}_t + q_t \bar{B}_{t+1}, \tag{8.39}$$

where P_t denotes the price level in period t. The left-hand side of this equation consists of government expenditures plus redemption of debt, the right-hand side consists of the seignorage revenue created by printing new money and by the issuance of new debt. The no Ponzi-game condition is

$$\lim_{T \to +\infty} D_T \bar{B}_T \leq 0, \tag{8.40}$$

where $D_0 = 1$ and $D_t = \prod_{s=0}^{t-1} q_s$ for $t \geq 1$ denote the nominal discount factors. The above two conditions are equivalent to the single lifetime budget constraint (solvency condition)

$$\sum_{t=0}^{+\infty} D_t P_t g + \bar{B}_0 \leq \sum_{t=0}^{+\infty} D_t (\bar{M}_{t+1} - \bar{M}_t). \tag{8.41}$$

A feasible government policy is a sequence $(q_t, \bar{M}_{t+1}, \bar{B}_{t+1})_{t=0}^{+\infty}$ satisfying $0 < q_t \leq 1$, $\bar{M}_{t+1} \geq 0$, and (8.41) (or, equivalently, (8.39) and (8.40)). Note that we can rewrite the solvency constraint (8.41) also in the form[7]

$$\sum_{t=0}^{+\infty} D_t P_t g + \bar{B}_0 + \bar{M}_0 \leq \sum_{t=1}^{+\infty} D_t \bar{M}_t (1/q_{t-1} - 1). \tag{8.42}$$

Let us now turn to the representative competitive agent. We denote by M_t and B_t the amount of money and bonds owned by the agent at the start of period t. The flow budget constraint of the agent can be written as

$$P_t c_t + M_{t+1} + q_t B_{t+1} = P_t \ell_t + M_t + B_t. \tag{8.43}$$

The left-hand side contains consumption expenditures and the purchases of assets, the right-hand side the revenue from selling output plus the value of the assets carried over from the previous period. As in the case of the government, we can aggregate this flow budget constraint into a single lifetime budget constraint of the form

$$\sum_{t=0}^{+\infty} D_t P_t c_t + \sum_{t=1}^{+\infty} D_t M_t (1/q_{t-1} - 1) \leq M_0 + B_0 + \sum_{t=0}^{+\infty} D_t P_t \ell_t,$$

where we have imposed the no-Ponzi game condition $\lim_{T \to +\infty} D_T (M_T + B_T) \geq 0$. The left-hand side of the lifetime budget constraint is the present value of lifetime

---

[7] The equivalence between the two formulations of the solvency constraint holds only under assumptions that ensure the absolute convergence of the infinite sums. We take these assumptions to be satisfied whenever we use the equivalence.

Dynamic optimization

consumption plus the opportunity cost of holding money. The right-hand side is the initial wealth plus the present value of lifetime earnings. Note that in a general equilibrium both asset markets and the output market must clear such that the conditions $\bar{M}_t = M_t$, $\bar{B}_t = B_t$, and (8.37) must hold for all $t \in \mathbb{N}_0$. This implies that the government's solvency constraint and the competitive agent's lifetime budget constraint are just two sides of the same coin and that they both have to hold with equality. Hence, the two conditions are in fact equivalent and we may impose a budget constraint either on the agent or on the government. We choose to impose it on the government and will therefore omit it from the competitive agent's problem.

In addition to the flow budget constraint, the agent has to respect the cash-in-advance constraint

$$M_t \geq P_t c_t. \tag{8.44}$$

This constraint says that consumption purchases must be made with cash carried over from the previous period. This means in particular that the agent cannot trade bonds for money before making consumption purchases. We can interpret this in the sense that the goods market opens before the asset market. The agent maximizes the utility in (8.38) with respect to $(c_t, \ell_t, M_{t+1}, B_{t+1})_{t=0}^{+\infty}$ and subject to (8.43) and (8.44). The Lagrangian function is

$$L = \sum_{t=0}^{+\infty} \beta^t \left\{ u(c_t) - \alpha \ell_t + \lambda_t (P_t \ell_t + M_t + B_t - P_t c_t - M_{t+1} - q_t B_{t+1}) + v_t (M_t - P_t c_t) \right\}$$

and the corresponding first-order conditions are

$$u'(c_t) - (\lambda_t + v_t) P_t = 0, \tag{8.45}$$

$$-\alpha + \lambda_t P_t = 0, \tag{8.46}$$

$$-\lambda_t + \beta(\lambda_{t+1} + v_{t+1}) = 0, \tag{8.47}$$

$$-\lambda_t q_t + \beta \lambda_{t+1} = 0. \tag{8.48}$$

Using (8.46) to eliminate λ_t and λ_{t+1} from (8.48), it follows that

$$r_t := P_t/(q_t P_{t+1}) = 1/\beta, \tag{8.49}$$

where r_t denotes the gross real interest rate from period t to $t + 1$. Equation (8.49) implies that

$$D_t P_t/P_0 = \prod_{s=0}^{t-1} r_s^{-1} = \beta^t. \tag{8.50}$$

Combining (8.45)–(8.47) and (8.49), we obtain

$$u'(c_{t+1}) = \lambda_t P_{t+1}/\beta = \alpha/q_t. \tag{8.51}$$

Equation (8.51) demonstrates that monetary policy is distortionary. A high nominal interest rate from period t to $t + 1$ (low value of q_t) causes high opportunity costs of holding money because the money has to be held across periods to satisfy the cash-in-advance constraint. This implies that the competitive agent will trade off utility of high consumption against the opportunity cost of holding the money that is necessary to buy consumption goods. As a consequence of (8.51), whenever $q_t < 1$ it must hold that $c_{t+1} < c^*$, where c^* is the first-best consumption level. Because (8.49) shows that q_t and the rate of inflation P_{t+1}/P_t are inversely related to each other, we can also say that inflation is costly in real terms.

Finally, note that $q_t < 1$ together with (8.47)–(8.48) imply that $v_{t+1} > 0$, and, hence, that $P_{t+1}c_{t+1} = M_{t+1} = \bar{M}_{t+1}$ hold. This means that the competitive agent does not hold more money than necessary whenever $q_t < 1$, and it follows that the money demand in period t is given by $M_{t+1} = P_{t+1}c_{t+1}$. On the other hand, if $q_t = 1$ holds, the two assets yield the same return and the money demand in period t is not uniquely pinned down. In order to eliminate this ambiguity, we assume that the competitive agent holds only as much money as it needs to carry out the consumption expenditures. In other words, we assume that condition (8.44) holds with equality for all $t \in \mathbb{N}_0$.

We are now ready to derive an optimal government policy under commitment. Dividing (8.42) by P_0 and using (8.50), we get

$$g/(1 - \beta) + (\bar{B}_0 + \bar{M}_0)/P_0 = \sum_{t=1}^{+\infty} \beta^t (\bar{M}_t/P_t)(1/q_{t-1} - 1). \tag{8.52}$$

Because of $\bar{M}_0 + \bar{B}_0 \geq 0$, $g > 0$, and $q_t \leq 1$ for all $t \in \mathbb{N}_0$, it follows from equation (8.52) that $q_t < 1$ must hold at least for some t. Thus, the government must use monetary policy at some point to generate seignorage income because it does not have any initial wealth out of which it could finance public consumption. The optimal government policy will balance the distortions created by monetary policy over all periods in an optimal way.

The government chooses its policy variables so as to maximize the welfare function (8.38) subject to the private sector's reaction function (8.51), the goods market clearing condition (8.37), and its own budget constraint (8.52). We follow the primal approach and eliminate the policy variables from this problem using (8.37) and (8.51). Because of (8.37), the objective functional of the government can be written as

$$\sum_{t=0}^{+\infty} \beta^t \left[u(c_t) - \alpha(c_t + g) \right]. \tag{8.53}$$

As for the budget constraint, we combine (8.52) with (8.51) and $\bar{M}_t/P_t = c_t$ to obtain

$$g/(1 - \beta) + c_0(1 + \bar{b}_0) = \sum_{t=1}^{+\infty} \beta^t [u'(c_t)/\alpha - 1]c_t, \tag{8.54}$$

where $\bar{b}_0 = \bar{B}_0/\bar{M}_0 \geq -1$. Note that this condition contains consumption as the only endogenous variable. The government maximizes (8.53) subject to (8.54). The Lagrangian for this problem is

$$L^G = \sum_{t=0}^{+\infty} \beta^t \left[u(c_t) - \alpha(c_t + g)\right] + \lambda \left\{ \sum_{t=1}^{+\infty} \beta^t [u'(c_t)/\alpha - 1]c_t - c_0(1+\bar{b}_0) - g/(1-\beta) \right\}$$

$$= u(c_0) - [\alpha + \lambda(1 + \bar{b}_0)]c_0 + \sum_{t=1}^{+\infty} \beta^t \left\{ u(c_t) + (\lambda/\alpha)u'(c_t)c_t - (\alpha + \lambda)c_t \right\} - \lambda_0,$$

where $\lambda_0 = (\alpha + \lambda)g/(1 - \beta)$ is a constant.

From the first-order conditions of the government's optimization problem, we obtain

$$u'(c_0) - \alpha = \frac{\alpha(1 + \bar{b}_0)}{\alpha + (\sigma - 1)u'(c_t)}[u'(c_t) - \alpha], \tag{8.55}$$

where $\sigma = -c_t u''(c_t)/u'(c_t)$ is the elasticity of marginal utility, which we assume to be constant (that is, independent of c_t) from now on.[8]

The following observations can be made from equation (8.55). First, it must be the case that $c_t = c_s$ holds for all $1 \leq t < s$, but, in general, $c_0 \neq c_t$ holds for all $t \geq 1$. Let us write c instead of c_t for $t \geq 1$. For the interpretation of (8.55), it is useful to interpret $u'(c_t) - \alpha = u'(c_t) - u'(c^*)$ as the wedge between the marginal utility of consumption in the first-best solution and the marginal utility of consumption under optimal policy. The left-hand side of (8.55) is this wedge at time 0 and the right-hand side is the wedge at any other period multiplied by a weight. We can therefore say that the government chooses the same distortion for all periods $t \geq 1$, but in general it chooses a different distortion for the initial period.

Whether $c_0 < c$ or $c_0 > c$ holds depends primarily on σ. To see this, assume for the moment that $\bar{b}_0 = 0$. In this case, it follows from (8.55) that $c_0 < c < c^*$ if $\sigma < 1$ and $c^* > c_0 > c$ if $\sigma > 1$. If $\bar{b}_0 > 0$, then the threshold level for σ is greater than 1, and if $-1 < \bar{b}_0 < 0$, then it is smaller than 1. Some intuition can be obtained from the following observation. The demand for consumption in period 0 is determined by the cash-in-advance constraint $c_0 = \bar{M}_0/P_0$. It has therefore the price elasticity 1. The demand function for $c = c_t$, on the other hand, is given by (8.51), that is, by the equation $u'(c_t) = \alpha/q_{t-1} = \alpha P_t/(\beta P_{t-1})$, which has a price elasticity of $1/\sigma$. According to a well-known principle of optimal taxation, the less elastic a good is, the more heavily it should be taxed. For example, if $\sigma > 1$, consumption demand in period $t \geq 1$ is less elastic than consumption demand in period 0, and the equilibrium value c is therefore more distorted than c_0. If $\sigma < 1$, the opposite relation holds. The presence

---

[8] This means that the utility function takes the form $u(c) = (c^{1-\sigma} - 1)/(1 - \sigma)$ for $\sigma \neq 1$ and $u(c) = \ln c$ for $\sigma = 1$.

of nominal debt creates an additional incentive to distort the initial consumption rate more heavily because surprise inflation reduces the real value of initial government debt and therefore relaxes the government's budget constraint.

Equation (8.55) is of course not enough to determine the allocation generated by the optimal policy, because it is a single equation with two unknowns c_0 and c. To obtain a second equation, we first divide (8.39) by $\bar{M}_t$ and use $M_t/P_t = c_t$ to get

$$\frac{g}{c_t} + \bar{b}_t = \mu_t - 1 + q_t\mu_t\bar{b}_{t+1}, \tag{8.56}$$

where $\bar{b}_t = \bar{B}_t/\bar{M}_t$ is the debt-to-money ratio and where $\mu_t = \bar{M}_{t+1}/\bar{M}_t$ is the gross nominal money growth rate. Combining $P_tc_t = M_t = \bar{M}_t$ with (8.49), it follows that

$$q_t = \frac{\beta c_{t+1}}{\mu_t c_t}. \tag{8.57}$$

We can use this equation together with (8.51) to eliminate q_t and μ_t from (8.56). This yields

$$g + (1 + \bar{b}_t)c_t = \frac{\beta u'(c_{t+1})c_{t+1}}{\alpha} + \beta\bar{b}_{t+1}c_{t+1}. \tag{8.58}$$

Furthermore, using $\bar{M}_t = P_tc_t$ and (8.50), the no-Ponzi game condition (8.40) can be written as

$$\lim_{t\to+\infty} \beta^t\bar{b}_tc_t = 0. \tag{8.59}$$

Since $c_t = c$ holds for all $t \geq 1$, equation (8.58) turns into $g + (1 + \bar{b}_t)c = \beta u'(c)c/\alpha + \beta c\bar{b}_{t+1}$. This is a linear difference equation for $\bar{b}_t$ which has a unique solution that satisfies (8.59), namely

$$\bar{b}_t = \bar{b} := \frac{\beta u'(c)c/\alpha - c - g}{(1 - \beta)c} \tag{8.60}$$

for all $t \geq 1$. For $t = 0$, on the other hand, equation (8.58) implies

$$g + (1 + \bar{b}_0)c_0 = \frac{\beta u'(c)c}{\alpha} + \beta\bar{b}c.$$

Combining the last two equations, we get

$$g + (1 - \beta)(1 + \bar{b}_0)c_0 = \frac{\beta u'(c)c}{\alpha} - \beta c. \tag{8.61}$$

The two unknowns c_0 and $c_t = c$ can now be obtained from (8.55) and (8.61). Note that the values of these variables depend on the initial state $\bar{b}_0$.

To conclude this example, we point out that the optimal policy is typically dynamically inconsistent. In period 0, the government plans to choose the same consumption level for all periods after $t = 1$. If the government would re-optimize in period 1, it would (in general) choose different consumption levels for periods 1 and 2. Such a solution can therefore only be implemented if the government has access to a commitment technology. For certain values of the initial debt, however, the dynamic inconsistency problem may vanish. This will be the case if (i) $\bar{b}_0$ is such that c_0 and c coincide and (ii) $\bar{b}$ coincides with $\bar{b}_0$ such that the coincidence between c_0 and c is perpetuated. In other words, the equilibrium must be a fixed point of the equilibrium dynamics. We state the conditions under which this happens in the following lemma.

Lemma 8.1

(a) The optimal policy is dynamically consistent if and only if $\bar{b}_0$ coincides with the value $\bar{b}$ from (8.60), where $c > 0$ satisfies the equation

$$g + c = \frac{[1 - (1 - \beta)\sigma]u'(c)c}{\alpha} = \frac{[1 - (1 - \beta)\sigma]c^{1-\sigma}}{\alpha}. \tag{8.62}$$

(b) If $\sigma \in (0, 1)$, then there exists $\bar{g} > 0$ such that equation (8.62) has two solutions if $g < \bar{g}$, a single solution if $g = \bar{g}$, and no solution if $g > \bar{g}$.
(c) If $\sigma = 1$, then equation (8.62) has the solution $c = (\beta/\alpha) - g$ whenever $g < \beta/\alpha$ and it has no solution otherwise.
(d) If $\sigma \in (1, 1/(1 - \beta))$, then equation (8.62) has a unique solution.
(e) If $\sigma \geq 1/(1 - \beta)$, then equation (8.62) has no solution.

PROOF: We have seen above that dynamic consistency requires that $c_0 = c$. Together with (8.55), this implies, $\bar{b}_0 = (\sigma - 1)u'(c)/\alpha$. Substituting this result and $c_0 = c$ into (8.61), we get equation (8.62). This proves the necessity part in statement (a). Since all steps can be reversed, sufficiency holds as well. The proofs of the remaining statements (b)–(e) are left as an exercise for the reader.

Finally, let us derive the sign of government debt in a fixed point. From the proof of lemma 8.1, we know that in a fixed point it must hold that $\bar{b}_0 = (\sigma - 1)u'(c)/\alpha$. This implies obviously that

$$\bar{b}_0 \begin{Bmatrix} > \\ = \\ < \end{Bmatrix} 0 \text{ if } \sigma \begin{Bmatrix} > \\ = \\ < \end{Bmatrix} 1.$$

The sign of government debt in a fixed point is therefore entirely determined by the elasticity of intertemporal substitution in consumption.

Discretionary optimal policy

In the examples of the previous section, we have seen that the optimal solution to the policy maker's decision problem is typically dynamically inconsistent. Hence, unless a commitment technology is available, such a solution cannot be implemented. It is therefore of interest to analyze the optimal policy problem also in the absence of commitment. According to the discussion in section 6.2, this can be done using the multiple-selves model, that is, we assume that in every period t a separate self of the policy maker has control over the policy variable g_t. This self takes the behaviour of all future selves as given and it also takes into account that the competitive agents react to policy choices in the form of a dynamic competitive equilibrium. We restrict attention to the sophisticated solution in which the separate selves of the policy maker are aware of their lack of commitment power and of the fact that later selves will decide on the basis of the preferences and constraints prevailing at that time. Policy making in which every self of the policy maker decides on its instrument settings from the point of view of its own preferences that prevail at the time when these instruments are chosen is referred to as *discretionary*.

In period $t \in \mathbb{N}_0$, the policy maker's objective functional is

$$\sum_{s=t}^{+\infty} \mathbf{U}(\mathbf{x}_s, \mathbf{x}_{s+1}, g_s, s).$$

The only task of self t is to choose $g_t \in \mathbf{G}$. Self t, however, is well aware of the fact that the choice of g_t affects the decision problems of the competitive agents and, hence, the individual system variables $(x_s^i)_{s=t}^{+\infty}$ as well as the aggregate system variables $(z_s)_{s=t}^{+\infty}$ via the aggregation condition

$$z_s = \mathbf{A}(\mathbf{x}_s, s).$$

As in the previous section, we assume that both the individual and the aggregate system variables are pre-determined, that is, that they are state variables. Furthermore, we assume that the policy maker uses a closed-loop strategy $\sigma = (\sigma_t)_{t=0}^{+\infty}$ of the form $g_t = \sigma_t(z_t)$, where σ_t (the strategy applied by self t) maps Z into $\mathbf{G}$.

Solving the model for an optimal policy without commitment (that is, for an optimal discretionary policy) is a formidable task. In realistic scenarios, numerical solution techniques are unavoidable. In what follows, we therefore restrict ourselves to explaining the basic features of the approach and to illustrating them by means of examples. Even defining the concept of optimal discretionary policy requires considerable effort. The following definition involves four steps and is based on the recursive formulation of a dynamic competitive equilibrium.

Recall that, according to the recursive approach, the competitive agents believe that the aggregate system variable evolves according to the perceived law of motion

$$z_{t+1} = \psi(z_t, t)$$

for all $t \in \mathbb{N}_0$. Recall furthermore that self t takes the strategies of its successor selves $s \in \{t+1, t+2, \ldots\}$ as given. Let us denote the strategy profile of all selves by Σ, that is, $\Sigma = (\sigma_t)_{t=0}^{+\infty}$.

The first step in the definition of an optimal solution consists of evaluating the policy maker's objective functional from period $t+1$ onwards (where $t \in \mathbb{N}_0$ is arbitrary) assuming that the profile of system variables at the beginning of period $t+1$ is an arbitrary element $\mathbf{x} \in \mathbf{X}$ and that the aggregate state at the beginning of period $t+1$ is an arbitrary element $z \in Z$. Because self $s \in \{t+1, t+2, \ldots\}$ of the policy maker uses the strategy σ_s it follows that, from the point of view of period $t+1$, the competitive agent $i \in \mathbf{M}$ seeks to maximize

$$\sum_{s=t+1}^{+\infty} U^i\left(x_s^i, x_{s+1}^i, z_s, \sigma_s(z_s), s\right)$$

subject to the constraints

$$x_{s+1}^i \in G^i\left(x_s^i, z_s, \sigma_s(z_s), s\right)$$

for all $s \in \{t+1, t+2, \ldots\}$ and given the perceived law of motion for the aggregate state variable. As in section 8.2, we assume that the solution to this problem can be described by an optimal policy function $h_{\psi,\Sigma}^i : X^i \times Z \times \mathbb{N}_0 \mapsto X^i$, that is, it holds for all $s \geq t+1$ that

$$x_{s+1}^i = h_{\psi,\Sigma}^i\left(x_s^i, z_s, s\right).$$

The subscripts ψ and Σ indicate that the competitive agent takes the perceived law of motion ψ and the policy maker's strategy profile Σ as given. Corresponding to this optimal policy function, we can also determine the optimal value function $V_{\psi,\Sigma}^i : X^i \times Z \times \mathbb{N}_0 \mapsto \mathbb{R}$, which must satisfy the recursive equation

$$V_{\psi,\Sigma}^i(x^i, z, s) = U^i\left(x^i, h_{\psi,\Sigma}^i(x^i, z, s), z, \sigma_s(z), s\right)$$
$$+ V_{\psi,\Sigma}^i\left(h_{\psi,\Sigma}^i(x^i, z, s), \psi(z, s), s+1\right) \tag{8.63}$$

for all $s \geq t+1$.

Analogously to section 8.2, we can use the individual optimal policy functions $h_{\psi,\Sigma}^i$ to write the dynamic competitive equilibrium dynamics of the entire profile of system variables in the form

$$\mathbf{x}_{s+1} = \mathbf{h}_{\psi,\Sigma}(\mathbf{x}_s, z_s, s).$$

Finally, this allows us to obtain the following recursive equation for the optimal value function of the policy maker's optimization problem:

$$\mathbf{V}_{\psi,\Sigma}(\mathbf{x}, z, s) = \mathbf{U}(\mathbf{x}, \mathbf{h}_{\psi,\Sigma}(\mathbf{x}, z, s), \sigma_s(z), s) + \mathbf{V}_{\psi,\Sigma}(\mathbf{h}_{\psi,\Sigma}(\mathbf{x}, z, s), \psi(z, s), s + 1).$$

$$(8.64)$$

In the second step, we basically repeat this exercise, but this time from period t onwards under the assumptions that self t of the policy maker chooses an arbitrary value $g \in \mathbf{G}$ and that the later selves use the strategy profile Σ. Taking into account the results from step one, the individual optimization problem of agent $i \in \mathbf{M}$ becomes the maximization of

$$U^i\left(x_t^i, x_{t+1}^i, z_t, g, t\right) + V_{\psi,\Sigma}^i\left(x_{t+1}^i, \psi(z_t, t), t + 1\right)$$

subject to the constraint

$$x_{t+1}^i \in G^i\left(x_t^i, z_t, g, t\right).$$

The optimal solution to this problem is assumed to be determined by the optimal policy function $\tilde{h}_{\psi,\Sigma_{>t}}^i : X^i \times Z \times \mathbf{G} \times \mathbb{N}_0 \mapsto X^i$, where the subscript $\Sigma_{>t}$ indicates that only the selves $s > t$ use their strategies, whereas self t chooses the fixed value g for its policy variable. This means in particular that agent i chooses

$$x_{t+1}^i = \tilde{h}_{\psi,\Sigma_{>t}}^i\left(x_t^i, z_t, g, t\right).$$

Aggregating this relation over all agents $i \in \mathbf{M}$, we obtain the dynamic competitive equilibrium dynamics induced by ψ, $\Sigma_{>t}$, and g as

$$\mathbf{x}_{t+1} = \tilde{\mathbf{h}}_{\psi,\Sigma_{>t}}(\mathbf{x}_t, z_t, g, t).$$

In the third step of the definition of discretionary optimal policy, we formulate the decision problem of self t of the policy maker. Given the profile of system variables $\mathbf{x}_t$ at the beginning of period t, this self chooses its policy variable $g_t \in \mathbf{G}$ so as to maximize

$$\mathbf{U}\left(\mathbf{x}_t, \tilde{\mathbf{h}}_{\psi,\Sigma_{>t}}(\mathbf{x}_t, z_t, g_t, t), g_t, t\right) + \mathbf{V}_{\psi,\Sigma}\left(\tilde{\mathbf{h}}_{\psi,\Sigma_{>t}}(\mathbf{x}_t, z_t, g_t, t), \psi(z_t, t), t + 1\right). \quad (8.65)$$

Note that the decision variable g_t, over which the maximization takes place, appears both as an argument of the policy maker's utility function $\mathbf{U}$ and as an argument of the competitive equilibrium dynamics $\tilde{\mathbf{h}}_{\psi,\Sigma_{>t}}$.

The final step of the definition of an optimal discretionary policy consists of two consistency conditions. The first condition is that the solution to the policy maker's optimization problem, that is, the maximizer g_t of the objective function in (8.65), coincides with the equilibrium strategy, that is

$$\sigma_t(z) = \mathrm{argmax}\big\{\mathbf{U}\big(\mathbf{x}, \tilde{\mathbf{h}}_{\psi,\Sigma_{>t}}(\mathbf{x}, z, g, t), g, t\big)$$
$$+ \mathbf{V}_{\psi,\Sigma}\big(\tilde{\mathbf{h}}_{\psi,\Sigma_{>t}}(\mathbf{x}, z, g, t), \psi(z, t), t+1\big) \mid g \in \mathbf{G}\big\}$$

holds for all $z \in Z$, all $t \in \mathbb{N}_0$, and all profiles $\mathbf{x} \in \mathbf{X}$ which satisfy $z = \mathbf{A}(\mathbf{x}, t)$. This condition amounts to the requirement that the strategy σ_t is a best response of self t to the strategies of its successors, that is, that the strategy profile Σ constitutes a Nash equilibrium of the game among the different selves of the policy maker. We should note that this condition implies obviously that $\tilde{\mathbf{h}}_{\psi,\Sigma_{>t}}(\mathbf{x}, z, \sigma_t(z), t) = \mathbf{h}_{\psi,\Sigma}(\mathbf{x}, z, t)$.

The second consistency condition is the requirement that the actual law of motion that is generated by the aggregation of the individual optimal policy functions coincides with the perceived law of motion. In the present context, this condition says that

$$\psi(z, t) = \mathbf{A}(\mathbf{h}_{\psi,\Sigma}(\mathbf{x}, z, t), t)$$

holds for all $z \in Z$, all $t \in \mathbb{N}_0$, and all profiles $\mathbf{x} \in \mathbf{X}$ which satisfy $z = \mathbf{A}(\mathbf{x}, t)$. This is of course the very same condition that we have already encountered in the recursive formulation of a dynamic competitive equilibrium without an active policy maker.

Both consistency conditions include the problematic qualifier that the stated condition has to hold for all profiles $\mathbf{x} \in \mathbf{X}$ which satisfy $z = \mathbf{A}(\mathbf{x}, t)$. We have already pointed out in our discussion of the recursive formulation of dynamic competitive equilibrium in section 8.2 that this qualifier is not likely to be satisfied without a homogeneity assumption on the set of competitive agents or strong structural assumptions on the model (like a linear-quadratic structure along with a linear aggregation condition). This is a consequence of the recursive approach which postulates that next period's aggregate state depends on the present profile of individual system variables only via the present aggregate state variable.

We would like to make two comments on the above definition. The first one is that despite the fact that we call the solution a discretionary 'optimal' policy, it is not an optimum but an equilibrium. More specifically, it is a Nash equilibrium in the game among the different selves of the policy maker, who jointly act as Stackelberg leaders against the competitive agents. As a consequence of being a Nash equilibrium, the discretionary optimal policy typically does not satisfy any efficiency properties. By its very construction, however, it is dynamically consistent.

The second comment is related to the first one. Recall that we pointed out the similarity between the optimal policy under commitment and an equilibrium of a Stackelberg game with an open-loop strategy space. Even if we assume in the present section that the policy maker, respectively the various selves of which it consists, uses closed-loop strategies, the reader should not draw any parallel between discretionary optimal policy and a Stackelberg equilibrium in closed-loop strategies. This would be wrong because there is no single Stackelberg leader who solves a dynamic optimization problem but countably many of them (the multiple selves), each of whom solves a one-period problem.

The following example demonstrates the derivation of discretionary optimal policy in the artificial linear-quadratic setting of example 8.5.

Example 8.8 Let us return to example 8.5 for which we could fully characterize the optimal policy under commitment. In what follows, we show that in this model there exists a discretionary optimal policy with the property that the policy maker's strategy and the equilibrium law of motion of the aggregate state are given by $\sigma_t(z) = \bar{g}$ and $\psi(z, t) = \bar{z}$, respectively, for all $t \in \mathbb{N}_0$ and all $z \in \mathbb{R}$. Here $\bar{g}$ and $\bar{z}$ are constants that can be expressed in closed form as functions of the time-preference factor β. Because the formulas for $\bar{g}$ and $\bar{z}$ are rather long, we discuss the analytical derivation of the equilibrium only for the special case $\beta = 7/10$ and present the results for general β in terms of a diagram.

We claim that in the case of $\beta = 7/10$, a discretionary optimal policy is given by $\sigma_t(z) = \bar{g} := 11/5$ and $\psi(z, t) = \bar{z} := 1/2$. For these specifications of $\Sigma = (\sigma_t)_{t=0}^{+\infty}$ and ψ, the current value Bellman equation for the dynamic optimization problem of the competitive agents in step one of the equilibrium definition takes the form

$$V_{\psi,\Sigma}^i(x, z) = \max \left\{ -[(x + y)^2 + (y - 11/5)^2 + (y - z)^2]/2 \right.$$
$$\left. + (7/10)V_{\psi,\Sigma}^i(y, 1/2) \mid y \in \mathbb{R} \right\}.$$

The unique concave quadratic polynomial that satisfies this equation is given by

$$V_{\psi,\Sigma}^i(x, z) = -(5/14)(x^2 + z^2) - (2/7)xz - (1/2)(x - z) - 187/30$$

and the corresponding optimal policy is

$$h_{\psi,\Sigma}^i(x, z) = 1/2 - (2/7)(x - z).$$

Using the aggregation condition $z_t = x_t$, the latter result implies immediately that the actual law of motion is given by $z_{t+1} = x_{t+1} = h_{\psi,\Sigma}^i(x_t, x_t) = 1/2$ and therefore coincides with the perceived law of motion. All we need to show is that every self of the policy maker finds it indeed optimal to choose $g_t = 11/5$.

The recursive equation determining the current value optimal value function of the policy maker is

$$\mathbf{V}_{\psi,\Sigma}(x, z) = -\left[h_{\psi,\Sigma}^i(x, z) \right]^2 / 2 + (47/10)h_{\psi,\Sigma}^i(x, z) - 11/5$$
$$+ (7/10)\mathbf{V}_{\psi,\Sigma}\left(h_{\psi,\Sigma}^i(x, z), 1/2 \right).$$

Substituting the expression for $h^i_{\psi, \Sigma}(x, z)$ that we derived above, it is straightforward to verify that the unique concave quadratic polynomial that satisfies this equation is given by

$$\mathbf{V}_{\psi, \Sigma}(x, z) = -(10/231)(x - z)^2 - (x - z) + (1/12).$$

We now turn to step two of the definition of discretionary optimal policy. Suppose that self t chooses an arbitrary value g_t and that all selves $s > t$ play the equilibrium strategy and therefore choose $g_s = \bar{g} = 11/5$. The competitive agents in period t therefore maximize

$$-[(x_t + x_{t+1})^2 + (x_{t+1} - g_t)^2 + (x_{t+1} - z_t)^2]/2 + (7/10)V^i_{\psi, \Sigma}(x_{t+1}, 1/2).$$

Using the formula for the optimal value function $V^i_{\psi, \Sigma}$ derived above and carrying out the maximization with respect to x_{t+1}, we obtain

$$x_{t+1} = \tilde{h}^i_{\psi, \Sigma_{>t}}(x_t, z_t, g_t) = -(9/70) + (2/7)(g_t - x_t + z_t).$$

Taking into account this equilibrium reaction of the competitive agents, self t chooses g_t so as to maximize

$$-\left[\tilde{h}^i_{\psi, \Sigma_{>t}}(x_t, z_t, g_t)\right]^2 / 2 + (47/10)\tilde{h}^i_{\psi, \Sigma_{>t}}(x_t, z_t, g_t)$$
$$- g_t + (7/10)\mathbf{V}_{\psi, \Sigma}\left(\tilde{h}^i_{\psi, \Sigma_{>t}}(x_t, z_t, g_t), 1/2\right)$$

which, after substitution of the formulas for $\tilde{h}^i_{\psi, \Sigma_{>t}}(x_t, z_t, g_t)$ and $\mathbf{V}_{\psi, \Sigma}(x, z)$ and after taking care of the aggregation condition $z_t = x_t$, boils down to

$$\frac{-583 + 880g_t - 200g_t^2}{4620}.$$

Obviously, this expression is maximized at $g_t = 11/5$ thereby confirming the first consistency condition stated in step four of the definition of discretionary optimal policy. Since we have already confirmed the second consistency condition (namely, that the actual law of motion of the aggregate state variable coincides with the perceived law of motion), the proof that $\sigma_t(z) = 11/5$ and $\psi(z, t) = 1/2$ form an equilibrium is now complete.

Analogous calculations can be carried out for general $\beta \in (0, 1)$, but they involve messy algebra.[9] Instead of stating these results here, we show the equilibrium values of $\bar{g}$ and $\bar{z}$ in figure 8.1. We can see that in the boundary case $\beta = 0$, it holds that $\bar{g} = 3$ and $\bar{z} = 1$, which coincide with the corresponding values g_0 and z_1 in the optimal solution under commitment. This should not come as a surprise because for β equal

---

[9] A second simple case is dealt with in exercise 8.8.

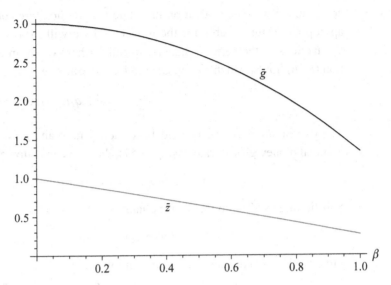

Figure 8.1 The equilibrium values $\bar{g}$ and $\bar{z}$ as functions of β

to 0 neither the policy maker nor the competitive agents care about the future and, hence, commitment or the lack thereof becomes completely irrelevant. As β grows, both values $\bar{g}$ and $\bar{z}$ become smaller and are therefore between the values g_0 and g_t and z_1 and z_t, respectively, from the commitment solution.

In the above example, we have verified the discretionary optimal solution following exactly the four steps that we used in defining this concept. In more realistic problems, the discretionary optimal policy is typically derived by a primal approach, that is, by using the dynamic competitive equilibrium conditions to eliminate the policy variables and by formulating the game among the different selves in terms of the system variables rather than in terms of the policy variables. We now use the primal approach to investigate the monetary policy problem from example 8.7 under the assumption that the central bank lacks commitment power.

Example 8.9 Let us reconsider the economy from example 8.7, but this time we assume that the policy maker (the government or the central bank) does not have commitment power, that is, we consider discretionary optimal policy. In this situation, the central bank in period t can optimally choose period-t policy variables, but it cannot fix policy variables for the future.

Our first task is to identify a low-dimensional aggregate state variable. To this end, we recall that the consumption levels c_0 and c implemented in the solution with commitment were dependent on the value $\bar{b}_0$. We therefore conjecture that this is an appropriate state variable for the model, and we will express all period-t variables as functions of the period-t state $\bar{b}_t$. Recall furthermore from example 8.7 that equation (8.56) holds, which we repeat here for convenience:

$$\frac{g}{c_t} + \bar{b}_t = \mu_t - 1 + q_t \mu_t \bar{b}_{t+1}.$$

The variable $\bar{b}_t = \bar{B}_t / \bar{M}_t$ is the debt-to-money ratio and $\mu_t = \bar{M}_{t+1} / \bar{M}_t$ is the gross nominal money growth rate. Using (8.57), the above equation can be written as

$$g + (1 + \bar{b}_t)c_t = \mu_t c_t + \beta \bar{b}_{t+1} c_{t+1}.$$

Substituting (8.57) into (8.51), we obtain

$$\beta u'(c_{t+1})c_{t+1} = \alpha \mu_t c_t.$$

From the last two displayed equations, it follows that

$$g + (1 + \bar{b}_t)c_t = \beta c_{t+1} \left[\frac{u'(c_{t+1})}{\alpha} + \bar{b}_{t+1} \right]. \qquad (8.66)$$

This equation is the government's budget constraint expressed only in terms of the system variables $\bar{b}_t$ and c_t. Following the primal approach, we have used the private-sector equilibrium conditions to eliminate the government's choice variables μ_t and q_t.

Because the model has a stationary discounted structure, we conjecture that the policy maker's strategy for consumption is independent of the time variable t. Denoting this strategy by $\mathcal{C}$, it follows that in equilibrium it must hold that $c_{t+1} = \mathcal{C}(\bar{b}_{t+1})$.[10] The government's flow budget constraint (8.66) therefore turns into

$$g + (1 + \bar{b}_t)c_t = F(\bar{b}_{t+1}), \qquad (8.67)$$

where

$$F(\bar{b}) = \beta \mathcal{C}(\bar{b}) \left[\frac{u'(\mathcal{C}(\bar{b}))}{\alpha} + \bar{b} \right]. \qquad (8.68)$$

Suppose for the moment that equation (8.67) can be solved uniquely for $\bar{b}_{t+1}$, say $\bar{b}_{t+1} = \mathbf{h}(\bar{b}_t, c_t)$.[11] We define the continuation value function for the government's optimization problem recursively by

$$\mathbf{V}_{\mathcal{C}}(\bar{b}) = u(\mathcal{C}(\bar{b})) - \alpha[g + \mathcal{C}(b)] + \beta \mathbf{V}_{\mathcal{C}}(\mathbf{h}(\bar{b}, \mathcal{C}(\bar{b}))).$$

---

[10] We have chosen to denote the consumption strategy by $\mathcal{C}$ rather than by σ as in the general discussion, because the symbol σ is already used in the present example to denote the elasticity of marginal utility.

[11] In order to simplify the notation, we suppress the dependence of the function $\mathbf{h}$ on the strategy and the perceived law of motion in the notation.

The value $\mathbf{V}(\bar{b})$ is the present value of the competitive agents' utility (that is, social welfare) from a certain period onwards if the state at the beginning of that period is equal to $\bar{b}$ and if all selves of the government from that period onwards stick to the policy rule $c_t = \mathcal{C}(\bar{b}_t)$. The above equation must hold identically for all values of $\bar{b}$ such that we may also differentiate the equation to get

$$\mathbf{V}'_{\mathcal{C}}(\bar{b}_t) = [u'(c_t) - \alpha]\mathcal{C}'(\bar{b}_t) + \beta\mathbf{V}'_{\mathcal{C}}(\bar{b}_{t+1})[\mathbf{h}_1(\bar{b}_t, c_t) + \mathbf{h}_2(\bar{b}_t, c_t)\mathcal{C}'(\bar{b}_t)]. \quad (8.69)$$

Given $\bar{b}_t$, the policy problem of the current government is to maximize

$$u(c) - \alpha(g + c) + \beta\mathbf{V}_{\mathcal{C}}(\mathbf{h}(\bar{b}_t, c))$$

subject to c. If $\mathcal{C}$ is the equilibrium strategy, then it must be the case that the value $c_t = \mathcal{C}(\bar{b}_t)$ maximizes the above function. The corresponding first-order condition is

$$u'(c_t) - \alpha + \beta\mathbf{V}'_{\mathcal{C}}(\bar{b}_{t+1})\mathbf{h}_2(\bar{b}_t, c_t) = 0.$$

Solving this equation for $\mathbf{V}'_{\mathcal{C}}(\bar{b}_{t+1})$ and substituting the result into (8.69), we obtain

$$\frac{u'(c_{t-1}) - \alpha}{\mathbf{h}_2(\bar{b}_{t-1}, c_{t-1})} = \frac{\beta[u'(c_t) - \alpha]\mathbf{h}_1(\bar{b}_t, c_t)}{\mathbf{h}_2(\bar{b}_t, c_t)}. \quad (8.70)$$

It remains to calculate the partial derivatives $\mathbf{h}_1(\bar{b}, \mathcal{C}(\bar{b}))$ and $\mathbf{h}_2(\bar{b}, \mathcal{C}(\bar{b}))$ in this expression. It follows from the definition of $\mathbf{h}$ that $g + (1 + \bar{b})c = F(\mathbf{h}(\bar{b}, c))$ and we obtain therefore from the implicit function theorem the relations

$$\mathbf{h}_1(\bar{b}_t, c_t) = \frac{c_t}{F'(\bar{b}_{t+1})} \quad (8.71)$$

and

$$\mathbf{h}_2(\bar{b}_t, c_t) = \frac{1 + \bar{b}_t}{F'(\bar{b}_{t+1})}. \quad (8.72)$$

Furthermore, from (8.68) it follows that

$$F'(\bar{b}_t) = \beta\left\{c_t + \mathcal{C}'(\bar{b}_t)\left[\bar{b}_t + \frac{(1 - \sigma)u'(c_t)}{\alpha}\right]\right\}. \quad (8.73)$$

Substituting (8.71)–(8.73) into (8.70), we finally obtain the *generalized Euler equation*

$$\frac{[u'(c_{t-1}) - \alpha]\{c_t + \mathcal{C}'(\bar{b}_t)[\bar{b}_t - (\sigma - 1)u'(c_t)/\alpha]\}}{1 + \bar{b}_{t-1}} = \frac{[u'(c_t) - \alpha]c_t}{1 + \bar{b}_t}. \quad (8.74)$$

It is called a generalized Euler equation because it contains the derivative of the unknown policy function $\mathcal{C}$.

Equations (8.66) and (8.74) together form a system of two implicit first-order difference equations in the variables $\bar{b}_t$ and c_t. It is obvious that the first-best allocation c^* along with $\bar{b} = -1 - g/[(1 - \beta)c^*]$ qualify as a fixed point of this system. We call this fixed point the Friedman rule steady state, because it corresponds to the first-best allocation. Furthermore, we see from (8.74) that in every fixed point in which the consumption level differs from c^* it must either hold that $C'(\bar{b}) = 0$ or that $\bar{b} = (\sigma - 1)u'(c)/\alpha$. Discarding the possibility of $C'(\bar{b}) = 0$, we recover equation (8.62) by substituting $\bar{b} = (\sigma - 1)u'(c)/\alpha$ into (8.66). It follows therefore that exactly those debt levels for which the dynamic inconsistency problem vanishes in the commitment solution emerge as fixed points under discretion.

The above example clearly demonstrates the limits of a pencil-and-paper approach to the analysis of discretionary optimal policy in models with reasonably realistic assumptions. There is little hope to obtain an analytical characterization of the optimal policy function C or to solve the generalized Euler equation (8.74) without resorting to numerical approximations. Computational approaches for the analysis of this problem, as well as of similar ones, do of course exist, but it is beyond the scope of the present book to deal with these methods.

8.5   EXERCISES

EXERCISE 8.1   Consider the dynamic competitive economy populated by a unit interval $\mathbf{M} = [0, 1]$ of agents with individual utility functions

$$U^i\left(x_t^i, x_{t+1}^i, z_t, t\right) = -(\beta^t/2)\left[\left(x_{t+1}^i - kz_t\right)^2 + \left(x_{t+1}^i - x_t^i\right)^2\right]$$

and transition possibility set $G^i(x^i, z, t) = \mathbb{R}$. Here, x_t^i is the system variable of agent i at time t, with x_0^i being exogenously given, $\beta \in (0, 1)$ is the common time-preference factor of all agents, and k satisfies

$$0 < k < \bar{k} := \sqrt{\beta} - 2 + \frac{2}{\sqrt{\beta}}.$$

The aggregate system variable z_t is related to the individual system variables via $z_t = \int_0^1 x_t^i \, di$.

(a) Derive the conditions for a dynamic competitive equilibrium in sequence formulation via the Euler equation approach.

(b) Assume that all agents have the same initial states $x_0^i = x_0$. Solve the model for a symmetric dynamic competitive equilibrium in sequence formulation via the Euler equation approach.

EXERCISE 8.2 Consider the model from exercise 8.1 again. Note that all agents have the same utility function but that they may have different initial states x_0^i. Write down the conditions for a dynamic competitive equilibrium in recursive formulation. Use the perceived law of motion $z_{t+1} = \psi z_t$, where ψ is an unknown coefficient, and conjecture that the optimal value function of agent i takes the form $V_\psi(x^i, z) = -v_0(x^i)^2/2 + v_1 x^i z - v_2 z^2/2$. Prove that the optimal policy function of the competitive agents takes the form

$$h^i(x^i, z) = \frac{2x^i}{2 + \beta + \sqrt{\beta^2 + 4}} + \frac{2kz}{\sqrt{4 + \beta^2} + \sqrt{4 + \beta^2 - 4\beta k}}.$$

EXERCISE 8.3 Suppose that there exists a unit interval $\mathbf{M} = [0, 1]$ of agents who can participate in a network. Denote by x_t^i (a non-negative real number) the level of involvement of the representative agent in the activities of the network in period t (for example, the number of maintained links). Furthermore, let $z_t = \int_0^1 x_t^i \, di$ be the average involvement of all agents. The benefits to agent i of participating in the network are given by $\sqrt{x_t^i z_t}$ and the costs are $A x_t^i$, where $A \in (0, 1/2)$ is a parameter. Changing the level of involvement creates the cost $g(u_t^i)$, where $u_t^i = x_{t+1}^i - x_t^i$ and where $g : \mathbb{R} \mapsto \mathbb{R}$ is a strictly convex function satisfying $g'(0) = 0$. Assume that an initial level x_0^i is given for every $i \in \mathbf{M}$.

(a) Formulate a dynamic competitive equilibrium model in which every agent $i \in \mathbf{M}$ takes the average involvement of the population as described by $(z_t)_{t=0}^{+\infty}$ as given and chooses its own involvement in order to maximize the discounted sum of benefits minus costs. The time-preference factor $\beta \in (0, 1)$ is assumed to be the same for all agents.

(b) Now assume that the agents have identical initial states $x_0^i = x_0$ for all $i \in \mathbf{M}$. Show that there exists a positive real number $\bar{u}$ and a dynamic competitive equilibrium in which every agent $i \in \mathbf{M}$ chooses $u_t^i = \bar{u}$ for all $t \in \mathbb{N}_0$. How does the value $\bar{u}$ depend on the cost parameter A?

EXERCISE 8.4 Consider an economy that is populated by a finite set $\mathbf{M} = \{1, 2, \ldots, n\}$ of agents. Agent $i \in \mathbf{M}$ is endowed with $k_0^i > 0$ units of capital in period 0 and with one unit of labour in every period $t \in \mathbb{N}_0$. The agent has access to a technology described by the production function $f(k, \ell, t) = B k^\alpha (A_t \ell)^{1-\alpha}$, where k and ℓ denote the capital and labour input of the agent, $B > 0$ and $\alpha \in (0, 1)$ are parameters, and A_t is labour productivity. The output produced by the agent can either be consumed or used as capital for the following period, that is, the capital holdings of the agent evolve according to

$$k_{t+1}^i = B\left(k_t^i\right)^\alpha \left(A_t \ell_t^i\right)^{1-\alpha} - c_t^i,$$

where c_t^i denotes the consumption by agent i. Agent i takes the sequence $(A_t)_{t=0}^{+\infty}$ as given and chooses $(c_t^i, k_{t+1}^i)_{t=0}^{+\infty}$ to maximize the objective functional

$$\sum_{t=0}^{+\infty} \beta^t \ln c_t^i$$

subject to the flow budget constraint stated above and non-negativity constraints for c_t^i and k_{t+1}^i. Note that there are no markets on which output, capital, or labour are traded. The connection between the agents arises solely from the fact that labour productivity A_t is determined by

$$A_t = \left(\prod_{i=1}^{n} k_t^i \right)^{1/n}.$$

(a) Show that the individual capital stocks evolve according to the equation

$$k_{t+1}^i = \alpha \beta B \left(k_t^i \right)^{\alpha} A_t^{1-\alpha}$$

and use this result to derive the equilibrium values of the aggregate system variable A_t. Determine the equilibrium paths of the individual state variables k_t^i, $i \in \mathbf{M}$. [Hint: it may be helpful to rewrite the dynamics in terms of logarithmic variables.]

(b) Write down the Bellman equations for the individual decision problems of the agents under the assumption that they expect the aggregate state to evolve according to the perceived law of motion $A_{t+1} = \psi A_t$. Show that an optimal value function of the form

$$V_{\psi}^i(k^i, A) = P \ln(k^i) + Q \ln(A) + R$$

with appropriately chosen coefficients P, Q, and R satisfies the Bellman equation and derive the corresponding optimal policy function of the individual optimization problems.

EXERCISE 8.5   Prove statements (b)-(e) of lemma 8.1.

EXERCISE 8.6   Consider the following dynamic competitive equilibrium model. There exist a policy maker and a unit interval $\mathbf{M} = [0, 1]$ of competitive agents. Competitive agent $i \in \mathbf{M}$ has preferences

$$\sum_{t=0}^{+\infty} \beta^t \left[\sqrt{x_t^i z_t} + \sqrt{g_t \left(1 - x_{t+1}^i \right)} + \sqrt{g_t z_t} \right],$$

where $\beta \in (0, 1)$ is the time-preference factor, $(x_t^i)_{t=0}^{+\infty}$ is a sequence of individual system variables under the control of agent i, $(z_t)_{t=0}^{+\infty}$ is a sequence of aggregate system variables, and $(g_t)_{t=0}^{+\infty}$ is a sequence of policy instruments under the control of the policy maker. The system variables satisfy $x_t^i \in X = [0, 1]$ for all $t \in \mathbb{N}_0$ and all $i \in \mathbf{M}$ and the initial values $x_0^i \in X$ are given. The aggregation condition is $z_t = \int_0^1 x_t^i \, di$ and the set of feasible values for the policy variables is $\mathbf{G} = [0, \beta^2]$.

(a) Assuming that the competitive agents are identical (that is, $x_0^i = x_0^j$ for all $(i, j) \in \mathbf{M}^2$) derive the unique symmetric dynamic competitive equilibrium corresponding to an arbitrary given sequence of policy variables $(g_t)_{t=0}^{+\infty}$ with $g_t \in \mathbf{G}$ for all t.

(b) Assume that the policy maker is benevolent, that is, that he or she seeks to maximize the utility of the representative competitive agent. Compute the optimal policy under commitment and show that it is periodic and dynamically consistent. [Hint: it may be helpful to refer to the results from example 5.11 and exercise 5.5.]

EXERCISE 8.7 Consider the following dynamic competitive equilibrium model. There exist a policy maker and a unit interval $\mathbf{M} = [0, 1]$ of competitive agents. Competitive agent $i \in \mathbf{M}$ has preferences[12]

$$\sum_{t=0}^{+\infty} \beta^t \left[\sqrt{(1 - x_{t+1}^i)(1 - z_{t+1})} + \sqrt{g_t x_t^i} + \sqrt{g_t(1 - z_{t+1})} \right],$$

where $\beta \in (0, 1)$ is the time-preference factor, $(x_t^i)_{t=0}^{+\infty}$ is a sequence of individual system variables under the control of agent i, $(z_t)_{t=0}^{+\infty}$ is a sequence of aggregate system variables, and $(g_t)_{t=0}^{+\infty}$ is a sequence of policy instruments under the control of the policy maker. The system variables satisfy $x_t^i \in X = [0, 1]$ for all $t \in \mathbb{N}_0$ and all $i \in \mathbf{M}$ and the initial values $x_0^i \in X$ are given. The aggregation condition is $z_t = \int_0^1 x_t^i \, di$ and the set of feasible values for the policy variables is $\mathbf{G} = [0, 1/\beta^2]$.

(a) Assuming that the competitive agents are identical (that is, $x_0^i = x_0^j$ for all $(i, j) \in \mathbf{M}^2$) derive the unique symmetric dynamic competitive equilibrium corresponding to an arbitrary given sequence of policy variables $(g_t)_{t=0}^{+\infty}$ with $g_t \in \mathbf{G}$ for all t.

(b) Assume that the policy maker is benevolent, that is, that he or she seeks to maximize the utility of the representative competitive agent. Compute the optimal policy under commitment and show that it is eventually periodic and dynamically inconsistent. [Hint: it may be helpful to refer to the results from example 5.11 and exercise 5.5.]

EXERCISE 8.8 Redo the calculations from example 8.8 with $\beta = 11/12$ instead of $\beta = 7/10$. The equilibrium values are $\bar{g} = 29/18$ and $\bar{z} = 1/3$.

---

[12] This model does not belong to the class of models discussed in the text, because the instantaneous utility function depends on z_{t+1} rather than on z_t. Nevertheless, all concepts and methods introduced in this chapter can be applied to this model as well.

8.6   COMMENTS AND REFERENCES

Dynamic competitive equilibria are primarily studied in macroeconomics. Excellent treatments that focus on the recursive formulation are Stokey and Lucas [86] and Ljungqvist and Sargent [62]. Example 8.2 is the Ramsey–Cass–Koopmans model originating from the work of Ramsey [77], Cass [17], and Koopmans [49]. The recursive formulation of dynamic competitive equilibrium goes back to Lucas and Prescott [63] and Prescott and Mehra [75].

The optimal policy problem under commitment, also called the Ramsey problem, takes its name from Ramsey [76], who studied the optimal design of a distortionary tax system in a static setting. The result that capital should not be taxed in the long run, as shown in example 8.6, was first derived by Chamley [19] and Judd [43]. Our exposition of that example follows Atkeson *et al.* [3]. The monetary policy problem treated in examples 8.7 and 8.9 is taken from Ellison and Rankin [30]; see also Díaz-Giménez *et al.* [27] and Martin [64]. Discretionary optimal fiscal policy, that is, a solution to the problem from example 8.6 for the case where the government lacks commitment power, can be found in Klein and Ríos-Rull [48] and Klein *et al.* [47]. We can also solve these policy problems under the assumption of partial commitment as discussed in section 6.3. For the case of fiscal policy, this is done in Debortoli and Nunes [24].

References

[1] D. Acemoglu, *Introduction to Modern Economic Growth*, Princeton University Press, 2008.

[2] R. P. Agarwal, M. Meehan, and D. O'Regan, *Fixed Point Theory and Applications*, Cambridge University Press, 2001.

[3] A. Atkeson, V. V. Chari, and P. J. Kehoe, 'Taxing capital income: a bad idea', *Federal Reserve Bank of Minneapolis Quarterly Review* **23** (1999), 3–17.

[4] C. Azariadis, 'Self-fulfilling prophecies', *Journal of Economic Theory* **25** (1981), 380–396.

[5] C. Azariadis, *Intertemporal Macroeconomics*, Blackwell, 1993.

[6] C. Azariadis and R. Guesnerie, 'Sunspots and cycles', *Review of Economic Studies* **53** (1986), 725–737.

[7] R. J. Barro and D. B. Gordon, 'A positive theory of monetary policy in a natural-rate model', *Journal of Political Economy* **91** (1983), 589–610.

[8] R. J. Barro and D. B. Gordon, 'Rules, discretion and reputation in a model of monetary policy', *Journal of Monetary Economics* **12** (1983), 101–120.

[9] T. Başar, 'On the uniqueness of the Nash solution in linear-quadratic differential games', *International Journal of Game Theory* **5** (1976), 65–90.

[10] T. Başar and G. J. Olsder, *Dynamic Noncooperative Game Theory*, SIAM Series in Classics in Applied Mathematics, 1999.

[11] R. Bellman, *Dynamic Programming*, Princeton University Press, 1957.

[12] L. M. Beneviste and J. A. Scheinkman, 'On the differentiability of the value function in dynamic models of economics', *Econometrica* **47** (1979), 727–732.

[13] O. Blanchard, *Macroeconomics*, 5th edn., Prentice Hall, 2009.

[14] M. Brin and G. Stuck, *Introduction to Dynamical Systems*, Cambridge University Press, 2002.

[15] J. Bullard and K. Mitra, 'Learning about monetary policy rules', *Journal of Monetary Economics* **49** (2002), 1105–1130.

[16] D. A. Carlson and A. Haurie, *Infinite Horizon Optimal Control: Theory and Applications*, Springer-Verlag, 1987.

[17] D. Cass, 'Optimum growth in an aggregative model of capital accumulation', *Review of Economic Studies* **32** (1965), 233–240.

[18] D. Cass and K. Shell, 'Do sunspots matter?' *Journal of Political Economy* **91** (1983), 193–227.

[19] C. Chamley, 'Optimal taxation of capital income in general equilibrium with infinite lives', *Econometrica* **54** (1986), 607–622.

References

[20] B. Champ and S. Freeman, *Modeling Monetary Economies*, 2nd edn., Cambridge University Press, 2001.

[21] R. Clarida, J. Galí, and M. Gertler, 'The science of monetary policy: a New Keynesian perspective', *Journal of Economic Literature* **37** (1999), 1661–1707.

[22] C. W. Clark, *Mathematical Bioeconomics: The Optimal Management of Renewable Resources*, 2nd edn., Wiley-Interscience, 1990.

[23] P. Collet and J.-P. Eckmann, *Iterated Maps on the Interval as Dynamical Systems*, Birkhäuser, 1980.

[24] D. Debortoli and R. Nunes, 'Fiscal policy under loose commitment', *Journal of Economic Theory* **145** (2010), 1005–1032.

[25] D. De la Croix and P. Michel, *A Theory of Economic Growth: Dynamics and Policy in Overlapping Generations*, Cambridge University Press, 2002.

[26] W. De Melo and S. Van Strien, *One-Dimensional Dynamics*, Springer-Verlag, 1993.

[27] J. Díaz-Giménez, G. Giovanetti, R. Marimon, and P. Teles, 'Nominal debt as a burden on monetary policy', *Review of Economic Dynamics* **11** (2008), 493–514.

[28] E. Dockner, S. Jørgensen, N. Van Long, and G. Sorger, *Differential Games in Economics and Management*, Cambridge University Press, 2000.

[29] S. N. Elaydi, *An Introduction to Difference Equations*, 3rd edn., Springer-Verlag, 2005.

[30] M. Ellison and N. Rankin, 'Optimal monetary policy when lump-sum taxes are unavailable: a reconsideration of the outcomes under commitment and discretion', *Journal of Economic Dynamics and Control* **31** (2007), 219–243.

[31] B. Ferguson and G. Lim, *Discrete Time Dynamic Economic Models: Theory and Empirical Applications*, Routledge, 2003.

[32] C. Fershtman and M. I. Kamien, 'Dynamic duopolistic competition with sticky-prices', *Econometrica* **55** (1987), 1151–1164.

[33] S. Frederick, G. Loewenstein, and T. O'Donoghue, 'Time discounting and time preference: a critical review', *Journal of Economic Literature* **40** (2002), 351–401.

[34] J. Galí, *Monetary Policy, Inflation, and the Business Cycle*, Princeton University Press, 2008.

[35] O. Galor, *Discrete Dynamical Systems*, Springer-Verlag, 2010.

[36] G. Gandolfo, *Economic Dynamics*, 4th edn., Springer-Verlag, 2009.

[37] J.-M. Grandmont, 'On endogenous competitive business cycles', *Econometrica* **53** (1985), 995–1045.

[38] J.-M. Grandmont, P. Pintus, and R. De Vilder, 'Capital-labor substitution and competitive nonlinear endogenous business cycles', *Journal of Economic Theory* **80** (1998), 14–59.

[39] H. Halkin, 'Necessary conditions for optimal control problems with infinite horizons', *Econometrica* **42** (1974), 267–272.

[40] J. Hofbauer and K. Sigmund, *Evolutionary Games and Population Dynamics*, Cambridge University Press, 1998.

[41] C. Hommes, *Behavioral Rationality and Heterogeneous Expectations in Complex Economic Systems*, Cambridge University Press, 2013.

[42] H. Humenberger, 'Iterationen, Grenzwerte und Spinnwebdiagramme – oder: warum ist 2 doch nicht 4?' *Internationale Mathematische Nachrichten* **213** (2010), 19–34.

[43] K. L. Judd, 'Redistributive taxation in a simple perfect foresight model', *Journal of Public Economics* **28** (1985), 59–83.

[44] N. Kaldor, 'A classificatory note on the determinateness of equilibrium', *Review of Economic Studies* **1** (1934), 122–136.

[45] T. Kamihigashi, 'A simple proof of the necessity of the transversality condition', *Economic Theory* **20** (2002), 427–433.

[46] A. Katok and B. Hasselblatt, *Introduction to the Modern Theory of Dynamical Systems*, Cambridge University Press, 1995.

[47] P. Klein, P. Krusell, and J.-V. Ríos-Rull, 'Time-consistent public policy', *Review of Economic Studies* **75** (2008), 789–808.

[48] P. Klein and J.-V. Ríos-Rull, 'Time-consistent optimal fiscal policy', *International Economic Review* **44** (2003), 1217–1245.

[49] T. C. Koopmans, 'The concept of optimal economic growth', in *The Econometric Approach to Development Planning*, Pontificae Academiae Scientiarum Scripta Varia, North-Holland, 1965.

[50] M. Kurz, 'The general instability of a class of competitive growth processes', *Review of Economic Studies* **35** (1968), 155–174.

[51] Y. Kuznetsov, *Elements of Applied Bifurcation Theory*, Springer-Verlag, 1995.

[52] F. Kydland and E. C. Prescott, 'Rules rather than discretion: the inconsistency of optimal plans', *Journal of Political Economy* **85** (1977), 473–491.

[53] D. Laibson, 'Golden eggs and hyperbolic discounting', *Quarterly Journal of Economics* **112** (1997), 443–477.

[54] J. Laitner, 'Dynamic determinacy and the existence of sunspot equilibria', *Journal of Economic Theory* **47** (1989), 39–50.

[55] S. Lang, *Linear Algebra*, 3rd edn., Springer-Verlag, 1987.

[56] J. LaSalle and S. Lefschetz, *Stability by Liapunov's Direct Method with Applications*, Academic Press, 1961.

[57] A. Lasota and J. A. Yorke, 'On the existence of invariant measures for piecewise monotonic transformations', *Transactions of the American Mathematical Society* **186** (1973), 481–488.

[58] D. Levhari and N. Liviatan, 'On stability in the saddle-point sense', *Journal of Economic Theory* **4** (1972), 88–93.

[59] D. Levhari and L. J. Mirman, 'The great fish war: an example using a dynamic Cournot–Nash solution', *The Bell Journal of Economics* **11** (1980), 322–334.

[60] T. Y. Li and J. A. Yorke, 'Period three implies chaos', *American Mathematical Monthly* **82** (1975), 985–992.

[61] T. Y. Li and J. A. Yorke, 'Ergodic transformations from an interval into itself', *Transactions of the American Mathematical Society* **235** (1978), 183–192.

[62] L. Ljungqvist and T. J. Sargent, *Recursive Macroeconomic Theory*, 3rd edn., MIT Press, 2012.

References

[63] R. E. Lucas Jr and E. C. Prescott, 'Investment under uncertainty', *Econometrica* **39** (1971), 659–681.

[64] F. Martin, 'A positive theory of government debt', *Review of Economic Dynamics* **12** (2009), 608–631.

[65] G. McCandless and N. Wallace, *Introduction to Dynamic Macroeconomic Theory – an Overlapping Generations Approach*, Harvard University Press, 1991.

[66] L. W. McKenzie, 'Optimal economic growth: turnpike theorems and comparative dynamics', in K. J. Arrow and M. D. Intriligator (eds.), *Handbook of Mathematical Economics*, vol. III, North-Holland, 1986, pp. 1281–1355.

[67] C. D. Meyer, *Matrix Analysis and Applied Linear Algebra*, SIAM, 2000.

[68] T. Mitra and G. Sorger, 'Extinction in common property resource models: an analytically tractable example', *Economic Theory* **57** (2014), 41–57.

[69] T. Mitra and H. Y. Wan Jr, 'Some theoretical results on the economics of forestry', *Review of Economic Studies* **52** (1985), 263–282.

[70] T. Mitra and H. Y. Wan Jr, 'On the Faustmann solution to the forest management problem', *Journal of Economic Theory* **40** (1986), 229–249.

[71] J. F. Muth, 'Rational expectations and the theory of price movements', *Econometrica* **29** (1961), 315–335.

[72] M. Nerlove and K. J. Arrow, 'Optimal advertising policy under dynamic conditions', *Economica* **29** (1962), 129–142.

[73] E. Phelps and R. A. Pollak, 'On second best national saving and game-equilibrium growth', *Review of Economic Studies* **35** (1968), 185–199.

[74] R. A. Pollak, 'Consistent planning', *Review of Economic Studies* **35** (1968), 201–208.

[75] E. C. Prescott and R. Mehra, 'Recursive competitive equilibria: the case of homogeneous households', *Econometrica* **48** (1980), 1365–1379.

[76] F. P. Ramsey, 'A contribution to the theory of taxation', *Economic Journal* **37** (1927), 47–61.

[77] F. P. Ramsey, 'A mathematical theory of saving', *Economic Journal* **38** (1928), 543–559.

[78] W. Roberds, 'Models of policy under stochastic replanning', *International Economic Review* **28** (1987), 731–755.

[79] P. A. Samuelson, 'Interactions between the multiplier analysis and the principle of acceleration', *Review of Economics and Statistics* **21** (1939), 75–78.

[80] P. A. Samuelson, 'Optimality of profit-including prices under ideal planning', *Proceedings of the National Academy of Sciences* **70** (1973), 2109–2111.

[81] A. N. Sarkovskii, 'Coexistence of cycles of a continuous map of a line into itself', *Ukrains'kyi Matematychnyi Zhurnal* **16** (1964), 61–71.

[82] E. Schaumburg and A. Tambalotti, 'An investigation of the gains from commitment in monetary policy', *Journal of Monetary Economics* **54** (2007), 302–324.

[83] K. Shimomura and D. Xie, 'Advances on Stackelberg open-loop and feedback strategies', *International Journal of Economic Theory* **4** (2008), 115–133.

[84] R. Shone, *Economic Dynamics*, 2nd edn., Cambridge University Press, 2002.

[85] R. Solow, 'A contribution to the theory of economic growth', *Quarterly Journal of Economics* **70** (1956), 65–94.

[86] N. Stokey and R. E. Lucas Jr, *Recursive Methods in Economic Dynamics*, Harvard University Press, 1989.

[87] R. H. Strotz, 'Myopia and inconsistency in dynamic utility maximization', *Review of Economic Studies* **23** (1955–1956), 165–180.

[88] W. Sutherland, 'On optimal development in a multisectoral economy: the discounted case', *Review of Economic Studies* **37** (1970), 585–589.

[89] T. W. Swan, 'Economic growth and capital accumulation', *Economic Record* **32** (1956), 334–361.

[90] K. Sydsæter, P. Hammond, A. Seierstad, and A. Strøm, *Further Mathematics for Economic Analysis*, 2nd edn., Pearson Education, 2008.

[91] K. Train, *Discrete Choice Methods with Simulation*, 2nd edn., Cambridge University Press, 2009.

[92] N. Van Long, *A Survey of Dynamic Games in Economics*, World Scientific, 2010.

[93] N. Van Long and G. Sorger, 'A dynamic principal-agent problem as a feedback Stackelberg differential game', *Central European Journal of Operations Research* **18** (2010), 491–509.

[94] J. Weibull, *Evolutionary Game Theory*, MIT Press, 1997.

[95] M. Woodford, 'Stationary sunspot equilibria: the case of small fluctuations around a deterministic steady state', http://www.columbia.edu/%7Emw2230/Sunspot.pdf.

[96] M. Woodford, *Interest and Prices*, Princeton University Press, 2003.

[97] D. Xie, 'On time inconsistency: a technical issue in Stackelberg differential games', *Journal of Economic Theory* **76** (1997), 412–430.

Index

Printed in the United States
By Bookmasters